F V

The Journey of Life is both a cultural history of aging and a contribution to public dialogue about the meaning and significance of later life. The book shows how Northern middle-class culture, first in Europe and then in America, created and sustained specifically modern images of the life course between the Reformation and World War I. During this period, old age was removed from its ambiguous place in life's journey, rationalized, and redefined as a scientific problem. In the late twentieth century, however, postmodern culture has begun to recover the spiritual dimensions of later life and to envision new opportunities for growth in an aging society.

The Journey of Life

The Journey
of
Life

A Cultural History of Aging in America

THOMAS R. COLE

Institute for the Medical Humanities
The University of Texas Medical Branch

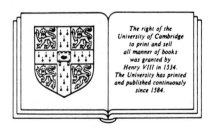

The right of the
University of Cambridge
to print and sell
all manner of books
was granted by
Henry VIII in 1534.
The University has printed
and published continuously
since 1584.

CAMBRIDGE UNIVERSITY PRESS

Cambridge

New York   Port Chester   Melbourne   Sydney

Published by the Press Syndicate of the University of Cambridge
The Pitt Building, Trumpington Street, Cambridge CB2 1RP
40 West 20th Street, New York, NY 10011, USA
10 Stamford Road, Oakleigh, Melbourne 3166, Australia

© Cambridge University Press 1992

First published 1992

Printed in Canada

Library of Congress Cataloging-in-Publication Data
Cole, Thomas R., 1949–
The journey of life : a cultural history of aging in America /
Thomas R. Cole.

p.   cm.

Includes bibliographical references and index.

ISBN 0-521-41020-7 (hardback)

1. Old Age – United States – History.   2. Aged – United States –
Social conditions.   3. Aging – Social aspects – United States.
4. Gerontology – United States – History.   I. Title.
HQ1064.U5C526   1992
305.26'0973 – dc20   91–8867
                                                              CIP

British Library Cataloguing in Publication Data
Cole, Thomas R.
The journey of life : a cultural history of aging in
America.
1. Old age   2. United States
I. Title
305.260973

ISBN 0-521-41020-7 hardback

To my wife Letha

Who initiated and completed her medical education, gave birth
to our two children, and supported me in many ways – all within
the decade between this book's conception and its completion

Down Time's quaint stream
Without an oar
We are enforced to sail
Our Port a secret
Our Perchance a Gale
What Skipper would
Incur the Risk
What Buccaneer would ride
Without a surety from the Wind
Or schedule of the Tide

Emily Dickinson

Contents

Illustrations

Preface

This book began as a dissertation in history at the University of Rochester in the late 1970s. Academic jobs in humanities departments then were as scarce as hens' teeth, but academic medicine and gerontology were awakening to the practical and heuristic necessity of humanities scholarship and its place in professional education.

I had the good fortune to benefit from these developments. Since 1982, I have been privileged to work at the Institute for the Medical Humanities of the University of Texas Medical Branch in Galveston. There, I apprenticed myself to Institute Director Ronald Carson, whose example, leadership, and support have been the major influence on my development as a humanist in medicine. My work at the Institute has required me to become intimately involved in medical education and practice; it has enabled me to develop strong working relationships with a broad network of colleagues in geriatrics and gerontological research, education, policy, and practice.

Conversations and exchanges with colleagues in these disciplines, as well as with colleagues in the humanities, have shaped my research and writing. Receiving critiques of my manuscript from such a diverse group of colleagues has admittedly been a mixed blessing. While my work is much improved thanks to all their time and effort, I realize that I cannot possibly respond satisfactorily to the suggestions of even a few of them.

Long before this book was conceived, I was introduced to a rare blend of intellectual integrity and spiritual wholeness in Merold Westphal, my philosophy mentor at Yale. Westphal's seminars in religion and politics, his compassion, and his willingness to put up with my know-it-all style of undergraduate radicalism have proved to be a decisive influence. From Donald B. Meyer at Wesleyan, I learned the importance of historical imagination, precise interpretation, and the excitement of open-ended empirical inquiry.

In the early years of this work, the National Science Foundation provided a valuable predoctoral grant. Toward the end of the dissertation, Glen Elder, Jr., played a key role in supporting me. My thanks to him and to Morton Weir and Luther Otto, who provided space and resources for me at the Boys

Town Center for the Study of Youth Development between 1979 and 1981. A special thanks to Dorothy Sato-Stohl, who helped me through a difficult time in 1981. James J. Farrell, William R. Leach, and Randy McGowen all read sections of the dissertation and offered critical suggestions. Leonard Sweet provided considerable help in religious history, as did Stephen Kunitz and John Romano in medical and geriatric issues. Theodore M. Brown and Stanley Engerman read a draft of the entire thesis and made valuable suggestions.

I am especially grateful to Christopher Lasch, my graduate mentor in history at the University of Rochester. I have learned much from Lasch's blending of historical scholarship and cultural criticism and benefited from both his friendship and his critical acumen. He supervised the dissertation and also critiqued a draft of the current manuscript.

In recent years, I have received assistance from many who read and commented on the entire manuscript. Andy Achenbaum has been a particularly strong supporter and astute critic. The final shape of the book owes much to his influence. Tom Bender also made a major contribution to this book, reading through two entire drafts and making invaluable comments. Carole Haber's careful reading, helpful suggestions, and strong objections forced me to clarify key issues. Ron Manheimer began sending responses back one chapter at a time until he got bogged down in too many mid-nineteenth-century Protestant sermons – most since removed.

Bob Abzug, Lois Banner, Dan Callahan, Randy McGowen, Tom Haskell, David Troyansky, Meredith Minkler, and Martin Kohli all read drafts and sent detailed comments. Rod Olsen offered ideas and support over several years, while serving as my editorial superego.

Others have also been helpful. Amy Stanley carefully critiqued an early version of the material on antebellum religion and helped identify iconographic material at the Folger Shakespeare Library. Megan Seaholm often lent a supportive presence and suggested relevant secondary sources on women in American history. From Terri Premo, I learned much about women's history and the importance of personal writings for understanding the inner life of older people.

Rick Moody provided a model of engaged, critical thinking about aging. Barbara Thompson, M.D., invited my participation in nursing home and hospital rounds at the University of Texas Medical Branch. She has taught me a great deal about what it means to care for older patients. Carter Williams and Nancy Wilson inspired me with their unflagging dedication to more humane forms of gerontological practice and policy. More than once, Marc Kaminsky revived my flagging spirits. "Keep your plow in the ground," he admonished me. "When you reach the end of the row, the tip will be sharp and shiny."

My colleagues at the Institute for the Medical Humanities have been especially supportive. Mary Winkler, who collaborated on both the research and the writing for the opening chapter, introduced me to visual thinking and methods of interpreting iconographic sources. She taught me that the properly educated eye is the soul's window. Chester Burns, Ron Carson, Ellen More, and Bill Winslade all commented on parts of the manuscript and helped me overcome obstacles to completing the book. Ellen especially urged me to be more explicit about issues of gender and aging. Colleagues formerly at the Institute also influenced me in substantial ways. From Sally Gadow, I learned much about the phenomenology of aging. David Barnard introduced me to the work of Abraham Heschel. He and I spent considerable time together, pondering the place of "meaning" in health care.

In my seminars on the history and philosophy of aging, graduate students at the Institute were helpful in various ways. Gretchen Aumann, Pat Jakobi, Jackie Low, Cielo Perdomo, and Larry Wygant responded thoughtfully to many fledgling ideas later worked out in this book. Gretchen, Pat, and Cielo provided editorial and bibliographical assistance as well, while Dale Meyer collaborated on the interpretation of Jasper Johns's *The Seasons*.

The Institute has also provided generous research time and support with the help of a Challenge Grant from the National Endowment for the Humanities. I am particularly indebted to Sheila Keating, who has worked patiently with me for nine years – checking bibliography, counting annual American publications of *Pilgrim's Progress*, and carefully preparing at least three "final" versions of the manuscript. Eleanor Porter lightened my load at the end by helping with permissions, reproductions, editing, and indexing.

Innumerable librarians, archivists, and print curators assisted me, and I acknowledge my great debt to them and their institutions: the Rush Rhees Library at the University of Rochester; Sterling Memorial Library and the Mellon Museum at Yale University; the Fondren Library at Rice University; the Winterthur Museum in Winterthur, Delaware; the Museum of Fine Arts in Boston; the Connecticut Historical Society; the Folger Shakespeare Library, the National Gallery of Art, the National Portrait Gallery, and the Library of Congress in Washington, D.C.; the British Museum, the British Library, and the Warburg Institute of the University of London in London; the Rijksmuseum in Amsterdam; the Atlas von Stolk in Rotterdam; the Bodleian Library at Oxford; the Frick Art Reference Library and the Pierpont Morgan Library in New York; the Huntington Library in San Marino, Calif.; Mead Art Museum in Amherst, Mass.; the Stowe-Day Foundation in Hartford; the American Antiquarian Society and the Goddard Library Archives, Clark University, Worcester, Mass.; New York State School of Industrial and Labor Relations, Cornell University; and the Deutsche Staatsbibliothek in Berlin.

At the Moody Medical Library, University of Texas Medical Branch, the people at the Interlibrary Loan office have always gone out of their way to be helpful: Laura Cambiano, Cindy Hanak, Jerry D. Gwinn II, and Deirdre Becker. Alex Bienkowski and Larry Wygant have often helped me through the library's maze in search of information.

Earlier versions of Chapters 1, 4, 6, 10, and the Epilogue appeared in the following publications and are used here with permission of the editors and publishers: "The 'Enlightened' View of Aging: Victorian Morality in a New Key," *Hastings Center Report* 13, no. 3 (1983): 34–40; "The Prophecy of *Senescence*: G. Stanley Hall and the Reconstruction of Old Age in America," *The Gerontologist* 24, no. 4 (1984): 360–66; "Aging, Meaning, and Well-Being: Musings of a Cultural Historian," *International Journal of Aging and Human Development* 19, no. 4 (1984): 331–37; "Aging and Meaning: Our Culture Provides No Compelling Answers," *Generations* 10, no. 2 (1985): 49–52; "Putting Off the Old: Middle-Class Morality, Antebellum Protestantism, and the Origins of Ageism," in *Old Age in a Bureaucratic Society*, ed. David D. Van Tassel and Peter N. Stearns (Westport, Conn.: Greenwood Press, 1986), 49–65; *What Does It Mean To Grow Old?: Reflections from the Humanities*, coedited with Sally Gadow (Durham, N.C.: Duke University Press, 1986); "The Specter of Aging: History, Policy, and Culture in an Aging America," *Tikkun* (September/October 1988): 14–18, 93–95; "Oedipus and the Meaning of Aging: Personal Reflections and Historical Perspectives," in *Passing Through Time: Aging, Meaning, and Social Policy*, ed. Nancy Jecker (New York: Humana Press, 1991); and "Aging, Metaphor, and Meaning: A View from Cultural History," in *Metaphors of Aging in Science and the Humanities*, ed. Gary Kenyon et al. (New York: Springer, 1991), 57–82.

Introduction

Old age is like a rock on which many founder
and some find shelter.

Anonymous

They shall bear fruit even in old age;
They shall be ever fresh and fragrant.
They shall proclaim: the Lord is just.
He is my Rock, in whom there is no flaw.

Psalm 92

When I was a young child, the old people in my family were a sheltering
rock. They occupied a place in my inner landscape that has changed only
recently. My grandparents and great aunts always seemed the same. They
were there every weekend, on holidays, whenever we needed them. My
brother, my sister, and I ate at their tables, roamed their houses, climbed
in their yards, ravished their presents, and assumed their immortality.

When my father died at the age of twenty-seven, I was immediately
transformed into an aged four-year-old, a *senex puer*. For many years, I carried
a burden of guilt and depression, punctuated by primal flashes of wisdom.
The sequence of generations in my life had been broken. I could not live
childhood's innocence and exuberance and felt that I too would die young.

My grandfathers died when I was nine and sixteen. Irving Michel – a
quiet, cigar-smoking owner of a blueprint shop – cried every day of his life
after the death of his son and disinherited us when my mother's second
husband adopted us. The night Irving died I had been on a local television
show with my Cub Scout pack. My mother said he must have died happily
after seeing me on TV. I wondered about that. And Jack Breslav, the hard-
driving, self-made son of a Jewish immigrant tailor. Grandpa Jack had
graduated from Yale; his intensity, ambition, and success inspired and
haunted me. I felt great pride being a pallbearer at Jack's funeral, where
my uncontrollable crying disturbed an otherwise dignified affair.

The deaths of my grandfathers were painful. But they did not undermine

xv

the sense of continuity derived from my grandmothers, who seemed to go on without change. Until my late thirties, they maintained their independence, each somewhat stern and difficult in her own way, each fiercely loyal and proud. Their existence helped frame my own. They demanded little and gave much.

In the spring of 1986, after being forced out of the blueprint business she had run for fifty years, Reba Michel (Irving's wife and my father's mother) began to lose the ability to direct her own affairs. Failing vision from cataracts, acute glaucoma, severe arthritis, stomach trouble, and finally Alzheimer's disease broke her. Yet she fought furiously against me when I arranged a conservatorship and round-the-clock care for her. By autumn, both she and my newborn daughter were in diapers. Neither could walk more than a few steps without falling. Neither lived in the adult world of secular chronological time.

In the spring of 1987, my mother's mother entered the hospital for the first time since giving birth to her youngest daughter. She died two weeks later. Helen Breslav was the family's matriarch. She possessed an upper-class bearing, an unwavering sense of dignity, and high standards – as well as the wealth accumulated by Jack. She had always seemed invulnerable, as if she might actually outlive death, if not the rest of us. Her death was shocking despite her eighty-seven years. It felt as if the rope of a great anchor had suddenly come unraveled. Six weeks later, my grandfather's sister died and was buried on the same family plot that held my maternal grandparents, their parents, and my father.

For three years, we (my brother, sister, and I) kept our grandmother Reba in her home with round-the-clock nursing care. At first, she tried to jump off her balcony and frequently hit or screamed at her caregivers, who once sent her to the emergency room in a straitjacket. Then she was put on large doses of Haldol, which reduced her to driveling compliance. By the time we got her medication down to a minimum, she had lost most of her sight, hearing, and control over bowels and bladder. Her fierce independence gave way to depressed acceptance. Yet Reba said she liked her nurses and seemed increasingly resigned to her fate. Despite my guilt at not being there with her myself, I think she received good care. I visited two or three times a year, thinking each time would be the last. Sometimes, when I yelled "I love you" across 2,000 miles of phone lines, she whispered back, "I love you too."

After grandmother Reba had made several more impersonal and traumatic visits to the hospital, I came to an understanding with her nurse's aides and physician: She would remain at home until she died. Reba had often expressed the wish for an end to her suffering, and we had already decided against heroic measures to prolong her life. In 1988, she stopped walking altogether.

Most of her time was spent sleeping or sitting in a wheelchair. Her legs contracted and curled up like chicken wings. Her skin broke down and the sores became painful. Toward the end, she still had daily periods of lucidity. She was aware of her surroundings and recognized friends, family, and her aides.

One evening in late May 1989, Reba's caregivers telephoned. She had lost weight from vomiting and diarrhea, was not eating adequately, and could not communicate. Would I give permission to insert an intravenous line for fluids and nutrition? I told them to keep feeding her with straws, bottles, or syringes, that we'd see how she was the next morning. After a guilt-ridden, sleepless night, I spoke to Beverly, who worked the day shift. "Do you think she would want an IV?" I asked. "No, I don't think she'd want to be poked any more. Last week she said to me, 'Get out my blue dress and my shoes because I'm going to die.' " "OK," I said, my heart sinking. "Keep feeding her as much as she'll take by mouth, hold her, and tell her that I love her." That day, Reba ate well and seemed to be rallying. She died the next morning, as Beverly and Geri were giving her a bath.

The rock of old age no longer seems so secure. My mother and second father have begun to navigate its waters, which seem stormier and closer than before. But if old age looks more frightening now, it still symbolizes the spiritual integrity and wisdom that have attracted me since childhood. In what Anne Sexton calls "the awful rowing toward God," amidst waves of brokenness, rage, and loneliness, I sense its possibilities for wholeness and self-transcendence. Perhaps, if I am blessed, I may someday become a *puer senex*, an innocent and playful old man.

During the last fifteen years, these feelings have fueled my inquiry into aging. Stirred by the search for personal meaning, I have been exploring the cultural shoreline of later life, charting its historical forms and sounding their philosophical depths. This book presents the results of that exploration. It is not so much a history of *attitudes toward old age* as it is a study of the historical *meanings of aging*.[1]

In *The Journey of Life*, the term *aging* refers broadly to the second half of

---

[1] Work in the history of meaning involves complex philosophical and historical issues that have not yet been fully articulated. For an early foray into this new territory, see William Bouwsma, "Intellectual History in the 1980's: From the History of Ideas to the History of Meaning," *Journal of Interdisciplinary History* 12 (Autumn 1981): 279–91. For a critical overview of recent work, see John E. Toews, "Intellectual History after the Linguistic Turn: The Autonomy of Meaning and the Irreducibility of Experience," *American Historical Review* 92, no. 4 (1987): 879–907. Eugene Rochberg-Halton's *Meaning and Modernity: Social Theory in the Pragmatic Attitude* (Chicago: University of Chicago Press, 1986) offers a penetrating analysis of the place of meaning in modern culture and social theory. For an interdisciplinary bibliography on the "problematic" of aging and meaning, see Harry R. Moody and Thomas R. Cole, "Aging and Meaning: A Bibliographical Essay" and "A Select Bibliography" in *What Does It Mean To Grow Old? Reflections From the Humanities*, ed. Thomas R. Cole and Sally A. Gadow (Durham, N.C.: Duke University Press, 1986), 247–73.

life – including the young old or the Third Age, the old old or the Fourth Age, and the passage to death.[2] It focuses not on a particular age group or on chronological age but on the overall process and experience of growing old.[3] I view the stages of life as necessary but limited and static categories of understanding. As my title suggests, I want to emphasize that each individual's experience of life is always potentially fresh. Growing – up and old – resembles a continuous journey down a river flowing inexorably toward the sea.

But what is meaning, and why does it matter? Meaning is a notoriously vague concept, applied to an infinite number of things, and used in at least eight different though interrelated modes. *Meaning* can refer to external causal relationship; external referential, semantic, or symbolic relation; intention or purpose; lesson; personal significance; objective meaningfulness; and total resultant meaning, or the entire web of the preceding modes.[4] Yet no matter how carefully one defines or analyzes it, there can never be an objective, predefined formula capable of externally grasping the meaning of *meaning*. As self-defining and self-interpreting animals, we humans must enter into our own webs of meaning to understand ourselves.[5]

In contemporary culture, *meaning* is generally used in one of two ways: as a generalized theory of language or as an intuitive expression of one's overall appraisal of living. The *scientific* questions about meaning are part of the human attempt to develop logical, reliable, interpretable, and systematically predictive theories. The *existential* questions about meaning are part of the human quest for a vision within which one's experience makes sense. The concept of meaning, then, contains a crucial ambiguity, what Herbert Fingarette calls a "point of intersection from which one may move either into living or into theories about living."[6] The generative power of meaning as a concept derives from this seminal ambiguity, which allows one to connect the world of public understandings with the inner struggle for wholeness. Unfortunately, the dominant public discourse of aging (and much else) generally dissolves this essential and creative tension; scientific meanings of aging are separated from and elevated above existential (or experiential) meanings.

[2] See Bernice Neugarten, "Age Groups in American Society and the Rise of the Young Old," *Annals of the American Academy of Political and Social Science* 415 (1974): 187–98 and Peter Laslett, *A Fresh Map of Life: The Emergence of the Third Age* (London: Weidenfeld and Nicolson, 1989), esp. chaps. 1, 6, 10–12.

[3] See Howard P. Chudacoff, *How Old Are You? Age Consciousness in American Culture* (Princeton: Princeton University Press, 1989).

[4] See Robert Nozick, *Philosophical Explanations* (Cambridge, Mass.: Harvard University Press, 1981), 574–75.

[5] See Charles Taylor, "Interpretation and the Sciences of Man," and Hans-Georg Gadamer, "The Problem of Historical Consciousness," in *Interpretive Social Science*, ed. Paul Rabinow and William M. Sullivan (Berkeley: University of California Press, 1979), 25–71, 103–60.

[6] Herbert Fingarette, *The Self in Transformation* (New York: Harper and Row, 1977), 63–64.

Introduction

In our century, vastly improved medical and economic conditions for older people have been accompanied by cultural disenfranchisement – a loss of meaning and vital social roles. At least since World War I, Western observers have sensed this impoverishment of later life. In 1922, G. Stanley Hall noted that modern progress both lengthened old age and drained it of substance.[7] During the 1930s C. G. Jung observed that many of his patients found little meaning or purpose in life as they grew older.[8] In 1949, A. L. Vischer wondered whether "there is any sense, any vital meaning in old age."[9] Fifteen years later, Erik Erikson argued that, lacking a culturally viable ideal of old age, "our civilization does not really harbor a concept of the whole of life."[10] Summarizing a large volume of research in 1974, Irving Rosow claimed that American culture provides old people with "no meaningful norms by which to live."[11] In 1980, Leopold Rosenmayr claimed that the position of the elderly in Western society "can only be reoriented and changed if viable ideals, 'existential paradigms,' become visible and receive some social support."[12] And in 1987, Daniel Callahan argued that rising health care costs of an aging society and problems of generational equity demanded renewed meaning for old age.[13]

The Journey of Life offers a historical interpretation of this "spiritual situation of the age."[14] It is essentially a genealogy that traces the long-term transition from existential to scientific tonalities in cultural compositions of aging. The genealogy follows two motifs – the ages (or stages) of life and the journey of life – which have provided the basic musical phrases for those who would sing about aging. In one sense, the book results from my own engagement with these motifs, my personal and intellectual grappling with their significance. I invite the reader to do the same. At the same time, the book follows several subthemes that amplify the historical overtones of the major motifs: death, generational relations, attitudes toward old age and older people, gender, and the role of science.

This book is also a contribution to the growing public dialogue about the meaning and significance of later life. It attempts to show how central texts

[7] G. Stanley Hall, *Senescence, The Last Half of Life* (New York: D. Appleton, 1922), 403.

[8] Carl Gustav Jung, "The Stages of Life," in *Modern Man in Search of a Soul*, trans. W.S. Dell and Cary F. Baynes (New York: Harcourt Brace Jovanovich, 1933), 95–114.

[9] A. L. Vischer, *On Growing Old*, trans. G. Onn (Boston: Houghton Mifflin, 1967), 23.

[10] Erik Erikson, "Human Strength and the Cycle of Generations," in *Insight and Responsibility* (New York: Norton, 1964), 132.

[11] Irving Rosow, *Socialization to Old Age* (Berkeley: University of California Press, 1974), 148.

[12] Leopold Rosenmayr, "Achievements, Doubts, and Prospects of the Sociology of Aging," *Human Development* 23 (1980): 60.

[13] Daniel Callahan, *Setting Limits: Medical Goals in an Aging Society* (New York: Simon & Schuster, 1987).

[14] The phrase derives from Karl Jaspers's essay of cultural criticism, "Die geistige Situation der Zeit" (1931). For contemporary German perspectives, see Jurgen Habermas, ed., *Observations on the Spiritual Situation of the Age*, trans. Andrew Buchwalter (Cambridge, Mass.: MIT Press, 1984).

and images of Northern middle-class culture – first in Europe and then in America – created and sustained specifically modern configurations of the ages and journey of life between the Reformation and World War I. During this long period, secular, scientific, and individualist tendencies steadily eroded ancient and medieval understandings of aging as a mysterious part of the eternal order of things. Old age was removed from its ambiguous place in life's spiritual journey, rationalized, and redefined as a scientific problem. In the last quarter of the twentieth century, as I suggest in the Epilogue, postmodern configurations of the ages and journey of life imply renewed awareness of the spiritual dimensions of later life and new opportunities for healing our culture's split between mastery and mystery.

America's contemporary culture of aging is characterized both by the absence or inadequacy of shared meanings of old age and by the multiplication and uncertain vitality of new meanings. In the late twentieth century, several broad trends have converged to compel our attention to these issues: the democratization of longevity and the aging of our population; ideological and fiscal crises of the welfare state; the rapid progress of biomedical technology; and the cultural crisis of the therapeutic ethos that grew out of the ruins of a relatively unified Christian world view. Hence, the quality of our answers to the question, What does it mean to grow old?[15] has important implications for medical ethics and practice, psychotherapy and education of older people, research on the biology of aging and the prolongation of human life, intergenerational equity and public policy, and religious and spiritual life.

I am a cultural historian whose questions are existential and moral: Why do we grow old? Does aging have an intrinsic purpose? Is old age the culmination or the dreary denouement of life's drama? Is there anything important to be done after children are raised and careers completed? Are there perduring "gifts reserved for age"? Has death always cast its shadow over old age? What are the rights and responsibilities of older people? What are the virtues of old age? Has there ever really been a "good" old age?

Despite the rapid aging of Western populations since the nineteenth century and the vast gerontological literature that has appeared since World War II, such moral and spiritual questions have received remarkably little attention.[16] Our culture is not much interested in why we grow old, how we ought to grow old, or what it means to grow old. Like other aspects of our biological and social existence, aging has been brought under the do-

---

[15] For recent interdisciplinary reflections, see Cole and Gadow, *What Does It Mean?* (see n. 1).

[16] Since the mid-1970s, a new literature has grown up at the intersection of gerontology and the humanities. See Donna Polisar et al., *Where Do We Come From? What Are We? Where Are We Going? An Annotated Bibliography of Aging and the Humanities* (Washington, D.C.: Gerontological Society of America, 1988). For an introduction to the basic issues, disciplines, methods, and problems constituting the new field of humanistic gerontology, see Thomas R. Cole, David D. Van Tassel, and Robert Kastenbaum, eds., *Handbook of Aging and the Humanities* (New York: Springer, 1992).

minion of scientific management, which is primarily interested in *how* we age in order to explain and control the aging process.

In the last fifteen years, scholars who have pioneered the new history of old age have taken their basic orientation from the social and biomedical sciences, which generally view old age as an engineering problem to be solved or at least ameliorated. Hence, historians have focused primarily on issues involving old age as an object of social policy: unemployment, poverty, disease, health care, retirement, and pensions. I offer an alternative perspective. I view the "problem of old age" in the historical context of the cultural and symbolic impoverishment that has beset the last half of life since the late nineteenth century.

Understanding aging in the past is not only a matter of the status of old age, "attitudes" toward the elderly, class and gender differences, or treatment of the poor or frail aged. These are important sociological questions that historians have inherited from gerontologists. Unfortunately, we have also inherited gerontology's traditional dissociation of ideas, images, and attitudes from the "facts" of aging – an epistemological stance which denies that the experience and cultural representation of human aging help to constitute its reality.[17] This dissociation makes aging an abstraction and places the historian at a comfortable distance away. It treats ideas, beliefs, and feelings about aging as if they were merely subjective reactions to an objective reality. Such empiricism impedes a richer understanding of growing old – both in the past and in the present. When internalized, it feeds a kind of false consciousness, a separation of body and self, that is common in our culture.[18]

By focusing solely on an abstract "problem of old age," apart from the actual lives and cultural representations of people growing older, the scientific management of aging also denies our universal participation and solidarity in this most human experience. We humans are spiritual animals, who need love and meaning no less than food, clothing, shelter, or health care.

Yet historians of aging have been slow to appreciate religion and spirituality as fundamental aspects of life.[19] Religious beliefs and practices are often regarded as reflections of more basic realities, such as psychological need or economic and political power. Both these assumptions – that the empirical facts of aging alone are ultimately real and that religious or spiritual

---

[17] This traditional positivist approach has been increasingly challenged in recent years. See, for example, Ronald J. Manheimer, "The Narrative Quest in Humanistic Gerontology," *Journal of Aging Studies* 3, no. 3 (fall 1989): 231–52; James E. Birren and Vern L. Benston, eds., *Emergent Theories of Aging* (New York: Springer, 1988), esp. chaps. 1 (Harry R. Moody), 2 (Gary M. Kenyon), and 11 (Gary T. Reker and Paul T. P. Wong); L. Eugene Thomas, ed., *Research on Adulthood and Aging: The Human Science Approach* (Albany: State University of New York Press, 1989).

[18] See Morris Berman, *Coming to Our Senses: Body and Spirit in the Hidden History of the West* (New York: Simon and Schuster, 1989). For a philosophical alternative, see Sally A. Gadow, "Body and Self: A Dialectic," *Journal of Medicine and Philosophy* 5 (1980): 172–85.

[19] For an exception, see Terri L. Premo, *Winter Friends: Women Growing Old in the New Republic, 1785–1835* (Urbana: University of Illinois Press, 1990).

life can be reduced to other factors – must be set aside before we can achieve a deeper understanding of aging. All societies establish systems of meaning that help people orient themselves toward the intractable limits of human existence.[20] Religion dominated such social meaning systems in the past; science and medicine dominate them today. In the future, we will need a rapprochement between ancient wisdom and modern science, between mystery and mastery.

Such a rapprochement begins with a critique of the assumption that biological changes constitute the underlying reality of aging, upon which are constructed psychological, social, political, and cultural responses.[21] Aging and old age are certainly real, but they do not exist in some natural realm, independently of the ideals, images, and social practices that conceptualize and represent them.[22] Growing old cannot be understood apart from its subjective experience, mediated by social condition and cultural significance. Contemporary quests for new meaning in old age underscore the fragile cultural significance of late life.[23] Indeed, they presuppose the decline of older religious meanings – a process whose origins and implications I hope to illuminate.

In the last fifty years, the central goal of the modern scientific enterprise – the conquest of premature death from acute disease and the prolongation of healthy, vigorous life – has become a realistic expectation for most people in Western, urbanized countries. Ironically, however, the very success of this enterprise has also created a new fate for the developed world: Most of us will live well into the "long, late afternoon of life" and suffer from chronic disease before we die. Much of the peculiar pathos of aging in American culture derives from our denial of this new fate.

Since the mid-nineteenth century, Americans have come to view aging not as a fated aspect of our individual and social existence but as one of life's problems to be solved through willpower, aided by science, technology, and expertise. According to this view, the road to a better future has been paved with the methodology of positivist science, which assumes that we know more about all aspects of aging than our historical predecessors. An accumulation of empirical facts will someday produce total understanding of the

---

[20] See Daniel Bell, *The Cultural Contradictions of Capitalism* (New York: Basic Books, 1976), 146ff.

[21] For an excellent critique of this prevailing assumption, see Stuart F. Spicker, "Philosophical Reflections on the 'Biology of Aging,' " in *Vitalizing Long-Term Care: The Teaching Nursing Home and Other Perspectives*, ed. Stuart F. Spicker and Stanley R. Ingman (New York: Springer, 1984), 29–45.

[22] For a similar perspective on the nature of disease, see François Delaporte, *Disease and Civilization: The Cholera in Paris, 1832*, trans. Arthur Goldhammer (Cambridge, Mass.: Harvard University Press, 1986), 6ff.

[23] See, for example, Erik and Joan Erikson's introduction to Stuart Spicker, Kathleen Woodward and David Van Tassel, eds., *Aging and the Elderly: Humanistic Perspectives in Gerontology* (Atlantic Highlands, N.J.: Humanities Press, 1978), 1–8; Richard B. Calhoun, *In Search of the New Old* (New York: Elsevier, 1978); and Manheimer, "Narrative Quest" (see n. 17).

natural and social worlds, allowing us to grow old without disease, suffering, conflict, or mystery.

The problem with this mythology of scientific management is not that it is altogether false, but that it is only half true. The scientific management of aging fundamentally misconstrues the "problem" of aging. As T. S. Eliot once remarked, there are two kinds of problems in life. One kind requires the question, What are we going to do about it? And the other calls for different questions: What does it mean? How does one relate to it?[24] The first kind of problem is like a puzzle that can be solved with appropriate technical resources and pragmatic responses. The second kind of problem is really a mystery rather than a puzzle. It poses a deeper range of challenges – which no particular policy, strategy, or technique will overcome. Mysteries require meaning. Born of moral commitment and spiritual reflection, the experience of meaning helps individuals to understand, accept, and imaginatively transform the unmanageable, ambiguous aspects of existence.

Clearly, growing old involves both puzzles and mysteries. Yet people do not face life with the clear light of reason alone. We are always informed by beliefs and values that are embedded in history and society. Whether we are aware of them or not, cultural beliefs and values always shape our understanding of life's big questions. Even universal questions have only historical answers. We mortals glimpse eternity only in history. And history is *in us*.

"If you've got your health, you've got everything," my grandmother Reba used to tell me. When she lost her health, my grandmother had nothing. "How could I have come to this?" she asked when I talked with her about various methods of care. "I hate myself, I have nothing to live for. I just want to die." Weeping continuously, depressed from lack of food, sleep, and human contact, my grandmother resisted the idea of entering a nursing home. "What do you think I am?" she demanded, "a no-goodnik, a pauper? I worked hard all my life, and I'll kill myself before anybody puts me in a poorhouse. Is that what you want? Keep this up and you'll kill your grandmother."

My grandmother was an orthodox Jew, who put off marriage to nurse her mother through a long terminal illness. Yet Reba had thoroughly assimilated middle-class American priorities of health, productivity, and self-reliance, and she had neither son nor daughter to look after her. No longer competent to handle her own affairs, she considered her life over. "You've ruined me, shattered my life," she complained after I had made legal and home-care arrangements for her. "But what can you do?" My grandmother was broken on the rock of old age. She suffered from illness, from isolation, from the

---

[24] Cited by William F. May, "The Virtues and Vices of the Elderly," in Cole and Gadow, *What Does It Mean To Grow Old?* (see n. 1). On this crucial distinction between puzzles and mysteries, see Gabriel Marcel, *Man Against Mass Society* (Chicago: Henry Regnery, 1962), 89–90.

cumulative traumas of a lifetime. All these were intensified by the historically conditioned feelings of failure that accompanied her failing body and mind.

My grandmother Helen was spared such suffering – not because she possessed religious or spiritual commitments that might have helped her transform the experience of a failing body, but because her body only failed at the end. After her first heart attack, the cardiac surgeon prepared to implant a pacemaker. She died before he got the chance. Like Reba, Helen despised the idea of being bathed, fed, and dressed by others. Unlike Reba, she did not have to repeat her own mother's long experience of dependence and dementia.

My grandmothers both felt a deep sense of shame and revulsion at their own failing bodies. These feelings reflect our culture's intractable hostility to physical decline and mental decay, imposed with particular vengeance on older women.[25] Their shame and revulsion also reflects the scientific management of aging – which encouraged them to think of growing old not as part of the human condition but as a solvable problem.

The scientific management of aging has its origins in the late eighteenth century, which marks the beginning of a profound shift in Western approaches toward aging.[26] Benjamin Franklin once articulated the new scientific approach: "The rapid progress *true* science now makes," he wrote in 1780, "occasions my regretting sometimes that I was born so soon. It is impossible to imagine the height to which may be carried . . . the power of man over matter. . . . All diseases may by sure means be prevented or cured, not excepting even that of old age, and our lives lengthened at pleasure."[27]

Franklin and other Enlightenment figures reflect the modern movement away from understanding aging primarily as an existential problem requiring moral and spiritual commitment, toward understanding it primarily as a scientific problem amenable to technical solution. Throughout this book, I use the term *existential* broadly. It refers not to any particular existentialist philosophy but to the lived experience of our inherent limitations, of human beings seeking "love and meaning in the face of death."[28] Since the early twentieth century, and especially after World War II, public discussion of aging has taken place largely within the frameworks of science and medicine. Biomedical and social scientists have effectively labeled aging as a problem

---

[25] Susan Sontag, "The Double Standard of Aging," in *Psychology of Women: Selected Readings*, ed. Juanita H. Williams (New York: Norton, 1979).

[26] See David Troyansky, *Old Age in the Old Regime* (Ithaca, N.Y.: Cornell University Press, 1989), esp. chaps. 3–5; and Gerald J. Gruman, "A History of Ideas About the Prolongation of Life," *Transactions of the American Philosophical Society*, n.s., 56, part 9 (1966): 3–102. For reflections on the epistemological status of the study of aging, see W. Andrew Achenbaum, "Can Gerontology Be a Science?" *Journal of Aging Studies* 1 (1987): 3–18.

[27] Cited in Gerald J. Gruman, "A History of Ideas" (see n. 26), 74.

[28] For a clear statement of this usage in the context of contemporary medicine, see David Barnard, "Love and Death: Existential Dimensions of Physicians' Difficulties With Moral Problems," *The Journal of Medicine and Philosophy* 13 (1988): 393–409.

that we can solve (or at least manage) given enough basic research and intervention.

Obviously, certain problems of aging – poverty, isolation, treatable disease – can and should be alleviated. Yet others – the gradual decline of physical vitality, the eventual path to death – are intractable. Our culture's ability to infuse these existential mysteries with vital meaning has been profoundly weakened over the last two centuries. Our ability to see the spiritual possibilities of aging has been equally impaired.

It is true that the line between scientific problem and existential mystery is neither perfectly clear nor historically stable. Fifty years ago, for example, pneumonia was a common cause of death, known as "the old man's friend." Today, pneumococcus pneumonia is routinely cured with antiobiotics. In the future, several of today's intractable illnesses (e.g., Alzheimer's disease or cancer) will probably yield up their secrets to biomedical research and technology. But no amount of biomedical research and technical intervention can bring aging fully under the control of human will or desire. Growing old and dying, like being born and growing up, will remain part of the cycle of organic life, part of the coming into being and passing away that make up the history of the universe. Human freedom and vitality lie in choosing to live well within these limits, even as we struggle against them.[29]

The scientific management of aging – in its one-sided drive to maximize health and organic functioning – generally ignores these limits. It obliterates this existential dimension of aging and overlooks the spiritual resources needed to redeem human finitude.[30] Yet the problem is not simply that science and medicine have replaced religion and philosophy. By the late nineteenth century, the dominant culture of middle-class Protestantism had itself lost the ability to face aging and death with existential integrity, bequeathing science a legacy of fear, evasion, and hostility toward aging. Indeed, the core of this book shows how nineteenth-century Protestantism's growing commitment to Victorian morality and scientific progress undermined its ability to understand and accept the intractable vicissitudes of later life.

All cultures maintain ideals of aging and old age. Existentially vital ideals reflect the ineradicable paradoxes of later life: aging is a source of wisdom and suffering, spiritual growth and physical decline, honor and vulnerability.[31] These ambiguities, and the ambivalent feelings they evoke, cannot

---

[29] See Merold Westphal, *God, Guilt, and Death: An Existential Phenomenology of Religion* (Bloomington: Indiana University Press, 1984), 95–102.

[30] For a critique of the attempt to make death into a technical problem, see Larry R. Churchill, "The Human Experience of Dying: The Moral Primacy of Stories over Stages," *Soundings* 62 (spring 1976): 24–37.

[31] See George Minois, *History of Old Age From Antiquity to the Renaissance*, trans. Sarah Hanbury Tenison (Chicago: University of Chicago Press, 1989), 303–307; Simone de Beauvoir, *The Coming of Age* (New York: Putnam, 1972), 96–98.

be neatly clarified and placed into separate categories without violating the nature of aging itself. Victorian images of aging, however, did not reflect its uncertain and paradoxical nature. In place of ambiguity and contingency, Victorians portrayed a rigid polarity of positive and negative stereotypes whose legacy would extend far into the twentieth century.

The rise of liberal individualism and of a moral code relying on physical self-control marked the end of early American culture's ability to hold opposites in creative tension – to accept the ambiguity, contingency, intractability, and unmanageability of human life. The Puritans had urged early American believers to seek spiritual strength and personal growth by accepting frailty and decay as inevitable aspects of flawed human existence. Hope and triumph were linked dialectically to decline and death. This existential integrity was virtually lost in Victorian culture, which found it necessary to separate strength and frailty, growth and decay, hope and death. Impelled by their perfectionism in physical and spiritual matters, and by their belief in the power of individual will, Victorian moralists dichotomized and rationalized experience in order to control it. These pressures to master old age, rather than accept it, generated a rigid dualism: Anyone who lived a life of hard work, faith, and self-discipline could preserve health and independence into a ripe old age, followed by a quick, painless natural death; only the shiftless, faithless, and promiscuous were doomed to premature death or a miserable old age.

I have no desire to denigrate the accomplishments of science and medicine or to return to the "good old days" of Calvinism when people were reconciled to the vicissitudes of aging and death by virtue of faith. I welcome the advances in productivity, nutrition, public health, and scientific medicine that have made it possible for most people to live to a great age. I applaud the contributions that gerontology and geriatrics have made to the health and well-being of older people. We need more of these things, and we need them distributed more equitably within our aging population.

But we need a cultural reorientation as well. For all its accomplishments, the cultural hegemony of science intensifies the pathos of aging in a society devoted to the limitless pursuit of individual health and wealth. In the last twenty years, we have witnessed an important social movement aimed at eliminating age discrimination and at generating new positive images of old age. But this recent attack on ageism – as valuable as it is – has yet to confront the de-meaning of aging rooted in modern culture's relentless hostility toward decay and dependency. In the late twentieth century, later life floats in a cultural limbo. Old age remains a season in search of its purposes.

We cannot understand or relieve the pathos of aging in contemporary American culture without stepping back from the assumptions of scientific management and its uncritical alliance with capitalist accumulation and liberal individualism. I criticize this cultural and institutional matrix, however, as an insider rather than an outsider.[32] I make my daily bread as a humanist in an academic health science center, teaching medical students, allied health students, graduate students, interns, and residents in both classroom and clinical settings. I regularly attend hospital rounds in family medicine and serve as a consultant for difficult cases, often involving elderly patients who are frail, dying, or demented. My critique does not derive from any naive assumption that the humanities can somehow "save" the life of an aging society or simply replace scientific medicine as a world view. My goal is to reform the scientific management of aging, rather than to abolish it.[33]

Nor can we expect satisfying answers to emerge from modern science and professionalism, which fall silent before the human need for metaphysical explanation and consolation.[34] Science and the professions possess no common language for articulating moral and existential issues. Their cultural dominance reflects the double bind of modernity: Our aging society cannot express its most fundamental problems without such a language, yet our commitment to pluralism forbids privileging any one religious or spiritual language over others.[35] If there is a solution to this double bind, it lies in a public dialogue that addresses these issues without creating a false consensus.[36]

The Journey of Life contributes to this dialogue by recovering older languages of meaning and critiquing their evolution in American history. I do not believe that an older, religiously sanctioned, communal culture had the "right" language for addressing existential questions about aging. The past does not have "answers" for the present. It does, however, contain the

---

[32] Michael Walzer, *Interpretation and Social Criticism* (Cambridge, Mass.: Harvard University Press, 1987).

[33] For an overview of recent contributions from the humanities to gerontology and geriatrics, see my introduction to Polisar, *Where Do We Come From?* (see n. 16); also, Harry R. Moody, "Toward a Critical Gerontology: The Contribution of the Humanities to Theories of Aging," in *Emergent Theories of Aging*, ed. James E. Birren and Vern L. Bengtson (New York: Springer, 1988), 19–40. For practical implications of my perspective in clinical care, see Thomas R. Cole and Patricia Jakobi, "Reflections on Ethics, Aging, and Rehabilitation," in J. Dermot Frengley, Patrick Murray, and May L. Wykle, eds., *Practicing Rehabilitation with Geriatric Clients* (New York: Springer, 1990), 191–205; and Gretchen Aumann and Thomas R. Cole, "In Whose Voice? Composing a Lifesong Collaboratively,"*Journal of Clinical Ethics* 2:1 (1991): 32–35.

[34] There are, of course, important exceptions to this generalization, including writers like Lewis Thomas, Stephen Jay Gould, and Robert Butler.

[35] On the double bind of modernity, see Bell, *Cultural Contradictions* (see n. 20), part 1. For a discussion of the loss of language adequate to spiritual needs in the welfare state, see Michael Ignatieff, *The Needs of Strangers* (New York: Viking, 1985), 19ff.

[36] For a general attempt to undertake this task in contemporary American culture, see Robert Bellah et al., *Habits of the Heart: Individualism and Commitment in American Life* (Berkeley: University of California Press, 1985). For a communitarian effort to discuss the meaning and significance of old age in the context of allocating health care, see Daniel Callahan, *Setting Limits: Medical Goals in an Aging Society* (New York: Simon and Schuster, 1987), chap. 2. In my view, Norman Daniels's *Am I My Parent's Keeper? An Essay on Justice Between the Young and the Old* (New York: Oxford University Press, 1988) avoids questions of meaning and purpose by retreating behind a Rawlsian "veil of ignorance" and a medicalized version of equal opportunity in discussing issues of generational justice.

fundamental human stock of ideas, images, beliefs, wishes, superstitions, feelings, dreams, hopes, and fears about aging. Unlike the history of science and technology, cultural history cannot be the story of progress. Culture, understood as the realm of symbolic forms through which we seek to explore and express the meanings of human existence, always contains an element of return to the timeless concerns of birth and death, growth and decline, heroism, tragedy, love, and obligation.[37] In illuminating the past, cultural history helps guide our "return" to the future.

Cultures meet the existential needs of elders by drawing on their core beliefs and values to construct ideals of aging, old age, and its place within the life cycle. Using myth, metaphor, and other forms of symbolic language, such ideals impart meaning to old age and convey the dominant social opportunities available to people as they chart their individual paths into late life. An ideal old age legitimizes roles and norms appropriate to the last stage of life, providing sanctions and incentives for living with the flow of time. Ideals of old age are not always existentially sound, even if widely shared. And since cultures are not monolithic, competing ideals (of varying degrees of existential vitality and ideological power) circulate within a complex society.

Ideals of aging and old age are not simply goals to be achieved or desires to be fulfilled when careers are completed and children reared. Nor are they merely pious illusions to be debunked empirically with more solid or sordid realities. Ideals of old age are images of higher peaks and greater depths that can *enrich reality* in later life. "To want our reality to grow in directions of height and depth," writes Robert Nozick, "is to want our lives to be marked by ideals, understanding, and deep emotion, to be governed by these and to pursue them."[38]

At the same time, however, ideals are always socially located and implicated in relationships of power and authority. My perspective differs from that of George Minois, who sees ideals of old age before the Renaissance primarily as forms of domination.[39] Minois looks to modern medicine and the social sciences as neutral means of understanding older people's real needs. In contrast, I see medicine and the social sciences as essential for understanding patterns of health and disease, but as inadequate for teaching us what kind of elders we want to be. In fact, medicine and science since the Renaissance have generally been infused with unacknowledged middle-class, masculine ideals. These ideals call for criticism and evaluation in social, moral, and existential terms.

Ideals of later life are carved out of three basic dimensions of meaning:

[37] This is Bell's formulation, *Cultural Contradictions* (see n. 20), 12ff. See also Daniel Bell, "The Return of the Sacred?" in *The Winding Passage* (Cambridge, Mass.: ABT Books, 1980), 332ff.

[38] Robert Nozick, *The Examined Life: Philosophical Meditations* (New York: Simon and Schuster, 1989), 139.

[39] See his *History of Old Age* (see n. 31).

cosmic, social, and individual.[40] Every culture fashions ideals from all three sources of meaning, prioritizing and blending these in the light of its own history, social structure, and belief system. The three-part structure of this book follows the historical evolution of Western ideals of later life – from classical and Christian ideals that gave pride of place to the *cosmic* sense of meaning, to a Victorian ideal based on the priority of *social* meaning (especially secular progress), to scientific ideals of "normal" or "successful" aging, based on the priority of *individual* meaning.

Part 1 describes ideals of transcendence, in which the goal of aging is to bring oneself into alignment with an order of the cosmos. Part 2 describes the ideals of morality, which articulate social behavior considered necessary for a good old age and its religious rewards. Part 3 describes ideals of "normal" aging that seek to maximize individual health and physiological functioning in old age through scientific research and medical management. This three-part division into cosmic, social, and individual dimensions of meaning (and their corresponding ideals of transcendence, morality, and normality) does not do justice to the complexity, counterpoint, and contradiction that the careful reader will find in the text. Nevertheless, it is a heuristic device to help readers keep in mind the basic conceptual framework and historical thrust of the book.

Chapter 1 provides essential background for understanding the basic direction and pattern of change in American ideas about aging. It briefly shows how several learned and folk versions of life's ages and its journey passed from ancient authors into medieval Christianity. The chapter then argues that quintessentially modern ideas and images of individual lifetime were born in Northern Europe between the late Middle Ages and the seventeenth century. In this period, abstract ideas about individual lifetime took on new religious and social significance. Imagining one's own life (and that of others) as a spiritual drama, as a career, and as a sequence of stages became increasingly common. In popular iconography, the old medieval circle of life was replaced by a rising and falling staircase. At about the same time, life's journey also found its characteristically modern and enormously popular form in John Bunyan's *Pilgrim's Progress* (1678). These, I suggest, are the forms in which the ages of life and the journey of life later made their way to the New World and shaped the sensibility of middle-class American Protestantism toward aging.

Chapter 1 suggests that the growing interest in individual lifetime is best understood in conjunction with the "spirit of capitalism" described by Max Weber and the "civilizing process" described by Norbert Elias. Envisioning each individual life from birth to death as a sacred career, in other words,

---

[40] See Harry R. Moody, "The Meaning of Life and the Meaning of Old Age," in Cole and Gadow, *What Does It Mean To Grow Old?* (see n. 1), 16.

developed alongside new commercial ideas about time and work, together with specifically Protestant notions of salvation and the gradual postmedieval shift of social controls from the community to the individual.[41] Later chapters show that when the "civilizing process" reached a high-water mark in Victorian America, the aging body posed intractable problems for the ideology of self-control, opening the way for new methods in science and medicine.

Chapters 2 through 10 reconstruct three specific ideals of aging and old age held by middle-class Americans since the seventeenth century. I have used the terms *late Calvinist*, *"civilized"* or *Victorian*, and *"normal"* or *"successful"* to refer to these ideals. These have not been the only models of old age available in American culture. We will need a great deal of more specialized research to have a fuller appreciation of the cultural history of aging. We need, for example, to learn more about the values and practices of aging among Native American peoples, among blacks in slavery and in freedom, among working-class immigrants, Mexican Americans, urban Jews, Midwestern farmers, and Southern yeomen. Then we will be able to see how the dominant middle-class ideals both shaped and were shaped by the values of other social groups. This book does not attempt to discuss challenges and alternatives to the dominant middle-class ideals of aging. Rather, it traces the evolution of these ideals and evaluates their legacy for contemporary American life.

Again stated baldly, the book describes a historical evolution from communal ideals of transcendence through societal ideals of morality to individual ideals of health. Its major insights derive from analyzing a broad transition from religious and communal to scientific and individualistic ways of conceiving the meaning of aging and old age. In the late twentieth century, I suggest in the Epilogue, this continuous evolution toward secular individualist meanings has reached its limit. We are living through the search for ideals adequate to a postmodern culture, in which the recovery of cosmic and collective sources of meaning may enable us to appreciate the spiritual and moral aspects of aging without devaluing individual development.

Every society creates symbols, images, and rituals that help people live meaningfully within the limits of human existence. Meanings of aging and old age are inevitably linked to these cultural forms that symbolize life's meaning. And such cultural representations of life's meaning finally involve some intuitive grasp of its wholeness or unity.[42] Until recently, Western culture has relied on two archetypal images to represent intuitions of the wholeness or unity of life – the division of life into ages (or stages) and the metaphor of life as a journey. These fundamental images, therefore, are the essential cultural forms for the history of the meaning of aging.

---

[41] Norbert Elias, *The Civilizing Process*, trans. Edmund Jephcott (New York: Urizen Books, 1978).
[42] Harry R. Moody, "The Meaning of Life" (see n. 40), 11–17.

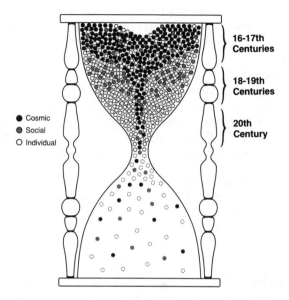

Figure 1. Sources of meaning: a pattern in Western history. (Gus Homann and Steve Schuenke, 1990.)

Classical antiquity first connected the ages of life and the journey of life, weaving them into its beliefs about the nature of human existence and the cosmos. In the Middle Ages, Christian writers adopted Greco-Roman ideas about the ages of life and conceived of the journey of life as a sacred pilgrimage. From the Reformation, which forged modern imagery of the life cycle, until World War I, which hastened its demise, various combinations of these images provided an existentially vital and culturally powerful framework that helped sustain the meaning of aging and old age in middle-class culture.

The archetypal power of these images derives from their capacity to help us approach the mystery of human temporality.[43] Virtually universal, they appear in many cultures not as cognitive abstractions but as ritualized elements of individual and social life.[44] Each offers a way of conceiving fragmented, sometimes chaotic, ever-changing "life time" as a unified whole.

[43] For valuable literary treatments of the journey of life, see Monica Furlong, *The End of Our Exploring* (London: Hodder and Stoughton, 1973), and Georg Roppen and Richard Sommer, *Strangers and Pilgrims* (Bergen: Norwegian Universities Press, 1964). Two theological works that have influenced me are Gabriel Marcel, *Homo Viator* (Chicago: Henry Regnery, 1951), and John S. Dunne, *Time and Myth* (New York: Doubleday, 1973).

[44] For anthropological discussions of the ages of life (known as age-grading), see Martha Nemes Fried and Morton H. Fried, *Transitions, Four Rituals in Eight Cultures* (New York: Norton, 1980), and Jennie Keith and David I. Kertzer, eds., *Age in Anthropological Theory* (Ithaca, N.Y.: Cornell University Press, 1984).

This imagined whole, within which various parts of life can be located, guarantees a coherent (and not always happy) place for aging and old age.

By the fifth century B.C.E. Greek legend and custom had divided human life into three ages, each corresponding to a generation, each possessing its own set of natural characteristics and prescribed behavior.[45] Aristotle formalized this threefold division in the *Rhetoric*, where he discussed the ages of growth, stasis, and decline.[46] Hippocrates described four physiologically determined ages – the most common scheme until the late Middle Ages, when the astrologically based system of seven ages was translated into the vernacular and eventually immortalized by Shakespeare's cynical Jaques:

> All the world's a stage,
> And all the men and women merely players.
> They have their exits and entrances;
> And one man in his time plays many parts,
> His acts being seven ages.
>
> *As You Like It*, act 2, scene 7

In *De Senectute*, Cicero identified the philosophical bedrock beneath the ages-of-life conception – the belief that despite the diversity of size, appearance, ability, and behavior that characterizes the different ages, the human lifespan constitutes a single natural order. "Life's racecourse is fixed"; wrote Cicero, "nature has only a single path and that path is run but once, and to each stage of existence has been allotted its appropriate quality."[47]

The ages of life offers a broadly unified view of a human lifetime; the processes of birth, growth, maturity, decay and death appear as parts of the cycle of organic life. But growing up and old is not only a *process*, rooted in our biological existence, structured by social and historical circumstances. It is also an *experience*, an incalculable series of events, moments, and acts lived by an individual person. This experience, this passage through the maze of the inner life, has been traditionally represented by the journey of life – a metaphor that operates by narrating diverse experiences in time and space, bringing them under control of a single unifying purpose.

The journey is among the most pervasive themes in world literature. Folk tales, poetry, drama, fiction, art, and religious teaching are filled with male heroes who set out from safe but constricting origins, undergo a series of adventures that transform them, and eventually reach or fail to reach a goal,

---

[45] See Laura Nash, "Concepts of Existence: Greek Origins of Generational Thought," *Daedalus* 107 (fall 1978): 1–22. See also a fable of Aesop, which combines primitive Germanic and Oriental ideas about the life cycle; cited in José Ortega y Gasset, "Idea of the Generation," in *Man in Crisis*, trans. Mildred Adams (New York: Norton, 1958), 48.

[46] Cited in James A. Burrow, *The Ages of Man* (Oxford: Oxford University Press, 1986), Appendix, 191–94.

[47] Cited in Burrow, *Ages of Man* (see n. 46), 1.

or prize, or spiritual home.[48] The stories of Gilgamesh, Job, Odysseus, and Aeneas reflect the power of this metaphor in antiquity, when poets first articulated the two major shapes of the journey: circular progression toward the renewal or restoration of the traveler, achieved through a homecoming; and linear progression from a situation of social or intellectual disorder to one of order.[49]

When the Jewish oral tradition was written down, the journey of life figured prominently in the teaching of Rabbi Akaviah ben Mahalalel: "Ponder three things and you will avoid falling into sin: Know your origin, your destination, and before Whom you will be required to give an accounting."[50] The Christian tradition, of course, has used the theme to convey the spiritual life of "strangers and pilgrims" in search of God (Hebrews 11:13).

Although both the ages motif and the journey motif offer images of life as a whole, each leaves out the other's essential insight. The ages of life envisions the biologically and socially structured process of the human life cycle. The journey of life emphasizes the fluid and unique qualities of individual experience, the spiritual drama of the traveler's search. A deeper understanding of human "life time" requires some imaginative fusion of the two themes, in which neither is reduced to the other and both together create a whole greater than the sum of their parts. Existentially adequate and culturally powerful meanings of aging emerge when artists, writers, theologians, philosophers, or scientists hold these two motifs together in creative tension and weave them into their culture's view of the relations between cosmos, society, and self.

As I have shown elsewhere,[51] Sophocles achieved such a dynamic vision in *Oedipus Rex*, the familiar story of patricide and incest, and *Oedipus at Colonus*, the story of the aged exile.[52] By juxtaposing the ages of life (Oedipus's

---

[48] Furlong, *End of Our Exploring* (see n. 43), 19, 20. See also Joseph Campbell, *The Hero With a Thousand Faces* (Princeton: Princeton University Press, 1949); and Tu Wei-ming, "The Confucian Perception of Adulthood," *Daedalus* 105 (spring 1976): 109–23.

[49] See William Bridges, "The Odyssey and the Myth of the Homeward Journey," in *Consciousness and Creativity*, ed. John-Raphael Staude (Berkeley: Pan/Proteus Books, 1977), 99–112; and Roppen and Sommer, *Strangers and Pilgrims* (see n. 43), 18–20.

[50] See R. Travers Herford, trans., *The Ethics of the Talmud: Sayings of the Fathers (Pirke Aboth)* (New York: Schocken, 1962), chap. 3, verse 1, p. 63.

[51] Thomas R. Cole, "Oedipus and the Meaning of Aging: Personal Reflections and Historical Perspectives," in *Ethics and the Elderly*, ed. Nancy Jecker (New York: Humana Press, forthcoming).

[52] Scholarly interest in *Oedipus at Colonus* seems to be increasing, which suggests that contemporary audiences might respond favorably to new adaptations of the play. See, for example, Nancy Datan, "The Oedipus Cycle: Developmental Mythology, Greek Tragedy, and the Sociology of Knowledge," unpublished paper presented at the annual meeting of the Gerontological Society of America, New Orleans, 1985; Christine Downing, "Your Old Men Shall Dream Dreams," in *Wisdom and Age*, ed. John-Raphael Staude (Berkeley: Proteus Books, 1981), 169–86; Thomas Falkner, "Strengthless, Friendless, Loveless: The Chorus and the Cultural Construction of Old Age in Sophocles' *Oedipus at Colonus*," in *From the Bard to Broadway*, vol. 7, University of Florida Comparative Drama Conference Papers (Lanham, Md.: University Press of America, 1987), 51–59; and Thomas Van Nortwick, " 'Do not Go Gently . . . ': *Oedipus*

answer to the Sphinx's riddle) and the journey of life (Oedipus's long wandering in exile and his triumphant death), Sophocles generated profound insights into the mysteries of aging, death, and generational succession.

Sophocles, like Freud, used the legend of Oedipus to emphasize the sad inevitability of generational conflict — conflict guaranteed by the tensions that arise because each generation is destined to rise, decline, and die, to be replaced by a new generation. But whereas Freud pointed an accusing finger at the young Oedipus, recent commentators have reminded us that the tragedy is set in motion by his father, King Laius.[53] Laius attempts to evade the oracle's prophecy (that he would be killed by his own son) by leaving the infant Oedipus on a hillside to die. But a compassionate shepherd then takes Oedipus to Corinth, where he is raised by a couple he believes are his real parents. Laius's actions, which signify the attempt to deny mortality and generational succession, only seal his fate, which he meets fifteen years later at the hands of the unknowing Oedipus.

Oedipus, we will remember, does not ascend to the throne of Thebes through the murder of his father, King Laius. Before the action of *Oedipus Rex* begins, he saves the city from the monster Sphinx, who is strangling its inhabitants for being unable to answer her riddle: "What goes on four legs in the morning, two legs at noon, and three legs in the afternoon?" "Man," replies Oedipus; man crawls as an infant, walks upright in his prime, and hobbles with a cane in old age. Man is the animal whose three ages of life demand different forms of movement. But what are the origins and destiny of this movement?

Here, Sophocles is nudging us toward a deeper understanding of the riddle: We come to know the ages of life by living a personal journey from vulnerable, dependent childhood to apparently independent adulthood and on to vulnerability and dependence again in old age. Moving from stage to stage, we come to know ourselves. For all its apparent brilliance, Oedipus's solution to the Sphinx's riddle cannot ultimately save him or save Thebes. Unrelated to his own origins or destiny, Oedipus's answer is incomplete, uninformed by self-knowledge. Oedipus remains a riddle to himself.

In identifying man as the creature whose life resembles the rising and setting of the daily sun, Oedipus seems to affirm the ineradicable limits of the human condition and the necessity of generational continuity. Yet the great problem solver must first set out on the tragic road to self-knowledge before he will fully understand the riddle of man's existence in time.

Years after the death of Laius, when the action of *Oedipus Rex* begins, the

---

at Colonus and the Psychology of Aging," in *Old Age in Greek and Latin Literature*, ed. Thomas M. Falkner and Judith de Luce (Albany: State University of New York Press, 1989).

[53] N. Datan, "The Oedipus Cycle" (see n. 52); and J. M. Ross, "Oedipus Revisited: Laius and the 'Laius Complex,' " in *The Oedipus Papers*, ed. G. H. Pollock and J. M. Ross (Madison, Wisc.: International Universities Press), 235–316.

city of Thebes is suffering from a plague sent by the gods for the unsolved murder of the old king. With the same intellectual self-confidence he displayed in solving the Sphinx's riddle, Oedipus proclaims that he will find the murderer and banish him from Thebes. Thus slowly unravels the mystery of Oedipus's own origins, the story of patricide and incest, leading to blindness, horror, and exile.

For most of us, I suspect, this is where the story of Oedipus ends. But for Sophocles, who completed *Oedipus at Colonus* at the age of eighty-nine, Oedipus's self-blinding and exile are the beginning of a long journey to insight, inner knowledge, and finally to what Thomas Mann describes as "smiling knowledge of the eternal."[54]

After twenty years of wandering, led by his daughter Antigone, the old, blind, bearded, and ragged Oedipus seeks a final home in the sacred grove of the Furies at Colonus, the birthplace of Sophocles himself. Here, Oedipus realizes that he has come upon the place where the oracle predicted he would become a blessing to those who received him. Through his long exile the elder Oedipus eventually sees that he has lived all of his life in accordance with the oracle's prophecy and that trying to evade this fate only intensified its power over him. His blessed death, Sophocles seems to be saying, is appropriate to one "who has lived long enough to understand the meaning of his own story."[55]

Yet for all its power, the triumph of Oedipus remains troubling. Oedipus prevails, but in *Antigone* his family line comes to a miserable end. Rather than forgive even one of his sons, he allows them to slaughter each other in battle. His daughters live out the mystery of undeserved fate. We are forced to wonder: Did Oedipus's children pay the price for his glory? Did he put his own spiritual welfare above obligations to their future lives? Does successful culmination of life's journey require undue sacrifices from those, like Antigone, who make it possible?

I do not know the answers to these questions. Standing in between my daughter and my grandmothers, I do recognize myself as the animal that goes on four legs in the morning, two legs at midday, and three legs in the afternoon. Cut loose from the anchoring old rocks of my childhood, I have embarked on my "awful rowing toward God," in search of an innocent and playful wisdom. Along the way, I hope to see if my own old age corresponds to my middle-aged ideal of it.

---

[54] Cited in Downing, "Your Old Men Shall Dream Dreams" (see n. 52), 172.
[55] Downing, "Your Old Men Shall Dream Dreams" (see n. 52), 176.

PART I

The ages of life and the journey of life: transcendent ideals

Aging in the Western tradition: cultural origins of the modern life course

Men die because they cannot join the end to the beginning.

Alcmeon of Groton

Our critical day is not the very day of our death but the whole course of our life.

John Donne

In contemporary urban society, we are accustomed to the notion that a precise chronological age marks the transition from one stage of life to another.[1] Children begin school at age five, young people go to work or college at eighteen, old people retire at sixty or sixty-five. Our awareness of chronological age is part of a more basic historical development – the emergence of individual lifetime as a structural feature of modern society.[2] Understood as a pattern of rules, expectations, and events ordering activities over a lifetime, the life course in Western society has become an important institution in its own right since the eighteenth century. In an increasingly rationalized, urban, industrial society, chronological age came to function as a uniform criterion for sequencing the multiple roles and responsibilities that individuals assumed over a lifetime.

Beginning in the late eighteenth century, the structure of the modern life course was created by changes in demography and family life, as well as by the growth of age-stratified systems of public rights and duties. Demographically, age-at-death was transformed from a pattern of relative randomness to one of predictability. Average life expectancy rose dramatically, especially after 1900; by the mid-twentieth century, death struck primarily in old age,

---

This chapter was written in collaboration with Mary G. Winkler.

[1] Howard P. Chudacoff, *How Old Are You? Age Consciousness in American Culture* (Princeton: Princeton University Press, 1989).

[2] Martin Kohli, "The World We Forgot: An Historical Review of the Life Course," in *Later Life: The Social Psychology of Aging*, ed. Victor W. Marshall (Beverly Hills, Calif.: Sage, 1986), 271–303.

and with much less variance than in the past.[3] Meanwhile, the experience of a modern family cycle (including marriage, children, survival of both partners to age fifty-five, "empty nest," widowhood) became increasingly common and chronologically standardized.[4]

In the century roughly between 1870 and 1970, the social transition to adulthood (end of school; first job; first marriage) became more abrupt and uniform for a growing segment of the population.[5] At the same time, the spread of universal age-homogeneous public school and chronologically triggered public pension systems divided the life course into three "boxes": education, work, and retirement. The chronological ages of twenty-one and sixty or sixty-five came to define the lower and upper boundaries of participation in the adult world – as well as the cultural definition of full humanity.[6]

The origins of our chronologically defined, bureaucratized course of life, however, lie not in relatively recent demographic changes or the heightened age consciousness and age grading of the late nineteenth century, but in the search for religious and social order in early modern Northern Europe. From the late fifteenth to the seventeenth century, abstract ideas about lifetime took on new religious and social significance. Imagining one's own life (and that of others) as a career, as a spiritual drama, and as a sequence of stages became increasingly common. In early modern Northern Europe, quintessentially modern ideas and images of human lifetime were born.

The primary evidence for this claim rests on the appearance and proliferation of a new iconography of the stages of life. Medieval cosmology represented the universe as a series of concentric circles. Hence, it is not surprising that medieval artists portrayed human life as a circle from womb to tomb. "Nothing more endless, nothing sooner broke,"[7] wrote John Donne

[3] Arthur Imhoff, "Life-Course Patterns of Women and their Husbands: 16th to 20th century," in *Human Development and the Life Course*, ed. Aage B. Sorenson, Franz E. Weinert, and Lonnie R. Sherrod (Hillsdale, N.J.: Lawrence Erlbaum, 1986); and James F. Fries and Lawrence M. Crapo, *Vitality and Aging* (San Francisco: Freeman, 1981), chap. 3.

[4] M. Mitterauer and R. Sieder, *The European Family*, ed. K. Oosteween and M. Horzinger (Chicago: University of Chicago Press, 1982), chap. 3; Peter Uhlenberg, "A Study of Cohort Life Cycles: Cohorts of Native Born Massachusetts Women, 1830–1920," *Population Studies* 23 (1969): 407–20; Peter Uhlenberg, "Cohort Variations in Family Life Cycle," *Journal of Marriage and the Family* 36 (1974): 284–89; and H. P. Chudacoff and T. K. Hareven, "From Empty Nest to Family Dissolution: Life Course Transitions into old Age," *Journal of Social History* 4 (1979): 69–83.

[5] Tamara K. Hareven and Kathleen J. Adams, eds., *Aging and Life Course Transitions* (New York: Guilford, 1982); John Model, Frank F. Furstenberg, Theodore Hershberg, "Social Change and Transitions to Adulthood in Historical Perspective," in *The American Family in Social Historical Perspective*, ed. Michael Gordon (New York: St. Martin's, 1978).

[6] Keith Thomas, "Age and Authority in Early Modern England," *Proceedings of the British Academy* 62 (1976): 248. As is often the case with historical writing, our ability to recognize and study the emergence of the modern life course comes at the very time when it is passing away, or undergoing significant alteration. See Martin Kohli, "The World We Forgot" (see n. 2), 294–97; and Michael Anderson, "The Emergence of the Modern Life Cycle in Britain," *Social History* 10 (1985): 69–87.

[7] Cited in Marjorie Hope Nicolson, *The Circle Broken* (New York: Columbia University Press, 1960).

of the circle in the seventeenth century. By Donne's era, the endless circle or *cycle* of human life had been iconographically broken and replaced by a life *course*, modeled on a rising and descending staircase. Within this iconography, the hourglass emerged as a symbol of the new prominence attributed to individual lifetime.

In the midst of changing attitudes toward time, the growth of pilgrimage as a religious theme, and growing fears of death and damnation, images of lifetime served to ease anxiety and focus worldly and otherworldly desires. The very concept of a life course fused time and space together, binding human growth and decline into an image that the new iconography made available for contemplation. At the beginning of the modern era, "the" life cycle, life course, or life span received its bourgeois cultural form – a form whose long-term implications for aging were later built into the structure of the modern life course. The new iconography, however, was itself rooted in ancient archetypal themes of the ages of life and the journey of life.

THE LEGACY OF ANTIQUITY

Until the mid-sixteenth century, *age* referred primarily to a stage or period of human life.[8] Since numerical age had virtually no social significance, few people knew exactly how old they were. This historical meaning of the word *age* reflected a universal assumption that during the course of time, men passed through several distinct phases of existence. No one doubted that women also passed through the ages of life, but until the seventeenth century, when scholars, writers, moralists, and artists wrote about or depicted the ages of life, they either subsumed women under the category of man or referred exclusively to men.[9]

Ancient authors established three principal traditions of the ages of life: divisions into three, four, and seven.[10] For the medieval world view, which assumed a divinely ordained correspondence between man, nature, and the cosmos, the fourfold division would prove most adaptable. Greek medicine and physiology had created the four ages: childhood, youth, maturity, and old age. Each of these ages possessed its special physical, mental, and behavioral characteristics, explained by its relationship to the four humors (black bile, phlegm, yellow or red bile, and blood), the four qualities (hot, dry, cold, and moist), the four elements (air, fire, earth, and water), and the four seasons.

Aristotle provided authority for the biological division of life into three

[8] Mary Dove, *The Perfect Age of a Man's Life* (Cambridge: Cambridge University Press, 1986), 11.
[9] See Dove, *Perfect Age* (see n. 8), chap. 3, "The Ages of Woman's Life."
[10] James A. Burrow, *The Ages of Man* (New York: Oxford University Press, 1986), chap. 1. It is important to note that less common divisions of life ranging from three to twelve stages also existed.

ages: growth, stasis, and decline. In the *Rhetoric*, Aristotle had also argued the moral superiority of middle age. Since men at the height of their powers are neither too trusting nor too cynical, he claimed that the ideal ruler is neither young nor old – an argument often repeated in medieval writings.[11] In general, the biological division of three ages, based on the rise and fall of physical power, was less hospitable to old age than the fourfold scheme, which easily fell into medieval patterns of harmony between microcosm and macrocosm.

The third major scheme of the life course depicted seven ages, each explained according to the influence of a planet. In his astrological treatise *Tetrabiblos*, the second-century astronomer Ptolemy provided the authoritative version of this scheme, which did not become popular in the West until the late Middle Ages. In Ptolemy's treatise, which provided the model for Jaques' monologue in *As You like it*, the last two ages are ruled by Jupiter and Saturn. The sixth age (from fifty-six to sixty-eight) brings "thoughtfulness, dignity and decorum," while the last age (sixty-eight until death) is old and cold, "dispirited, weak, easily offended, and hard to please."[12]

"To every thing there is a season, and a time to every purpose under heaven," medieval people learned from Ecclesiastes. They believed that appreciating the harmonious relations between the course of life and all of God's creation opened one's soul to divine transcendence. Neither the number of ages nor the exact chronology of each age was as important as the basic assumption that the natural divisions of a lifetime belong to the divine order of the universe.

Christian writers developed a doctrine of spiritual ages to complement the theory of bodily ages. As Thomas, Bishop of Brinton, preached in 1380, "Just as we speak of bodily age, whereby we proceed from infancy to boyhood . . . and so forth, . . . so spiritual age is a progress from virtue to virtue, from grace to grace, from good to better, from perfection to greater perfection."[13] The concept of spiritual ages allowed for the paradoxical unity of physical decline and spiritual ascent. This unity played a central role in medieval thinking about aging and the life course.[14]

In *Il Convivio*, for example, Dante accepted Aristotle's theory of three ages. But he protested against the implication that "our life is no other than

---

[11] For Aristotle's views and influence, see Burrow, *Ages of Man* (see n. 10), 5–11.

[12] The relevant section of Ptolemy's *Tetrabiblos* is reproduced in Burrow's *Ages of Man* (see n. 10), Appendix, 197–98.

[13] Burrow, *Ages of Man* (see n. 10), 110. I have relied heavily on Burrow's discussion (in chap. 3) of this important doctrine. Burrow, in turn, acknowledges his debt to Christian Gnilka, *Aetas Spiritualis: Die Überwindung der natürlichen Altersstufen als Ideal frühchristlichen Lebens* (Bonn, 1972).

[14] Compare Elizabeth Sears, *The Ages of Man* (Princeton: Princeton University Press, 1986) and Burrow, *Ages of Man* (see n. 10), on aging. Sears misses the doctrine of spiritual ages and therefore falls prey to the cliché that youth was unequivocally considered good and old age bad.

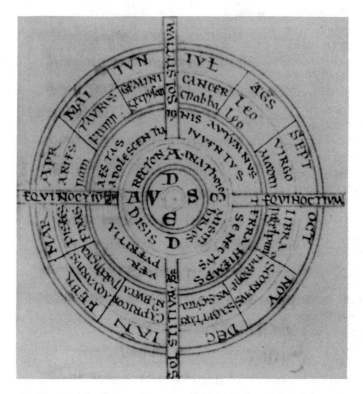

Figure 2. Diagram of a theocentric cosmos, linking the four ages and four seasons of life, from Byrhtferth's *Manual* (early eleventh century). (MS Ashmole 328, Bodleian Library, Oxford University.)

a mounting and descending." While he agreed that the physical and intellectual peak of life occurred in middle age, Dante believed that spiritual development continued – the "enobled soul proceeds in due order [toward] . . . its ultimate fruit."[15] Medieval authors generally assumed that spiritual development proceeded apace with the physical ages. The wisdom to embrace the mutability of life, the rhythm of generation and corruption, did not come to a man "until he has had many winters in the kingdom of earth," wrote an Anglo-Saxon poet.[16]

Theologians, however, did acknowledge the possibility of transcending one's bodily age and reaching a more advanced spiritual age. By a miracle of grace, a rare child (a *puer senex* or *puella senecta*) might possess the wisdom and virtue that could not ordinarily develop in the natural order until old age. Or an older person might display the virtues of *infantia*

[15] Burrow, *Ages of Man* (see n. 10), 7.
[16] Burrow, *Ages of Man* (see n. 10), 107.

spiritualis, the simplicity and purity of a small child. Anglo-Saxon literature shows a clear preference for the wisdom of old age over the innocence of childhood — for young people achieving the spiritual condition
of old age rather than older people achieving the virtues of childhood or
the powers of youth. In a culture that valued eternal life rather than
eternal youth, this preference is not surprising. Transcending one's age
allowed a person to triumph over secular time, to enter into the timeless
world of eternity.[17]

From antiquity, the Middle Ages received not only general ideas about
the course of life but also specific theories about the nature and causes of
aging. Aristotle, Galen, Hippocrates, and Cicero were the principal authorities. In *On Youth and Old Age, on Life and Respiration*, Aristotle defined
old age as that period of life when the body's innate heat diminishes.[18] Heat
was the essence of life according to Hippocratic medicine, the source being
the heart, conceived as a sort of furnace. From the heart, heat was sent to
the whole body for the purpose of maintaining a healthful balance of humors.[19] Both health and character depended on the regulation of the four
humors.[20] Each individual possessed a finite amount of heat that steadily
diminished in the natural course of life. Although it could be fortified or
replenished temporarily, vital heat could never wholly be restored. In time,
the fire of life would eventually be quenched.

Galen added another dimension to this classical theory of aging. Arguing
that blood and semen, as sources of generation, required a drying element
to produce tissue, he posited that vital heat began to dry these substances,
producing an embryo. The drying process did not stop after formation of
the embryo but continued throughout the individual's life. Thus Galen
believed that an infant is moist and an old person quite dried out. In his
theory, old age meant desiccation: "For that which all men commonly call
old age is the dry and cold constitution of the body resulting from many
years of life."[21]

Behavioral changes accompanied physical signs. Aristotle considered old
age a time when normal failings were magnified, when physical decline and
the loss of inward heat depressed the spirit. Passions waned, a development
that philosophers, equating passion with animal nature, considered one blessing in a rather baleful process.[22]

---

[17] Burrow, *Ages of Man* (see n. 10), 105.

[18] Richard L. Grant, "Concepts of Aging: An Historical Review," *Perspectives in Biology and Medicine*
6 (summer 1963): 450.

[19] Grant, "Concepts of Aging" (see n. 18), 449.

[20] Raymond Klibansky, Erwin Panofsky, and Fritz Saxl, *Saturn and Melancholy: Studies in the History
of Natural Philosophy, Religion and Art* (New York: Basic Books, 1964), 3.

[21] Grant, "Concepts of Aging" (see n. 18), 452.

[22] David H. Fowler, Lois Josephs Fowler, and Lois Lamdin, "Themes of Old Age in Pre-Industrial

Such was the scientific legacy that the Greco-Roman world bequeathed to scholars of the Middle Ages.[23] Beginning at conception, the physiological process of drying out and growing cold continued inexorably until death. The stages of life were milestones marking diminution of natural heat and increased desiccation. Each change dictated its own behavior patterns. This approach to aging and the ages of life arose in an intellectual milieu without boundaries between science and philosophy. Medieval writers combined the physical and the moral, interpreting behavioral signs in the light of physiology and individual character.

Christianity added a new cause for sickness, aging, and death that went far beyond Hippocratic medicine's natural explanation. In medieval Christian theology, sickness, aging, and death were not the original condition of mankind. Rather they resulted from rebellion against God's commandment. In paradise, Adam and Eve had lived in perfect health, their humors in balance – immune to the aging process. Saint Augustine explained Adam's and Eve's youthful health: "[Their] bodies were not indeed growing old and senile, so as to be brought in the end to an inevitable death. This condition was granted them by the wonderful grace of God, and was derived from the tree of life which was in Paradise. . . . "[24] Once expelled from Paradise, however, they were no longer protected by the tree. They became subject to the processes of aging and illness that have been the fate of humankind ever since (see Fig. 3).

Whereas Greco-Roman writers stressed the physical causes of aging, Christianity added a spiritual or moral cause. Aging and death result from original sin; they are necessitated by man's enforced separation from his primal source of youth and health. Medieval Christian writers, however, did not reject natural explanations. Rather, they took Hippocratic remnants and stitched them into the fabric of scriptural and patristic teaching to create a world view in which physical processes were ordained and directed by God.[25]

In the medieval synthesis, medicine and theology interact. Although it is natural to age and die, the ultimate cause lies in the fall of man. This religious belief conceived of aging as preparation for death and eternity. Ancient philosophers had understood aging as part of a journey from birth

Western Literature," in *Old Age in Pre-Industrial Society*, ed. Peter N. Stearns (New York: Holmes & Meier, 1982), 22.

[23] For fuller expositions of ancient life course theories and their passage into the Middle Ages, see Burrow, *Ages of Man* (see n. 10); Sears, *The Ages of Man* (see n. 14); and F. Boll, "Die Lebensalter," *Neue Jahrbücher für das Klassische Altertum* 21 (1913): 7–145.

[24] Saint Augustine, *City of God*, trans. Henry Bettenson (Harmondsworth, England: Penguin, 1972), 533.

[25] Charles H. Talbot, "Medicine," in *Science in the Middle Ages*, ed. David C. Lindberg (Chicago: University of Chicago Press, 1978), 391.

Figure 3. *The Expulsion from Paradise*, a woodcut from *La Cité de Dieu* (Abbeville, 1486), a French translation by Raoul de Presle of Saint Augustine's *City of God*. (Pierpont Morgan Library, New York.)

to death.[26] Now the journey had become a pilgrimage to God, the eternal source of life.

Medieval Christian culture, in other words, subordinated the ages of life to the pilgrimage of life. Under the guiding hand of theology, it wove theories of the life course into a rich tapestry of astrology, humoral pathology, and natural philosophy. Until the end of the Middle Ages, these ideas remained the province of a courtly, ecclesiastical, or learned minority. Among the common folk, formal knowledge of these ideas and images was limited to what might be heard in an occasional sermon or seen on a wall-hanging or church window.

[26] See chap. 1 of *The Republic*, where Socrates says, "I regard the aged as travelers who have gone on a journey which we too may have to go, and of whom we ought to inquire whether the way is smooth and easy, or rugged and difficult." *The Republic of Plato*, trans. F. M. Cornford (New York: Oxford University Press, 1968), 4.

In agrarian peasant culture, life's divisions were not a matter of formal knowledge but of local custom and language, popular songs, rhymes, and rituals. A rhyme popular among German-speaking peoples in the fifteenth and sixteenth centuries probably reflects widespread ideas about the ages of life:

> 10 years – a child
> 20 years – youth
> 30 years – a man
> 40 years – standing still
> 50 years – settled and prosperous
> 60 years – departing
> 70 years – protect your soul
> 80 years – the world's fool
> 90 years – scorn of children
> 100 years – God have mercy.

Accompanying this folk rhyme was a little song attributing the qualities of an animal to each age.[27] A man at the peak of his physical powers, for example, was likened to a lion. An old man waiting for death was an ass. This rhyme and sequence of animals later found an important place in the new urban iconography of the life course during the Reformation.

Most people had little idea of their chronological age. Their age of life was determined largely by rites of passage – the rituals surrounding birth, marriage, and death.[28] Since retirement had no place in traditional European folk culture, old age as a stage of life was not set apart by specific transition rituals or customs.[29] Plagues, famines, epidemics, and infectious diseases prevented most people from growing old, giving it much thought, or associating death exclusively with old age. Nevertheless, long before the late eighteenth century, when life expectancy and population began to rise, a flexible and individualized form of retirement had developed.

In fact, the practice of retirement by contract was an integral feature of medieval marriage and household formation in central and northwestern Europe. Three basic features characterized this pattern: relatively late marriage for both sexes (at about age twenty-six for men and age twenty-three for women), control of the household by the newly married couple, and the circulation of young people among households as servants.[30]

[27] Karl Goedeke, *Pamphilius Gengenbach* (Amsterdam: Editions Rodopi, 1966), 573, 576.
[28] See Arnold Van Gennep, *The Rites of Passage*, trans. Monika B. Vizedom and Gabrielle L. Caffe, introduction by Solon T. Kimball (Chicago: University of Chicago Press, 1960); and Martha Nemes and Morton Fried, *Transitions, Four Rituals in Eight Cultures* (New York: Norton, 1980).
[29] Rudolph Schenda, "Bewertungen und Bewaltigungen des Alters aufgrund volkskundlicher Materialien," in *Gerontologie und Sozialgeschichte: Wege zu Eirerhistorischen Betrachtung des Alters*, ed. Christoph Conrad and Hans-Joachim von Kondratowitz (Berlin: Deutsches Zentrum für Altersfragen, 1983), 59.
[30] J. Hajnal, "Two Kinds of Pre-industrial Household Formation System," *Population and Development Review* 8 (1982).

This pattern, which had great significance for Western economic development, linked the transmission of resources to the marriage of the younger generation and discouraged coresidence of parents and married children. Older people occupied a relatively weak position. If a peasant or farmer lived long enough to see his children married, he might make a retirement contract with his heir, transferring the farm or rights of tenancy in the seignorial system in return for lifelong maintenance for himself and his wife. Widows were also known to make retirement contracts, sometimes with persons who were neither heirs nor kin.[31]

Aging, then, occupied a necessary if minor place in medieval thought and retirement practice. High rates of mortality and low life expectancy obviously limited the number of older people. But along with demographic constraints, cultural perspectives on time and lifetime inhibited thought about growing old. Medieval Catholics aspired to eternity, not longevity. For them, profane time, the passing of days on earth, was a mere shadow of sacred time, imminent death more expected than long life. The idea of a lifetime played virtually no part in achieving eternity. Salvation was attained through a succession of separate good works rather than through a system of being good that permeated one's whole life.

Not until new versions of life's ages and its journey became more widespread and socially important did Western society have the cultural cognitive maps necessary for long-range thinking and planning about individual lifetime. These themes began to grow in popularity and significance during the late medieval period, when imagining one's own life as a spiritual drama and as a sequence of stages became increasingly common.

Beginning in the fourteenth century, both the ages-of-life and the journey-of-life motifs circulated more widely in European villages, towns, and cities. Early church fathers had conceived life on earth as a pilgrimage, and the power of the metaphor grew enormously after the actual practice of pilgrimage became popular. As early as the sixth century, but especially from the eleventh to the thirteenth centuries, thousands of ordinary Christians made pilgrimages to Jerusalem, Rome, Canterbury, Compostela, Chartres, and other sacred places.[32] Whereas these pilgrims mystically traversed roads and pathways, monastic contemplatives often expressed their search for God as interior pilgrimages.[33] Others expanded the pilgrimage theme into an allegorical motif in morality plays.

---

[31] Mitterauer and Seider, *European Family* (see n. 4), chaps. 7, 8.

[32] Victor and Edith Turner, *Image and Pilgrimage in Christian Culture* (New York: Columbia University Press, 1978); and Christian K. Zacher, *Curiosity and Pilgrimage: The Literature of Discovery in Fourteenth-Century England* (Baltimore: Johns Hopkins University Press, 1976).

[33] For an insightful discussion of the journey metaphor among medieval mystics like Bernard of Clairvaux, Bonaventura, and Meister Eckhart, see Steven Ozment, *The Age of Reform* (New Haven, Conn.: Yale University Press, 1980), chap. 3, "The Spiritual Traditions."

The theme of pilgrimage pervades late medieval poetry, from Chaucer's description of characters traveling to the tomb of Saint Thomas à Becket in *Canterbury Tales*, to Dante's *Divine Comedy*, with its powerful opening lines: "In the middle of the journey of our life, I came to myself within a dark wood where the straight way was lost. Ah, how hard it is to tell of that wood, savage and harsh and dense, the thought of which renews my fear. So bitter is it that death is hardly more."[34]

In the fourteenth century, writers first structured entire works around the theme. Over the next several centuries, the motif gradually crystallized into a separate genre,[35] which reflected the growing religious and moral significance of both the individual and the course of life.[36] Typically, poems like Deguilleville's *Pèlerinage de vie humaine* (1330–31) begin with a dreamer whose story is an extensive answer to the question, What shall I do to save my soul? Written in a vernacular and often translated into other European languages, these poems used the journey to teach the standard religious material of parish priests: the Ten Commandments, the Articles of the Creed, the seven vices and virtues, the seven sacraments.

The dreamer's quest for eternal bliss generally led him (not her) through two stages: a struggle against vice and worldly temptations, and "then a more positive journey in which he, with superior counsel and aid, progresses from strength to strength."[37] The medieval synthesis of the ages and pilgrimage of life emerges clearly in this genre, which often used the female body or youth allegorically to symbolize vice and obstacles to spiritual growth. With the notable exception of Bunyan's *Pilgrim's Progress* (1678), discussed in the next chapter, the genre explicitly addressed the dreamer's own aging in the framework of the ages of life.[38]

During the late Middle Ages, the ages of life found their way into the repertoire of a new army of mendicant friars, who urged the lax Christian folk to turn from their wicked ways. Amidst a heightened sense of sin and mortality, the mendicants emphasized the transitory, mutable character of this life and the temptations awaiting the unwary on their journey from stage to stage. In such preaching and in the writings and illustrations of newly published encyclopedias such as *De Proprietatibus rerum*, the ages of life were increasingly used for instruction in proper conduct.[39] Images of the

---

[34] Dante Alighieri, *The Divine Comedy*, in *The Norton Anthology of World Masterpieces*, 4th ed., ed. Maynard Mack et al. (New York: Norton, 1979), 855–58.

[35] Siegfried Wenzel, "The Pilgrimage of Life as a Late Medieval Genre," *Mediaeval Studies* 35 (1973): 370–88.

[36] See Colin Morris, *The Discovery of the Individual, 1050–1200* (New York: Harper and Row, 1972), for a study of the emergence of the individual as a category in European thought.

[37] Wenzel, "Pilgrimage of Life" (see n. 35), 377.

[38] Wenzel, "Pilgrimage of Life" (see n. 35), 378.

[39] Sears, *The Ages of Man* (see n. 14), chap. 6, "The Ages of Man in the Preacher's Repertory."

Figure 4. Christ-centered wheel of life, from a Psalter (1339) belonging to Robert de Lisle of Yorkshire. (MS Arundel 83, fol. 126v., British Library, London.)

ages of life were also woven into tapestries and painted on walls throughout the continent.[40]

Adapting old motifs like the tree of life, the wheel of life, and the wheel of Fortune, artists increasingly depicted the ages of life to enhance pious meditation.[41] A beautiful example of the ages of life arranged around the wheel of life survives in a fourteenth-century Psalter that belonged to Robert de Lisle of Yorkshire (see Fig. 4). Here, Christ at the center governs the

---

[40] Sears, *The Ages of Man* (see n. 14), 136–37.
[41] Sears, *The Ages of Man* (see n. 14), chap. 7.

wheel on which the fate of man revolves. Radiating from the center are eight medallions illuminating four ages of life; two medallions – a coffin and a tomb – emphasize the natural end of life. The image conveys a sense of eternal turning, as the life of natural man progresses from season to season until death breaks the cycle, opening the passage to eternal life. Each age is equidistant from God, who stresses their subordinate but equal status. The inscription around the central medallion reads, *Cuncta simul cerna totum racione guberno* (I perceive all ages at once, I rule all with reason). In redeeming man from his natural cycle, this Christ-centered vision subordinates seasonal time to sacred time. Earthly time becomes a mere shadow of eternity.[42] The tomb becomes the womb of the timeless.[43]

In the late medieval countryside, only the bells of the monastery or parish church would have broken the natural rhythms of daily life. An individual life cycle corresponded to the cycles of the seasons, of day and night. Seasonal and diurnal time, in turn, were part of the world's time, which began with Creation and would end with the Apocalypse. Ultimately, all time belonged to God. It was, therefore, not for sale, nor was it precisely divided into linear segments.

Gradually, however, this serene, otherworldly image of time and lifetime was eroding. In the new cities of the late Middle Ages, merchants and artisans became aware that the orderly conduct of business required more exact measurement of time.[44] Churches and town halls installed mechanical clocks to ring the hours.[45] Out of this awareness grew the modern notion that time was a precious commodity, to be used before it fled.[46] In the confusion and bustle of urban life, artistic symbols of time merged with those of death, decay, and destruction. By the late fifteenth century, Father Time appeared as a destroyer, brandishing a scythe in one hand, holding an hourglass in the other (see Fig. 5).[47]

During the years preceding the Protestant Reformation, this sense of time merged with widespread anxiety about individual salvation to create a new sense of uncertainty and uneasiness.[48] In the cities, accepted boundaries were breached, traditional relationships between men and their neighbors undermined.[49] Society appeared selfish, opportunistic,

[42] Emile Mâle, *The Gothic Image* (New York: Harper Torchbooks, 1958), 56.

[43] I owe this phrase to Harold Stahmer in a personal communication.

[44] Jacques Le Goff, *Time, Work and Culture in the Middle Ages*, trans. Arthur Goldhammer (Chicago: University of Chicago Press, 1980), 35.

[45] Carlo M. Cipolla, *Clocks and Culture, 1300–1700* (London: Collins, 1967), chap. 1.

[46] David Landes, *Revolution in Time* (Cambridge, Mass.: Harvard University Press, 1983), 89.

[47] Erwin Panofsky, "Father Time," in his *Studies in Iconology: Humanistic Themes in the Art of the Renaissance* (New York: Harper and Row, 1972).

[48] William Bouwsma, "Anxiety and the Formation of Early Modern Culture," in *After the Reformation*, ed. Barbara C. Malament (Philadelphia: University of Pennsylvania Press, 1980), 220.

[49] Stephen E. Ozment, *The Reformation in the Cities* (New Haven, Conn.: Yale University Press, 1975), 15–46.

Figure 5. *Time in the Garden of Eden*, a woodcut in Thomas Peyton's *The Glasse of Time in the Second Age* (London, 1620). (The Huntington Library, San Marino, Calif.)

brutal. Moralists descried the sinful nature of the times and announced the coming of the Last Judgment. For some, anxiety about purgatory or hell reached the point of obsession; fears about the passage of time became increasingly haunting.[50] Could one perform enough good works to balance the heavenly account books? What if time "ran out" and one died in a state of sin?[51]

The earliest ages-of-life broadsheets printed for a popular audience reflect this anxiety about time, sin, and death. A late fifteenth-century *Lebensalter* print from Augsburg, for example, merges the ages of life with the wheel of Fortune (see Fig. 6). Here, ancient wisdom about the ages of life is joined to late medieval thought about death.[52] Although the design retains a circular composition, it lacks the serene harmony of the Delisle Psalter; Christ no longer occupies the center, the "still point of the turning world." Inscriptions of impending death admonish the viewer to meditate on the final disposal of his soul. These inscriptions are descriptive less of man's physiological development than of his moral weakness. Humankind is sinful, and the time we have been given is short: "Oh, that I was ever born, that I have let my time slip away. Yet, Lord, I put my soul in your hands, for I must journey to that other land."

The Augsburg woodcut introduces the basic components of the motif that

[50] H. G. Koenigsberger and George L. Mosse, *Europe in the Sixteenth Century* (London: Longman, 1968), 85ff.

[51] The metaphor of time "running out" derives from the hourglass, a symbol of the limited quantity of an individual's lifetime.

[52] Eduard de Keyser, "Le thème des degrés des âges dans l'estampe et l'imagerie populaire," *Bulletin de la Société Archeologique, Historique et Artistique, Le Vieux Papier* (July 1976): 489.

Figure 6. *The Seven Ages of Life and the Wheel of Fortune*, an anonymous woodcut (ca. 1470). (Fol. xy 1, Deutsche Staatbibliothek, Berlin.)

soon came to dominate iconography of the life cycle: personifications of the stages of life, warnings of the shortness of life and the imminence of death, suggestions of judgment or apocalypse. It also reveals the transition from modes of thought characteristic of agrarian, feudal society to those of an urban, market society with a growing middle class. The print conveys anxiety about the passage of time and the necessity of death, but also provides comfort. Life remains, literally, a cycle, a circle from cradle to grave. But an angel is now required to hold together the beginning (*generatio*) and the end (*corruptio*) of life. The wheel of Fortune turns, and all are sinners doomed to damnation or saved in paradise. In the sixteenth century, when the basic shape of lifetime was transformed from a circle to a rising and falling staircase, the *Lebensalter* (ages of life) would become the *Lebenstreppe* (steps of life) and later, in English, the "stages of life."

For both social and religious reasons, the upwardly mobile, urban middle classes of early modern Europe were intensely concerned with the problems of time, appropriate behavior, and salvation – giving the ages of life new significance in popular culture. One of the most influential works in sixteenth-century German literature, Pamphilus Gengenbach's "The Ten Ages of This World," written and presented in 1515 for the pre-Lenten festivities in Basel,[53] reveals this significance. Merging folk tradition and learned doctrine, Gengenbach's play reflects the newly crystallized thought concerning the stages of life, sin, death, and redemption. This crystallization reflected mounting pressure to combat sin with virtue at each age.

In Gengenbach's play, Hermit carries the moral and religious message in a dialogue with ten actors representing the ten ages of man. After reciting the well-known story of the fall of man, Hermit announces the evil nature of the times and the nearness of the Apocalypse. The ages then sequentially announce their besetting sins, which follow a rising course to age fifty and then fall in old age. With its careful moral prescription for each stage, "The Ten Ages of this World" reveals the importance of the life cycle in the "civilizing process" – the long transformation in the mechanisms of social order from the use of hierarchy and external force to more egalitarian, individual, internalized constraints.[54]

THE CIRCLE BROKEN: IMAGINING A MODERN COURSE OF LIFE

The cultural resonance of Gengenbach's play, which was presented again in Basel in 1516 and soon printed with illustrations throughout German-speaking Europe, lay in its presentation of the conflicts experienced most keenly by the urban middle classes. Its sense of approaching doom, of the struggle to find appropriate behavior, of time's being "out of joint," was

---

[53] Goedeke, *Pamphilius Gengenbach* (see n. 27), 572.
[54] Norbert Elias, *The Civilizing Process*, trans. Edmund Jephcott (New York: Urizen, 1978).

resolved by creating a new cognitive map of the life course, complete with virtues and vices for each age grade. This vision of the life course, the new schedule of life as a career, found its definitive iconographic representation in a rising and falling staircase (or a pyramid of stairs) – a shape which became the standard bourgeois image of a lifetime for the next 350 years.

Working separately but from the same idea, two sixteenth-century artists created this image, which fuses the popular tradition of the ten ages of life with the more learned traditions inherited from the Middle Ages. Jorg Breu executed his woodcut at Augsburg in 1540 (see Fig. 7).[55] On a bridgelike stepped arch, ten personifications of the ages of man are seated. Beneath are animals that traditionally symbolized each age.[56] Behind the apex of the arch, the figure of Death turns to shoot his arrows toward the ascending side of the bridge. On that side, the sky is naked and clear. But on the side where the elderly men sit, the sky is dark and cloudy – an allusion to the evening or winter of life. Beneath the arch, Breu engraved a scene of the Last Judgment, with John the Baptist and the Virgin Mary pleading for the souls of the faithful.

At about the same time, Cornelis Theunissen of Amsterdam created the other original source for what became the standard motif (see Fig. 8). Thennissen makes use of the classical arch of triumph and a more elaborate conception, but both artists attempt to convey the necessity of preparing for death and judgment, using common symbols to suggest the greenness of youth and the aridness of old age. In the morning or springtime of life, the sun rises over budding trees and flowery vegetation. In the evening or winter of life, bare branches are set against a darkening landscape.

In a world seeking new religious and social boundaries, the ages-of-life motif provided a model of correct behavior. Made to adorn the homes of good burghers, the German *Lebenstreppe* (or Dutch *Trap des Ouderdoms*) aimed to teach a lifetime of probity and self-discipline in the face of death and divine judgment. Rather than Gengenbach's emphasis on sinfulness, Breu and Theunissen present the viewer with an ideal self at each age. In Theunissen and virtually all subsequent examples, the new symbol of the hourglass reveals a growing preoccupation with the time available to each. The hourglass, as in Theunissen's engraving *Nascendo Morimur* (Fig. 9), shows the importance of properly understood righteousness by emphasizing the *velocitas temporia* – the speed of time. By stress-

[55] P. Joerissen, "Lebenstreppe und Lebensalterspiel in 16 Jahrhundert," in *Die Lebenstreppe, Bilder der menschlichen Lebensalter*, kommission bei R. Habelt (Bonn: Rheinland-Verlag, 1983), 26.

[56] Lists of animals corresponding to the ages varied from case to case; later representations of the ages of women often used various birds. See Sears, *The Ages of Man* (see n. 14), 154; and Boll, "Die Lebensalter" (see n. 23), 21. For a rendering of animals and ages in "high art," see Titian's *Allegory of Prudence*, in which the three ages of man are represented by a fox, lion, and wolf. This painting is reproduced on the cover of Burrow, *Ages of Man* (see n. 10).

Figure 7. *The Ten Ages of Man*, an engraving by Jorg Breu the Younger (Augsburg, 1540). (The British Museum. London, and elsewhere.)

Figure 8. *The Nine Ages of Life*, an engraving by Cornelis Theunissen (Amsterdam, 1540). (Rijksmuseum, Amsterdam.)

Figure 9. *Nascendo Morimur* (We Are Born to Die), an engraving by Cornelis Theunissen (Amsterdam, 1537). (Rijksmuseum, Amsterdam.)

ing the proper use of time in a world of transience and death, these Renaissance prints paradoxically set up the ideal of a long, orderly, and secure life.[57] Created to soothe anxiety and uncertainty, the sequence of calm figures in this new ideal transcends the fear of death by manifesting an inner faith and conviction throughout the whole course of life. Ironically, *Memento mori* (remember death) subtly conveys the wish for longevity – a wish given support in Reformation theology.

With the Reformation, a new relationship between time and work emerges to infuse all of earthly life with significance. Luther's revolutionary idea of justification by faith rather than works promised personal certitude of salvation in this life. In the Reformed tradition, good works were not to be merely a series of pious acts designed to secure salvation, but manifestations

---

[57] In this way, the ages-of-life motif anticipates by several hundred years the emergence of mass longevity and an increasingly orderly course of life. Cf. Kohli, "The World We Forgot" (see n. 2), 270–303. Hence it is not true, as many contemporaries assume, that modern longevity has no cultural foundation, that we have to learn to grow old as we once had to learn to grow up; this is a version of "cultural lag" theory and very misleading to an understanding of the historical phenomenology of aging and the life course.

of an inner conviction, the tenor of a whole life. In the pre-Reformation period, the deathbed had been a battlefield determining a soul's eternal fate. By the seventeenth century, the whole of an individual's life became important. In a funeral sermon of 1628, John Donne declared with certainty, "Our critical day is not the very day of our death but the whole course of our life."[58] Donne's words echo those of Jesus in John 9:4, "I must work the works of him that sent me, while it is day; the night cometh when no man can work." Implied is a lifetime (symbolically a day) of work, which can only be judged at the end (or at night.)

This attitude toward work and the life span has been aptly described in Max Weber's famous work, *The Protestant Ethic and the Spirit of Capitalism*. Discarding as selfish the monastic ideal of retirement from active life, Luther and his followers found the highest form of activity in fulfilling the duties and obligations of one's station in life. According to Weber, the moral justification of worldly activity was "one of the most important results of the Reformation."[59] Once one's whole life became consecrated for work, time acquired a new, more poignant meaning. The old anxieties about time and death acquired a new focus – the health and control of the physical body – which has grown ever more intense down to the present day.

The new interest in individual lifetime and in the physical body was also rooted in the "civilizing process" that facilitated the long transition from medieval feudalism to modern capitalism. As Norbert Elias has shown, this "civilizing process" involved a growing focus on the individual, whose capacity for internalizing moral norms became a primary source of self-control.[60] Rather than rely on hierarchical authority or external force, an emerging urban, market-oriented society gradually cultivated internalized self-control as a means of regulating social life. Both the ages and the journey of life were central to this process.

Reformed ideas about time and its preciousness as a commodity gave clear priority to the characteristics of middle age – the age when men were most capable of participating in the market. The new iconographic shape of a man's life from cradle to grave implied a hierarchy of values consistent with the northwestern and central European marriage pattern, where power over economic resources rested primarily with middle-aged men. The growth of urban markets intensified this hierarchy, encouraged efficiency in intergen-

---

[58] John Donne, "Death's Duell or, a Consolation to the Soule, Against the Dying Life, and Living Death of the Body," in *The Complete Poetry and Selected Prose of John Donne*, ed. Charles M. Coffin (New York: Random House, 1952), 58ff.

[59] Max Weber, *The Protestant Ethic and the Spirit of Capitalism*, trans. Talcott Parsons (New York: Scribner, 1976), 81.

[60] Elias, *Civilizing Process* (see n. 54), Appendix I, 221–63.

erational transmission, and fostered a more economically "rational" approach to aging.[61]

STAGING LIFE'S JOURNEY

In the cities of Northern Europe, and especially in England, the emergence of a market society in the sixteenth and seventeenth centuries dissolved the old medieval structure of estates. Particularly in Elizabethan England, the theater flourished as an arena where playwrights experimented with new forms of social representation.[62] These developments helped transform the ancient metaphor of the *theatrum mundi* from a simple otherworldly statement about human vanity into a secular commentary on the social world.

As the stage assumed this fertile cultural significance, new possibilities for imagining the life course arose.[63] Shakespeare's cynical Jaques pronounced the most enduring version. While Jaques first announces that both men *and* women are players on the stage of life, he goes on to render life's seven ages from a male perspective:

> All the world's a stage,
> And all the men and women merely players.
> They have their exits and entrances;
> And one man in his time plays many parts,
> His acts being seven ages.[64]

It was but a small step from the *ages* to the *stages* of life, a metaphor represented by the emergent iconographic shape of the life cycle, where each step became a stage for the performance of certain roles.[65] Many of the early continental examples of the *Lebenstreppe* motif were in fact executed as illustrations for stage productions of plays.[66] Neither of the older motifs, the dance of Death and the wheel of Fortune, was able to capture the complex message of the ages of life, which juxtaposed the swiftness of

---

[61] See Rolf Sprandel, *Altersschicksal und Altersmoral: die Geschichte der Einstellungen zum Altern nach der Pariser Bibelexegese des 12–16 Jahrhunderts* (Stuttgart: Anton Hiersemann, 1981).

[62] Jean-Christophe Agnew, *Worlds Apart: The Market and the Theatre in Anglo-American Thought, 1550–1750* (New York: Cambridge University Press, 1986).

[63] See, for example, the stages-of-life engravings, *Theatrum Humanae Vitae* (1577), executed in Antwerp by Petras Bast, held in the Shakespeare Folger Library, Washington, D.C.

[64] William Shakespeare, *As You Like It*, act 2, scene 7, in *The Complete Works of William Shakespeare*, ed. William Aldis Wright (Garden City, N.Y.: Garden City Books, 1936), 677. I am grateful to Lois Banner for pointing out to me that Jaques' speech subsumes women under a masculine view of the ages of life. See also the later visual rendering of Jaques' seven ages of man by Robert Smirke (1798) in the Yale Center for British Art.

[65] It is important to remember that "stage" theories in modern psychology and "role" theories in sociology have their roots in the search for proper behavior and for ways of representing one's self in early modern culture.

[66] Joerissen, "Lebenstreppe" (see n. 55), 35.

time and the power of death with the wish for an orderly, long, and productive life. The rising and falling staircase attempted to span the uncertainty, ambiguity, and helplessness of life. It depicted the middle-class struggle for success, as well as its fear of falling into social decline and eternal punishment.[67]

The stage metaphor also made it possible for every individual to understand himself (and by the seventeenth century, herself) as the central actor in his or her own pilgrimage. The motif provided a visual means for each person to step outside his own life experience and view it as a whole.[68] Thus the central drama of each life was shown to be salvation, a highly individual struggle that each person nevertheless shared with all mankind. At the same time, the methods and purposes of this drama were increasingly secular. By the eighteenth and nineteenth centuries, when the motif had become a common element in popular culture, the tension between its sacred and secular dimensions had largely dissolved – leaving bourgeois society with a cultural blueprint for the rationalized life course.[69]

Sixteenth-century examples of the motif depicted a balance between life and death, sacred and secular. Though the timing of death was uncertain and judgment loomed ahead, the fabric of a pious life, woven together with good manners (or *civilité*)[70] and faith in God, promised eternal salvation. Although the staircase motif clearly favored the secular power and productivity of middle age, aging still implied an uncertain journey to eternal life.

During the mid-seventeenth century, many of the intense feelings of anxiety and dislocation eased.[71] The pace of social change slowed and religious, political, and intellectual conflicts found resolution.[72] In this environment, the evolving bourgeois image of the life course achieved its full flowering. As we have seen, the rising and falling staircase of life ingeniously

[67] See P. Joerissen, "Die Lebensalter des Menschen – Bildprogramm und Bildform im Jahrhundert der Reformation," in *Die Lebenstreppe, Bilder der menschlichen Lebensalter*, kommission bei R. Habelt (Bonn: Rheinland-Verlag, 1983), 44. This motif is an important visual source for idiomatic language still used in English today – e.g., "going downhill," "slipping fast."

[68] By depicting "life time" in spatial terms – as a journey upward to one's peak and down again – the motif served as a visual chronotope. See M. M. Bakhtin, "Forms of Time and of the Chronotope in the Novel," in *Dialogic Imagination: Four Essays*, ed. Michael Holquist, trans. Caryl Emerson (Austin: University of Texas Press, 1981), 84–258.

[69] See Carl Ulrich Meyer and Walter Müller, "The State and the Structure of the Life Course," in *Human Development and the Life Course*, ed. Aage B. Sorensen, Franz E. Weinert, and Lonnie R. Sherrod (Hillsdale, N.J.: Lawrence Erlbaum, 1986), 217– 245.

[70] On the importance of *civilité* in Western society amidst the decline of feudalism and breakup of thé Catholic church, see Elias, *Civilizing Process* (see n. 54), 53–59.

[71] Theodore K. Rabb, *The Struggle for Stability in Early Modern Europe* (New York: Oxford University Press, 1975).

[72] Charles Webster, *The Great Instauration: Science, Medicine and Reform, 1626–1800* (New York: Holmes and Meier, 1976); and Jeffrey Stout, *The Flight From Authority* (Notre Dame, Ind.: Notre Dame Press, 1981).

played on fears of sinfulness, mutability, and transience, while creating an ideal of longevity and an orderly succession of life's stages.

When the *Lebenstreppe* prints began to reach a wider audience in the seventeenth century, the theme itself broadened to include women and couples. Women had been literally invisible in medieval stages of life doctrine and iconography. During the early modern period, they make their first appearance in the stages of life, albeit still through the eyes of men.[73] New representations of an ideal female life cycle reflect the growing significance accorded to women in male-dominated, bourgeois culture.

Much of this significance centered on women's new responsibility for health, beauty, and physical comportment. Medieval Christianity considered the human body a vessel of sin, an abomination. "The height of abomination, the worst of the body and of sexuality, was the female body . . . the devil's stomping ground."[74] By the sixteenth century, Neoplatonic views of the body as a pathway to divine love legitimated the notion that a beautiful body reflected a beautiful soul. In some bourgeois and aristocratic circles, beauty became a kind of vocation or sacred duty for women. Medical manuals on feminine beauty and body care appeared alongside books about court ceremonial and table manners.

Women, in other words, were assigned a prominent role in the "civilizing process." Cleanliness, care of the skin, hair, teeth, and face – these and other aspects of hygiene were considered essential responsibilities for women properly concerned about pleasing their husbands.[75] The new iconography of women's life cycle focused on daily life and women's duties to create and maintain a proper family. Male renderings of women's lives (I am not aware of any female artists in this genre) stressed the toll that family life took on aging women, frequently depicting physical disability and ugliness.[76] The verse accompanying François van Beusecom's *Trap des Ouderdoms* (1650; Fig. 10), for example, describes a mother descending from the peak of her life with "once-smooth wrinkled skin." She approaches her grave "worn out by work." The scrolls above and below warn both young and old: "Listen petting woman and good old mother, who stand on these steps. Beware and seek the right path before you go any further. . . . Maintain your house for your

---

[73] See Joerissen, "Bildprogramm und Bildform" (see n. 67), 51ff.

[74] Jacques Le Goff, *The Medieval Imagination*, trans. Arthur Goldhammer (Chicago: University of Chicago Press, 1988), 83.

[75] See Alison K. Lingo, "Santé et beauté feminines dans la France de la Renaissance," in *Le corps et la santé*, Actes du 110 Congrès National des Sociétés Sanvantes, Montpellier, 1985 (Paris, 1986), I: 191–99. I am grateful to Alison Lingo for sharing her work with me, and in particular for pointing out the place of women in the "civilizing process." See also her "A Medical and Literary Perspective of the Older Woman in Early Modern France: A Preliminary View," unpublished paper delivered at the Conference on Aging and the Life Cycle in the Renaissance, University of Maryland, College Park, Md., April 1988.

[76] See Joerissen, "Bilprogramm und Bildform" (see n. 67), 52ff.

Figure 10. *Trap des Ouder-doms* (The Stages of Woman's Life), an engraving by François van Beusecom (Amsterdam, 1650). (Atlas Van Stolk, Rotterdam.)

well-being. Thou shalt die and not stay alive. . . . So seek a city that lasts eternally."

By depicting the life cycle of couples, seventeenth-century artists also reveal a new emphasis on domesticity. Jan Houwens's *Trap des Ouderdoms* (Fig. 11), for example, clearly presents the man's duty to uphold the virtues of order and thrift alongside the woman's responsibility for the physical and spiritual health of the family, especially children.

For the aged, the traditional injunction to trust in God and hope for the future remained prominent, as expressed in the epigrams beneath Houwens's rendering of the decline of life: "But on the fifth [step] it's just that day in which the sun may not go higher. The sixth makes the hair gray. . . . The seventh for their sorrow sees with joy child's children. But once one treads on the eighth step, one drags on with nothing but sorrow. And on the ninth step, one sees what one already was and will be; when 100 years shuts the eyes, then the traveler's life is over."

It is important to remember that the motif developed in Northern Europe, where late medieval piety fused with new humanist learning to produce the Protestant Reformation. The motif achieved its most definitive form in the seventeenth century, that of the Thirty Years' War and the scientific revolution. It became a truly popular motif in the eighteenth and nineteenth centuries, long after its theological, medical, artistic, and scientific origins had been discarded.

The motif was a refuge and an expression of the longings of the urban middle classes, who sought *their* order in self-discipline, probity, and piety. Amidst the confusion of shifting cultural and religious boundaries, old certainties were sought out and dressed up. Ancient scientific teaching about the cycle of life, now moralized, put on the uniform of acceptance and self-control. On the steps of life, each man and woman stands, submissive to nature's law. No overwise child, no gamboling octogenarian parades before the viewer.

The ages-of-life prints, then, provided a visual antidote to the fear of disarray and disintegration typical of the sixteenth and early seventeenth centuries. By depicting the appropriate appearance and behavior for each age of life, the motif taught that *each* age had its necessary place in the order of things. To submit to the physical exigencies of the aging process was to acquiesce in divine purpose. Thus the motif attempted to restore or create order, and especially *religious* order, by focusing on a newly imagined course of life. This new cultural ideal of a long, orderly, and secure lifetime would not become a social and demographic reality for 300 years. In the process, its original spiritual commitments were lost and replaced by those of science, medicine, and technology.

In England, as on the continent, the ages of man and the pilgrimage of life had been familiar motifs in medieval learned culture. From 1485, when

Figure 11. *Trap des Ouderdoms* (The Life Cycle of Man and Woman), an engraving by Jan Houwens (Rotterdam, seventeenth century). (Atlas Van Stolk, Rotterdam.)

the Tudor dynasty was founded, until the outbreak of civil war in 1642, these themes became increasingly popular among English theologians, writers, artists, and physicians.[77]

Although English artists in this period produced much less than their counterparts in Europe, visual images of life's ages and its journey could be seen in books of hours, on church frescoes, in figures woven into tapestry or painted on clothes, and – toward the end of the period – on woodcuts and engravings. Ten ages of life, for example, hung on tapestries from the ceiling of Sir Thomas More's childhood home in London.[78] Four ages of life were engraved on the frontispiece of Francis Bacon's *History of Life and Death* (1645 edition).

Until the seventeenth century, the symbols representing the ages of life and the pilgrimage of life remained elusive and fluid. The old theme appeared in new forms or with fresh associations. The virtues and the vices were personified sometimes by masculine and sometimes by feminine characters. Death, the destroyer, was a skeleton who could kill with his bow and arrows, or cut men down with his scythe. He held the hourglass of time in one picture, and the scales of justice in another. Similarly the animals and their corresponding ages followed no fixed pattern. The cat, for example, could symbolize either childhood, because it liked to play, or old age, because it liked to doze near the fire.[79]

The new life course motif – with its fixed symbolism of order, longevity, and the struggle for salvation – seems to have made its way across the English Channel slowly. The seventeenth-century English epigrammatist Thomas Bancroft must have seen it when he wrote:

> We climbe the slippery stairs of Infancy,
> Of Childhood, Youth, of middle age, and then
> Decline, grow old, decrepit, bed-rid lye,
> Bending to infant-weakness once agen,
> And to our Cophines (as to Cradles) goe,
> That at the staire-foot stand, and stint our woe.[80]

Crude seventeenth-century versions of the motif appear to have been copied by English engravers or hurriedly redone and shipped to England.[81] By the

---

[77] See Samuel Chew, *The Pilgrimage of Life* (New Haven, Conn.: Yale University Press, 1962), chap. 6. The most widely quoted advice about the ages of life in seventeenth-century England was penned by the physician Sir Thomas Browne. For Browne's thoughts on time, aging, death, the virtues, and salvation, see his *Religio Medici* (1636) and "Christian Morals" (1716), reprinted in *Sir Thomas Browne: Selected Writings*, ed. Sir Geoffrey Keynes (Chicago: University of Chicago Press, 1968).

[78] Alice Tobriner, "Thomas More on Old Age: A Prolegomenon to the History of Gerontology," unpublished paper presented at the annual meeting of the Society for Health and Human Values, 1986.

[79] Chew, *Pilgrimage of Life* (see n. 77), xxiii.

[80] Cited by Chew, *Pilgrimage of Life* (see n. 77), 149.

[81] See, for example, the seventeenth-century English "Ye Steppes of Old Age," clearly copied from a Dutch original, in the Winterthur Museum, slide catalogue no. G69.838 a, b.

eighteenth century, cheap penny broadsheets depicting the ages of life were widely distributed among the poor.[82]

Popularization of life cycle imagery in England, and later America, favored life's journey over the ages and stages, though the two motifs remained intertwined. In representing the pilgrimage of life, Renaissance writers, poets, painters, sculptors, engravers, and weavers in England drew from a rich corpus of symbols. The theme remained masculine and medieval: Having forfeited immortality through sin, every man must pass through the world of time and fortune. Although man is free to choose one of two paths, he will face peril even along the straight and narrow way. He will face assaults from the infernal trinity and the seven deadly sins, which he can survive in the armor of Saint Paul and the company of virtues. At the end of the journey, Death awaits him, but beyond death lies the Celestial City.[83]

By 1678, when John Bunyan transformed this theme into a religious folk epic known as *Pilgrim's Progress*, he appealed to the growing belief that in order to live, men *and* women had to lift up their eyes unto the hills.

---

[82] Ruth Richardson, *Death, Dissection and the Destitute* (London: Routledge & Kegan Paul, 1987), 10–11.

[83] Chew, *Pilgrimage of Life* (see n. 77), xxiii.

2

The aging pilgrim's progress in the New World

So they lefte that goodly & Pleasant citie, which had been ther resting place, nere 12 years; but they knew they were pilgrimes, & looked not much on these things; but lift up their eyes to the heavens, their dearest cuntrie; and quieted their spirits.

William Bradford, on setting out from Leiden for the New World

In the 1620s and 1630s, thousands of English religious dissenters set out on an "errand into the wilderness" – to build the new Jerusalem, a godly city to lead lost humanity toward the millennium.[1] Modeling themselves on the Israelites' ancient exodus from Egypt, the first New Englanders established an identity and a view of history that strongly influenced early American culture.[2] With their theology, literature, and devotional practice, these English colonists brought Protestant ideas about aging to the New World. The Puritans and Pilgrims, of course, did not ponder the meaning of growing old *per se*. Rather, such meaning was embedded in their religious practice, addressed in an occasional sermon, and represented through the controlling image of life's pilgrimage.

Along with their communal identity as a people journeying from bondage to the promised land, the Puritans also carried a biblical ideal of each individual's passage from the slavery of sin to the freedom of salvation. Up through the Reformation, Christian ideas about human development and maturity had reflected two competing ideals. First was the Greek goal of manhood, in which the rational man pits his reason against the chaos within and around him. Second was the biblical goal of adulthood, in which the individual grows constantly toward the unreachable stature of God.[3]

---

[1] See Perry Miller, *Errand Into The Wilderness* (Cambridge, Mass.: Harvard University Press, 1956).

[2] Harry S. Stout, *The New England Soul: Preaching and Religious Culture in Colonial New England* (New York: Oxford University Press, 1986), Introduction, chaps. 13, 14. While showing the continuous influence of Puritan religious beliefs down to the Revolutionary era, Stout carefully avoids the trap of reading America as New England writ large.

[3] William J. Bouwsma, "Christian Adulthood," *Daedalus* 105 (spring 1976): 77–92. I have relied heavily on Bouwsma's article and on his *Calvin: A Sixteenth Century Portrait* (New York: Oxford, 1988) in the following discussion.

The Greek conception of manhood was rooted in the second age of life. It referred exclusively to males and allowed no room for individuality. Greek philosophers considered manhood both qualitatively distinct from and superior to childhood and old age, phases distinguished by their lack of reason. When Christian writers adopted this perspective in the Middle Ages, they conceived human life as a series of transits from one distinct phase to another, rather than a process of continuous development. Although medieval writers differed on the number, explanation, and chronology of the ages of life, they did agree that the transitions were not gradual processes but datable events. They displayed no interest in the actual experience of moving from one age of life to another.[4]

On the other hand, the biblical conception of adulthood, rooted in Jewish and Pauline ideas, emphasized the continuity of an individual's journey through the stages of life.[5] Several distinctive features characterize the biblical ideal. Childhood and old age can be understood metaphorically, and the qualities of both may coexist at different ages. The biblical ideal associates maturity with personal stability and loving solidarity with all humanity. The true measure of adulthood is "the full stature of Christ" – an absolute and unreachable standard. In the biblical ideal, women are considered spiritually but not socially equal to men; the body and its passions are not regarded as evil.[6] Time and change are seen as necessary and good.

The biblical ideal contains an essential paradox: since no individual, regardless of age, can attain the transcendent stature of Christ, no one can ever consider himself or herself a fully completed person. If no individual ever reaches full maturity, then neither old age nor adulthood can claim spiritual priority over youth or childhood. The biblical ideal of adulthood, therefore, affirms that all ages of life are equal in God's eyes. We are all as little children. A wise old man or woman is still somehow young, retaining a child's capacity for growth.[7]

Championing Augustine's view of the Christian life as a "journey or voyage home," Reformation theologians generally supported biblical over classical conceptions of maturity. Reformed thinkers accordingly saw conversion not as a precise stage that divided damnation and salvation but as the beginning of a lifelong journey to God. As Luther contended, "it is not sufficient to have done something, and now to rest. . . . [T]his present life is a kind of movement and passage, or transition . . . a pilgrimage from this world into the world to come, which is eternal rest." Calvin expressed the same idea:

[4] James A. Burrow, *The Ages of Man* (New York: Oxford University Press, 1986), 178.

[5] See Thorlief Boman, *Hebrew Thought Compared With Greek*, trans. Jules L. Moreau (New York: Norton, 1970).

[6] For recent scholarship on this issue, see Elaine Pagels, *Adam, Eve, and the Serpent* (New York: Random House, 1988), esp. chaps. 1, 6; also Peter Brown, *The Body and Society: Men, Women, and Sexual Renunciation in Early Christianity* (New York: Columbia University Press, 1988).

[7] Bouwsma, "Christian Adulthood" (see n. 3), 81.

"Let each one of us, then, proceed according to the measure of his puny capacity and set out upon the journey we have begun. . . . Let us not cease so to act that we may make some unceasing progress in the way of the Lord."[8]

The biblical ideal of Christian maturity, while never uncontested by its classical counterpart, played an important role in the religious piety that the Puritans brought to the New World. The biblical view that spiritual growth was both possible and necessary at every age implied that all of Christian life was a continuous process of change or "progress" toward salvation.[9] Conversion, therefore, did not lead immediately into a safe harbor but rather to a voyage of discovery – a metaphor that aptly described both the collective and the individual experience of those who set sail rather than conform to the Church of England or submit to persecution.

Despite their rejection of the Catholic and Anglican churches, Puritans maintained devotional practices closely allied with these traditions.[10] Particularly in prayer and meditation, Puritan piety retained the hallmarks of Augustinian spirituality: primary emphasis on personal experience, human sinfulness, and divine initiative in salvation through grace.

Following Calvin, the Puritans attempted to free men and women from a childish state of bondage to priestly authority. They rejected monastic separation from the world and aimed their devotional practices at ordinary people engaged in secular pursuits. In personal writings, sermons, manuals, and rules for meditation and prayer, the Puritans addressed the lay person caught up in the daily world.[11]

Puritans promoted the individual practice of piety by revitalizing the Sabbath, by printing manuals and devotional aids, and by encouraging believers to read, meditate, and pray on their own. Although they banned actual pilgrimages to holy places, the Puritans embraced the pilgrimage metaphor. In fact, pilgrimage was the major theme or controlling metaphor of Puritan spirituality and devotional practice. With the first-generation New England preacher Thomas Hooker, Puritans believed that England had become a self-seeking rather than a God-seeking nation, a country of spiritual vagabonds.[12] The pilgrimage motif, set in a hostile environment, reminded

---

[8] Cited by Bouwsma, "Christian Adulthood"(see n. 3), 90, fn. 30.

[9] Bouwsma writes that for the biblical ideal, all of Christian life is like adolescence, "that stage in which the adult seems, however ambiguously, trembling to be born." See "Christian Adulthood" (see n. 3), 81.

[10] The following discussion of Puritanism as a devotional movement relies on Charles E. Hambrick-Stowe, *The Practice of Piety: Puritan Devotional Disciplines in Seventeenth-Century New England* (Chapel Hill: University of North Carolina Press, 1982). The scholarly literature on Puritanism is enormous. See, for example, Michael Walzer, *The Revolution of the Saints* (New York: Atheneum, 1968); Perry Miller, *Errand Into the Wilderness* (Cambridge, Mass.: Harvard University Press, 1956); and Edmund Leites, *The Puritan Conscience and Modern Sexuality* (New Haven, Conn.: Yale University Press, 1986).

[11] Hambrick-Stowe, *Practice of Piety* (see n. 10), 46ff.

[12] See Hambrick-Stowe, *Practice of Piety* (see n. 10), 69.

Puritans of the "progress" that was possible if one sought out the well-marked "stages" on the road to their holy destination.

The original New Englanders traveled across a dangerous ocean to an uncharted world for the right to their own spiritual pilgrimages. As William Bradford, Plymouth colony's founding governor, reflected in later life,

> [God] call'd me from my native place
> For to enjoy the means of grace.
> In wilderness he did me guide,
> And in strange lands for me provide.
> In fears and wants, through weal and woe
> A pilgrim passed I to and fro.[13]

The Puritans and Pilgrims (those separatists who established Plymouth colony) risked their lives to come to a wilderness and hear the word of God preached correctly. Twice on Sunday and often once during the week, every minister in colonial New England preached for up to two hours. Ministers delivered over five million sermons during the colonial period, the vast majority devoted to regular preaching on salvation. The average weekly churchgoer listened to roughly 7,000 sermons in a lifetime. Throughout the colonial period, preaching on the sequence of salvation remained a minister's primary responsibility. And in a society where there were few competing public speakers, the minister's sermon served as the principal voice of authority.[14]

Puritanism grew up in an era that witnessed the appearance of "masterless men" – political exiles, vagabonds, pilgrims, rogues, and adventurers – who lived outside the grasp of traditional authority. Like Calvin, the Puritans felt a keen anxiety about human sinfulness and the dangers of social disorder.[15] Like the Reformed tradition in general, Puritans placed great emphasis on the virtues and behaviors appropriate to each stage of life. Freed from medieval commitments to passivity and feudal loyalty, Puritan saintliness involved a conscious decision to repress oneself and others in pursuit of a holy life. At the center of their moral vision was an ethic of constancy characterized by relentless sobriety, self-control, and emotional steadiness.[16]

Despite their emphasis on personal experience and their commitment to "growth in grace" throughout life, the Puritans never accepted the potential freedom and flexibility implicit in the biblical ideal of adulthood. Although the pilgrimage of life was their primary metaphor for spirituality, the Puritans constrained each individual's pilgrimage by prescribing appropriate experience and behavior according to one's age of life. The spiritual dimension

---

[13] Cited in N. H. Keeble, "The Way and the Ways of Puritan Story: Biblical Patterns in Bunyan and His Contemporaries," *English* 33 (autumn, 1984): 212.

[14] Stout, *New England Soul* (see n. 2), 30–31, 4.

[15] Bouwsma, *Calvin* (see n. 3), 35ff.

[16] Leites, *Puritan Conscience* (see n. 10), 1ff.

of constancy involved careful self-examination and assessment of one's place along a well-marked road to salvation.

Wary of spawning a society of unruly spiritual vagabonds, New England ministers took considerable pains to label every stage of the journey from humiliation to saving faith to true obedience. They imposed harsh sanctions on people like Anne Hutchinson, who denied the necessity of a staged order of redemption. First-generation preachers like Thomas Hooker and Thomas Shepard carefully detailed the acceptable sequence of spiritual stages. Progress along these stages was the major theme of Hooker's preaching. Paraphrasing Romans 8:30, Hooker outlined the sequence: "Christ by the virtue of his Resurection, and by the power of his Spirit, he doth rescue the soul, and humble him, and call him, and justify him, and sanctify him, and glorify him, and then deliver him up to the Father at the great day."[17]

For New England Congregationalists, a public relation of one's spiritual experience – a "confession" of faith – was the test for admission to full church membership. But how could such public confessions of personal experience be evaluated? To judge the claims of those aspiring to visible sainthood and church membership, ministers and congregations relied on a shared vocabulary of spiritual stages. This vocabulary was absorbed through many years of Bible study, introspection, gospel preaching, and observation of those farther along on the road to salvation.[18]

It is impossible to know how many ordinary people internalized the vocabulary of spiritual stages and applied it to their own experience. Thomas Shepard's notes on the confessions of fifty-one young men and women who joined the Cambridge Church between 1638 and 1645 suggest that this staged approach to one's spiritual journey may have been widespread.[19] The outpouring of diaries, poetry, meditations, and spiritual autobiography from the more literate members of Puritan New England also attests to popular understanding of this framework.[20]

The vocabulary of spiritual stages mingled freely and easily with images of the ages and pilgrimage of life. In her poem "Of the Four Ages of Man," Anne Bradstreet relied on several traditional images to express the respect Puritan culture attributed to old age and the end of life:

---

[17] Cited by Hambrick-Stowe, *Practice of Piety* (see n. 10), 82.

[18] Stout, *New England Soul* (see n. 2), 40; see also Edmund Morgan, *Visible Saints* (New York: New York University Press, 1963), chap. 3.

[19] Bruce Chapman Woolley, "Reverend Thomas Shepard's Cambridge Church Members, 1636–1649: A Socio-Economic Analysis" (Ph.D. diss., University of Rochester, 1976), 96.

[20] See Daniel B. Shea, Jr., *Spiritual Autobiography in Early America* (Princeton: Princeton University Press, 1968); Patricia Caldwell, *The Puritan Conversion Narrative: The Beginnings of American Expression* (Cambridge, England: Cambridge University Press, 1983); Milo Kaufman, *The Pilgrim's Progress and Traditions in Puritan Meditation* (New Haven, Conn.: Yale University Press, 1966); Kenneth Lockridge, *Literacy in Colonial New England: An Inquiry into the Social Context of Literacy in the Early Modern West* (New York: Norton, 1974).

And last of all to act upon this stage
Leaning upon his staff came up Old Age,
Under his arm a sheaf of wheat he bore,
An harvest of the best, what needs he more?
In's other hand a glass ev'n almost run,
This writ about: *This out then I am done.*
His hoary hairs, and grave aspect made way,
And all gave ear to what he had to say.[21]

Here we see a series of conventional themes that became sentimental fare in the nineteenth century: the stage metaphor, the correspondence between old age, autumn, and the harvest, and the hourglass motif.

In her more personal reflections, Bradstreet began meditating on death when still in her teens. In 1632 she responded to "a Fit of Sickness" with a poem of preparation:

Twice ten years old, not fully told
Since nature gave me breath,
My race is run, my thread is spun,
lo here is fatal Death.[22]

Bradstreet wrote many such meditations in response to childbirth, illness, and the deaths of relatives.[23] In 1669, exhausted and suffering from a painful disease, Bradstreet wrote "As weary pilgrim, now at rest," an exquisite expression of her yearning for Christ through death:

A pilgrim I, on earth perplext
with sinns with cares and sorrows vext
By age and paines brought to decay
and my Clay house mouldring away
Oh how I long to be at rest
. . . .
Lord make me ready for that day
then Come deare bridgrome Come away.[24]

While Bradstreet's father Thomas Dudley did not have the poetic gifts of his daughter, he and other Reformed Christians did have a virtually universal vocabulary and tradition of preparation for death which persisted well into the nineteenth century. The following poem was found in Dudley's pocket after he died:

[21] Reprinted in *Poems of Anne Bradstreet*, ed. Robert Hutchinson (New York: Dover, 1969).
[22] Anne Bradstreet, "Upon a Fit of Sickness," in *Poems of Anne Bradstreet* (see n. 21), 78.
[23] See Ross W. Beales, "Anne Bradstreet and her Children," in *Regulated Children/Liberated Children: Education in Psychohistorical Perspective*, ed. Barbara Finkelstein (New York: Psychohistory Press, 1979), 10–23.
[24] Anne Bradstreet, "As Weary Pilgrim," in *Poems of Anne Bradstreet* (see n. 21), 78.

Dim eyes, deaf ears, cold stomach show
My dissolution is in view.
My shuttle's shut my race is run
My sun is set, my deed is done.
My span is measured
[My] tale is told,
My flower's faded and grown old.
My life is vanished, shadows fled,
My soul's with Christ, my body dead [25]
. . . .

Puritan conversion narratives rarely reveal a sudden change of heart. Instead, they reflect an ongoing process marked by the emotional highs and lows of people struggling to bring themselves into closer communion with God. The narratives generally reach their climax at the point of full repentance for sin, the common criterion for church membership. Conversion, the process of preparing for the infusion of faith, might take as long as ten years and was generally completed about the time of marriage.[26] By prescribing a correspondence between spiritual and secular stages, New England Puritans – like their early modern European counterparts – turned to life time as a tool of social and religious order.

Yet even full church membership, the final stage of conversion, marked only another phase in the Puritan's lifelong devotional practice and preparation for death. Ahead lay the difficult work of sanctification – the gradual bending one's life to the will of God, along with constant self-examination for signs of election. Although no Puritan dared take his election for granted, older Puritans generally benefited from the opinion that old age itself might be a sign of election.[27] As they grew older, aging believers could continue to grow toward – but never reach – perfection in Christ.

Contemporary psychiatrists and psychologists are increasingly convinced that a fully mature human identity depends, among other things, upon each individual reviewing the contents of a lifetime, telling one's own story to another.[28] This work helps us understand why Puritan views of maturity and religious experience were particularly well-suited to the spiritual and emotional needs of the older believer. But we also need to realize that the contemporary vogue of life review and reminiscence represents a secular variation of Protestantism's traditional ideal of maturity. Even the puzzling

---

[25] Cited in Hambrick-Stowe, *Practice of Piety* (see n. 10), 238.

[26] Philip J. Greven, Jr., "Youth, Maturity, and Religious Conversion: A Note on the Ages of Converts in Andover, Mass., 1711–1749," *Essex Institute Historical Collection* 108 (1972): 119–34.

[27] David Hackett Fischer, *Growing Old in America*, expanded ed. (New York: Oxford University Press, 1978), 29–37.

[28] The seminal article in this area is Robert Butler, "The Life Review: An Interpretation of Reminiscence in the Aged," *Psychiatry* 26 (1963): 65–76. See also Marc Kaminsky, ed., *The Uses of Reminiscence: New Ways of Working With Older Adults* (New York: Haworth, 1984).

passage from Shakespeare's *As You Like It* – "And thus from hour to hour we ripe and ripe,/ and then from hour to hour we rot, and rot./ And thereby hangs a tale" – becomes clear when we remember the biblical description of old age as "a tale that is told."[29]

Puritanism maintained a keen interest in the personal past, and in each individual's careful reflection on the past before God. The belief that personal experience formed a divinely ordered, rational whole, that "life was a tightly knit fabric of providences,"[30] encouraged aging Puritans to clarify their souls by reviewing the past, searching for signs of election that might ease doubt and renew feelings of assurance.[31] Since "remarkable providences" (God's interventions) in history sanctified time and revealed God's personal interest in each soul, a pilgrim's progress depended as much on looking backward as on looking ahead.

Puritanism surrounded the journey of the aging pilgrim with social conventions, beliefs, and symbols that esteemed the end of life. By restricting membership to those old enough to examine themselves, by extending the conversion process, by emphasizing sanctification through experience and reflection, by often seating the oldest members of the congregation in front, and by prescribing veneration, the Puritans infused aging with a wealth of social and religious meaning.[32] They encouraged even the oldest individual to cherish each moment of life while preparing to relinquish it. Living on the edge of uncertainty about both their earthly and their eternal fate, Puritans of all ages faced death "with an intensity virtually unknown in modern American life."[33]

Unlike Victorian culture, Puritanism did not envision life's pilgrimage merely as a linear journey that prized the goal and devalued the process. Nor did Puritans restrict their journey to men only, in contrast to classical and medieval writers.[34] Indeed, the sanctification of experience and the strong

---

[29] Awareness of the traditional religious roots of life review and reminiscence poses many interesting questions about the form of late-life spirituality encouraged by modern gerontology. For an overview of recent work, including the danger of reifying the concepts of life review and reminiscence, see Robert Disch, ed., "Twenty-Five Years of the Life Review: Theoretical and Practical Considerations," *Journal of Gerontological Social Work* 12, nos. 3 and 4 (1988). See also Marc Kaminsky, "The Art of Life Review," unpublished manuscript, Myerhoff Center, New York City.

[30] Shea, *Spiritual Autobiography* (see n. 20), 210.

[31] See, for example, Asahel Nettleton's sermon "Self-Examination," in *Remains of the Late Reverend Asahel Nettleton* (Hartford, Conn.: Robins & Smith, 1845).

[32] Not all churches gave priority to age as the criterion of seating; after the mid-eighteenth century, churches increasingly sold seats to the highest bidder rather than assigning them according to age or estate. See Fischer, *Growing Old* (see n. 27), 38–40, 78–79.

[33] David E. Stannard, *The Puritan Way of Death* (New York: Oxford University Press, 1977), ix.

[34] During the later Middle Ages, women's formal and informal participation in religious life grew considerably; specifically female influences on the development of piety emerged. See Caroline Walker Bynum, "Religious Women in the Later Middle Ages," in *Christian Spirituality: High Middle Ages and Reformation*, ed. Jill Raitt (New York: Crossroad Press, 1987), 121–38; also Clarissa W. Atkinson, *Mystic and Pilgrim: The Book and World of Margery Kempe* (Ithaca N.Y.: Cornell University Press, 1983).

value placed on "growth in grace" provided support for women as well as men in the latter half of life.

John Bunyan's treatment of Christiana in Part Two of *Pilgrim's Progress* is the most important example of Puritanism's view of women, aging, and spirituality. Even today, when this work is no longer commonplace, people who have never read John Bunyan's *Pilgrim's Progress* recognize the names of characters, places, and events from this masterpiece. Vanity Fair, the Iron Cage, the Slough of Despond, Beulah, Madam Bubble, Mr. Worldly Wiseman – these are only some of the places and characters that have passed into the popular imagination of the English-speaking world. Unfortunately, Christiana's journey has been less appreciated than that of her husband Christian.

Part One of this folk epic, written at least partially during Bunyan's first imprisonment for Nonconformity and sectarian preaching, describes the fictional journey of Christian, a kind of Everyman whose passage through the stages of redemption takes the form of an exciting adventure through unknown and dangerous territory. Within a decade of its appearance in 1678, *Pilgrim's Progress* had exhausted eleven English editions and been translated into Dutch, French, and German. In America, where the lonely hero's struggle in an unknown land resonated with the experience of settling a wilderness, this *Pilgrim's Progress* eventually came to have even more influence than in England.[35]

Bunyan refused to "conform" to the Church of England. He was imprisoned for twelve years under Charles II for organizing and preaching at sectarian meetings. The enormous success of Bunyan's work reflected in part the maturity of a large class of small tradesmen and shopkeepers – haberdashers, cordwainers, candlemakers, grocers, ostlers, buttonmakers, combmakers, braziers – who were claiming the right to think for themselves in religious and political matters.[36]

Pilgrim's Progress also reveals the growing stature that Puritanism accorded women. As we saw in the preceding chapter, women made their first iconographic appearance on the stages of life in the seventeenth century.[37] In that century, they also first entered the pilgrimage motif as protagonists in Part Two of Bunyan's work (first published in 1684), which treats the journey of Christiana and her children. *Pilgrim's Progress* not only appealed to people across class and gender lines, it also beautifully painted the universal quest for salvation amidst the local settings of daily life – meandering footpaths,

---

[35] David E. Smith, *John Bunyan in America* (Bloomington: Indiana University Press, 1966), 3–16.

[36] Monica Furlong, *Puritan's Progress* (New York: Coward, McCann & Geoghegan, 1975), 14. See also Christopher Hill, *A Tinker and a Poor Man: John Bunyan and His Church, 1628–1688* (New York: Knopf, 1989), esp. 197–230.

[37] As far as I know, the only exception to this generalization is Bertelli's *Nine Ages of Woman*, engraved in the late sixteenth century. See Samuel Chew, *The Pilgrimage of Life* (New Haven, Conn.: Yale University Press, 1962), fig. 102.

frightening bogs, flowery meadows, flatlands, rectories, marketplaces.[38]

Interestingly, Puritanism's most influential and enduring piece of literature – Bunyan's *Pilgrim's Progress* – depicts the archetypal male journey as one of middle age and the archetypal female journey as one that extends from young adulthood to old age. In Part One, the middle-aged Christian completes his journey almost overnight – a far cry from Oedipus's decades of wandering or from medieval pilgrims' long years of searching. On the other hand, Christiana begins her journey in Part Two as a young mother and completes it as an "aged matron." Although she remains bound by conventions of female subordination, Christiana experiences the culmination of her spiritual quest in old age.

Part One of *Pilgrim's Progress* is a long description of a dream. A man appears in rags. Carrying a great burden (of sin) on his back, he breaks into tears while reading his Bible. "What shall I do?" he cries in desperation.[39] The man goes home to his wife and family but finds no relief from this terrible distress. Walking in the fields, reading his book and crying aloud, the man meets Evangelist, who asks, "Wherefore dost thou cry?" The man answers that he fears death and judgment: the burden of sin on his back will surely sink him into Hell. He is given a parchment roll, inscribed with the words "Fly from the wrath to come." Evangelist points him across a very wide field toward a Wicket Gate, telling him to follow a shining light. The man, now called Christian, runs from his family and jeering neighbors, fingers in his ears, shouting "Life, life, Eternal life."[40]

Thus begins Christian's mid-life journey. No sooner has he escaped from the City of Destruction than he falls into the Slough of Despond, a putrid bog filled with the scum and filth of human sinfulness. Sinking up to his neck in the mire, struggling with his heavy burden, Christian finds Help, a man who pulls him out and explains that men fall into the Slough of Despond when they realize how sinful they are. Next Christian meets Mr. Worldly Wiseman, who suggests that he consult Legality, a gentleman living in the village of Morality. Legality, or his son Civility, will be able to ease the oppressive burden on Christian's back.

But Christian is quickly rescued from this false path of conventionality. Evangelist reappears and explains that Christian will face many false paths – crooked and wide – but that only one "straight and narrow" path leads to the Celestial City. At the House of the Interpreter, he learns about sanctification, patience, and Christ's saving grace. He enters a dark room where a man in an iron cage suffers unspeakably from the belief that he has sinned beyond all hope of forgiveness. "I am now a man of despair, and am

---

[38] Ronald Blythe, *Divine Landscapes* (San Diego: Harcourt, Brace, Jovanovich, 1986), 103.

[39] John Bunyan, *Pilgrim's Progress*, ed. Roger Sharrock (Harmondsworth, England: Penguin, 1965), 39. All further citations of *Pilgrim's Progress* refer to this edition.

[40] *Pilgrim's Progress*, Part One, 40, 41.

shut up in it, as in this iron cage. I cannot get out, O now I cannot."[41]

Alarmed, Christian runs with great difficulty up a steep highway, fenced on both sides by the Wall Salvation. At the top of a hill, he stands before a Cross. Suddenly, his burden drops from his shoulders and falls down the hill into an open tomb. But even after this experience of grace, there are many dangers ahead.

After glimpsing the Delectable Mountains from the House of the Virgins Discretion, Prudence, Piety, and Charity, Christian must endure the slippery slope downward into the Valley of Humiliation, where he encounters the hideous monster Apollyon, "who was clothed with scales like a fish . . . wings like a dragon, feet like a bear, and out of his belly came fire and smoke."[42]

Apollyon, Prince of this World, tries to force Christian to return to the City of Destruction. Christian kills him in a terrible fight and narrowly escapes from the Valley of Humiliation. He enters the Valley of the Shadow of Death, full of darkness, dragons, and hobgoblins. Amidst great fear and trembling, Christian is comforted by the voice of a man reciting the Twenty-Third Psalm: "Though I walk through the Valley of the Shadow of Death, I will fear none ill, for thou art with me."[43]

At the end of this Valley, Christian comes across the blood, bones, ashes, and mangled bodies of men, even of pilgrims that had preceded them. These are the victims of two giants, Pope and Pagan. Pagan is long since dead. Pope is alive. But he is so old and "grown so crazy and stiff in his joints that he can now do little more than sit in his cave's mouth, grinning at pilgrims as they go by, and biting his nails because he cannot come at them."[44]

Rejoicing at his deliverance from the Valley of the Shadow of Death, Christian meets Faithful and they journey together to the town Vanity, named (Bunyan tells us) from the ancient phrase in Ecclesiastes: "All that cometh is vanity." This town sponsors a perpetual festival, Vanity Fair, where everything is for sale. The two are imprisoned for their strange dress and behavior. The judges are unimpressed by the explanation that "they were pilgrims and strangers in the world, and that they were going to their own country, which was the heavenly Jerusalem."[45] Faithful meets a horrible death at the stake, and Christian escapes to continue his journey.

Christian and his new companion Hopeful make the mistake of leaving the stony path and cutting over a stile through By-Path Meadow. They are quickly surrounded by darkness, almost drowned in the flood of an immense thunderstorm. When they awaken next morning, Giant Despair imprisons

---

[41] *Pilgrim's Progress*, Part One, 66.
[42] *Pilgrim's Progress*, Part One, 90.
[43] *Pilgrim's Progress*, Part One, 98.
[44] *Pilgrim's Progress*, Part One, 99, 100.
[45] *Pilgrim's Progress*, Part One, 127.

them in the dungeon of his Doubting Castle for trespassing. After days of torture, Christian is sorely tempted to suicide. But he is comforted by Hopeful and in the midst of prayer remembers that he already has a key called Promise that unlocks all doors in the Giant's castle.

There are only a few more trials to face. Christian and Hopeful come to the Delectable Mountains. They have to avoid the steep drop Errour and a smoking door for hypocrites cut straight through to Hell. They encounter Ignorance, a brash young man who is also traveling to the Celestial City. Ignorance suffers from the ultimate error of believing that he can effect his own salvation.

The pilgrims finally arrive at the country of Beulah, safe at last. They reach the Enchanted Ground, which resembles the sacred grove of the Furies in *Oedipus at Colonus*. Yet they cannot sleep here, but must remain sober and watchful. Hopeful then gives an autobiographical account of his spiritual life that reveals his personal experience of sinfulness and God's saving grace. Since there is no bridge across the River of Death, the two brave the water together, Hopeful saving the exhausted Christian from drowning. A heavenly host receives them, clothes them in heavenly garments, and they enter the King's city amidst the sounding of trumpets and bells.

Still believing in his own sufficiency, Ignorance gets a ferryman to take him across the river but cannot produce a Certificate to prove his Election. He is taken and flung through the doorway of the hill leading to Hell. "Then I saw that there was a way to Hell, even from the Gates of Heaven, as well as from the City of Destruction. So I awoke, and behold it was a dream."[46]

In Christian's journey, Bunyan brilliantly fuses the pilgrimage motif with the spiritual stages of Puritan orthodoxy. He adapts the ballads and adventure stories that he loved as a child to the medieval figure of the lonely wayfaring man who sets out on a journey for truth. Christian is neither a prince nor a nobleman. He has no special gifts of strength or intelligence. He is a peasant folk-hero, with all the fears, mistakes, gullibility, and limitations of ordinary men. Christian is driven from the City of Destruction by his desperate need for a righteousness not his own. He dare not lose his integrity by conforming to "this world" – by pleasing others or accepting superficial, legalistic religion. His exhaustingly dramatic journey reveals the difficulty of achieving a genuine belief that is nevertheless a gift from God.

Pilgrim's Progress universalizes the myth of individual growth within the intensely demanding framework of Calvinist orthodoxy. Bunyan accomplishes this not only by creating a peasant folk-hero, but also by emphasizing the pilgrimage of female believers. Bunyan describes Christiana's journey in Part Two of *Pilgrim's Progress*, published in 1684, six years after the pub-

---

[46] *Pilgrim's Progress*, Part One, 185, 205.

lication of Part One. Never as prominent in Anglo-American culture as Christian's more solitary story of hazardous adventure, Christiana's story describes loving relationships in a Christian community. It contains insights about aging that are notably absent in Part One. And it reflects Bunyan's identification with both suffering and love from a woman's point of view.

Bunyan's spiritual autobiography *Grace Abounding to the Chief of Sinners* and Part One of *Pilgrim's Progress* also testify to the importance of women in his own spiritual development. His first wife seems to have stimulated Bunyan's initial interest in religion and churchgoing. This interest led to the intense spiritual crisis described in *Grace Abounding* and in Part One of *Pilgrim's Progress*. Shortly after his marriage and the birth of a blind daughter in 1650, Bunyan's encounter with several poor women played a key role in his conversion, lifting him out of his loneliness and spiritual despair.

Walking through Bedford in his occupation as a traveling tinker (making and repairing household pans, kettles, and farm implements), Bunyan came across several poor women sitting and talking about religion. He listened to them talk about new birth, about Christ's love and their wretchedness without his love. Listening to these women, Bunyan felt a deep and sudden awareness of love, an experience that saved him from despair and alienation.[47]

When he sat down to write Part Two of *Pilgrim's Progress*, Bunyan had become a highly successful and admired preacher, pastor, and writer. He had remarried after his first wife's death. His children were almost grown, and his family no longer suffered acutely from poverty. Nor, to judge from his writings, did he suffer from the inner torments of guilt and despair. But the more relaxed pace and tone of Part Two reflect more than Bunyan's changed circumstances. They also reflect a radically different focus for the pilgrimage theme. In Part Two, Bunyan leaves behind the sinner's terror and desperation. His attention moves from the individual to the family, from the male to the female.[48]

Both parts of *Pilgrim's Progress* use the device of a dream-vision to represent their protagonists' journeys to salvation. Both Christian and Christiana set out from the City of Destruction toward the Celestial City. In Part One, Christian suddenly leaves his wife Christiana and their children, setting out alone and in great distress. His journey runs its course within a few brutal weeks or months through a lonely and hostile landscape. Bunyan radically telescopes Christian's passage through Puritanism's spiritual stages, severing the traditional connection between time, physical aging, and spiritual growth.

Christiana, on the other hand, takes time to pack before embarking with

---

[47] Furlong, *Puritan's Progress* (see n. 36), 58, 21ff.

[48] Margaret Olofson Thickstun, "From Christiana to Stand-fast: Subsuming the Feminine in the *Pilgrim's Progress*," *Studies in English Literature, 1500–1900* 26 (summer 1986): 439–40. The following discussion of gender differences in *Pilgrim's Progress* relies on Thickstun's seminal article.

her four sons and her neighbor Mercy. Her journey takes place over many years, during which time she is transformed from a young mother into an elderly matron. Whereas Christian directly faces the spiritual and physical dangers of masculine independence, Christiana faces spiritual dangers peculiar to women and receives physical protection appropriate to female subordination.

Christian personifies the embattled Puritan, fighting onward through the narrow way, the strenuous hill, the valley of peril, the dangers and persecutions of the city.[49] He fights the monster Apollyon in the Valley of Humiliation. When Christiana reaches the same spot, she comes upon a beautiful green valley filled with lilies. She and her companions find guidance and instruction from Mr. Great-heart. Several Christian communities also shelter the group, which grows larger as more and more believers join the quest.

Both Christian and Christiana experience "progress" through the stages of spiritual life. They both learn that the claims of this world lead one to stray from the path of salvation. Yet each follows a separate path layed out by the conventions of gender. Christiana experiences temptations and seeks virtues that differ from those of Christian. Her relationship to God is conceived in radically different terms. Bunyan expresses Christian's relationship to God through the metaphor of king and subject, making loyalty a cardinal virtue and treason the corresponding sin. Christiana's relationship to God, on the other hand, is initially modeled on that of bride to bridegroom. Like Anne Bradstreet's, Christiana's longing for God echoes the Song of Solomon 3:1–2:

By night on my bed I sought whom my soul loveth; I sought him, but I found him not.

I will rise now, and go about the city, and in the broad ways I will seek him whom my soul loveth.

Through this metaphor, Bunyan presents chastity as the primary female virtue and sexual misconduct (including adultery, promiscuity, prostitution, and even being raped) as the characteristic female sin. The Puritan belief in female insufficiency prevails.

For the Puritans, a woman's relationship to God was always mediated through her husband, God's representative to her. Accordingly, Christiana initially conceives her own sinfulness in terms of duty to her husband: "Sons, we are all undone. I have sinned away your father." At the same time, Christiana imagines her future salvation as reunion with Christian: "Pack up," she urges her children, "and be gone to the Gate that leads to the

---

[49] See E. Beatrice Batson, *John Bunyan: Allegory and Imagination* (Totowa, N.J.: Barnes & Noble, 1984), 38ff.

Celestial Country, that we may see your father and be with him and his companions in peace."[50]

Part One of *Pilgrim's Progress* seems to suggest that each individual must face the dangers of the spiritual road alone.[51] Christian learns to rely only on God's intervention and his word (symbolized by Evangelist) for protection against evil. Part Two warns against female social and spiritual independence. When they are rescued from an attempted rape by "two ill-favoured ones," Christiana and Mercy learn that they must rely on male protectors. Although the women vigorously resist their would-be rapists, Bunyan equates this episode with sexual temptation and spiritual pollution. Christiana fears that the rape experience may have reflected her own suppressed desires, expressed in an earlier dream. Both she and Mercy must be purified in the "Bath of Sanctification" – a ritual bath designed to cleanse them of their fallen nature and impure sexuality.

After the party leaves the House of the Interpreter, Great-heart takes up his Sword, Helmet, and Shield to protect the women on their way to the House Beautiful. Bunyan's portrayal of female frailty and subordination eliminates adventure from women's lives, replacing it with domesticity and relationship.[52] Roughly midway through Part Two, Bunyan's emphasis shifts from the experience of Christiana and Mercy to the exploits of men like Old Honest, Valiant-for-Truth, Mr. Stand-fast, and Mr. Great-heart. For the remainder of *Pilgrim's Progress*, Christiana and Mercy mend clothes and care for the sick while the men launch expeditions and slay giants.

Just before the party reaches the Land of Beulah, the bright and beautiful waiting-place for those who will cross the river to the Celestial City, they come across a man kneeling in prayer. Mr. Stand-fast is thanking God for delivering him from the harlot Madam Bubble, "Mistriss of the World." Like Christiana, Stand-fast has resisted sexual advances. But unlike Christiana, he is not condemned for secretly desiring Madam Bubble or for encouraging her persistent "enticements." Instead Bunyan uses Madam Bubble to personify sexual evil, a scapegoat who represents all the sins of "this vain world."[53]

Christiana's death takes place in the warmth and security of a Christian community, but Bunyan does not allow Christiana to consummate her relationship as a perfect bride of Christ. She has been cleansed of sexual evil, but her aging female body remains the symbol of earthly imperfection. Bunyan therefore completes *Pilgrim's Progress* with Stand-fast, whose last words, "Take me, for I come unto thee,"[54] transform his death into a form

[50] *Pilgrim's Progress*, Part Two, 223, 226.
[51] Thickstun, "Christiana to Stand-fast" (see n. 48), 445.
[52] Furlong, *Puritan's Progress* (see n. 36), 119.
[53] *Pilgrim's Progress*, Part Two, 361.
[54] *Pilgrim's Progress*, Part Two, 372, 373.

of sexual surrender. Feminine chastity has been replaced and completed by male perfection. Stand-fast – not Christiana – becomes the most perfect bride of Christ.[55]

Bunyan's depiction of a female protagonist marks a major departure from earlier works in the "pilgrimage of life" genre. With Christiana, women appear prominently on the stages of life's way in popular literature as well as iconography. Bunyan's treatment of Christian also differs from traditional characterizations of the pilgrim. In medieval versions, the male hero's journey through the stages of the spirit took him through the stages of life as well. Finding true bliss meant enduring the ravages of time and the body's vicissitudes.[56] Christian, in contrast, passes through all the required spiritual stages of Calvinist orthodoxy – calling, conviction, faith, repentance, justification, forgiveness, sanctification, and perseverance – in a matter of weeks or months.[57]

We can only speculate about why Bunyan's treatment of Christian broke the traditional links between the ages of life and the ages of the spirit. Perhaps it reflected a rapid personal transformation forged in the experiences of persecution and imprisonment. Perhaps Bunyan endowed Christian with his own rare capacity for achieving a spiritual condition far beyond that of the ordinary middle-aged man. In the future, however, this segregation of spiritual growth from physical aging would become widespread in Protestant America. It would dovetail neatly with secular priorities of middle-aged, male self-control and would intensify fears of decay, dependence, and decline.

Christian represents a new kind of hero in modern literature: a kind of Everyman who is ordinary, vulnerable, liable to mistake the way, but certain of his goal.[58] In Victorian America, when *Pilgrim's Progress* reached the height of its influence, Christian became a model for the view that men, given enough faith and willpower, could somehow triumph over time and transcend its effects on the body. By splitting the spiritual from the physical, Bunyan also foreshadowed the instantaneous conversion favored by nineteenth-century evangelicals, who focused on youth and devalued later life. Christiana's journey, on the other hand, retains the traditional pattern of physical decline and spiritual growth. As we will see, some early American women of faith, adequate means, and good fortune were able to approximate Christiana's example.

[55] Thickstun, "Christiana to Stand-fast" (see n. 48), 451.
[56] Siegfried Wenzel, "The Pilgrimage of Life as a Late Medieval Genre," *Mediaeval Studies* 35 (1973): 378.
[57] Furlong, *Puritan's Progress* (see n. 36), 108.
[58] Keeble, "Ways of Puritan Story" (see n. 13), 226.

3

"Death without order": the late
Calvinist ideal of aging

Man is the most dependent creature in the world. He cometh forth like a
flower, weak, frail, delicate. He grows up, lives and dies in a state of dependence. . . . [T]hrough every stage of life we are constrained to lean more
or less upon the power, wisdom, and kindness of our fellowmen. . . . [T]he
young depend upon the old, and the old upon the young.

Nathaniel Emmons

None can either read or hear the word of God properly and profitably without
numbering their days aright, and realizing whether they are in the morning,
the meridian, or decline of life.

Nathaniel Emmons

THE SOCIAL CONTEXT OF AGING IN
EARLY AMERICA

The Puritans understood aging as a sacred pilgrimage to God and final judgment. They also held a patriarchal ideal of family life and assumed that the
young should venerate the old. Their images of aging and ideals of old age
would seem to justify a rosy picture of old people in early America.[1] But cul-

[1] Although historians have spilled a good deal of ink debating the power and status of old age in
early America, we do not yet have enough empirical data – especially outside of New England – to
justify strong generalizations. On this debate, see David Hackett Fischer, *Growing Old in America*,
expanded ed. (New York: Oxford University Press, 1978), chaps. 1, 2, and Bibliographical Appendix;
Lawrence Stone, "Walking Over Grandma," *New York Review of Books*, May 12, 1977; D. H. Fischer
and Lawrence Stone, "Exchange," *New York Review of Books*, September 15, 1977; Daniel Scott Smith,
"Old Age and the 'Great Transformation': A New England Case Study," in *Aging and the Elderly:
Humanistic Perspectives in Gerontology*, ed. Stuart F. Spicker, Kathleen M. Woodward, and David D. Van
Tassel (Atlantic Highlands, N.J.: Humanities Press, 1978), 285–302; John Demos, "Old Age in Early
New England," in *Aging, Death, and the Completion of Being*, ed. David D. Van Tassel (Philadelphia:
University of Pennsylvania Press, 1979), 115–64; W. Andrew Achenbaum, *Old Age in the New Land*,
pts. 1, 2 (Baltimore: Johns Hopkins University Press, 1978); Carole Haber, *Beyond Sixty-Five: The
Dilemma of Old Age in America's Past* (New York: Cambridge University Press, 1983), chaps. 1, 2; and
Gene W. Boyett, "Aging in Seventeenth-Century New England," *New England Historical and Genealogical
Register* 134 (July 1980): 181–93.

tural ideals and social experience often diverge. Prescriptions and practice are never identical. Although veneration of the elderly was an important ideal, age alone was no guarantee of respect, power, or well-being. Wealth, race, and gender also structured the social experience of aging. Elderly slaves were the most vulnerable and powerless, while the aged poor – especially women without family – often became objects of scorn and abuse.[2]

Some older people undoubtedly benefited from the hierarchical ideal of society and family that prevailed in early modern Anglo-American culture. According to this ideal, "the young were to serve and the old to rule."[3] This ideological preference for age and seniority was reinforced by the doctrine of spiritual ages (the idea that the soul grew along with the body) and by the widespread image of God as an old man, the "Ancient of Days."[4] Although the Puritans had steadfastly rejected patriarchal doctrine in the political realm, they embraced it in family life, insisting on the authority of the husband and father.[5] The patriarchal ideal in turn was supported by a commitment to hierarchy, stability, and continuity – values that were not effectively challenged until the latter half of the eighteenth century.

On the other hand, patriarchal ideals were *not* accompanied by conventions or laws vesting lifelong control over resources in the hands of fathers. In colonial New England, average wealth tended to be lowest for men in their twenties, rising to a peak in the fifties, and declining thereafter.[6] Substantial wealth and power in church or state lay generally in the hands of men aged forty to sixty.[7] The same trends have been found in England from the sixteenth to the mid-eighteenth century and can be attributed to a common convention in northwestern and central Europe: that the older generation must yield scarce and valuable resources to assist the next generation. Because the economic independence of newly married couples required the transmission of property before their parents' death, the senior generation occupied a relatively weak position compared to their counterparts in Eastern Europe and Asia.[8]

---

[2] Fischer, *Growing Old in America* (see n. 1), 60–67.

[3] Keith Thomas, "Age and Authority in Early Modern England," *Proceedings of the British Academy* 42 (1976):207.

[4] Thomas, "Age and Authority" (see n. 3), 210; Fischer, *Growing Old in America* (see n. 1) 34–35.

[5] See Gordon J. Schocet, *Patriarchalism in Political Thought* (New York: Basic Books, 1975), 86, 99, 100; T. H. Breen, *The Character of a Good Ruler: A Study of Puritan Political Ideas in New England, 1630–1730* (New Haven, Conn.: Yale University Press, 1970), 17–21; and Lawrence Stone, *The Family, Sex, and Marriage in England, 1500–1800*, abridged ed. (New York: Harper and Row, 1979), chap. 5.

[6] Demos, "Old Age" (see n. 1), 137.

[7] See D. S. Smith, "Old Age and the 'Great Transformation' " (see n. 1), 285–302.

[8] See J. Hajnal, "European Marriage Patterns in Perspective," in *Population in History*, ed. D. V. Glass and D. E. C. Eversley (Chicago: University of Chicago Press, 1965), 101–43; also Hajnal, "Two Kinds of Preindustrial Household Formation," *Population and Development Review* 8 (1982): 449–94; and Jack Goody, "Aging in Non-industrial Societies," in *Handbook of Aging and the Social Sciences*, ed. Robert H. Binstock and Ethel Shanas (New York: Van Nostrand Reinhold, 1976), 117–29.

While most older men continued to work and hold productive property, they may not have done so out of free choice alone. Instead, the rarity of retirement probably reflects hostility toward the unproductive and reluctance to expend limited resources on their maintenance. It was risky for a man to release his property and become a "sojourner" or a "tabler" with his children.[9] Aging fathers often took care to specify the heir's obligations and the surviving spouse's rights in the legal documents authorizing transmission of property.

Conventional wisdom held that old parents should avoid becoming dependent on their children. But most people who lived long enough found it difficult to meet obligations to the next generation without becoming dependent and vulnerable. In Europe, especially during the eighteenth century, increasing longevity and a growing population pressed against a limited land supply, giving rise to considerable bitterness toward fathers who held on to their farms too long.[10]

In early America, available land dampened the intensity of intergenerational conflict. Some of the first settlers who came to the vast wilderness of the New World were even able to approximate the patriarchal ideal. In Andover, Massachusetts Bay Colony, for example, men who settled between 1646 and 1662 generally lived long lives, sired large families, and garnered enough land to place their sons on plots near the parental homestead without surrendering title until death. Even in Andover's third and fourth generations, marked by declining land availability and increasing geographical and occupational mobility of sons, a majority of those inheriting land did not assume title until their father's death.[11] Not all New England towns – even in their early years – offered such power to the men who settled them.

In Plymouth, for example, the ideal of a compact Christian community quickly gave way to the establishment of new townships as ambitious sons and new immigrants dispersed to take possession of unsettled land.[12] Geographical mobility distressed the General Court and original settlers like William Bradford, who feared the decline of the colony's religious ideals. In mourning the town's loss of cohesion, Bradford used a metaphor suggesting that fear of abandonment and destitution in old age was not unknown. Plymouth, he wrote, was "like an ancient mother grown old and forsaken of her children, though not in their affections yet in regard of their bodily

---

[9] Thomas, "Age and Authority" (see n. 3), 237–38.

[10] See Lutz K. Berkner, "The Stem Family and the Development Cycle of the Peasant Household: An Eighteenth-Century Austrian Example," *American Historical Review* 77 (1972): 398–418; also David Troyansky, *Old Age in the Old Regime: Image and Experience in Eighteenth-Century France* (Ithaca, N.Y.: Cornell University Press, 1989), chap. 1.

[11] Philip J. Greven, *Four Generations: Population, Land and Family in Colonial Andover* (Ithaca, N.Y.: Cornell University Press, 1970), chap. 4.

[12] John Demos, *A Little Commonwealth: Family Life in Plymouth Colony* (New York: Oxford University Press, 1970), 9–12.

presence and personal helpfulness; her ancient members being most of them worn away by death, and these of later time being like children translated into other families, and she like a widow left only to trust in God. Thus, she that had made many rich became her self poor."[13]

Occasionally, aged New Englanders did find themselves destitute and without relatives living nearby. Most likely, a local meeting or governing body would supervise their care, assigning particular tasks and services to various townspeople and reimbursing the expenses. In local records, such people are often referred to by names like "old Bright," "old Bunnill," and "old Woodward."[14] Nevertheless, old people receiving public assistance were expected to be of service in whatever ways were possible. In 1671, for example, the elderly John Martin was receiving several pounds a year but failed to occupy himself productively. The Wenham Congregational Church declared him guilty of idleness and asked the selectmen to find him work.[15]

Bradford's metaphor of an "ancient mother grown old and forsaken of her children" suggests the special vulnerability of older widows. Poor, elderly widows and unattached women were sometimes neglected, scorned, or even driven away and forced to wander from town to town.[16] In a patriarchal household, the legal personhood of a wife was incorporated into that of her husband. Upon the death of a father or husband, a family was legally dissolved.

But the legal power of male household heads did not necessarily mean that women were actually powerless. By common law and custom, widows usually inherited one-third of the household goods and received the use of or income from one-third of the real estate until she died or remarried. While final disposition of family property was determined by court order or by her husband's will, a widow generally received enough to maintain herself at a level appropriate to the estate.[17] New England wills generally spelled out the arrangements for care and maintenance of elderly widows, often empowering widows themselves to see to their fulfillment.[18]

By cultural norm, adult women were expected to marry and subordinate themselves to their husbands, who were to rule, protect, and provide for them. Milton neatly summed up the Puritan view of gender and subordination: "He for God only, she for God in him." In this ideological climate,

---

[13] Cited in Demos, *A Little Commonwealth* (see n. 12), 178.

[14] Demos, "Old Age" (see n. 1), 141–49; John J. Waters, "The Traditional World of the New England Peasants: A View From Seventeenth-Century Barnstable," *New England Historical and Genealogical Register* 130 (1976): 11ff.

[15] Boyett, "Aging in Seventeenth-Century" (see n. 1), 191, fn. 67.

[16] Fischer, *Growing Old in America* (see n. 1), 63.

[17] Laurel Thatcher Ulrich, *Good Wives* (New York: Knopf, 1982), 7; see also Alexander Keyssar, "Widowhood in Eighteenth-Century Massachusetts: A Problem in the History of the Family," *Perspectives in American History* 8 (1974): 83–119.

[18] Demos, "Old Age" (see n. 1), 141.

images of poor or struggling widows commonly evoked pity, charity, or outrage. These images proliferated not because they reflected a widespread social reality but because they reinforced the assumption that a woman could not live independently of a man's protection. On the other hand, wealthy widows, freed from the need for surrogate husbands and constant work, represented a disturbing anomaly to the expectations of female subordination. Such widows were commonly ridiculed in literature as licentious, vulnerable to unscrupulous suitors, and unable to handle their freedom from male authority.[19]

Widowhood in early America was a common female experience, in which older women lived for many years outside the boundaries of male authority. In southeastern Pennsylvania, for example, a married woman had a slightly better than even chance of becoming a widow during the late eighteenth and early nineteenth centuries. The average age at which a woman became a widow during this period was forty-eight. She had lived for twenty-five years in marriage and faced another thirteen years of widowhood before remarrying (which was rare) or dying.[20]

Many women apparently handled widowhood with strength and competence, often gained from marriages characterized by mutual obligation and cooperation for the benefit of the family as a whole.[21] While death usually struck at least one partner in a marriage before their last child had come of age, parents in the Northern colonies lived unusually long lives. Compared to Europe or the Chesapeake, colonial New England especially offered a higher standard of living, characterized by better nutrition, greater resistance to disease, and longer life expectancy.[22] Records from a number of seventeenth-century New England towns suggest that men who reached maturity and women who survived their childbearing years may have enjoyed a life expectancy approximating seventy years.[23] Although infant mortality

---

[19] Charles Colton, "The Widow's Tale: Male Myth and Female Reality in 16th and 17th-century England," *Albion* 10 (summer 1978): 118–29; and Lisa Wilson Waciega, "Widowhood and Womanhood in Early America: The Experience of Women in Philadelphia and Chester Counties, 1750–1850" (Ph.D. diss., Temple University, 1986).

[20] Waciega, "Widowhood and Womanhood" (see n. 19), 14.

[21] See Terri Premo, *Winter Friends: Women Growing Old in the New Republic, 1785–1835* (Urbana: University of Illinois Press, 1989); Waciega, "Widowhood and Womanhood" (see n. 19), chaps. 2–6.

[22] On mortality in the Northern colonies, see Fischer, *Growing Old in America* (see n. 1), Appendix, Tables IV, V, VI; also John Duffy, *Epidemics in Colonial America* (Baton Rouge: Louisiana State University Press, 1953), 107; and Kenneth Lockridge, *A New England Town: The First Hundred Years* (New York: Norton, 1970), 67. On the Chesapeake region, see Lorena S. Walsh and Russell R. Menard, "Death in the Chesapeake: Two Life Tables for Men in Early Colonial Maryland," *Maryland Historical Magazine* 69 (1974): 224, Table 3. For European mortality in the early modern period, see, for example, T. H. Hollingsworth, *Historical Demography* (Ithaca, N.Y.: Cornell University Press, 1960), 189; Pierre Goubert, *The Ancient Regime: French Society, 1600–1750*, trans. Steve Cox (New York: Harper & Row, 1974), pt. 2; and E. A. Wrigley, ed., *An Introduction to English Historical Demography* (London: Weidenfeld & Nicolson), 166.

[23] Lockridge, *A New England Town* (see n. 22), 67; Demos, *A Little Commonwealth* (see n. 12), 192,

was quite high by today's standards, it was not unusual to grow old. In established communities, people aged sixty or older made up between 4 and 7 percent of the colonial population.[24]

The survival of so many men and women into old age has led one observer to suggest that grandparents were "invented" in New England.[25] Few ordinary Englishmen in this period ever lived to see their grandchildren; most males married in their late twenties and died in their early fifties, leaving behind only unmarried children.[26] By comparison, it seems likely that grandparent-grandchild relationships were relatively widespread and at least potentially close in early New England.[27]

Older women of some means benefited considerably from this new longevity. Having fulfilled their culturally defined roles as housewives, deputy husbands, consorts, mothers, mistresses, neighbors, and Christians, older women in early New England grew into considerable stature.[28] In villages, they were entrusted with upholding the moral standards enunciated by the church and enforced by the court. Having proven their integrity and presumably beyond lust themselves, old women could recognize and condemn sexual sins. Experience rather than innocence constituted the primary female virtue in rural New England.[29] Because many children never saw their first birthday, great prestige was accorded fertility and survival. The crown of mothering arrived in old age, when a sturdy and fortunate woman saw her children's children come into the world (see Fig. 12).[30]

During the eighteenth century, patriarchal authority and hierarchical forms of community and religious practice faced increasing opposition.[31] With the growth of a market economy and of economic individualism, the power of kings, lords, masters, clergymen, fathers, and elders was increasingly circumscribed. The Enlightenment praised the capacity of ordinary men and women to reason and to know. Evangelicalism affirmed the capacity

Table 2; Demos, "Old Age" (see n. 1) 124ff; Greven, *Four Generations* (see n. 11), 24ff, Tables 2, 27; Fischer, *Growing Old in America* (see n. 1), 28, fn. 7.

[24] Demos, "Old Age" (see n. 1), 130. For more detailed analyses, see Maris A. Vinovski, ed., *Studies in American Historical Demography* (New York: Academic Press, 1978).

[25] John M. Murrin, "Review Essay," *History and Theory* 10 (1972): 238.

[26] Peter Laslett, *The World We Have Lost*, 2d ed. (New York: Scribner, 1971), 94, 96–99; see also Laslett, "The History of Aging and the Aged," in his *Family Life and Illicit Love in Earlier Generations* (London: Cambridge University Press, 1977), 174–213.

[27] Demos, "Old Age" (see n. 1), 129.

[28] Ulrich, *Good Wives* (see n. 17), 9.

[29] Ulrich, *Good Wives* (see n. 17), 103; for a fascinating account of an older woman's part in convicting a man of attempted adultery for advances toward his daughter, see pp. 89–92. The moral authority of older women seems to have continued well into the early nineteenth century. See Premo, *Winter Friends* (see n. 21).

[30] Ulrich, *Good Wives* (see n. 17), 160.

[31] See Richard Bushman, *From Puritan to Yankee: Character and the Social Order in Connecticut, 1690–1765* (Cambridge, Mass.: Harvard University Press, 1967); and Bernard Bailyn, *New England Merchants in the Seventeenth Century* (Cambridge, Mass.: Harvard University Press, 1955).

Figure 12. *The First, Second, and Last Scene of Mortality*, a needlework picture by Prudence Punderson (late eighteenth century). (Connecticut Historical Society, Hartford.)

of their hearts to feel and believe. And republicanism insisted on the political rights of propertied, adult males.

In this climate, veneration was an ideal whose days were numbered. Throughout Anglo-American society, the gentry and urban middle classes set in motion new ideas about parental responsibilities and filial rights, moral obligation and personal autonomy, the character of God and the nature of sin, and the role of the family and education in society.[32] By the mid-eighteenth century, a new parental ideal was successfully competing with patriarchal values. The new ideal cherished more affectionate and egalitarian relationships between parents and children.[33] It placed considerable emphasis on companionship and affection within marriage, as well as on the right and obligation of all children to become autonomous and rational adults. A central text for enlightened familial relations was John Locke's *Some Thoughts on Education* (1693). Locke's belief that the child's mind was a *tabula rasa* and

[32] For citations, see Jay Fliegelman, *Prodigals and Pilgrims: The American Revolution Against Patriarchal Authority* (New York: Cambridge University Press, 1982), 269, fn. 2.
[33] Fliegelman, *Prodigals and Pilgrims* (see n. 32), 1.

that character was formed by experience rather than inheritance helped many to reject the traditional idea of original sin.

Lockean child rearing emphasized the development of reason, the "internal governor," together with habits of self-control and self-denial as the proper preparation for adulthood. While Scottish moral philosophers like Hume emphasized innate moral sociability (in contrast to Locke's stress on individual rationality), they too rejected an authoritarian model of the family and urged development of an "internal governor" to lead individuals to virtue throughout the course of life.

By the revolutionary era, the moral education of free, self-governing individuals had become a dominant theme in Anglo-American culture. Parents increasingly abandoned the belief that their primary responsibility was to break the evil tendencies in their children and bring their fallen natures into conformity with external authority.[34] Instead, such parents – increasingly female parents by the late eighteenth century – sought to educate and prepare children for their futures as independent citizens.[35]

During the late eighteenth and early nineteenth centuries, social and demographic changes both reflected and reinforced the new familial ideals, weakening the power of one generation over another. Throughout the seventeenth and early eighteenth centuries, young men had remained dependent and directly responsible to fathers or masters until marriage or their father's death. Yet the pressure of a limited land supply in original areas of settlement increasingly prevented even wealthy fathers from settling all their sons on the family estate.[36] Expansion and diversification of economic life created new forms of employment over which fathers had no control.

By the 1820s, increasing numbers of young men began leaving home in their late teens, abandoning agriculture for construction work on canals and turnpikes or for commercial and industrial employment in expanding towns and cities. Migration to the city, growing separation of work from the home, and the decline of apprenticeship generated large numbers of unattached young men – the raw material of capitalist industry and a frightening symbol of social disorder.[37] Especially between 1770 and 1820, increased premarital sex and premarital conception, declining generational cohabitation and reduced frequency of parental permission for marriage were further signs that patriarchal authority and power were eroding.[38]

[34] Fliegelman, *Prodigals and Pilgrims* (see n. 32), 1.

[35] See Mary Beth Norton, *Liberty's Daughters: The Revolutionary Experience of American Women, 1750–1800* (Boston: Little, Brown, 1980), 96–97.

[36] James A. Henretta, *The Evolution of American Society* (Lexington, Mass.: Heath, 1973), chap. 1; and Kenneth Lockridge, "The Evolution of New England Society, 1630–1790," *Past and Present* 39 (1968): 68–82.

[37] Joseph Kett, *Rites of Passage* (New York: Basic Books, 1977), 86–107.

[38] See Norton, *Liberty's Daughters* (see n. 35), 71–109; Daniel Blake Smith, *Inside the Great House: Planter Family Life in Eighteenth-Century Chesapeake Society* (Ithaca, N.Y.: Cornell University Press, 1980),

The new conception of parental duty and authority altered the tone and temporal perspective of generational relations. Fathers came to view their farms and land not so much as reflections of familial tradition as the basis for future prosperity of their children.[39] Those that kept their children in a prolonged state of dependence came to appear unjust and tyrannical.

The autonomy and equality of adult generations was a fundamental principle of republican politics no less than of republican families. American revolutionaries often compared George III to a father who exercised illegitimate power over colonial children who had come of age. In *The Rights of Man* (1791), Tom Paine argued that the equality of man implied equality of generations – as if each individual endowed with natural rights "had been conceived by creation instead of generation." Each generation was therefore free to act for itself.[40] Paine's ideas were of a piece with Jefferson's famous dictum that the earth belongs to the living, not to the dead hand of the past.

As these ideas about society and family undercut patriarchal and hierarchical authority, old age lost its ideological prestige. By the end of the eighteenth century, the ideal of veneration ill suited a society of individuals who were less and less willing to submerge their identities or constrain their activities within the communal confines of family, church, and town.[41] Several changes symbolized the cultural devaluation of old age. New England meetinghouses increasingly used wealth rather than age as the primary criterion for seating arrangements. State legislatures began to require public officials to retire at age sixty or seventy. Before 1790, people tended to report themselves to census takers as older than they actually were. After that date they generally reported themselves as younger. Men's dress styles increasingly flattered youth rather than old age. And group portraits tended to represent family members on a horizontal plane, as opposed to the older composition of the patriarch standing above his wife and children.[42]

The case against patriarchal authority also entailed an attack on the God of Calvinism, whose absolute sovereignty and power of predestination were increasingly unacceptable to men and women who believed in shaping their own earthly and eternal futures. Following Lord Shaftesbury's argument that the true God must possess the qualities of Locke's ideal parent, republican

25–54; and Carl Degler, *At Odds: Women and the Family in America from the Revolution to the Present* (New York: Oxford University Press), 144–248.

[39] Henretta, *Evolution of American Society* (see n. 36), 10; Fliegelman, *Prodigals and Pilgrims* (see n. 32), 9–11.

[40] Cited by Fliegelman, *Prodigals and Pilgrims* (see n. 32), 169.

[41] See Fischer, *Growing Old* (see n. 1), chap. 2. Fischer claims here that the growing spirit of liberty and equality "snapped the ties of obligation between generations as well as between classes" (p. 109), leading to a "revolution in age relations." This is too strong a characterization for changes that appear to have been more gradual and symbolic. See Haber, *Beyond Sixty-Five* (see n. 1), 28–46.

[42] Fischer, *Growing Old in America* (see n. 1), 77–97.

deists and liberal Congregationalists characterized God as benevolent and compassionate. Within the ranks of Calvinism itself, a growing number of ministers could no longer affirm the basic Protestant paradox of divine sovereignty and human accountability for sin.

Parishioners who wanted to be saved but could not find their way to the foot of a sovereign, inscrutable God, wondered how they could be blamed. Increasingly, believers demanded a rational and moral understanding of human accountability. The New Divinity movement, founded in the 1750s and 1760s by Joseph Bellamy and Samuel Hopkins, attempted to provide this understanding and to reconcile the increasingly strident conflict between theocentric piety and humanitarian morality.[43] Despite such challenges, orthodox Calvinism remained the religion of most churchgoing Americans down to the end of the eighteenth century. As late as 1790, more than 60 percent of American churches upheld the Five Points of Calvinism as defined by the Synod of Dort in 1619. Theologically speaking, the Puritan Congregationalists of New England agreed on most points with other Protestant inhabitants of British America, major exceptions being Lutherans and Quakers.[44]

By the 1820s, the inscrutable and omnipotent God of Calvin had given way to the benevolent and just God that characterized the second Great Awakening. One influential New England minister, however, lived far enough into the nineteenth century to keep alive Calvinist ideas about life and death, growing up and growing old in a universe ruled by a sovereign and inscrutable God.

NATHANIEL EMMONS AND THE CALVINIST IDEAL OF OLD AGE

When ninety-five-year-old Nathaniel Emmons died in 1840, New England lost the last of its great Puritan divines. Like many ministers of his generation, Emmons emerged from obscure, rural origins. Born in East Haddam, Connecticut, he studied theology at Yale and was ordained to preach in 1769. After several years as an itinerant preacher, he settled into a church in the small town of Franklin, Massachusetts. This entirely rural parish steadfastly supported his old-fashioned Calvinism during a period that many lamented as a time of "declension." During his fifty-year career in Franklin, Emmons achieved considerable renown: He taught theology to eighty-seven theology students, helped found the Massachusetts Missionary Society, became an editor of its magazine, and commented freely on public matters.

---

[43] See Joseph Haroutunian, *Piety versus Moralism* (New York: Holt, 1932); Joseph Conforti, *Samuel Hopkins and the New Divinity Movement* (Grand Rapids, Mich.: Christian College Consortium, 1981).

[44] Fischer, *Growing Old in America* (see n. 1), 32, fn. 16.

57

Emmons was a firm patriot during the Revolution and a Federalist thereafter. When he preached a bitter denunciation of Jefferson's deistic heresies, Federalists welcomed the sermon as a major political diatribe.[45]

Emmons's unusually long life attracted widespread interest. "Few men in their old age ever excited so much attention as he," noted the editor of his *Works*. "Clergymen of all denominations and gentlemen of every other profession, far and near, . . . manifested a peculiar interest in him." Long before he showed any of its infirmities, Emmons often talked about old age with his friends, expressing his dread of its sufferings and trials. "By and by I shall be thrown behind the door, and you have no idea what a dreadful thing it is to be laid aside as good for nothing." But more than "any degree of suffering or neglect," Emmons feared "the continuation of his public labors beyond their usefulness." Convinced that old ministers generally held on too long, Emmons took the first indication that his powers were failing as an opportunity to avoid this embarrassment.[46]

In May 1827, the eighty-two-year-old minister fainted while delivering a Sunday sermon. Two weeks later, he resigned with a letter to his parishioners renouncing "all claims upon future ministerial support; relying entirely upon your wisdom to grant or not to grant, any gratuity to your aged servant during the residue of his life."[47] His parish voluntarily granted him an annuity of $150 per year for life, sparing him the indigent plight of many retired ministers.[48] When congratulated on his "green" old age by a man who wondered if he had not retired too soon, Emmons replied, "I meant to retire while I had SENSE enough to do it."[49]

During the last fifteen years of his life, Emmons was regarded as an intellectual and physiological curiosity. His "hoary age" provided a convenient symbol, both for assaults on Calvinist orthodoxy and for its defenders. Lecturing to the senior class at Andover Theological Seminary, Edwards A. Park remembered Emmons "as the representative of choice men among the ancient clergy of New England. He often spoke of himself as being left alone, all the old familiar faces long since veiled from his view. There has even been a melancholy and sombre interest flung over such a man, staying

---

[45] Charles G. Cole, *The Social Ideas of the Northern Evangelists, 1826–1860* (New York: Columbia University Press, 1954), 19.

[46] Jacob Ide, "Memoir," in Nathaniel Emmons, *The Works of Nathaniel Emmons* (Boston: Congregational Board of Publication, 1842), 1:97, 100. For an example of one such minister's "ungraceful" old age, see D. S. Smith's discussion of Ebenezer Gay in "Old Age and the 'Great Transformation' " (see n. 1), 285–302.

[47] Ide, "Memoir" (see n. 46), 1:100.

[48] Maris A. Vinovskis, " 'Aged Servants of the Lord': Changes in the Status and Treatment of Elderly Ministers in Colonial America," in *Aging from Birth to Death*, ed. Mathilda White Riley, Ronald P. Abeles, and Michael S. Teitelbaum (Boulder; Colo.: Westview Press, 1982), 2:105–37.

[49] Emmons, *Works* (see n. 46), 1:101.

Figure 13. Portrait of Nathaniel Emmons. (From *Memoir of Nathanael Emmons*, by Edwards A. Park [Boston: Congregational Board of Publication, 1861].)

so long behind his time, and watching over the fourth generation of his successors."[50]

Emmons preserved the fashions of his youth to the end. As if he were the Gray Champion of Hawthorne's tale, boys flocked after him through the streets of a New England town, with his three-cornered hat, bright buckles on shoes and knees, and long white hair flowing down around his shoulders.[51] While he lived, the Franklin meetinghouse remained unaltered. The last religious service in this old-style church, with high pulpit and square pews, was his funeral. "But he has gone," concluded Park, "numbered at last with the friends of his youth, allowed to rejoin the company from which he has been severed for so long. The last of our patriarchs has left us; and men whom he baptized in infancy wept at his funeral when they had well-nigh reached their seventieth year. 'Nothing was more affecting to me,' said one

[50] Edwards A. Park, "Miscellaneous Reflections," in Emmons, *Works* (see n. 46), 1:clxvi.
[51] On "gray champions" in early New England, see Fischer, *Growing Old in America* (see n. 1), 48–52.

who witnessed his obsequies, 'than to see these old men weeping over the corpse of their father.' "[52]

What did Nathaniel Emmons preach to his congregation on the subject of age? How did this last man of New England's Calvinism interpret the meaning of aging, the value of old age, and the trials, comforts, responsibilities of the aged? The answers require prior understanding of Emmons's broader theology. Emmons's religious ideas evolved from the evangelical Calvinism of Jonathan Edwards and Samuel Hopkins. He preserved the sovereignty of God and the depravity of man, yet allowed room for human agency in regeneration. Although he claimed that man was utterly dependent on God, Emmons believed that active repentance might win God's mercy. At ninety-three, he expressed this belief: "I go with the Old School of New England divines half way, and then turn around and oppose them with all my might. I go with the New School half way, and then turn around and oppose them with all my might. The Old School must say less of passivity, the New School more of dependence."[53]

In Emmons's cosmology, both social relations and relations between man and God were characterized by dependence, servility, and mutuality. His sermon of January 1826, for example, depicted a world of reciprocity: "Through every stage of life we are constrained to lean more or less upon the power, wisdom, and kindness of our fellow men . . . the young depend upon the old, and the old upon the young. The poor depend upon the rich and the rich upon the poor." Nevertheless, Emmons continued, God "never meant that our dependence upon each other should be a just ground for renouncing our supreme dependence upon himself. He is the only self-existent and independent being. He carries all other things in his hand."[54]

Emmons's views on life, death, and salvation lay midway between those of his seventeenth-century ancestors and his nineteenth-century successors. Until the Great Awakening of the mid-eighteenth century, Puritans held rigorously to the doctrines of human depravity, predestination, and God's inscrutability. Stained by the sin of Adam, few seventeenth- or early eighteenth-century Calvinists considered themselves worthy of salvation, a status God had predetermined for the select few. These Puritans constantly searched their souls for signs of saving grace. After lifelong journeys of harrowing introspection, even the most pious Puritans did not take salvation for granted. Nevertheless, at least some achieved a serene confidence and sense of peace in the face of death.[55]

By the time of Emmons's birth, many New England churches had accepted

---

[52] Park, "Miscellaneous Reflections" (see n. 50), 1:clxxii.
[53] Park, "Miscellaneous Reflections" (see n. 50), 1:clx–clxi.
[54] Emmons, "Dependence on Man Forbidden," *Works*, (see n. 46), 3:313.
[55] For a different view, see David Stannard, *The Puritan Way of Death* (New York: Oxford University Press, 1977).

George Whitefield's message that it was possible to determine with certainty who was marked for salvation and who was not. Mid-eighteenth-century Puritans also believed with Jonathan Edwards that "assurance is to be attained not so much by self-examination as by active piety."[56] A merciful God could be moved to give his saving grace to those sinners who actively sought regeneration. From this position, it was a short but important step (one that Emmons refused to take) to the evangelical Arminianism of Charles Finney, Lyman Beecher, Nathaniel Taylor, and Albert Barnes.[57] These preachers, discussed in the following chapter, entirely subverted the doctrine of predestination, already weakened by the first Great Awakening. Upholding the doctrine of free grace, they claimed that an individual's spiritual fate lay in his own hands – salvation was free for the asking.

"DEATH WITHOUT ORDER"

If Emmons granted human beings a modicum of influence over their eternal lives, such influence barely extended to earthly life. Volume 3 of his collected *Works*, subtitled "Instructions to the Afflicted," resounds again and again with the message of human frailty and the need to prepare for death. At the funeral of Daniel Thurston in 1802, Emmons stressed the fundamental principle of "Death Without Order." He claimed that God sent the "King of Terrors" to visit people without respect to age, stage of life, health, character, station in life, or human feelings. "In a word, God discovers no order in calling men out of the world. As he gave them life, so he takes it away at his pleasure. . . . " Since God revealed no order in death, Emmons assailed the sinful presumption of those who observed an order in preparing for death: "though they expect to die, and intend to prepare for death, yet they imagine they may safely neglect [this], til age, infirmity, or sickness place them in the rank of the dying. This is the order in which thousands and thousands resolve to prepare for eternity; and it is next to impossible to convince them of the folly and danger of their presumption."[58]

In New England's increasingly humanized and rationalized religious tradition, death remained the last bastion of Calvinism's absolute, incomprehensible, and sovereign God. Emmons's God cared little for the health, strength, and usefulness of the young. "The oldest person on earth cannot give a reason why he did not die in infancy, or in childhood, or in any period or circumstance of life in which others have died. The living are a wonder to themselves. They can assign no reason why they have not, before

[56] Jonathan Edwards, *An Humble Inquiry*, cited by Stannard, *Puritan Way of Death* (see n. 55), 154.

[57] On the roots of English Arminianism, see Ellen More, "John Goodwin and the Origins of the New Arminianism," *Journal of British Studies* 22 (fall 1982): 50–70.

[58] Emmons, "Death Without Order," *Works* (see n. 46), 3:36–37.

now, been numbered with the dead. They are the monuments of God's sparing, distinguishing and sovereign mercy."[59] Life was God's precious and mysterious gift – not a reward for proper behavior. The old merited this gift no less than the young. The young stood no farther from death than the old.[60]

When he preached about health and longevity, Emmons tried to accommodate Puritanism's inscrutable God to the Enlightenment's benevolent natural laws. Expectation of long life was unwise, he argued, not only because people might meet death at any moment but also because God had gradually curtailed the human life span for nearly four thousand years. Antediluvian patriarchs of the Bible once lived a thousand years, their lives amazingly prolonged by the "general laws of nature." During the time of Moses, God began to reduce the "common period of life" down to seventy or eighty years, using a variety of more particular providences.

Emmons claimed that although seventy or eighty years marked the "full measure of a man's useful life," God retained an absolute right either to lengthen out a man's life to as much as a century, or to deprive him of the "residue of his years." In fact, God's interventions so frequently counteracted the laws of nature that no one could state with certainty the precise span of human life, leaving open the possibility of radically longer life spans: "we have great reason to conclude that God has most commonly deprived mankind of the residue of their years, and never allowed one in a thousand or a million of the human race to reach the bounds of life which nature has set."[61]

Since God occasionally blessed individuals by prolonging their lives, Emmons urged his congregation "always to pray that God would lengthen out [their] own lives, and the lives of others, as long as they fulfill the designs of providence." At the same time, however, if "God so often deprives men of the residue of their years, then it is extremely unreasonable and dangerous to flatter ourselves with hopes of living a great while in the world." An essential tension resided at the core of Emmons's theology of longevity and death. While the general laws by which God governed the natural world enabled mankind to live far longer than at present, He still exercised an unqualified right to lengthen or shorten any individual life – to remind humans of their "constant and absolute dependence upon himself."[62]

In one sense, the tension in Emmons's vision reflected the conflict between Calvinism and the Enlightenment. Though he insisted that God brought death into the world "without order," Emmons also accepted the desirability

[59] Emmons, "Death Without Order," *Works* (see n. 46), 3:38.
[60] Seventeenth-century English ministers delivered the same message to young people. See Stephen R. Smith, "Religion and the Conception of Youth in Seventeenth-Century England," *History of Childhood Quarterly* 2 (1975): 493–516.
[61] Emmons, "Shortening of Life," *Works* (see n. 46), 3:82.
[62] Emmons, *Works* (see n. 46), 3:82ff.

of natural death – the orderly culmination of living according to natural law.[63] Indeed, portions of Emmons's sermon "Expectation of Long Life Unwise" (1826) paradoxically approach the position of hygienic reformers who argued that the length of a person's life is largely a matter of that person's own behavior. "Very few of mankind," he wrote, "at this day, die a proper natural death." Most people died prematurely, due to improvidence, intemperance, or excessive labor. Careless of their health and safety, they brought upon themselves "a premature and painful old age, which they might retard and render vastly more easy, pleasant, and useful."

Yet ultimately, Emmons returned to God's inscrutable power over death. Paradoxically, he argued that it was "dangerous," "absurd," the "strongest and most fatal practical error that mankind ever imbibed," to rely on hopes of longevity. Such hopes "stupefied" the minds of the godly, who would neglect their duties to God, themselves, and their fellow creatures. Belief in longevity encouraged the "hearts of the wicked to neglect their spiritual concerns."[64]

Emmons's equivocation reveals far more than intellectual or theological inconsistency. It epitomizes the existential integrity of a waning Calvinist realism. Emmons refused to rationalize or evade the most basic and irreconcilable conflict of the human condition – the contradiction between one's self and one's body, between one's limitless desires, dreams, and ambitions, and one's fragile, decaying, physical existence. Emmons exhorted his congregation to face this reality without flinching: to cherish "every moment, every hour, and every year added to our lives." Yet he urged them simultaneously to prepare for the judgment of God. Later evangelicals proved much less willing to accept the intractable and tragic contradictions of human life, including those of aging and old age.

Emmons devoted one entire sermon to the subject of old age. He began by asking, "Who may properly be called old people?" Common usage "affixed no definite meaning" to the term, and Emmons declined to resort to simple chronology. "Old and young are relative terms," he noted, "and may admit of different significations. Children always think their parents old." Hence, many called men of forty, fifty, or sixty old. Emmons believed that seventy years marked the most commonly accepted boundary. "There seems to be no impropriety however, in calling any man old rather than young, who has passed the meridian of life, which is commonly supposed to be at about forty-five."[65]

The fluidity and elusiveness of the term *old* did not, according to Emmons, excuse a person from the obligations appropriate to his or her age. God

---

[63] On natural law and natural death, see James J. Farrell, *Inventing the American Way of Death* (Philadelphia: Temple University Press, 1980).

[64] Emmons, "Shortening of Life," *Works* (see n. 46), 3:87–88.

[65] Emmons, "Piety A Peculiar Ornament to the Aged," *Works* (see n. 46), 2:492.

required each individual to "judge for himself when the precepts to the young bind him, and when the precepts to the old bind him." Emmons insisted that determination of one's stage of life was made by each individual rather than by what others thought of one. "None can either read or hear the word of God properly and profitably," he wrote, "without numbering their days aright, and realizing whether they are in the morning, the meridian or decline of life."[66]

When God prolonged a person's usefulness, health, and life into old age, He granted a "distinguishing favor." More often than not, Emmons asserted, old age brought with it "so many infirmities of body and mind" that most people turned away from it "with pain or disgust." "You can hardly bear to see a man," Emmons intoned, "with whom you have been acquainted in his better days, after he has lost his bodily activity, his hearing, his seeing, his memory, and all his sociability." Yet these were the "usual effects" of old age – "certainly great corporeal and mental imperfections which need something to cover them." The only possible source of compensation for aging's multiple losses lay in the title of Emmons's sermon: "Piety a Peculiar Ornament to the Aged."[67]

Piety – tested, refined, and vital – was both the salvation and the obligation of the old. Emmons hinted that those who had lived a long time in the path of holiness and obedience to God might see themselves reflected in the Book of Proverbs: "The hoary head is a crown of glory, if it be found in the way of righteousness." Although the oldest Christians never arrived at sinless perfection in this life, they could "grow in grace" as the years went by, reconciling themselves to decay, death, and the Lord's judgment. Aged saints, Emmons declared, ought to renounce the world and spend the "residue of their days in praise, retirement, and devotion."[68]

If piety was a "peculiar ornament" in old age, its absence was a peculiar blemish. Absence of piety in earlier life was so common, Emmons argued, that it was "but little noticed." Older people, however, who neglected their relationship to God displayed "a vain mind, a hard heart, a stupid conscience, and an unwise disregard to their future and eternal happiness." Without piety, the various "species of inward and moral disorders" that plagued old age would leave old people melancholy, querulous, and generally wretched. Old age, Emmons implied, was insupportable without piety.[69]

For both the older individual and his community, aged piety transformed darkness into light. Not only did it hide "imbecility of body and mind," piety also rendered old people useful "when they would otherwise be useless and burdensome to the world." Long after their "laboring days" were over,

---

[66] Emmons, "Piety," *Works* (see n. 46), 2:493.
[67] Emmons, "Piety," *Works* (see n. 46), 2:496.
[68] Emmons, "Piety," *Works* (see n. 46), 2:503.
[69] Emmons, "Piety," *Works* (see n. 46), 2:501–502.

pious old people could serve God, their families, and their communities by their example, prayers, instructions, and admonitions. The pious old represented "visible monuments of sovereign grace," revealing the Lord's righteousness, His faithful support and comfort of friends. Aged piety, in other words, enabled old people to transcend the "moral disorders . . . and natural infirmities of unrenewed human nature," even as it inspired and fortified younger people who looked ahead.

If old people without piety were useless, wretched, and morally and physically infirm, what consideration did others owe them? Even strangers to piety in old age, Emmons asserted, deserved the "respect and tenderness" of their children. Even a family burdened with old parents "perpetually murmuring, and complaining . . . under an insupportable load of guilt and misery," was obligated. Age merited respect in itself. Both in his own personal expectations and in his social and religious prescriptions, Emmons retained the ideal of veneration: "An old patriot, an old valiant general, an old faithful soldier, and every old parent and old man, ought to be respected, whether pious or not. All old people have served and suffered in the world, and done something in God's view for the benefit of mankind, and therefore have a claim to their respect on account of age."[70]

Despite the decline of patriarchal authority and the demise of orthodox Calvinism, traditional formulations of the ages and journey of life persisted well into the nineteenth century. Death could strike at any time and still demanded preparation and submission from the living, but it no longer occupied the throne of the "King of Terrors." The deaths of older people were commonly used as occasions for instruction for each age of life. "Let the young remember," said Reverend John Channing Abdy at Britannia Faulkner's funeral in 1824, "that she whose loss we deplore was early pious, that she preferred to go with the children of God rather than to enjoy the pleasures of sin for a season. Let those who are in the middle of their earthly course be reminded, that she was an example of all that a wife and mother should be. Let widows look to her as realizing all that St. Paul held excellent. . . . Let those who . . . are approaching to the end of their race, be admonished by her example to make advanced life respectable by its conduct, and not repelling by its manners; to unite, as she did, the wisdom of age with the cheerfulness of youth."[71]

When the elderly Bathsheba Sanford died in November 1800, Nathaniel Emmons addressed the widower in familiar terms: "She accompanied you a

---

[70] Emmons, "Piety," *Works* (see n. 46), 2:499–500.

[71] Reverend John Channing Abdy, funeral sermon for Mrs. Britannia Faulkner, delivered November 28, 1824, p. 21. See also Jonathan L. Pomeroy, "Sermon Preached at the Funeral of Mr. Jededia Wilbur" (Northampton, Mass.: William W. Clapp, 1816). Both sermons can be found in the Yale University Divinity School Library, Archives and Manuscripts Division, Commemorative Addresses, Group 29, Box 37.

great way in the journey of life. With you she joined, morning and evening, in addressing the throne of divine grace. . . . " Emmons did not spare the widower, his colleague Reverend David Sanford, from the typical exhortation to accept divine will. Since God was the "agency of death," He required "you to be dumb, and not open your mouth, *because he has done it.* . . . You have long been preaching submission to others; but you are now called to feel and express it to yourself."[72]

Emmons's message was typical of countless funeral sermons delivered in the first half of the nineteenth century.[73] Although ministers, health reformers, physicians, and scientists would soon launch a concerted effort to define death as appropriate and natural only in old age, most Americans still considered the timing of death unpredictable and its cause providential.[74] When twenty-seven-year-old Ebenezer Grant Marsh died in 1803, Yale President Timothy Dwight preached the traditional *memento mori* message to the assembled students: "The race of Adam are all travelers in the journey of life. . . . At every stage of their progress death ambushes their path, and unseen graves open to receive them. . . . Infancy, Childhood, Youth, Manhood, and Age descend to the tomb . . . ."[75] In funeral sermons, ministers often spoke to the young, middle-aged, and old in turn, reminding each age of life of the frailty of its hopes. God had predetermined the timing and manner of each individual's death.

"Every moment brings us nigher to eternity," noted John Gardner at the funeral of Protestant Episcopal Bishop Samuel Parker. "We glide the stream of time with imperceptible rapidity, and shall soon be carried into the ocean of futurity." Gardner reiterated the old assumptions about mortality and the seasons of life: "Some are blown from the tree of life early in the spring, others drop off withered by the heat of the summer, few survive the chilling blasts of autumn, and those few are shrunk and scattered by the deadly breath of winter."[76] Death in the winter of life was the exception rather than the rule – both in fact and in expectation.

[72] Sermon delivered at the funeral of Mrs. Bathsheba Sanford, November 17, 1800 (Wrentham, Mass.: Nathaniel Heaton, Jr., 1801), Yale University Divinity School Library, Archives and Manuscripts Division, Commemorative Addresses, Group 29, Box 36.

[73] Early nineteenth-century funeral sermons emphasizing the spirit of submissiveness and preparation can be found in the Yale University Divinity School Library, Archives and Manuscripts Division, Commemorative Addresses, Group 29, Boxes 35–37.

[74] For a discussion of ordinary Americans' ideas about death, see Lewis O. Saum, *The Popular Mood of Antebellum America* (Westport, Conn.: Greenwood Press, 1980), chap. 4.

[75] Timothy Dwight, "A Sermon on the Death of Mr. Ebenezer Grant Marsh" (Hartford, Conn.: Hudson and Goodwin, 1804), 16–17. The same views were expressed in Bancroft Fowler's memorial sermon, "An Oration on the Death of Mr. Ebenezer Grant Marsh" (Hartford, Conn.: Hudson and Goodwin, 1804), 13. Both sermons can be found in the Yale University Divinity School Library, Archives and Manuscripts Division, Commemorative Addresses, Group 29, Box 35.

[76] Sermon by John Sylvester J. Gardner, preached December 9, 1804, on the death of the Reverend Samuel Parker (Boston: Gilbert and Dean, 1804), Yale University Divinity School Library, Archives and Manuscripts Division, Commemorative Addresses, Group 29, Box 36.

CONSOLATION FOR OLD AGE: THE FIRST AMERICAN
AGING MANUAL

During the middle third of the nineteenth century, books containing instruction, inspiration, consolation, and advice about aging appeared in the literary marketplace. Generally written by older ministers or female authors, this literature reflected the expansion of publishing, the growth of a middle-class reading public, and the barrage of self-help manuals aimed at providing new standards of conduct following the demise of communal traditions.[77] Taken broadly, advice about aging in the nineteenth century underwent a shift from consolation and mystery to exhortation and mastery – what a later era might label from pessimism to optimism. In Chapter 7, we will observe this shift in some detail.

Just as traditional images of the ages and journey of life persisted well into the nineteenth century, so did the late Calvinist ideal of aging and old age. Yet even as the first self-help manual for elders was being written in the late 1820s, the religious, social, and ideological sources of its Calvinist vision were quickly eroding.

In 1829, Reverend John Stanford published *The Aged Christian's Companion*, advertised as "the first attempt to provide a book adapted especially for those . . . entering the vale of years." Stanford, described by a friend as a lifelong "son of consolation," had served for many years as chaplain of New York City's public welfare institutions, promoting the "temporal comfort and spiritual welfare" of thousands of inmates of New York's asylums, prisons, almshouses, hospitals, and other houses of refuge. At age seventy-six, Stanford took the opportunity to address a presumably more fortunate audience by writing a book "adapted to the improvement, consolation, and encouragement of persons advanced in life." He died in 1831, while working on a second volume. *The Aged Christian's Companion* went through three editions by 1852, initiating the genre of American advice literature for older people.[78]

Like Emmons, Stanford defined old age, with biblical sanction, as seventy years or more. His general perspective emerges clearly in his essay on the familiar theme, "Winter, An Emblem of Old Age."[79] Stanford's vision of late life remained squarely within the tradition of Reformed theology. His imagery reached back to the integrated world view of the Middle Ages, with

---

[77] Charles A. Madison, *Book Publishing in America* (New York: McGraw-Hill, 1966); and William Charvat, *Literary Publishing in America 1790–1830* (Philadelphia: University of Pennsylvania Press, 1959).

[78] John Stanford, *The Aged Christian's Companion* (New York: Stanford and Sword's, 1852). For a less popular aging manual, see Joseph Alden, *The Aged Pilgrim* (Boston: Massachusetts Sabbath School Society, 1846).

[79] Despite this chronological definition, Stanford retained the looseness of preindustrial age-grading: "At fifty or sixty, men are called aged, but they do not arrive to old age until they reach the number seventy." *Aged Christian's Companion* (see n. 78), 190.

its harmonious synthesis of the ages of life and the journey of life and its assumption that each stage of life is equidistant from God.[80] The same imagery abounds in the diaries and letters of older women who were probably among his readers.[81]

Stanford reaffirmed the ancient belief in divinely ordained limits of human life: "As in the natural world, so it is in the human creation. Times, seasons, and periods of existence are fixed, and they cannot pass their bounds."[82] Like Emmons, Stanford noted that most people hoped to live to old age, but "death often blasts the prospect!" Since God had spared the aged from the common fate of early mortality, Stanford argued that gratitude, humility, and hope were the appropriate attitudes for old Christians completing their earthly pilgrimage.[83] In contrast, once expectation of long life achieved widespread cultural sanction in the mid-nineteenth century (and this preceded the actual demographic accomplishment of increased longevity), gratitude and humility came to appear less appropriate. The sense of being fortunate gave way to the desire to remove the misfortunes and infirmities of age.

Wintry days, according to Stanford, were short, dark, and cold, permitting little activity or service. Rheumatic complaints, palsy, and muscular stiffness made old people "feel somewhat like the stream which, by the effects of cold, is congealed into ice. . . . Remember, aged friend, with you it is winter, and no winter is without its fogs and storms" – an insight intended to help cultivate submission to the will of God.[84] Unlike later sentimental writers and painters who placed old age comfortably beyond the turbulence of middle age, Stanford did not exempt old age from the storms of life.

Throughout *The Aged Christian's Companion*, Stanford reiterated his claim that old people met the most severe afflictions at the end of their pilgrimage, "when they most need[ed] the cup of consolation."[85] Comparing the tears of the aged with the "tears of infants," he pointed with acute insight to the essential helplessness of both infancy and infirm old age. While the infant relied on its earthly mother, the aged Christian turned to the heavenly Father. In the language of the 131st Psalm, Stanford affirmed the spiritual necessity of mourning: "Surely I have behaved and quieted myself, as a child that is weaned of its mother: my soul is even as a weaned child."

Like Emmons, Stanford confirmed the essential cycle of human dependency – a human quality increasingly anathema to middle-class male culture. "In

---

[80] Stanford, *Aged Christian's Companion* (see n. 78), 357–58.

[81] See Premo, *Winter Friends* (see n. 21), chap. 4.

[82] As our discussion of Trollope and Osler in Chapter 9 will show, "fixed" periods do not necessarily contain fixed cultural content.

[83] Stanford, *Aged Christian's Companion* (see n. 78), 358–59.

[84] Stanford, *Aged Christian's Companion* (see n. 78), 358–59, 361–62.

[85] Stanford, *Aged Christian's Companion* (see n. 78), 20.

your infirm age," he addressed his readers, "you are realizing the whole in your own person, for old age is little else than a return of the weeping babe! A sense of this cannot fail to produce a long train of pious reflections."[86]

For Stanford then, the weaning of old age led one to that review of life central to the Calvinist tradition of evangelical Protestantism. Since the regenerate "new man" coexisted throughout life with the "old man . . . corrupt according to the flesh," even the most pious Christian suffered an "internal warfare," stimulating a search for final reconciliation. "Review the history of your own life," urged Stanford. "Bring to your recollections the sins and evils which have attended it, and [realize] . . . the great importance of finding grace in the eyes of the Lord, that by faith you may enter into the true ark, the Lord Jesus Christ."[87]

This life review, however, did not emerge full-blown out of a previously repressed past; ideally it followed a lifetime of introspection and examination, enabling the aged Christian to complete earlier efforts.[88] A diary, containing the record of previous efforts, could provide "a valuable aid" to a man's failing memory: "he will esteem the little book next to his *Bible*, and call it a part of his most valuable treasure, because it contains the history of God's mercy to himself."[89]

Stanford's ideal aged Christian would achieve both reconciliation with the past and calm hope for the future. Reflecting an older tradition that had not sundered the private sphere from the public, Stanford saw these personal accomplishments as social obligations of old age. Citing Saint Paul's letter to Titus (Titus 2:2–5), he outlined the proper character of old men and women: "that the aged men be sober, grave, temperate, sound in faith, in charity, in patience. The aged women likewise, that they be in behavior as becometh holiness, not false accusers, not given to much wine, teachers of good things. . . ."

Like Emmons, Stanford maintained that old men had solemn obligations to fulfill. By 1829, however, this biblically sanctioned sober, grave old man was increasingly a remnant of dying patriarchal values. By mid-century, as we will see, advice manuals exhorted aged men not to behave according to the dignity and distant sobriety of a powerful patriarch, but to exhibit the more emotional characteristics increasingly associated with feminine virtue.

Male and female differences notwithstanding, in the fading Reformed tradition, aged piety served as public instruction and pointed to a single source of goodness: "There is something so lovely and encouraging to young

---

[86] Stanford, *Aged Christian's Companion* (see n. 78), 60, 62.

[87] Stanford, *Aged Christian's Companion* (see n. 78), 15–17, 105.

[88] It is worth noting that Butler's notion of the life review does not conceive reminiscence in old age as the culmination of ongoing introspection throughout life. See Robert Butler, "The Life Review: An Interpretation of Reminiscence in the Aged," *Psychiatry* 26 (February 1963): 65–76.

[89] Stanford, *Aged Christian's Companion* (see n. 78), 19.

persons to behold the aged in the house of God, that it cannot fail to enforce the duty upon them. It teaches them that God has blessings to bestow both upon the aged and the young, that although nature wears out, grace grows stronger and bears the richest fruit."[90] Stanford often spoke directly to his aged readers, offering his concern and consolation. He urged those in sickness and pain to seek deeper communion with God, rekindling hope in "the final state of rest in heaven." Celebrating the "rich and abundant encouragement" of the Gospel, Stanford extracted fourteen biblical "Promises Adapted to the Aged," recommending them in time of need.

If *The Aged Christian's Companion* retained orthodox Reformed conceptions of consolation, life review, and the relations between the seasons, ages, and generations, it also hinted both at an incipient age consciousness and the increasing disjunction between traditional images of aging and American secular values. "The history of old age [i.e., the life histories of old people] seldom meets with that attention which it deserves," claimed Stanford. Most young people had no interest in those who "have penetrated into the vale of years."

Assuming that most people preferred reading about the lives, infirmities, and habits of others "who bear nearly the same date of years with themselves,"[91] he produced the first of a proliferating series of lists celebrating the accomplishments of well-preserved prodigies of old age. These lists, which became longer and more monotonous throughout the nineteenth century and into the twentieth,[92] were designed both to defend old age against charges of uselessness and to inspire old people with models of accomplishment and triumph. Stanford's list included Moses, Saint John the Divine, and a host of English and American ministers, doctors, and scholars, as well as the ten antediluvian patriarchs who lived to an average of 875 years.[93] While aging manuals following *The Aged Christian's Companion* rarely referred to patriarchal longevity or its decline, virtually all of them took the decline of patriarchal authority for granted.

---

[90] Stanford, *Aged Christian's Companion* (see n. 78), 134–35, 266.

[91] Stanford, *Aged Christian's Companion* (see n. 78), 377.

[92] For a contemporary counterpart, see Alex Comfort, *A Good Age* (New York: Crown, 1976).

[93] Stanford, *Aged Christian's Companion* (see n. 78), 389ff.

PART 2

The dualism of aging in
Victorian America

4

Antebellum revivals and Victorian morals: the ideological origins of ageism

The day of earth's redemption can never come, til the traditions of the elders are done away. . . . These traditions of the elders are the grand sources of most of the fatal errors of the present day.

Charles G. Finney

The conversion of an aged sinner is an event that justly strikes the mind with astonishment.

Nathaniel Taylor

The time of youth compared with old age has about the same relation to salvation, which spring-time and summer, compared with winter, have with reference to a harvest. The chills and frosts of age are about as unfavorable to conversion to God as the frosts and snows of December are to the cultivation of the earth.

Albert Barnes

On July 4, 1825, a speaker at ground-breaking ceremonies for a new canal urged Ohio citizens to mobilize "the vigor and firmness of youth, the strength and firmness of manhood, and the wisdom of age" to complete the huge project. "Great as is the undertaking," he continued, "your powers are equal to its completion; be but united, firm and persevering, and if heaven smile on your labors, success is sure."[1] Before the Civil War, the belief that every age of life could help build a new society was commonplace. Yet this same unbounded optimism and passion for material progress generated both a distaste for the living representatives of an outmoded past and a need to compensate for cutting them loose.

Exactly one year later, Thomas Jefferson and John Adams died within hours of each other. The passing of the revolutionary generation and the rise

---

[1] Cited in W. Andrew Achenbaum, *Old Age in the New Land* (Baltimore: Johns Hopkins University Press, 1978), 9. Achenbaum comments in chap. 1, "The Usefulness of Old Age," p. 10, that ministers, scientists, essayists, and editors commonly asserted that "a lifetime of experience made older persons remarkable promoters of healthful longevity, ideal custodians of virtue, and seasoned veterans of productivity."

of Jacksonian democracy corresponded with a major transformation in American society. Westward migration, the growth of cities, the rise of manufacturing, and the creation of national transportation, communication, and financial networks testified to liberal capitalism's economic power. As communal forms of life eroded, generational continuity in families became more tenuous.[2] Enormous material progress revealed its dark side – fear of decline, of degeneration, of being left behind. Romantic images of the old man as stranger reflected these fears; sentimental images of old fathers, ministers, and soldiers concealed them.

Amidst the quickening pace of everyday life, Northern ministers often turned to the biblical text "Our fathers, where are they?" to remember the men who had lived through the American Revolution.[3] Their deaths were commonly mourned in patriarchal terms.[4] In 1811, Zebulon Ely used the biblical death of Abraham to eulogize Connecticut's last surviving signator of the Declaration of Independence: "Then Abraham gave up the ghost and died in a good old age, an old man and full of years; and was gathered to his people" (Genesis 25:8). Before his death at the age of eighty-one, William Williams had served in both national and state public life for more than fifty years. Although Ely entitled his sermon "A Ripe Shock Seasonably Gathered," he did not consider Williams's death in old age the normal state of affairs. Instead, he emphasized the "peculiarly favorable circumstances" that allowed Williams to serve God for so many years.[5]

As old age was being infused with increasingly sentimental images of lost patriarchal authority,[6] a new kind of old man appeared in Anglo-American literature.[7] Coleridge's Ancient Mariner, Wordsworth's Old Cumberland Beggar, and Washington Irving's Rip Van Winkle all convey a strangeness mixed with the poignancy of nostalgia.

Unlike Oedipus or Christian these men do not find a secure resting place.

---

[2] For examples of generational discontinuity reflected in American literary culture, see Steven Mintz, *A Prison of Expectations: The Family in Victorian Culture* (New York: New York University Press, 1985), chap. 2; and Rodney Olsen, *Dancing in Chains: The Youth of William Dean Howells* (New York: New York University Press, 1990).

[3] See, for example, the following sermons, which can be found in the Yale University Divinity School Library, Archives and Manuscripts Division, Commemorative Addresses, Group 29: Alfred L. Bowery, "The Brevity of Human Life" (Boston: n.p., 1841), preached at the funeral of Zibeon Hooker, an officer in the Continental Army (Box 78); Samuel Nott, sermon preached at the funeral of Mary Hanford Williams (Hartford, Conn.: Peter G. Gleason, 1815) (Box 37); and David McClure, "The Death of the Righteous Desirable" (Hartford, Conn.: Hudson and Goodwin, 1803) (Box 37).

[4] George B. Forgie, *Patricide in the House Divided* (New York: Norton, 1979).

[5] Zebulon Ely, *A Ripe Shock Seasonably Gathered, A Discourse Occasioned by the Death of the Honourable William Williams, Esq.* (Hartford, Conn.: Hudson and Goodwin, 1812), 3, 4.

[6] On the figure of the patriarch in sentimental literature, see Ann Douglas, *The Feminization of American Culture* (New York: Avon, 1978), 236–39.

[7] David Luke, " 'How Is It That You Live, And What Is It That You Do?' The Question of Old Age in English Romantic Poetry," in *Aging and the Elderly*, ed. Stuart F. Spicker, Kathleen Woodward, and David Van Tassel (Atlantic Highlands, N.J.: Humanities Press, 1978), 221–40.

The Ancient Mariner is condemned to wander eternally. These old, alienated travelers do not reflect the reality of old age in the late eighteenth and early nineteenth centuries. Instead they represent younger authors' fears, anxieties, and desires about growing old in a rapidly changing society that stressed individualism and youth. Rip Van Winkle, in particular, foreshadows both the marginality *and* the sentimental devotion that American society would soon associate with old men.

Published in 1819, "Rip Van Winkle" recounts the story of a man who fell asleep before the American Revolution and awoke twenty years later to discover an alien world. American school children still learn about this "poor fellow" who grew old overnight. Irving's story suggests the disruption of identity created by rapid social change: "God knows . . . I'm not myself — I'm somebody else . . . I was myself last night, but I fell asleep on the mountain, and they've changed my gun, and every thing's changed, and I'm changed, and I can't tell what's my name, or who I am!"[8]

"Rip Van Winkle" is also an ironic protest against the "civilizing process" — the continuing rationalization of individual behavior in a market society.[9] As a young man, Rip is completely unattuned to the individualism and self-interest expected of a successful farmer. Indeed, he has allowed his "patrimonial estate" to dwindle away to little more than a "mere patch of Indian corn and potatoes." Rip loves to drink, hunt, and help his neighbors. He is a favorite of children who lives in accord with the communal rhythms and values of New York's Dutch folk tradition. Despite his wife's constant lecturing about his idleness, Rip would rather "starve on a penny than work for a pound." To escape Dame Van Winkle, Rip often withdraws to the "outside of the house — the only side which, in truth, belongs to a henpecked husband."

When Rip returns to his town on the Hudson River, he is amazed and saddened to find "himself thus alone in the world." Finally, however, he is recognized and reunited with his daughter, who takes him home to live with her. "Having nothing to do at home, and being arrived at that happy age when a man can be idle with impunity, he took his place once more on the bench at the inn door, and was reverenced as one of the patriarchs of the village. . . ."[10] Rip's fate foreshadows the obsolescence of the old man in a secular society where women become rulers of the home, productivity becomes the primary criterion of a man's worth, and patriarchy becomes a maudlin compensation for powerlessness.

[8] Washington Irving, "Rip Van Winkle," in *Anthology of American Literature*, ed. George McMichael (New York: Macmillan, 1974), 1:613. For a perceptive study of Irving, see Jeffrey Rubin-Dorsky, *Adrift in the Old World: The Psychological Pilgrimage of Washington Irving* (Chicago: University of Chicago Press, 1988).

[9] See Bryan Jay Wolf, *Romantic Re-Vision: Culture and Consciousness in Nineteenth-Century American Painting and Literature* (Chicago: University of Chicago Press, 1982), 107–10.

[10] Irving, "Rip Van Winkle" (see n. 8), 614–15.

Figure 14. *The Return of Rip Van Winkle*, an oil painting by John Quidor (ca. 1829). (Andrew W. Mellon Collection, National Gallery of Art, Washington, D.C.)

In 1829, the year Andrew Jackson took office, John Kerr's play based on Rip Van Winkle opened in Washington and quickly became a favorite of American audiences.[11] The same year, John Quidor exhibited his painting *The Return of Rip Van Winkle*.[12] Quidor's figure is bearded, tattered, and bewildered – reminiscent of the old Oedipus, Lear in exile on the heath, or the Ancient Mariner. Baffled and angry, he neither belongs to the present nor possesses his past. He has become a stranger in his own town, a victim of time. Rip wears a noose around his neck, suggesting mortality. Yet he has no sacred story to tell, no pilgrimage to complete.[13] Trapped in a present characterized by unaccountable loss, Quidor's Rip Van Winkle represents the old man as a stranger who is no longer a pilgrim. In 1829, Quidor's perceptive if eccentric painting was a harbinger of things to come. For most

[11] Douglas T. Miller, *The Birth of Modern America, 1820–1850*, (New York: Western, 1970), 19–20.
[12] For an excellent interpretation, see Wolf, *Romantic Re-Vision* (see n. 9), 153–67.
[13] Wolf, *Romantic Re-Vision* (see n. 9), 159.

Americans, the pilgrimage of life remained a powerful metaphor, still in tension with the pressures of economic rationality and secular values.[14]

"CIVILIZED" MORALITY, ANTEBELLUM REVIVALISM, AND THE RHETORIC OF AGEISM

By the time Nathaniel Emmons died in 1840, the world of Puritan patriarchs, hierarchy, and communalism had given way to the independence, individual enterprise, and passion for material wealth that characterized Jacksonian America. In this democratic, competitive, increasingly urban culture, middle-class moralists developed ideals that came to dominate popular morality throughout the nineteenth century.[15] These ideals were rooted in a value system or moral code of "civilized" or Victorian morality that placed primary emphasis on personal responsibility and internalized self-restraint.[16] Northern Protestant religious culture at once participated in and reflected these changes, with important consequences for its approach to aging and old age.

By 1800, the demise of the "well-ordered" eighteenth-century town had undermined the power of the ministry and removed its traditional means of enhancing public order.[17] Disestablishment of religion shattered the Puritan unity of piety and politics, while the rise of a national party system deprived clergymen of uncontested influence as public officers. Emphasizing habits of deference, subordination, and mutuality, eighteenth-century pastors had attempted to weave their parishioners tightly into an institutional fabric. When this fabric unraveled, early

[14] See Lewis O. Saum, *The Popular Mind of Antebellum America* (Westport, Conn.: Greenwood Press, 1980), chap. 4.

[15] For useful discussions of the term *middle class*, see Peter Stearns, "The Middle Class: Toward a Precise Definition," *Comparative Studies in Society and History* 21 (1979): 377–96; Steven Mintz, *A Prison of Expectations: The Family in Victorian Culture* (New York: New York University Press, 1985), 203–206; and Stuart M. Blumin, *The Emergence of the Middle Class: Social Experience in the American City, 1760–1900* (New York: Cambridge University Press, 1989), chap. 1.

[16] My use of the term *"civilized" morality* derives from the work of Sigmund Freud, Nathan G. Hale, Jr., and Norbert Elias. In 1908, Freud's essay " 'Civilized' Sexual Morality and Modern Nervousness," *Complete Psychological Works*, S.E. (London: Hogarth Press, 1959), 9:181–204, voiced a limited protest against the dominant Victorian moral code, which restricted the expression of sexuality to procreation within marriage through internalized control of sexual behavior and impulse. Discussing the early reception of Freud's thought in America, Nathan Hale, Jr., *Freud and the Americans: The Beginnings of Psychoanalysis in the United States, 1876–1917* (New York: Oxford University Press, 1971), chap. 2, points out that "civilized" morality operated as a coherent set of social, economic, and religious norms, regulating not only sexuality but virtually the entire routine of daily life. Although we still do not have a definitive study of this subject, Victorian culture seems to embody the high-water mark of the "civilizing" process described by Norbert Elias and referred to in Chapter 2 of this volume.

[17] See Edward M. Cook, "The Fathers of the Towns" (Ph.D. diss., Johns Hopkins University, 1972); also Michael Zuckerman, *Peaceable Kingdoms: New England Towns in the Eighteenth Century* (New York: Knopf, 1970).

nineteenth-century clergymen did not surrender their role as guardians of public order. Instead, they abandoned public office to party politics and set about promoting moral order and social discipline through separately organized voluntary institutions.[18]

The resulting "evangelical conception of social order" premised the permanence of republican institutions on spreading the word of God.[19] As Lyman Beecher put it, "The universal extension of our religious institutions is the only means of reconciling our unparalleled prosperity with national purity and immortality. Without the preserving power of religious and moral influence, our rapid increase in wealth will be the occasion of our swift destruction."[20] Accordingly, the first quarter of the nineteenth century witnessed the construction of an enormous evangelical empire. Tract, Bible, education, home missionary, temperance, and Sabbath school societies sprang up, forming a network of regional and benevolent associations designed to convert and reform the American people.[21]

The "evangelical conception of social order" relied heavily on female child rearing and voluntary church associations to instill an intensely repressive code of individual conduct in children, especially males, who would soon enter civil society without institutional guidance or control. Evangelicals fashioned the spiritual dimension of this code, best summarized by the terms "civilized" or Victorian morality. The culmination of the "civilizing" process that originated in the sixteenth century, Victorian morality placed extreme demands on individuals to shape their physical, social, and spiritual destinies. When evangelicals embraced Victorian morality's heavy emphasis on physical health and economic self-reliance, they unwittingly secularized their own tradition. Leaving behind traditional ideas about human imperfection and divine omnipotence, they adopted a hygienic utilitarianism that had little room for either the vicissitudes of old age or the glory of God.

Designed to guide people through the dangers and temptations of the marketplace, "civilized" morality was the secular value system of the modern middle-class individual, free to pursue the main chance unfettered by parents or past. Elaborated by health, sex, and temperance reformers, ministers, parents, and public officials, this ideal of conduct required tight inner control over "the passions" in order to harness the body for work and restrain the excesses of individual competition. Disciplining his desire for material wealth and calming the persistent anxieties of his lonely struggle for advancement,

---

[18] See Donald M. Scott, *From Office to Profession* (Philadelphia: University of Pennsylvania Press, 1978), chap. 2.

[19] Scott, *Office to Profession* (see n. 18), chap. 3.

[20] Lyman Beecher, "The Memory of Our Fathers," in *Sermons Delivered on Various Occasions* (Boston: T. R. Marvin, 1828), 309.

[21] Scott, *Office to Profession* (see n. 18), 51.

the ideal self-made man followed a strict regimen of industry, self-denial, and restraint.[22] The ideal Victorian woman would follow a similar regimen specifically adapted to "woman's sphere."

For nineteenth-century evangelicals, the purpose of religion was not to glorify God but to make virtuous men. Post-Calvinist piety consisted of proper behavior – obedience to the laws of God and morality for the attainment of happiness. In contrast, Jonathan Edwards had described the virtues of honesty, sobriety, industry, faithfulness, and thrift as "secondary virtues." Edwards argued that these instrumental virtues were essential elements of social morality. But he insisted that they not be confused with "true virtue" or absolute love of God and "benevolence to Being in general." Edwardian piety demanded respect for God-given reality – "Being in general" – for man's connection to and dependence on a world often indifferent to personal welfare. Post-Edwardian evangelicals, arguing that obedience to God would make men happy, gradually suppressed the inherent tragedy of human life. Transforming theocentric piety into humanitarian moralism, they unwittingly raised bourgeois values to the status of religious truths and reduced love of God and His creation to one of several virtues required for happiness.[23]

After 1820, evangelicals used revivals to sweep large numbers into the church and anchor the internal restraints of "civilized" morality. Antebellum revivalists revised the Puritan orientation to the past and its living symbols, the aged, to accord with the decline of communalism and the altered character of generational relations. Charged with converting large numbers of people who were moving westward and into rapidly growing cities, post-Puritan clergymen could no longer appeal to an organic community.[24]

Even as they abandoned traditional Calvinist doctrine, evangelicals intensified the traditional Puritan concern with the morally instructed individual. Identifying social order with individual piety, men like Albert Barnes and Charles Finney freely attacked intemperance or godlessness among elders or betters, identifying them as obstacles in the path of religious perfection and national progress. Whereas Puritans drew inspiration by looking back to a covenant of the fathers, revivalists in particular looked ahead to a millennial future cut loose from the imperfections of the past.[25] Mirroring the expansive optimism of bourgeois culture, they emphasized the individual's ability to shape the future unencumbered by what Finney called the "traditions of the elders."

---

[22] See Martin C. Van Buren, "Indispensable God of Health: A Study of Republican Hygiene and the Ideology of William Alcott" (Ph.D. diss., University of California at Los Angeles, 1977).

[23] For a fascinating critique of New England theology after Edwards, see Joseph Haroutunian, *Piety versus Moralism* (New York: Holt, 1960).

[24] On the history of community in America, see Thomas Bender, *Community and Social Change in America* (Baltimore: Johns Hopkins University Press, 1978), chap. 3.

[25] Perry Miller, "From Covenant to Revival," *The Life of the Mind in America* (New York: Harcourt Brace & World, 1965).

During the first Great Awakening, Jonathan Edwards had regarded quickened religious fervor as an outpouring of divine grace; revivalists of the second Great Awakening did not wait for God to work. Traveling throughout towns and villages of the South and West, as well as older cities on the east coast, these evangelists created special techniques for promoting revivals, transforming revivalism into something of a peripatetic profession.[26] Closely linked to various antebellum reform movements, professional revivalists helped shape the reformation of private life – the careful analysis and rationalization of daily conduct that replaced agrarian rhythms with morals and manners shaped for an urban, middle-class society.[27] Revivalists, in other words, belonged to a larger reform movement led by "religious virtuosos" – men and women in search of a new sacred order.[28]

Puritanism had not encouraged conversion in childhood or adolescence, in part because young people remained dependents in patriarchal households during the seventeenth and most of the eighteenth centuries. Daily supervision and control and a future of well-defined roles permitted the slow absorption of religious tradition. Nineteenth-century revivalists, on the other hand, emphasized teenage conversion, reflecting the evangelical preoccupation with both the liberation and control of young people. Evidence from several New England Congregational churches between 1730 and 1835 suggests that not until the second Great Awakening did a significant number of teenagers gain church membership.[29]

Rather than gradual conversion, which required reflection, doctrinal education, and patience, antebellum revivalists called for immediate repentance and conversion. The new evangelical style of conversion had no place for "growth in grace" or the doctrine of spiritual ages. It required an abrupt and deeply transforming experience of rebirth. New converts felt that they had "died in sin and been born again into righteousness," that they had broken completely with their sinful past.[30] Revivalists of the second Great

---

[26] See William McLoughlin, *Modern Revivalism* (New York: Ronald Publishers, 1959).

[27] Van Buren, "Indispensable God of Health" (see n. 22), 382. For the impact of revivalism on social and familial relations in commercial cities in upstate New York, see Paul Johnson, *A Shopkeeper's Millennium* (New York: Hill and Wang, 1978); and Mary Ryan, "A Women's Awakening: Evangelical Religion and the Families of Utica, NY, 1800–1840," *American Quarterly* 30 (winter 1978): 602–23.

[28] Max Weber's term *religious virtuoso* has been insightfully applied to antebellum reform leaders by Robert H. Abzug. I have benefited greatly from Abzug's interpretive overview of antebellum reform movements, *The Origins of American Reform*, vol. 1, *Religion*, chap. 1 (New York: Oxford University Press, forthcoming).

[29] I am grateful to Richard D. Shields for sharing these data with me. See his "Revivals of Religion among New England Congregationalists, 1730–1835" (unpublished paper, Department of History, Ohio State University at Newark, 1979).

[30] Scott, *Office to Profession* (see n. 18), 77. Compare the revivalist style of conversion with the remarks of Andover's Samuel Phillips in 1716: "Man does not at once come to be perfect in goodness. But, gradually, therefore, there are means appointed for our growth in Grace." Cited by Philip J. Greven, Jr., "Youth, Maturity, and Religious Conversion: A Note on the Ages of Converts in Andover, Mass., 1711–1749," *Essex Institute Historical Collection* 108 (April 1972): 123.

Awakening aspired to sweep away all hindrances to the pietistic perfection that would usher in the millennium. Aging and old age were either irrelevant or antithetical to these aspirations.

REVISING THE STAGES OF LIFE

Antebellum Americans recognized four loosely distinguished stages of life: infancy (or childhood), youth, manhood, and old age.[31] Of these stages, evangelicals generally agreed with Albert Barnes that "youth is the most favorable time always for becoming a Christian." God made a special promise that those who sought him early in life would find him. Old age, on the other hand, was not the season to seek salvation: "The chills and frosts of age," argued Barnes, "are about as unfavorable to conversion to God as the frosts and snows of December are to the cultivation of the earth."[32] In youth, claimed Nathaniel Taylor, one's character was formed for eternity. "All that follows is cause for fear and anxiety, and in the case of multitudes, as God sees it, for despair."[33]

Rather than wait for God's grace, revivalists compressed the older morphology of conversion,[34] eliminated the value of doubt, and demanded active transformation of the heart. "There is no need of young converts having or expressing doubts as to their conversion," claimed Finney. "It has long been supposed to be a virtue, and a mark of humility, for a person to doubt whether he is a Christian. . . . A real Christian has no need to doubt."[35]

Each additional day of waiting threatened to turn probation into reprobation. "How long, sinner, have you lived?" pressed Finney. "Sailing along unknown seas in the voyage of life, have you ever paused to take in sails, get out your instruments, and take your bearing?"[36] Finney dramatized the

[31] See Joseph F. Kett, *Rites of Passage* (New York: Basic Books, 1977); Thomas Cole's series of paintings *The Voyage of Life*; and Nathaniel Taylor, "The Goodness of God Designed to Reclaim," in *Practical Sermons* (New York: Clark Austen and Smith, 1858).

[32] Albert Barnes, "The Harvest Past," in *Practical Sermons: Designed for Vacant Congregations and Families* (Philadelphia: H. Perkins, 1841), 349–50.

[33] Nathaniel Taylor, "The Harvest Past," in *Practical Sermons* (New York: Clark Austen and Smith, 1858), 442–43.

[34] Before being reduced to the instantaneous experience of antebellum revivalism, the old Puritan morphology underwent a gradual evolution during the eighteenth century. Philip Greven's figures (see n. 30) show that the time required to complete the conversion process decreased in Andover, as mid-century men and women acquired earlier independence from their parents. Jonathan Edwards, whose *A Faithful Narrative* recorded his observations of Northampton conversions during 1734 and 1735, described a three-stage morphology that, contrary to his intentions, became a standardized norm during the eighteenth and early nineteenth centuries. See C.C. Goen, "Introduction," *Works of Jonathan Edwards*, vol. 2 (New Haven, Conn.: Yale University Press, 1959), 25–32.

[35] Charles G. Finney, "Instructions to Converts," *Lectures on Revivals of Religion* (Cambridge, Mass.: Harvard University Press, 1960), 386–87.

[36] Charles G. Finney, "All Things Conspire for Evil to the Sinner," *Sermons on the Way of Salvation* (Oberlin, Ohio: E. J. Goddrich, 1891), 237.

Figure 15. Portrait of Albert Barnes at age 32, an oil painting by John Neagle (1830). (Presbyterian Church, USA, Department of History, Philadelphia.)

"fearful rocks of damnation" and dark tempests increasingly poised to overturn the frail bark of aging travelers.

Both Taylor and Finney agreed that individuals over age twenty were less likely to convert than younger people. They often cited conversion lists that appeared to confirm this view. Since revivalists designed their preaching specifically to bring young men into the church (women of all ages generally constituted the majority of communicants), this argument was obviously self-serving. Like later scientific findings about the relations between age and productivity, physical strength, mental functioning, and reaction time, these conversion lists confirmed their own ideological bias toward youth.

In 1868, Baptist Jacob Knapp recalled the more gradual methods of nonrevivalist ministers who told potential converts to "go home, read their Bibles, reflect upon their condition, look within, dig deep, and be not deceived." Knapp, who traveled throughout the North and stopped counting after converting over a hundred thousand souls, rejected the traditional requirements of "introspection" or waiting for God's saving grace. He insisted on "speedy admission" of young converts.[37]

---

[37] Jacob Knapp, *Autobiography of Elder Jacob Knapp* (New York: Sheldon and Co., 1858), 217; and Finney, "Instructions to Converts" (see n. 35), 389.

Revivalists claimed that conversion of young people uncorrupted by worldly experience was essential preparation for adult life. Complete regeneration would insulate an individual from the moral blandishments of the world and point the way to perfection on earth. Clergymen, however, did not rely on thoughts of God alone to guarantee a moral life. The act of surrendering to God simultaneously opened one to the norms of "civilized" behavior. Instructions to young converts invariably linked piety with self-denial and obedience to God with control over "the passions," thereby linking qualifications for salvation and middle-class ideals of conduct. Charles Finney, for example, became an advocate of Sylvester Graham's dietary reforms (explored in Chapter 5), attacking luxury, idleness, novel reading, theatergoing, card playing, dancing, gluttony, and sexual indulgence.[38]

The Puritans had considered life God's mysterious gift. Decisions about longevity and death remained in God's hands. In contrast, nineteenth-century evangelicals and revivalists conceived life as individual property and longevity as a reward for proper behavior. Just as salvation had become a matter of personal volition, length of life and quality of old age came to hinge on self-discipline. "The duration of human life," claimed Lyman Beecher in *Six Sermons on Intemperance* (1827), "will manifestly vary according to the amount of ardent spirits consumed in the land." Beecher continued: "The prospect of a destitute old age, or of a suffering family, no longer troubles the vicious portion of our community. They drink up their daily earnings, and bless God for the poorhouse."[39] "Who does not know," asked Finney, "that the time of every man's death, as far as he himself is concerned, is a matter of entire contingency; that his days may be lengthened or shortened by his own conduct; that years, or scores of years, may be added to or subtracted from, his life, through the instrumentality of his own agency."[40]

Revivalist sermons contain a wealth of imagery about aging and old people, invoked to contrast with supposedly youthful qualities of vigor, immediacy, action, and self-control. Unlike the sentimental imagery foreshadowed by "Rip Van Winkle" and discussed in later chapters, revivalist sermons often bristle with hostility toward old age – suggesting that old people are seen as powerful impediments to progress, unwelcome reminders both of the oppressive weight of the past and of humankind's inevitable weakness and dependence.[41] Antebellum revivalists commonly attacked the "prudent old professors" who denied Finney's claim that "religion is something to do,

[38] William McLoughlin, "Introduction," in Finney's *Lectures on Revivals of Religion* (Cambridge, Mass.: Harvard University Press, 1960), xxix.
[39] Lyman Beecher, "Six Sermons on Temperance," in *Sabbath and Temperance Manuals* (New York: American Tract Society, n.d.), 48.
[40] Charles G. Finney, "Reprobation," in *Sermons on Important Subjects* (New York: J.S. Taylor, 1836), 242.
[41] I want to thank Carole Haber for suggesting that revivalist hostility toward old age may reflect perceptions that old people had too much power.

not something to wait for."[42] They encouraged young people to rise in church and exhort the congregation to greater spiritual efforts – a practice objected to by those who opposed revivals.

Jacob Knapp, recalling his efforts in Jefferson County, New York, in the autumn of 1833, criticized the Congregationalists who barred revivalists from the pulpit and refused to allow young converts to speak or pray: "The 'old fogies' went poking along . . . like an old lazy yoke of oxen, keeping a little ahead of the converts, and hooking them back lest they should go too fast."[43] Finney charged that the elders of many Presbyterian churches had a "blighting influence" in prayer meetings. He rejected the custom of teaching young converts to "file in behind the old, stiff, dry, cold, members and elders. . . . " Unless young converts were encouraged to take an "active part in religion," they would grow "cold and backward." Against the formal and dignified approach to prayer meetings, Finney even urged rebellion against church officers in the name of pious zeal.[44]

Methodist preacher Peter Cartwright exemplifies a muscular approach to revivalism that was more common in rural areas. Cartwright was converted at age fifteen and soon began riding circuits in Kentucky, Tennessee, Indiana, Ohio, and Illinois. Though he was appointed a "presiding elder" at age twenty-one, this title scarcely inhibited his physical approach to opposition. When describing those who opposed the intensely emotional, rollicking camp meetings of his revivals, Cartwright scorned the "old dry professors" and "old starched Presbyterian preachers." Like the corpulent "old lady" he knocked onto her backside in Knox County, Kentucky, recalcitrant old people failed to restrain the great revival in which "our country seemed all coming home to God."[45]

In one of his most famous sermons, "Traditions of the Elders," Finney combined the heresies of the Jews, Catholics, Antinomians, and Universalists together: "The day of earth's redemption can never come, til the traditions of the elders are done away. . . . These traditions of the elders are the grand sources of most of the fatal errors of the present day."[46] Although Finney directed his attack more at "tradition" than at "the elders," he made no effort to separate the two.

Old age suffered another important symbolic setback at the hands of revivalists. Their belief in human perfectibility gave new prominence and meaning to the ancient biblical metaphor for regeneration, putting "off the old man" and putting "on the new man" (Ephesians 4:22–24; Colossians 3:9–10). Perfectionism challenged the old Calvinist view that the Adamic nature of sin

[42] Cited by McLoughlin, "Introduction" (see n. 38), xxix.
[43] Knapp, *Autobiography* (see n. 37), 88.
[44] McLoughlin, "Introduction" (see n. 38), fn. 130.
[45] Peter Cartwright, *The Autobiography of Peter Cartwright* (New York: Abingdon, 1956), 43.
[46] Finney, "Traditions of the Elders," *Lectures* (see n. 35), 88.

could never be fully transformed by even the most pious convert. For Calvinists, the "old man" of human sinfulness and the "new man" of God's grace existed side by side in all Christians. In contrast, revivalists argued that born-again Christians could remove sin from their lives entirely. They could completely "put off the old man." Emerson Andrews, for example, described the "Great Change" of conversion: "There is no patchwork, no sewing new cloth into the old garments. . . . The old man is put off and the new put on."[47]

Revivalists feared that if a man lived too long without Christ, God would abandon him to the helplessness and decrepitude of old age. "Perhaps some of you are fifty or sixty," pressed Finney. "[H]ow seldom can you find one of your age converted. There is only one here and there one . . . just to keep old sinners from absolute despair. Aged sinner, it is more than fifty chances to one that you are a reprobate!"[48] "The conversion of an aged sinner," claimed Nathaniel Taylor, "is an event that justly strikes the mind with astonishment."[49]

For all their prescription, revivalists never instructed young people on proper conduct toward old people. This suggests that unlike the Puritan ideal of veneration, prescribed attitudes and conduct toward old people play no essential role in the ideology of "civilized" morality. Yet the decline of veneration as an ideal did not challenge the universal assumption that adult children should attend to the needs of old, infirm parents. A pious Christian, "temperate in all things," did not have to be told to care for his or her aged parents. "Civilized" morality, then, did not alter the structure of intergenerational family life. It did weaken ideological and psychological support for the hierarchical authority of elders.

Revivalists not only abandoned the practice of advising the young to venerate the old, they also withheld the traditional gestures of consolation for the aged. Revivalists never addressed the trials of aging. They simply demanded immediate conversion of all sinners before it was too late.[50] Their implicit assumption – that old age was closer to death than to life – was shared and articulated by the settled members of the ministerial profession.

AGING AS DYING

Unlike the revivalists, settled preachers and theologically conservative ministers did address the spiritual and emotional needs of their older parishioners.

---

[47] Emerson Andrews, "The New Birth," in *Revival Sermons Preached in Protracted Meetings* (Boston: J. H. Earle, 1870), 37.

[48] Finney, "Reprobation" (see n. 40), 251.

[49] Taylor, "The Harvest Past" (see n. 33), 443.

[50] Older believers who attended church faithfully but showed little interest in revivals sometimes experienced pressure for reconversion. See for example Heman Humphrey, *Revival Sketches and Manual* (New York: American Tract Society, 1859), 460.

Their sermons, while presumably directed to older women as well as older men, framed issues of aging in exclusively male terms.[51] Before the mid-century romantic evangelicals (discussed in Chapter 6), advice and consolation for the aged persisted mainly in the late Calvinist style of Emmons and John Stanford. Old age remained a time of "peculiar" care and sorrow, a succession of irreparable losses. Friends, senses, memory, health, and sociability all departed, evoking, as one old-school Presbyterian put it, "an inexpressible loneliness and desolation of the soul."[52] Nonperfectionist ministers made little attempt to disguise the ravages of time. They belabored the infirmities of age to underscore the saving qualities of faith. With the Puritans, they believed that old age was insupportable without the fruits and consolations of religion.[53]

Preaching to settled congregations, nonrevivalists (and mellowing revivalists) showed leniency toward unregenerate old age. "Aged friend! Stop! There is mercy in heaven!" implored the old-school Presbyterian Cortlandt Van Rensselaer at a funeral in 1841. "Relatives, friends, pray for him! The star of Bethlehem yet shines, though on the very edge of his horizon! . . . Pray that even in old age, his youth may be renewed by the strength of an immortal hope!"[54] Nevertheless, Van Rensselaer stressed that the period of earthly probation reached an irreversible point in old age. Like walking to the end of an isthmus, there was no going back and only one step to death.[55] The aging Albert Barnes drew the inevitable conclusion: "That man is indeed desolate who has reached the period of 'three-score and ten' with no hope of a future," he asserted. "What plan, what hope can he now have if it is not derived from religion? . . . What a blank must existence now be to him if he has no prospect of life and joy beyond the grave!"[56]

Ministers argued that aged faith transformed darkness into light in two basic ways: It endowed life on earth with individual security and broader social purpose, and it secured safe passage through death to eternal life. Charles Porter, pastor of the first Presbyterian church in Utica, put it this way in 1842: Just when "existence . . . seems an intolerable burden," when "nature bends under the weight of years, and seems to ask imploringly for the undisturbed rest and quiet of the grave," the aged Christian could turn confidently to God and the fulfillment of divine promise. "Even to good old

---

[51] Published sermons provide very few clues about the actual practice of ministering to older women and men. To explore the issue of gender in relations between ministers and aged parishioners, we need a more biographical focus and archival research focused on specific churches, ministers, and congregations.

[52] Charles Summerfield Porter, *Abandonment of God Deprecated by the Aged* (Utica, N.Y.: n.p., 1842), 8.

[53] See Joseph Alden, *The Aged Pilgrim* (Boston: Massachusetts Sabbath School Society, 1846).

[54] Cortlandt Van Rensselaer, *Old Age: A Funeral Sermon* (Washington, D.C.: n.p., 1841), 21.

[55] Van Rensselaer, *Old Age* (see n. 54), 21.

[56] Albert Barnes, *Life at Three-score and Ten*, 2d ed. (Philadelphia: H. B. Ashmead, 1869): 58–59.

age I am He, and even to hoar hairs will I carry you. I have made and I will bear, even will I carry you and deliver you."[57]

Long after his days of public service were over, the aged saint continued to perform important duties. An "impressive spectacle to men," he revealed both the progress of sanctification and the efficacy of God's grace in renewing depraved human nature "to the similitude of the divine!" "The peaceful life and triumphant death of an old man," Van Rensselaer took pains to argue, "beautifully attest to the power of early training."[58]

Following their late Calvinist predecessors, settled antebellum ministers also insisted that the usefulness of age depended on fulfillment of "solemn responsibilities." Barnes, who saw himself enter the land of old age between sixty and seventy, advised old people to seek confirmed assurance of their regeneration and reconciliation with God, through "solemn reflections on the past," reflections that would bring evidence of piety to consciousness.[59]

Along with prayer and reflection, the duties of the aged included a special class of moral exercises: "love, joy, peace, long-suffering, gentleness, goodness, faith, meekness, temperance." For theologically conservative antebellum ministers, attempting to reinforce the fading value of submission to God's will, socially useful conduct overlapped with qualifications for salvation. The patience, meekness, and faith of the aged provided essential lessons for others. "The patient, cheerful, active piety of the aged, may and does, speak impressively to the hearts of the young," noted Porter. Age has its advantages for moral purposes; and gray hairs may sow seed that shall spring and bear fruit into everlasting life. . . ."[60]

Ministers also encouraged older men to release their worldly interests to the next generation and recognize that their real interests lay beyond the grave. In the late nineteenth century, such ministerial advice would no longer be necessary; by then, fewer old people would have significant resources to pass on. "The older a Christian grows, the more does he desire to enter Heaven," claimed Van Rensselaer. "The aged saint is, as it were, a mediator between life and death, interceding through his decaying frame for his speedy departure to glory. He would rather be in Heaven than on earth, yet the breath of his prayer is, 'Not my will, but thine be done.' "[61]

The hope of immortality, more than any other doctrine or belief, encouraged aged believers to view their old age not as a period of terminal decline, but as a final stage of earthly probation leading to eternal glory.

[57] Porter, *Abandonment of God* (see n. 52), 9–10.
[58] Van Rensselaer, *Old Age* (see n. 54), 12. See also Barnes, *Life at Three-score and Ten* (see n. 56), 51–52.
[59] Barnes, *Life at Three-score and Ten* (see n. 56), 146; Porter, *Abandonment of God* (see n. 52), 11.
[60] Porter, *Abandonment of God* (see n. 52), 11, 13.
[61] Van Rensselaer, *Old Age* (see n. 54), 5.

Unlike the aged Puritan, who might express hope and faith but not absolute assurance, the aged Protestant of the mid-nineteenth century might quiet his fears with the belief that God granted immortality freely to all believers. The most difficult and dangerous part of life lay behind. A future of endless peace and joy lay ahead. "A few more conflicts and toils – a few more sighs and tears, disappointments and pains, and then comes the blessed, blissful moment that separates him from infirmities and grief," exclaimed Porter.[62]

Antebellum Protestant ministers, irrespective of denominational differences or their view of revivalism, narrowed the conceptual distance between old age and death. In 1850, almost 50 percent of all deaths occurred under the age of fifteen. Less than 15 percent occurred at age sixty or over.[63] In other words, death still visited children far more than old people. Yet long before changes in the age distribution of death had significantly reduced infant and childhood mortality, evangelicals placed new emphasis on the ancient truism that old age was the "extreme limit of natural life" – that, although one *might* die in any stage of life, one *had* to die once one reached old age. Although settled clergymen showed much more concern and respect for old people than revivalists (whose own views softened with age), their commitment to the values of "civilized" morality ineluctably led them to the depreciation of old age. The decaying body in old age, the "old man," signified precisely what evangelical culture hoped to avoid.

Even the conservative Cortlandt Van Rensselaer, who urged young people to honor wise old men, saw the aging body in punitive terms. Delivering the funeral service for old Joseph Nourse in 1841, he suggested that disease and decay in old age are especially powerful signs of innate human sinfulness: "If old age be the utmost boundary of life, how forcibly are we reminded by it of the certainty of death. . . . The decay of age, as of death, is the sinner's accomplishment. Every old man, therefore, presents in his body the testimony of nature to SIN and DEATH. Two dread realities!"[64]

This remarkable passage illustrates the frightening character of the aging body in a culture where control of that body forms the linchpin of secular morality and its mortification is the condition of salvation. Surrounded by liberals who believed in childhood innocence rather than infant damnation, even the conservative Van Rensselaer articulates the growing connection between the aging body and death as punishment for sin. Having abandoned death as the arbitrary punishment of a sovereign God, Northern Protestants intensified the frightening aspects of physical decline as punishment for sinful conduct. When they held the traditional view that the ills of old age – like

---

[62] Porter, *Abandonment of God* (see n. 52), 13–14.

[63] Howard Spierer, *Major Transitions in the Human Life Cycle* (New York: Academy for Educational Development, 1977), 39–40.

[64] Van Rensselaer, *Old Age* (see n. 54), 7.

all forms of decay, disease, and infirmity – resulted from innate depravity, conservative ministers were swimming against the tide. Yet like the liberals, their views reveal newly intensified anxiety about physical decline and dependence as well as the growing identification of old age with death.

The growing tendency to identify old age with death dovetailed nicely with decline of patriarchal authority and the Jeffersonian vision of generational succession. Albert Barnes, himself seventy years old, illustrated this vision in his sermon "Life at Threescore and Ten" (1868). Barnes argued that the biblical passage "The days of our years are three-score years and ten" (Psalms 90:10) reflected a benevolent law of nature. Seventy years was an appropriate term of probation for man; longer life spans would benefit neither the individual nor the nation. "It is an advantage to the world that men should die; that, having accomplished the great purpose of life, they should give place to others."[65]

Barnes, a New School Presbyterian who wrote eleven volumes of biblical commentary while preaching in Philadelphia, identified himself as a self-made man of the clergy. Describing a typical seventy-year-old man who might well have been himself, Barnes claimed: "The purpose of life is accomplished; the changes have all been passed through." An old man, according to Barnes, had no new plans to form, no place in business, social circles, politics, or the professions. "One task alone remained for the old man: to tread his solitary way, already more than half forgotten, to the grave. He has had his day, and the world has nothing more to give him or to hope from him."[66]

Charles Porter painted a similar picture of age as the anteroom of death in his sermon "Abandonment of God Deprecated by the Aged" (1842). Even more vividly than Barnes, Porter used imagery that links the decline of patriarchal authority with the representation of old age as death. "Our fathers, where are they?" he asks. "One by one we carry them forth from our dwellings to the place of sepulchre; nor are they missed, except by the surviving few who have grown old with them, or have been the companions of their declining years. So disconnected have they become with the associations of the multitude, their quiet exit scarcely raises a ripple on the sea of life. And this fact shows that they are liable to be too much neglected while living."[67]

When William Ellery Channing delivered a tribute to the memory of Reverend Noah Worcester, who died in his eightieth year in 1837, he remarked that older men seemed to pass rapidly into obscurity. Even eminent men were quickly forgotten. Society had become such a "quick-shifting

---

[65] Barnes, *Life at Three-score and Ten* (see n. 56), 28.
[66] Barnes, *Life at Three-score and Ten* (see n. 56), 43–44.
[67] Porter, *Abandonment of God* (see n. 52), 5.

Figure 16. Portrait of Albert Barnes at age 70, an oil painting by Edward Dalton Merchant (1868). (Presbyterian Church, USA, Department of History, Philadelphia.)

pageant" that "he who retires from active pursuits is as little known to the rising generation as if he were dead."[68]

For the aged, "perpetually receding from earth's busy scenes," "liable to be forgotten," death was all that remained of life. "I take it that old age is the only natural death for mankind," asserted Theodore Parker, "the only one that is unavoidable, and must remain so. As virtue is the ideal life of man, so old age is the ideal death; it is the only one that mankind approves."[69] Whether they viewed death primarily as punishment, as heavenly reunion, or as a natural end to life, Northern Protestants gradually tightened the conceptual links between old age and death. In so doing, they performed the last rites for patriarchal authority and unwittingly added old age to the Victorian legacy of repression, denial, and fear.

The origins of ageism,[70] then, lie *both* in the revolt against hierarchical authority *and* in the rise of Victorian morality. If old age in America had

---

[68] William Ellery Channing, "The Philanthropist," *Complete Works* (Boston: American Unitarian Association, 1893), 602.

[69] Theodore Parker, "The Nature of Man," *The Works of Theodore Parker* (Boston: American Unitarian Association, 1910–1913), 5: 65–66.

[70] I am using the term *ageism*, with some hesitation, to refer to prejudice, stereotyping, avoidance, and discrimination against older people. My concerns about the very real limitations of *ageism* as a concept are discussed in the Epilogue.

only suffered the usual misfortune of being identified with an old order, the impact might have been short-lived. But old age came to symbolize not only the old world of patriarchy and hierarchical authority; it also represented an embarrassment to the new morality of self-control. The primary virtues of "civilized" morality – independence, health, success – required constant control over one's body and physical energies. The declining body in old age, a constant reminder of the limits of physical self-control, came to signify dependence, disease, failure, and sin. The devastating implications of ageism lay not in negative images alone but in the splitting apart of positive and negative aspects of aging, along with the belief that virtuous individuals could achieve one and escape the other.

New England Calvinists had constructed an integrated view of aging, emphasizing *both* inevitable loss and hope of redemption. Their successors created a dualistic vision, splitting later life into sin, decay, and dependence on the one hand, and virtue, self-reliance, and health on the other. According to this Victorian consensus, anyone who lived a life of hard work, faith, and self-discipline could preserve health and independence to a ripe old age and die a natural death. The shiftless, faithless, and promiscuous, however, doomed themselves to premature death or miserable old age. In the next two chapters, we will see how health reformers and romantic evangelicals developed this dualistic vision.

5

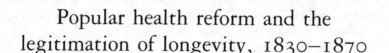

Popular health reform and the
legitimation of longevity, 1830–1870

The true principles of health and longevity, and the true principles of virtue and religion, are inseparable. . . . [I]f without any special regard to health and longevity, my only desire were to promote the highest and most perfect degree of virtue and piety in mankind, I would teach precisely the same principles that I do now.

Sylvester Graham

Old age, whenever it is wretched, is made so by sin. Suffering has no necessary connection with old age, any more than with youth or manhood. . . . If Methuselah suffered from what we call the infirmities of age, it was his own fault. God, his Creator, never intended it.

William Alcott

EVANGELICAL HEALTH REFORM: THE AUTHORITY
OF THE BODY

Between 1830 and 1870, the leaders of physiological societies, sexual reform, dietary reform, preventive medicine, hydropathy, phrenology, and the initiation of hygiene and physical education in the schools generated an unprecedented enthusiasm for individual health and medical self-help.[1] In doing so, they transformed popular ideas of sickness and death – with crucial implications for the cultural meanings of aging and old age. Migrating from rural areas and small towns to growing industrial cities, these sons and daughters of Calvinist New England expressed both horror at high rates of mortality and sickness and unbounded optimism at the prospects for improvement.[2]

[1] For a recent study of antebellum health reform in the context of a broader historical interpretation of American concern about physical fitness, see Harvey Green, *Fit For America* (New York: Pantheon, 1986), pt. 1, "Millennial Dreams and Physical Realities, 1830–1860."
[2] On regional and temporal variations in New England morality rates, see John W. Florin, *Death in New England* (Chapel Hill: University of North Carolina Press, 1971); and Louis I. Dublin, Alfred J. Lotka, and M. Spiegelman, *Length of Life: A Study of the Life Table* (New York: Ronald Press, 1949).

Anglo-American culture in the Victorian era placed special value on bodily health.[3] Hygienic health reform proved particularly well-suited to the needs of a growing middle class.[4] It functioned both as a defense against the physical and spiritual traumas of urban capitalist life and as a means for attaining economic independence. Health reform, however, was not simply an instrument of social mobility but part of a much broader reform movement that included revivalism, temperance, feminism, sabbatarianism, abolition, and various utopian experiments. Reformers looked to natural law for help in creating a new sacred order based on the voluntary sanctification of everyday life.[5]

Rejecting hierarchical communalism, as well as the traditional European sources of social discipline – the established church and the hereditary monarch – Jacksonian custodians of order opted for an especially rigid code of moral self-government. The power of this code derived from its ability to discipline the fierce desire for material wealth through careful rationalization and control of bodily impulses. Choosing the morally disciplined, autonomous individual as the ultimate unit of secular authority, the spokesmen of "civilized" morality placed special emphasis on physical control and on structuring human energies to meet the demands of the marketplace. If evangelicals fashioned the spiritual dimension of "civilized" morality, popular health reformers constructed its physiological rationale and technique. Blending the secondary virtues of Calvinism (self-control, rationality, discipline, frugality) with the eighteenth-century tradition of personal hygiene, health reformers created a method of anchoring authority in the independent individual. Self-government would be achieved through a regimen of ascetic bodily hygiene.[6] As William Alcott put it in 1859, summing up a career in religious health reform: "Credulous as everybody is and will be in this matter of health and disease, till they can daily be taught the laws of hygiene, they will lean upon somebody."[7]

Hygienic perfectionists were no more able than evangelical perfectionists to maintain a realistic view of aging – neither could abide the uncontrollable

---

[3] See Bruce Haley, *The Healthy Body in Victorian Culture* (Cambridge, Mass.: Harvard University Press, 1978).

[4] The middle-class constituency of health reform has been verified by studying membership lists of reform organizations. See Stephen Nissenbaum, *Sex, Diet, and Debility in Jacksonian America* (Westport, Conn.: Greenwood Press, 1980), chap. 9; and Regina Morantz, "Making Women Modern: Middle-Class Women and Health Reform in Nineteenth Century America," *Journal of Social History* 10 (June 1977): 472–89.

[5] See Robert Abzug, *The Origins of American Reform*, vol. 1, *Religion*, chap. 6 (New York: Oxford University Press, forthcoming).

[6] I have learned much about the ideological significance of health reform from Martin C. Van Buren, "The Indispensable God of Health: A Study of Republican Hygiene and the Ideology of William Alcott" (Ph.D. diss., University of California at Los Angeles, 1977).

[7] William Alcott, *Forty Years in the Wilderness of Pills and Powders; or, the Cogitations and Confessions of an Aged Physician* (Boston: J. P. Jewett, 1859), 43.

contingencies of the body's temporal destiny. Splitting later life into health and self-reliance on the one hand and undisciplined decay and dependency on the other, health reformers argued that all properly disciplined individuals might achieve the one and avoid the other. By making such extravagant claims about physical self-help, health reformers unwittingly set the stage for a radical reversal of their argument by late nineteenth-century medical authorities. Yet many of their valuable ideas surfaced again in the 1970s and 1980s, decades of a renewed search for a healthy old age.[8]

The reminiscences of Mary Gove Nichols (1810–84), a dedicated advocate of hygienic education, vegetarianism, and hydropathy, typify the orthodox origins of many health reformers. Born in a small New Hampshire town, where "Calvinistic Puritanism [was] the State Religion," Nichols recalled with revulsion the Congregationalist minister who also practiced the heroic style of medicine: "predestination to hell or heaven; long Sunday services in unventilated meeting-houses . . . calomel and bleeding." To orthodox ministers and doctors, parishioners and patients had a duty "to swallow alike the doctrines and drugs prescribed."[9] Like her male counterparts William Alcott (1798–1859) and Sylvester Graham (1794–1851), Mary Gove Nichols sought to free people from blind obedience to "dogma" and to establish the rational reign of natural law.

Historians have noted that health reformers preached a physical perfectionism that dovetailed nicely with evangelical perfectionism. As the American Physiological Society, founded in 1837, claimed, "the millennium can never reasonably be expected to arrive, until those laws which God has implanted in the physical nature of man are, equally with his moral laws, universally known and obeyed."[10] The Kingdom of God required perfect bodies as well as perfect souls. From this perspective, disease and suffering owed their existence not to God's inscrutable will but to human transgression. Sin alone – understood as ignorance or disobedience of God's natural laws – caused physical pain, disease, and infirmity. Since all individuals possessed the capacity for sinless perfection, all might achieve a state of perfect health.[11]

[8] See, for example, James F. Fries and Lawrence M. Crapo, *Vitality and Aging* (San Francisco: Freeman, 1981).

[9] Mary S. Gove Nichols, "Reminiscences of the First Ten Years of My Life," in Thomas L. Nichols, *Nichols' Health Manual: Being Also a Memorial of the Life and Work of Mary S. Gove Nichols* (London: Allen, 1887), 3–4.

[10] Cited in Ronald G. Walters, *American Reformers 1815–1860* (New York: Farrar, Straus & Giroux, 1978), 149. On the American Physiological Society, see Nissenbaum, *Sex, Diet, and Debility* (see n. 4), chap. 9; and E.H. Houff and J.F. Fulton, "The Centenary of the First American Physiological Society Founded at Boston by Sylvester Graham and William Alcott," *Bulletin of the Institute of the History of Medicine* 8 (October 1937): 687–734.

[11] See, for example, Orson S. Fowler, *Physiology, Animal and Mental* (New York: Fowlers & Wells, 1850), chap. 1; and Sylvester Graham, *Lectures on the Science of Human Life* (New York: S. R. Wells, 1858), 266ff.

The health reform movement assumed above all else that individuals were naturally healthy and that disease was caused by transgression of natural law. Whatever their particular specialty, all health reformers attempted to educate the public to the various laws of health. In her *Lectures to Women on Anatomy and Physiology* (1846), Mary Gove argued that "many people seem to think that all diseases are immediate visitation from the Almighty, arising from no cause but his *immediate* dispensation. Many seem to have no idea that there are established laws with respect to life and health, and that transgression of these laws is followed by disease."[12]

Similarly, Sylvester Graham's magnum opus, *Lectures on the Science of Human Life* (1839), claimed that matters of "life, health, disease and diet" were ultimately governed by fixed laws, capable of observation by the methods of exact science. "Our disquietudes, and diseases, and ultimately death must therefore spring not from the fulfillment, but from the infraction of the laws of God." To ascertain those laws and obey them meant fulfilling God's benevolent purposes.[13] "We beg those who would lengthen out their lives and see good days," wrote William Alcott, "to study those laws of God which we have been attempting briefly to investigate. But . . . It is not sufficient to know that a law exists, unless we obey it."[14]

Prolongation of human life was the central goal of both popular health reform and the public health movement.[15] This is hardly surprising, given that in mid-century Massachusetts, for example, as many as three infants in ten died before their first birthday, and life expectancy at birth was 40.4 years for men and 43.0 years for women.[16] What could be more desirable? Here, it would seem, lies a successful example of the nineteenth-century commitment to unequivocal progress. But historical progress always carries a price. In this case, the popular legitimation and pursuit of longevity harbored evasive and hostile attitudes about the realities of aging. Rather than simply liberating them from orthodox dogma, the quest for perfect health eventually saddled many middle-class Americans with feelings of failure and shame in the face of physical decline.

[12] Mary S. Gove, *Lectures to Women on Anatomy and Physiology* (New York: Harper Bros., 1846), 20.
[13] Graham, *Science of Human Life* (see n. 11), 23. On Graham's life and influence, see Jayme A. Sokolow, *Eros and Modernization: Sylvester Graham, Health Reform, and the Origins of Victorian Sexuality in America* (Rutherford, N.J.: Fairleigh Dickinson University Press, 1983).
[14] William Alcott, *Breathing Bad Air* (Boston: G. W. Light, 1839), 56.
[15] See John Bell, *On Regimen and Longevity* (Philadelphia: Haswell and Johnson, 1842), 31ff; Dublin, Lotka, and Spiegelman, *Length of Life* (see n. 2), chap. 2, "The Life Table as a Record of Progress"; and Barbara Rosenkrantz, *Public Health and the State* (Cambridge, Mass.: Harvard University Press, 1972).
[16] Paul H. Jacobson, "An Estimate of the Expectation of Life in the United States in 1850," *Milbank Memorial Fund Quarterly* 35 (1957): 197–201. Maris Vinovskis has argued that the Jacobson life table underestimates life expectancy at birth by two to four years. See Maris A. Vinovskis, "The Jacobson Life Table of 1850: A Critical Examination from a Massachusetts Perspective," *Journal of Interdisciplinary History* 8 (spring 1978): 703–24.

HYGIENE AND THE GOSPEL OF LONGEVITY

People of all times and places have dreamed of longer life, if not immortality. In the West, various systems of hygiene – ascribing health and longevity to individual regimen and diet – have offered the most common methods of achieving long life. Though dating back to the Roman physician Galen (130–200 C.E.), the hygienic tradition generally languished throughout the many centuries when few believed that the duration of human life could be affected by individual conduct. During the Renaissance, this attitude was challenged by the publication of Luigi Cornaro's *Discorsi della vita sobria* (1558), soon translated into Latin, English, French, German, and Dutch.[17]

In the eighteenth century, Cornaro's system received the enthusiastic endorsement of Joseph Addison and *The Spectator* in 1711, and a growing number of eminent European physicians published hygiene manuals for the literate public.[18] Western hygiene received its greatest popular dissemination in the *Encyclopédie*.[19] Enlightened French thinkers rejected traditional calls for old people to turn away from the world and urged instead a "virile" old age.[20]

Although eighteenth-century hygiene made some headway on the western shores of the Atlantic, not until the first half of the nineteenth century did the religious, scientific, and ideological climate in America become suitable to the popular pursuit of health and longevity as legitimate goals of individual life. At the turn of the century, as we have seen, Emmons's preaching on health and longevity attempted to shore up the crumbling structures of Calvinism. While Emmons conceded the existence of natural law and the desirability of natural death, he nevertheless held firmly to the fundamental principle of "death without order." God retained an unqualified right to suspend natural law and call humans out of the world at any moment. Those who neglected to prepare for death and confidently expected long life displayed a foolish disregard for their condition in the next world.

By the 1830s, these arguments commanded little assent. The orthodox clergy's move to intensify its power over death no longer frightened those

---

[17] See Gerald J. Gruman, "A History of Ideas About the Prolongation of Life," *Transactions of the American Philosophical Society* 56 (1966): chap. 7.

[18] See, for example, George Cheyne, *An Essay of Health and Long Life* (London: n.p., 1724); Samuel Tissot, *Advice to the People in General, with regard to Their Health*, trans. J. Kirkpatrick (London: T. Becket and P.A. De Hondt, 1781); Christopher Hufeland, *The Art of Prolonging Life*, 2 vols. (London, 1797); and Thomas Beddoes, *Hygeia, or Essays Moral and Medical* (Bristol, England: Mills, 1802).

[19] William Coleman, "Health and Hygiene in the Encyclopédie: A Medical Treatise for the Bourgeoisie," *Journal of the History of Medicine* 29 (1974): 399–421.

[20] David Troyansky, *Old Age in the Old Regime* (Ithaca, N.Y.: Cornell University Press, 1989), 77–108.

whose efforts brought increasing power over life.[21] Falling back on doctrines like predestination and infant damnation, late Calvinists provoked a strenuous rebellion against the God of death in the name of health, morality, and rationality.[22]

The men and women who freed themselves from the power of an absolute sovereign eventually set themselves at the mercy of an equally repressive regime. But the terrors of the God of health were not immediately apparent. Those who migrated from relatively healthful rural areas to rapidly growing industrial cities had ample reason to be concerned about their health. In Boston, New York, and Philadelphia, for example, poverty, overcrowding, and poor sanitation created higher rates of mortality and infectious disease in the half century after 1815.[23] The transition from a childhood where daily life had been regulated by household production, communal tradition, and seasonal rhythms, to an adulthood organized around the impersonal laws of the market proved emotionally as well as physically distressing. Letters appearing in the short-lived *Graham Journal of Health and Longevity* (1837–39), for example, reveal a general portrait of fear, alienation, physical debility, and uncertainty about how to cope with life.[24]

The genius – and the pathos – of health reform was its attempt to eliminate middle-class suffering by grounding identity and authority in the rationalized body of the entrepreneurial self. Yet the body would prove a highly unreliable locus of identity. Despite their pursuit of science, rationality, and control, the Puritans had always demanded respect for the ultimately ambiguous and unmanageable qualities of human life. In contrast, evangelical health reform brooked neither mystery nor contradiction. The fixed constitutional laws governing the universe guaranteed harmony between humankind's physical and spiritual nature and promised to keep evil and uncertainty at bay. Sylvester Graham, who began his career as a Presbyterian minister, declared: "the true principles of health and longevity, and the true principles of virtue and religion, are inseparable. . . . [I]f without any special regard to health and longevity, my only desire were to promote the highest and most perfect degree of virtue and piety in mankind, I would teach precisely the same principles that I do now."[25]

---

[21] For a description of this process in eighteenth-century France, see Bernard Groethuysen, *The Bourgeois*, trans. Mary Ilford (London: Holt, Rinehart & Winston, 1968), chaps. 5, 6.

[22] The children of Lyman Beecher exemplify this rebellion. See Kathryn Sklar, *Catharine Beecher* (New Haven, Conn.: Yale University Press, 1973); and William G. McLoughlin, *The Meaning of Henry Ward Beecher* (New York: Knopf, 1970).

[23] Judith R. Leavitt, "An Overview," in *Sickness and Health in America*, ed. Judith R. Leavitt and Ronald L. Numbers (Madison: University of Wisconsin Press, 1978), 3.

[24] Nissenbaum, *Sex, Diet, and Debility* (see n. 4), 140.

[25] Graham, *Science of Human Life* (see n. 11), 265.

Health reformers invariably claimed that expectation of long life was not foolish (as Emmons had argued) but pious. Since God intended men to live out their lives in health, it was both wise and prudent to seek a ripe old age. Since God's physical and moral laws worked in perfect harmony, there was no danger that concern for bodily health would endanger spiritual welfare.[26] The phrenologist Orson Fowler, for example, scorned the traditional injunction to prepare for the next life by weaning oneself from this life: "The very best preparation for a future life is to live a perfect present one, physiological included, in order that we may 'be gathered in like a shock of corn fully ripe.' "[27]

Without exception, health reformers devoted themselves to prolonging life. They portrayed longevity not simply as a desirable goal, but also as a moral one, the emblem and reward of an upright life. "Each of us has but a single life to live," wrote Fowler in *Practical Phrenology* (1847). "Hence . . . it should be spun out as long as the laws of nature will allow, and everything which tends either immediately or remotely to induce disease or shorten life, is, to all intents and purposes, murder or suicide." In *Education and Self-Improvement* (1844), Fowler assumed a moral equivalency between health and longevity: "If, therefore, it is wicked to shorten life, then it is wicked to impair the health; for such impairment is but diminishing life, and inviting and hastening death."[28] William Alcott predicted that "the child of future blessed ages" would die at 100 years old – if he were a Christian. The wicked, however, would not live out half their days.[29]

Fusing possessive individualism with the physiology of vitalism, health reformers often referred to the individual's fund of vital energy as his "physical capital."[30] Like other forms of capital, vital energy required as much protection as possible from capitalism's boom–bust cycle. If an individual lived too fast, or squandered his fixed supply of "physical capital," he would quickly fall into sickness or bankruptcy. "Health – life – is a sum of money in the bank," argued Orson Fowler, "the interest of which, economically used, will support you. But you spend foolishly, and draw on principal. This diminishes the income, and you draw the oftener and the larger drafts, till you exhaust it and become bankrupt."[31]

If, on the other hand, an individual carefully hoarded his energies, the accumulated capital would yield dividends of longevity – the culmination

---

[26] Graham, *Science of Human Life* (see n. 11), 264.

[27] O.S. Fowler, *The Family* (New York: n.p., 1859), 214.

[28] O.S. Fowler, *Practical Phrenology* (New York: O. S. and L. N. Fowler, 1847), 27; *Education and Self-Improvement* (New York: O. S. and L. N. Fowler, 1844), 52.

[29] William Alcott, *The Home-Book of Life and Health* (Boston: n.p., 1856), 46.

[30] See Nissenbaum, *Sex, Diet, and Debility* (see n. 4), chap. 4.

[31] Fowler, *Physiology* (see n. 11), 41. See also Alcott, *Home-Book* (see n. 29), 42; J. Milner Fothergil, *The Maintenance of Health* (London: Smith, Elder, 1874); and Reuben Diamond Mussey, *Health* (Boston: Gould & Lincoln, 1862).

of perfect health. "Every animated organism is created with a determinate fund of vitality, which constitutes its capital stock of life," wrote Russell Trall. "This may be expended slowly or rapidly; but it can never be increased. . . . Health and longevity depend on its judicious expenditure."[32] William Alcott made similar claims. "As it is in pecuniary matters, so it is in the manufacture of health," he wrote. "The more active capital a person can really use, and use profitably, the greater his gains."[33]

Long after popular health reform faded in the last quarter of the nineteenth century, the metaphor of body as capital remained commonplace. In 1905, Colonel Nicholas Smith recounted a story of the late Vermont Senator Justin S. Morrill:

One day he was accosted by a friend with this question: "How is it, Senator, that you at eighty-eight or eighty-nine are hale and hearty, while I, at seventy-six, am a cripple, full of rheumatism and all manner of aches and pains and general disabilities?" "Why," said Senator Morrill, "I can't account for it unless it is that I am drawing dividends and you are paying assessments."[34]

The hygienic pursuit of physiological dividends consisted essentially of rooting out "artificial" habits that constituted "immoderate drafts" on old age. All reformers agreed that tobacco, coffee, tea, alcohol, and sexual indulgence overstimulated the nervous system, leading to premature exhaustion and death. To protect the economy of the body from "panic" and "depression" (or debility), reformers attacked these unnatural stimulates which threatened to create a "feeble and constantly deteriorating race."[35] In 1844, William Alcott estimated the yearly amount spent on tea and coffee at $40 million. He argued that if Americans stopped buying these poisons, "the soil now devoted to tea and coffee, might be made to produce an abundance of vegetable substances highly conducive to health and longevity."[36] Water-cure specialist Joel Shew cited a salutary letter written by John Quincy Adams after the latter's renunciation of tobacco: "I have often wished that every individual of the human race afflicted with this passion, could prevail upon himself to try but for three months the experiment which I have made! Sure that it would turn every acre of tobacco-land into a wheat field and add five years of longevity to the average of human life."[37]

[32] Russell Trall, *Nervous Debility* (New York: Davies and Kent, 1861), vi.
[33] Alcott, *Home-Book* (see n. 29), 42.
[34] Nicholas Smith, *Masters of Old Age* (Milwaukee: The Young Churchman Co., 1915), 226–27.
[35] See Alcott, *Home-Book* (see n. 29), 20ff; Trall, *Nervous Debility* (see n. 32), iii; and Grove, *Lectures to Women* (see n. 12), 205.
[36] William Alcott, *Tea and Coffee: Their Physical, Intellectual, and Moral Effects* (Boston: G. W. Light, 1844), 96ff.
[37] Joel Shew, *Tobacco: Its History, Nature, and Effects on the Body and Mind* (New York: Fowler and Wells, 1850), 96; see also Russell Trall, *Tobacco: History, Nature, and Effects* (New York: Fowler and Wells, 1855).

Many reformers followed the lead of Sylvester Graham, who suspected that meat eating was one of the "customs and circumstances of artificial life" that caused overstimulation, disease, and debility.[38] In 1832, Graham argued that the cholera epidemic owed some of its virulence to the consumption of meat. "A plain, simple, nourishing vegetable diet is decidedly most conducive to permanent health and longevity," he wrote.[39] By mid-century, the regimen of health reform included an amalgam of vegetarianism, phrenology, temperance, water cure, sexual restraint, fresh air, and exercise.[40]

Mary Gove, who also espoused vegetarianism, lectured to women on anatomy and physiology and practiced hydropathy in New York City. Gove married free-love advocate Thomas Nichols in 1848. They subsequently moved to Cincinnati and opened a large hydropathic establishment in nearby Yellow Springs. Like her fellow reformers, Mary Gove Nichols attributed the urban declension in health to unnatural habits; "civilized" living had multiplied human pain and disease. Pure and nutritious vegetable diet, pure air maintained by well-ventilated buildings, bathing, and frequent changes of clothing were sole requirements for the rehabilitation of a population enfeebled by bad habits. "Any person," claimed Nichols, "born with a decent constitution, by observing these principles and living up to them, may be sure – accidents and the evil influences of others excepted – of living in health and happiness to a good old age."[41]

If moral physiology and hygiene promised to remove the causes of premature death, then just how long might the perfectly healthy individual live? Answers to this question ranged from eighty years to a thousand, without unduly straining contemporary credulity. Before the days of life insurance records and vital statistics registration, even informed opinion enjoyed a degree of freedom unimaginable in today's world of demographic exactitude. Not statistical probability but examples of alleged individual longevity seemed to provide the most reliable source of knowledge. If Methuselah lived 969 years, or if Thomas Parr lived 152 years (William Harvey performed the autopsy in 1635 without doubting Parr's actual age), or Luigi

---

[38] William Lambe's *Water and Vegetable Diet* (New York: Fowler and Wells, 1850), first published in London in 1815, argued that animal diet shortened life expectancy: "[T]he system becomes prematurely exhausted and destroyed. We become diseased and old when we ought to be in the middle of life" (p. 71). On vegetarianism, see Nissenbaum, *Sex, Diet, and Debility* (see n. 4), chap. 3; and James C. Whorton, " 'Tempest in a Flesh-Pot': The Formulation of a Physiological Rationale for Vegetarianism," *Journal of the History of Medicine* 32 (1977): 115–39.

[39] Cited in Nissenbaum, *Sex, Diet, and Debility* (see n. 4), 99.

[40] See William B. Walker, "The Health Reform Movement in the United States, 1830–1870" (Ph. D. diss., Johns Hopkins University, 1955); Richard Shryock, "Sylvester Graham and the Popular Health Movement," *Mississippi Valley Historical Review* 18 (1931): 172–83; and Sidney Ditzion, *Marriage, Morals, and Sex in America: A History of Ideas* (New York: Octagon, 1953), 322–39.

[41] Nichols, *Health Manual* (see n. 9), 405, citing Mary S. Gove Nichols.

Cornaro lived 98 years, then perhaps others could reach similar ages by obtaining the secrets of these prodigies.

In *The Hydropathic Encyclopedia* (1852), Russell Trall claimed that "if it can be proved that one man may live two or three hundred years under the most favorable hygienic circumstances, we want no further evidence of the existence of a physiological law that *all* may, under precisely similar circumstances."[42] Such reasoning explains why even professional medical journals published lists of centenarians, and reports of centenarian autopsies and surgery, down to the twentieth century.[43]

Health reformers and professional physicians who promised to prolong life well over a century drew comfortably on both biblical and Enlightenment sources.[44] In the eighteenth century, for example, the eminent physician Benjamin Rush discussed the tendency of extremely old people to regenerate certain functions or organs. According to Rush, "frequent renovation of different parts of the body" accounted for the ancient achievement of "antediluvian age."[45]

As long as biblical literalism survived, and no one critically scrutinized the birth or baptismal certificates of prolongevity's prodigies, belief in the incredible ages of various antediluvian patriarchs or hygienic heroes remained widespread.[46] "Facts and testimony," wrote Sylvester Graham, "constitute our only authority on this point. . . . [T]he Sacred Books written by Moses are unquestionably the most ancient and perhaps the only authentic testimony." Graham confidently asserted that within a few generations, "good habits" would prolong life to several hundred years, with "a much greater degree of youthfulness" throughout the life span.

[42] Russell Trall, *The Hydropathic Encyclopedia* (New York: Fowler and Wells, 1852), 384. Graham made the same argument in *Science of Human Life* (see n. 11), 261ff.

[43] See, for examples, Archer Atkinson, "Longevity, With a List of Persons Known to Have Lived One Hundred Years or More," *Virginia Medical Monthly* 20 (1893–94): 256–64; R. D., "Some Account of John Gilley, Who Died at Augusta, Maine, at the Age of 124 Years," *Boston Medical and Surgical Journal* 80 (1869): 423–33; Richard Jarrot, "Amputation for Gangrene of the Foot, Successfully Performed on a Negro, at the Advanced Age of One Hundred and Two Years," *Charleston Medical Journal and Review* 4 (1849): 301–303; and "Centenarians," *Medical Record* 10 (1875): 317–19.

[44] See, for examples, Homer Bostwick, *An Inquiry into the Cause of Natural Death, or Death From Old Age* (New York: Springer and Townsend, 1851); William Sweetser, *Human Life: Considered in its Present Condition and Future Developments, Especially With Reference to its Duration* (New York: Putnam, 1867); and Daniel H. Jacques, *Hints Towards Physical Perfection* (New York: Fowler and Wells, 1859).

[45] Benjamin Rush, "An Account of the State of the Body and Mind in Old Age . . . ," *Medical Inquiries and Observations*, 1st ed. (Philadelphia: J. Grigg, 1805), 445. For an eminent eighteenth-century physician who argued for a two-hundred-year life span, see Hufeland, *Art of Prolonging Life* (see n. 18).

[46] The first work to definitively refute claims of longevity over a century was W. J. Thoms, *Human Longevity, Its Facts and Its Fictions* (London: J. Murray, 1873). Using records from twelve British life insurance companies, Thoms showed that between 1670 and 1857, not a single policy had been paid to the family of any individual over ninety-seven. Subjecting several celebrated cases to critical scrutiny, Thoms said that there was "not a tittle of evidence" to prove that old Parr lived to 152, that Henry Jenkins survived to 169, or that the Countess of Demond reached 140 (p. vii).

Graham even held out hope for a millennium of health, in which perfect obedience might restore, if not patriarchal authority, at least patriarchal longevity.[47]

THE SANCTIFICATION OF HEALTHY OLD AGE

Popular legitimation of longevity required more than a revolt against premature death and the sickening conditions of urban life. Health reformers also had to confront both the traditional Christian view of aging as punishment for original sin and the specter of debilitating, dependent old age that darkened the appeal of long life. When we remember the emotional and physical dislocation that gave popular hygiene much of its resonance, it is clear that the prolongation of melancholy, dyspepsia, and debility would hardly seem an enticing prospect. These considerations were not lost on the rural-born, middle-aged artisans and tradesmen who joined the new American Physiological Society in the 1830s. Their society hoped to become "not only a means of increasing the average duration of human life, but of securing its highest comfort and happiness."[48]

This vision of long life accompanied by the "highest comfort and happiness" required a substantial revision of traditional Calvinist and even Jeffersonian rationalist views of the aging body. Cotton Mather's *The Angel of Bethesda* (1724) exemplified the Puritan view. Mather could not find a publisher for this work, the first general medical text in America. Interestingly, it bears some resemblance to the English physician George Cheyne's *An Essay of Health and Long Life*, published the same year that Mather completed his *Angel*. Without qualifying God's power to punish original sin through sickness and death, this Puritan preacher recommended the rational methods of temperance to achieve long life. The belief that humans should cherish life and simultaneously prepare for death did not confuse Mather. "After all, we see, death unavoidable," he wrote. "My *Angel of Bethesda*, that has express'd so much concern to arm his readers against the approaches of death, yett confesses, I cannot by any means redeem thee; nor find out a remedy for thee, that thou shouldest live forever, and not see corruption."[49]

In his chapter entitled "Liberatur, or the Thanksgiving of One Advanced in Years, and Praeserved from Grievous and Painful Diseases," sixty-one-year-old Mather marveled at his exemption from death and the common infirmities and illnesses of age – the stone, gout, cancer, palsy, and broken

[47] Graham, *Science of Human Life* (see n. 11), 264, 266–67.
[48] American Physiological Society, *Constitution, With a Catalogue of Its Members and Officers* (Boston, n.p., 1837), 5.
[49] Cotton Mather, *The Angel of Bethesda*, ed. Gordon W. Jones (Barre: American Antiquarian Society, 1972), 317.

bones.[50] In Mather's medical theology, disease and debility constituted the normal conditions of old age – proof of the imperfection and corruption of humanity. Individuals might offer humble thanksgiving if spared these ills, but no amount of human effort could alter or eliminate them.

When Enlightenment hygiene appeared in Jeffersonian circles, its version of benevolent natural law softened but did not eliminate the infirmities of age. Whereas nineteenth-century health reformers claimed that proper obedience to natural law eliminated all sickness and evil, eighteenth-century rationalists argued that natural law helped people accept the "natural evils" of existence. Benjamin Rush, for example, whose commitment to republican hygiene was as important as his belief in heroic medicine, offered hope for ameliorating rather than eliminating the diseases of old age.[51] After studying men and women aged eighty or more for five years, Rush offered "An Account of the State of the Body and Mind in Old Age, with Observations on its Diseases, and their Remedies."

Along with virtually all medical investigators before the late nineteenth century, Rush offered more information on how to achieve old age than on how to treat its infirmities. Among those "circumstances favoring longevity," Rush listed "descent from long-lived ancestors" and "temperance in eating and drinking." Virtually all the old people Rush studied had used coffee and tea for the last forty or fifty years of their lives, apparently without adverse effects on longevity. For Rush, temperance meant just that – moderation, not abstinence. Although he had written the first American attack on "the intemperate use of spirits" in 1785, Rush did not advocate the elimination of alcohol. Contrary to most evangelical health reformers who succeeded him, Rush sanctioned the use of tea and coffee, favored a diet of "animal matter," and even prescribed moderate use of wine, "the milk of old age."[52]

Whereas Calvinists insisted that unregenerate human nature brought moral degeneration in old age, Rush claimed to have observed no instance of "impaired moral or religious faculties." He attributed this to human rather than divine will. "I do not believe that these faculties of the mind are preserved by any supernatural power, but wholly by the constant and increasing exercise of them in the evening of life."[53]

Among the chronic diseases of old age, Rush listed weakness in the knees and ankles, pain in the bones or "rheumatalgia," the involuntary flow of tears, coughing, difficulty in breathing, inability to retain urine, wakeful-

[50] Mather, *Angel* (see n. 49), 315–16.

[51] Van Buren, "Indispensable God of Health" (see n. 6), and Nissenbaum, *Sex, Diet, and Debility* (see n. 4), both make this point. Rush's *Sermons to Gentlemen upon Temperance and Exercise* (Philadelphia: John Dunlap, 1772), was an early American hygiene manual. For a perceptive account of Rush's work, see Abzug, *Origins of American Reform* (see n. 5), chap. 2, "Benjamin Rush and Enlightened Christian Reform."

[52] Rush, "An Account of the State of the Body" (see n. 45), 451.

[53] Rush, "An Account of the State of the Body" (see n. 45), 444.

ness, giddiness, deafness, and failing vision. For these ills, he recommended an essentially hygienic regimen, spiced with a dose of heroic drugs: heat, warm clothing, generous diet, youthful company, gentle exercise, cleanliness, and opium to relieve chronic rheumatism, coughing, and wakefulness. For the acute diseases of old age – inflammation of the eyes, pneumonia notha, the colic, palsy and apoplexy, the piles, difficulty in making water, and quartan fever – Rush admitted therapeutic impotence, except for bleeding in cases of "plethora and an inflammatory action of the pulse."[54] Confronted with the evils of old age, Rush sought not to eliminate but to assuage them – to show how they fit into the benevolent design of nature.[55]

The Philadelphia physician would certainly have appreciated the exchange between Adams and Jefferson on the question of grief. "I have often wondered for what good end the sensations of grief could be intended," wrote seventy-three-year-old Jefferson in 1816. The octogenarian Adams replied that pleasure and pain seemed inseparably bound up with each other. As one of life's ineradicable evils, grief raised the question of the ultimate origin and cause of evil. "This perhaps is known only to omniscience. We poor mortals have nothing to do with it, but to fabricate all the good we can out of all inevitable evils, and to avoid all that are avoidable." To this eloquent answer, Jefferson added only his agreement. "You have exhausted the subject. I see that, with the other evils of life, [grief] is destined to temper the cup we are to drink."[56]

Acknowledgment of the intractable sorrows and infirmities of age remained culturally acceptable as long as men and women lived in families, churches, and communities regulated by principles of hierarchy, dependency, and reciprocal obligation. But how could the ideology and psychology of self-reliance be squared with decay of the body? Only by denying its inevitability and labeling it as failure.

Health reformers promised a solution that would eliminate dependency in old age through physical perfection. "Many say it is not desirable to live to be so old and decrepit, and full of infirmities and ailments," noted Sylvester Graham. "Who . . . would wish to outlive their usefulness, and enjoyment, to lean in trembling feebleness upon the staff, to sink into the helplessness of second childhood . . . ?" Whereas Graham's ancestors had defined these conditions as inevitable consequences of original sin, he and other health reformers defined them as results of individual moral failure.[57]

William Alcott responded in a similar manner to those who preferred a short and merry life, or assumed that longevity meant a dull and weary old

---

[54] Rush, "An Account of the State of the Body" (see n. 45), 453.

[55] Rush, "An Account of the State of the Body" (see n. 45) 446. See Daniel Boorstin, *The Lost World of Thomas Jefferson* (Boston: Beacon Press, 1948), 50, 262, n. 24.

[56] Lester J. Cappon, ed., *The Adams-Jefferson Letters* (Chapel Hill: University of North Carolina Press, 1959), 2:472–73, 483.

[57] Graham, *Science of Human Life* (see n. 11), 265–66.

age. The view that "old age must necessarily be wretched," Alcott insisted, was a serious error. "Old age, whenever it is wretched, is made so by sin. Suffering has no necessary connection with old age, any more than with youth or manhood." Alcott claimed that both infectious and chronic diseases could be eradicated by the regimen of Christian physiology and hygiene. Old age "need not have rheumatism, or gout, or any other of those diseases misnamed the infirmities of age," argued Alcott. "If Methuselah suffered from what we call the infirmities of age, it was his own fault. God, his Creator, never intended it. The very common belief, that old age necessarily brings with it bodily infirmities, besides being a great mistake, reflects dishonor on God."[58]

This argument startlingly reverses the views of Alcott's Puritan and republican predecessors. For them, infirmity in old age reflected innate human limitation. They would have found it preposterous to claim that men could exercise such complete control over their bodies. God alone possessed such powers of perfection. The health reformers' ideal of old age reveals at once nostalgic longing for the patriarchal authority they had dethroned, and intense, unacknowledged fear of decay and dependence in old age.[59]

THE NATURE OF A NATURAL DEATH

If human rationality and morality could eliminate premature death and guarantee a healthy old age, why should anyone die at all? Why not conquer death completely, substituting natural for supernatural salvation? Although this line of thought would surface at the end of the century, antebellum health reformers never raised human perfectibility to the level of divinity. Sylvester Graham went so far as to suggest that death as well as sickness might spring not from fulfilling but from disobeying God's laws. But he never pursued the idea — perhaps sensing that it would put God out of business altogether.[60]

While they differed over how long human beings might live, health reformers never doubted that human beings must die. Once violence, disease, and accidents were removed as causes of death, reformers predicted that humanity would enjoy painless natural death from "pure" old age. Aside from Oliver Wendell Holmes's One-Hoss Shay (which ran "one hundred years to the day" before collapsing "all at once and nothing first"), no

---

[58] William Alcott, *The Laws of Health* (Boston: J. P. Jewett, 1860), 9–10; see also Russell Trall, *Sexual Physiology* (New York: Miller, Wood, 1866), 304.

[59] See, for example, Graham, *Science of Human Life* (see n. 11), 268.

[60] From the French physiologist Bichat, Graham absorbed a theory that implicitly denied that death was an integral part of life. Bichat argued that "life is the totality of those functions which resist death." Cited by Nissenbaum, *Sex, Diet, and Debility* (see n. 4), 60.

physician or health reformer ever reported a single natural death.[61] The evasions and implications of this ideal lay comfortably submerged until later in the century, when vital statistics and clinical investigation helped force them into the open, provoking a desperate attempt to salvage biological self-reliance by curing the disease of old age.

The ideal of natural death reflected a broader cultural effort to eliminate death as a force in life and to remove both the pain and preparation previously considered essential to dying well.[62] Natural death complemented the evangelical certainty of supernatural salvation. The individual who died naturally would not suffer pain or debility or anxiety about his fate. Dying would be the orderly, peaceful culmination of a well-ordered life. For antebellum health reform, natural death meant "dying of old age." "Isaiah has indicated a period in human history when the child shall die a hundred years old," noted William Alcott. "I see no reason at all why we should be required to wait many centuries for the full realization of this blessed promise, would we but follow out the path of pure and perfect obedience, physically and morally."[63]

Eighteenth-century American versions of natural death had not entailed such a rosy scenario. Benjamin Rush, whose writings served as a source book for Graham and other health reformers, painted a different picture. "Death from old age," he wrote, "is the effect of a gradual palsy. It shows itself first in the eyes and ears, in the decay of sight and hearing; it appears next in the urinary bladder, in the limbs and trunk of the body; then in the sphincters of the bladder and rectum; and finally in the nerves and brain, destroying in the last, the exercise of all the faculties of the mind."[64]

A similar description appears in Thomas Jefferson's correspondence to John Adams (August 1, 1816). The two old men had been speculating about whether they would rather live their lives over again or accept a better life in the next world. Between the ages of twenty-five and sixty, Jefferson wrote, he would happily live again. But after sixty, "the powers of life are sensibly on the wane, sight becomes dim, hearing dull, memory constantly enlarging its frightful blank . . . spirits evaporate, bodily debility creeps on palsying every limb, and so faculty after faculty quits us, and where then is life?" These considerations immediately precede his often quoted remarks about death and generational relations. "There is a ripeness of time for death,

[61] Alcott freely acknowledged this; see his *Home-Book* (see n. 29), 19. When old age was reported on antebellum death certificates, it functioned as a synonym not for disease-free, natural death, but for disease.

[62] For a classic manual on preparation for death see Jeremy Taylor, *Holy Living and Holy Dying* (London: G. Bell and Sons, 1918), first published in the sixteenth century. On the "dying of death," see James J. Farrell, *Inventing the American Way of Death, 1830–1920* (Philadelphia: Temple University Press, 1980); and also Philippe Ariès, *The Hour of Our Death*, trans. Helen Weaver (New York: Knopf, 1981).

[63] Alcott, *The Laws of Health* (see n. 58), 18.

[64] Rush, "An Account of the Body and Mind" (see n. 45), 454.

regarding others as well as ourselves, when it is reasonable we should drop off, and make room for another growth. When we have lived our generation out, we should not wish to encroach on another."[65]

Jefferson's unflinching acceptance of bodily infirmity probably owed some of its realism to age. At seventy-three, he had more experience with old age than the middle-aged antebellum health reformers who later envisioned painless aging. Moreover, Jefferson possessed a sense of generational continuity ("reasonable we should drop off and make room for another growth") that eased the pain and loss of aging and death. A sense of generational continuity is precisely what many Victorian Americans lacked.[66] Breaking with their parental past to establish themselves as democratic individuals, many middle-class city dwellers cut themselves off from the intergenerational solidarity needed to reconcile themselves to decline and death.[67] Hence decay and dependency in old age appeared intolerable.

The health reformers' vision of natural death promised to purify old age and regulate generational succession. Graham's *A Lecture to Young Men on Chastity* (1834) linked the ideal of natural death with the regimen of "civilized" morality. If men lived "precisely as they ought to live," Graham argued, they would pass through the various stages of life "without sickness and pain – enjoying their long-protracted years, health and serenity, and peace, and individual social happiness; [they would] gradually wear out their vital energies, and finally, lie down, and fall asleep in death, without an agony – without a pain."[68] Whereas Rush and Jefferson as well as the Calvinists had assumed that death was invariably painful, Orson Fowler, for example, argued that premature death alone was painful. Painful death, he claimed, would never "come, unless . . . summoned by violated law, till old age folds us up gradually in a natural and therefore pleasurable decline, after we have no more desire for life or dread of death."[69]

The health reform vision of natural death diverged from the Jeffersonian vision in another important respect. For Jefferson, "ripeness for death" was both a social and a biological question, regulated by the rhythm of gen-

---

[65] Cappon, *Adams-Jefferson Letters* (see n. 56), 2:469, 470, 483–84.

[66] See Rodney Olsen, *Dancing in Chains: The Youth of William Dean Howells* (New York: New York University Press, 1990) for an acute discussion of home-leaving and generational relations in the antebellum North.

[67] Emotional solidarity between generations provides an important form of symbolic immortality. See Robert Lifton, *The Broken Connection* (New York: Simon & Schuster, 1979). I suspect that men suffered from feelings of isolation and uselessness more often than women. In *Winter Friends: Women Growing Old in the New Republic* (Urbana: University of Illinois Press, 1989), Terri Premo shows the moral authority and continuity in older women's lives between 1785 and 1835. The persistence of strong female networks of family and friends probably strengthened and comforted older widows throughout the nineteenth century. See Carroll Smith-Rosenberg, "The Female World of Love and Ritual: Relations Between Women in Nineteenth-Century America," reprinted in her volume *Disorderly Conduct: Visions of Gender in Victorian America* (New York: Oxford University Press, 1985), 53–76.

[68] Sylvester Graham, *A Lecture to Young Men on Chastity* (Boston: Light and Stearns, 1834), 12.

[69] Fowler, *Physiology* (see n. 11), 50.

erational succession: "When we have lived out generation out, we should not wish to encroach on another." Health reformers attempted to define "ripeness for death" entirely within the natural rhythms of the individual. Joel Shew, lecturing on the prevention of cholera in 1848, recommended the precept "TEMPERANCE IN ALL THINGS." With adequate study and God's blessing, he told his audience, "you may live to a ripe old age, without suffering, without pain." Life would end quietly in natural death, when, " 'Like a clock, worn out with eating time, the wheels of weary life at last stand still!' "[70] Similarly, Mary Gove Nichols claimed that the "only natural death is the gradual and painless wearing out of the vital energy in old age, 'like a shock of corn fully ripe.' "[71]

Contemporary biomedical science, still unable to definitively explain biological aging or the finite human life span, remains divided on the possibility and meaning of natural death from old age. On the one hand, geriatricians in the 1970s launched a vigorous campaign to separate disease from physiological aging, reflected in Sharon Curtin's title *Nobody Ever Died of Old Age*.[72] On the other hand, a new version of natural death appeared in the work of James Fries and Lawrence Crapo (1981): "Natural death is the inevitable outcome of linear decline of function in vital organ systems. At some point, declining organ function must become insufficient to sustain life." Aging involves the declining capacity of organs to compensate for stress and to restore homeostasis.[73] Since acute and chronic disease, as well as other external threats to homeostasis, must be acknowledged as natural (in the sense of common and universal), dying in old age from disease or even a slight accident must also be understood as "natural."

Antebellum notions of natural death are remarkably analogous to Fries and Crapo's discussion of declining organ reserve and ability to restore homeostasis. Drawing somewhat eclectically on Galenic and vitalist theories, health reformers, even as they addressed middle-class needs and anxieties, constructed a theory that grew out of the internal logic of scientific theory.[74] Following European physiologists,[75] health reformers believed that aging was caused by the gradual deterioration of vital force. Since this vital force activated all bodily processes, its deterioration was somehow responsible for the basic phenomena of aging – the drying out of the body, the diminution

[70] Joel Shew, *The Cholera, Its Prevention and Cure* (New York: Fowler and Wells, 1850), 41.
[71] Nichols, *Health Manual* (see n. 9), 21.
[72] Sharon R. Curtin, *Nobody Ever Died of Old Age* (Boston: Little, Brown, 1972). See Robert Butler, *Why Survive? Being Old in America* (New York: Harper & Row, 1975).
[73] Fries and Crapo, *Vitality and Aging* (see n. 8), 98.
[74] Richard L. Grant, "Concepts of Aging: An Historical Review," *Perspectives in Biology and Medicine* (summer 1963): 443–78.
[75] In particular, Xavier Bichat, *Physiological Researches Upon Life and Death*, trans. T. Gold (Boston: Richardson & Lord, 1827); and Hufeland, *Art of Prolonging Life* (see n. 18).

and putrefaction of the humors, the constriction of the vessels, the ossification of the organs, and the accumulation of earthy deposits in the body.

From Galen, Graham and various physicians and reformers took the view that the body was originally formed from warm fluids and became progressively drier and colder. From Bichat and Hufeland, they learned that declining vital energy led to the changing proportion of solids and fluids, eventually ending in accumulation of earthy material that ossified and finally choked the body. As Russell Trall put it, "Natural death results from a gradual consolidation of the structures. . . . In a perfectly normal condition of the organism, all the functions, powers, and senses decline in the same harmonious relation in which they were developed. . . . [D]eath occurs without a struggle or a groan."[76]

[76] Trall, *The Hydropathic Encyclopedia* (see n. 42), 386–87. See also Graham, *Science of Human Life* (see n. 11), 268–69, 442–43; S. Rowbotham, *An Inquiry Into the Cause of Natural Death; or Death From Old Age* (Manchester, England: A. Heywood, 1842), 10; Bostwick, *An Inquiry Into the Cause* (see n. 44), 2ff; and Alcott, *Forty Years in Wilderness* (see n. 7), chap. 21, "Ossified Veins."

6

Aging, popular art, and Romantic religion in mid-Victorian culture

There is something . . . beautiful in the thought of a man leaning upon his own staff. In youth you are cutting the staff that you are to lean upon in old age.

Henry Ward Beecher

Such is the spectacle that we witness in many instances. . . . One dreads to see grey hairs in poverty, in beggary, dependent upon . . . charity. . . . One shrinks from old age when it is full of pains, when it is crippled, . . . helpless, hopeless, and hapless.

Henry Ward Beecher

So have I seen a pine tree in the woods, old, dry at its roots, capped with age-resembling snow; it stood there, and seemed to stand; but a little touch of wind drove it headlong, and it fell with a long, resounding crash. . . . This is natural death, for the old tree and the venerable old man.

Theodore Parker

THE AGES OF LIFE AND THE VOYAGE OF LIFE IN POPULAR ART

Victorians were not unique in their desire to avoid poverty, infirmity, and disease in old age. What distinguished them was their belief that everyone could actually do so: God's laws of morality and health enabled all to live to a healthy old age, die a natural death, and enter the kingdom of heaven. Failure resulted from individual ignorance or lack of will, not from human limitation or divine providence. As we have seen, this vision evolved from the search for a rational, orderly, and secure course of life, which originated in early modern Europe.

In Chapter 2, we saw that modern imagery of the life course emerged during the sixteenth and seventeenth centuries in Northern European cities. Amidst religious upheaval, war, famine, plague, intellectual uncertainty, and the decline of feudal society, urban middle classes sought stability and longevity in an orderly course of life. Artists, craftsmen, ministers, writers, and moralists mapped a life course complete with virtues and vices for each age of life. This new schedule of life as a career found its definitive iconographic representation in a rising and falling staircase (or a pyramid of stairs), the shape that became the standard middle-class image of individual lifetime for the next 350 years. The evolution of this iconography between the seventeenth and nineteenth centuries reveals a great deal about changing attitudes toward death, the decline of eternal time, and the growing hope for longevity in secular time (see Fig. 17).

Whereas seventeenth-century versions of the ages of life contained the baroque message of *memento mori*, eighteenth-century images portray a more tamed secular vision of death. Frightening pictures of death and the Last Judgment were softened or eliminated altogether. In the increasingly affluent and literate eighteenth century, older prints were copied and extensively distributed in Europe. A more rational life course appeared – a visually formulaic image, sometimes accompanied by texts full of nostalgia and sadness.[1] Robert Burns's ballad "John Anderson," for example, written from the perspective of an aging woman, evokes the sweet sadness of a couple growing old together:

> John Anderson my jo, John
>   We clamb the hill thegither;
> And mony a canty day, John,
>   We've had wi'ane anither:
> Now we maun totter down,
>   John
> But hand in hand we'll go;
> And sleep thegither at the foot,
>   John Anderson my jo.[2]

By the mid-nineteenth century, this iconography of the life course reached a mass audience in Europe and America. Its evolution reveals the middle-class quest for a normal life course, increasingly defined in terms of health and material self-reliance. As steam engines, railroads, and modern factories transformed the urban landscape, the sequences of an individual life were no longer lived against the backdrop of a relatively changeless environment, itself surrounded by eternity. Eternity, or sacred time, continued to recede

---

[1] See, for example, H. Numan, "De Trap des Ouderdoms," in *Die Lebenstreppe, Bilder der menschlichen Lebensalter*, kommission bei R. Habelt (Bonn: Rheinland-Verlag, 1983), 125–26. On eighteenth-century French iconography of the life cycle, see David Troyansky, *Old Age in the Old Regime* (Ithaca, N.Y.: Cornell University Press, 1989), 20–26. Troyansky devotes an entire chapter to the new presence of the aged in French art; see pp. 27–49.

[2] Allan Cunningham, *The Complete Works of Robert Burns, Illustrated* (London: George Virtue, 1840), 2:160.

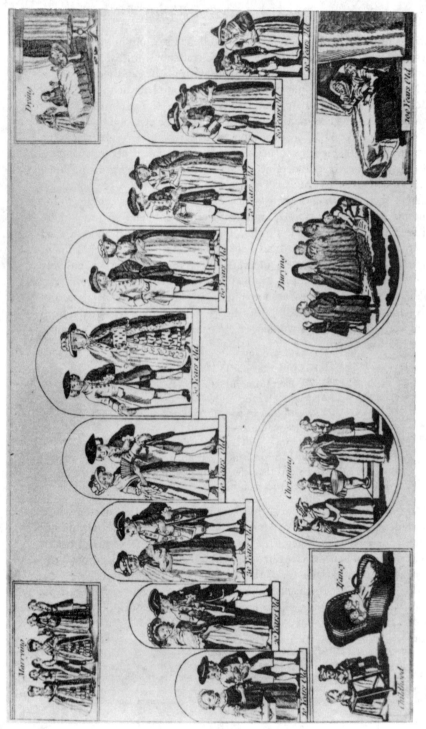

Figure 17. *The Life Cycle of Man and Woman*, an anonymous print (London, ca. 1773). (Catalogue British Museum Satires II, 1873, No. 1995. Photograph Warburg Institute, University of London.)

Figure 18. *John Anderson My Jo*, an engraving by J. M. Wright and S. Smith (1840).
(From *The Complete Works of Robert Burns*, vol. 2, London, 1840.)

in popular consciousness. Time and history were conflated.[3] The modern
sense of the word *generation* was born in an environment where, like Washington Irving's Rip Van Winkle, one might go to sleep at night and wake
up an old man – a stranger in one's own place.[4]

In the seventeenth-century ages-of-life motif, the arch had framed a "window" onto eternity – a way of seeing "through" chronological time, guided
by a religious vision of the right relations between lifetime and the timeless.

---

[3] John Berger and J. Mohr, *Another Way of Telling* (New York: Pantheon, 1982), 104–109.
[4] John Kerr's play based on "Rip Van Winkle" was standard American theater fare in the 1830s and
1840s; see Douglas Miller, *The Birth of Modern America, 1820–1850* (New York: Western, 1970), 19–
20. The word *generation*, however, did not connote the increasingly different experience of successive
generations until the early twentieth century. See Robert Wohl, *The Generation of 1914* (Cambridge,
Mass.: Harvard University Press, 1979), 2–3.

By the nineteenth century, didactic instruction in bourgeois values dominated the message. The edifying and devotional aspects of the motif were disappearing.[5] Under the arch, scenes of work or the Garden of Eden often replaced the Last Judgment. Sentimental images of comfortable old age or natural death began to replace images of the cold, dry old man or woman slipping from cane to coffin.

Throughout Europe and the United States, the secularized motif could be found – on Spanish cigarette wrappers, German beer mugs, English board games, calendars, ceramic stove tiles, book illustrations, and almanacs. Now we can see the ideal of a firmly entrenched middle class: an orderly society, which permits upward mobility without conflict, while assuming the subservience of women and the inferiority of childhood and old age.[6] The subordination of women is clearly reflected in an American print from 1836 (Fig. 19).

If medieval culture subordinated the ages of life to the pilgrimage of life in the interests of Christian eternity, Victorian culture reversed these priorities for the sake of productivity, progress, and health. In the early modern period, as our discussion of Bunyan and the Puritans has shown, the pilgrimage motif had resisted the priorities of worldly success and social usefulness. By the nineteenth century, this oppositional quality was largely muted. The pilgrimage of life was tamed and assimilated to the quest for the normal life course in Victorian society.

Even as the old religious, medical, and artistic traditions originally embedded in the motif became moribund, the imagery reached its broadest audience, thanks in part to the spread of lithography during the 1830s. The motif found its way into the workshops of American lithographers like Nathaniel Currier.[7] Prints like *Life and Age of Man* (Fig. 20) and *Life and Age of Woman* (Fig. 21) retained the traditional early modern form and much of its symbolism. The decades of a man's life, for example, are still likened to various animals: the lamb, goat, eagle, bull, lion, fox, wolf, dog, cat, and ass. Trees on the left and right mark the traditional spring and winter of life. In contrast, the weeping willow tree above the last four decades of woman's life reflects a softer symbolization of decline.

By the nineteenth century, serious artists had long since abandoned the traditional motif. To the educated and urbane, these images appeared "artless but unforgettable" – Jakob Grimm's description of the *Lebenstreppe* print that

---

[5] Cornelia Will, "Was ist des Lebens Sinn? Lebensalterdarstellung im 19 Jahrhundert," in *Die Lebenstreppe* (see n. 1).

[6] Rudolf Schenda, "Die Alterstreppe – Geschichte einer Popularisierung," in *Die Lebenstreppe* (see n. 1), 23–24.

[7] See Walton Rawls, *The Great Book of Currier and Ives' America* (New York: Abbeville Press, 1979), 263–67.

Figure 19. *The Life and Age of Woman*, a print by A. Alden (1836). (Library of Congress, Washington, D.C.)

Figure 20. *Life and Age of Man, Stages of Man's Life from the Cradle to the Grave,* a print by Currier and Ives (ca. 1850). (Library of Congress, Washington, D.C.)

Figure 21. *Life and Age of Woman, Stages of Woman's Life from the Cradle to the Grave,* a print by Currier and Ives (1850). (Library of Congress, Washington, D.C.)

hung in his childhood home.[8] The rising and falling staircase was so familiar that it became caricatured and used for other purposes. For example, an 1846 Currier print, *The Drunkard's Progress* (Fig. 22), portrays the woeful life course of a fallen pilgrim. The drunkard "progresses" through the stages of poverty, disease, loneliness, desperation, and finally suicide. Beneath the arch, in place of the Second Coming, we see a widow and young child sadly leaving the ruins of what was once a home.

The traditional motif of the rising and falling staircase was never as popular in America as in Europe. Its fixed ordering of the ages and urban flavor clashed with American individualism and taste for natural settings. By far the most popular artistic rendering of the life course in Victorian America was Thomas Cole's series of paintings, *The Voyage of Life* (1842). This grand allegory, representing human lifetime as a journey down a river, consists of four canvases, each over five feet high and six feet wide: childhood, youth, manhood, and old age. Each age corresponds to a season and a time of day.

The Voyage of Life has rightly been called a landmark in American cultural history,[9] reflecting Romantic ideas about nature along with the optimism and anxiety of urban middle-class culture. The paintings won Cole more popular acclaim than any of his landscapes or other allegories. Even before *The Voyage of Life* achieved mass circulation through engravings and reproductions in popular periodicals, it was widely known. Between 1850 and 1875, printed editions of the series were as popular as engravings of George Washington had been in an earlier generation.[10]

When Cole began working on the series in 1839, he was reading Bunyan's *Pilgrim's Progress*, which enjoyed enormous influence in antebellum America.[11] The themes and imagery of *The Voyage of Life* were common not only in the Puritan tradition but in the broad vernacular tradition of dissent that included Baptists of all kinds, Presbyterians, Quakers, Congregationalists, and Independents. Ironically, the most specific and direct influence on Cole's visualization of life's voyage may have been the Anglican clergyman Reginald Herber's "Farewell Sermon," preached in England in 1823 before Herber's departure for Calcutta.[12] Cole may also have been influenced by Samuel

[8] Jakob Grimm, *Reden und Aufsatze*, ed. Wilhelm Schaaf (Munich: Winkler Verlag, 1966), 155–56.
[9] E. P. Richardson, *A Short History of Painting in America* (New York: Crowell, 1956), 128.
[10] Cited in "The Voyage of Life: Youth," anonymous mimeograph from the National Gallery of Art. See also Louis L. Nobel, *The Life and Works of Thomas Cole*, ed. Elliot S. Vessell (Cambridge, Mass.: Harvard University Press, 1964).
[11] Before the nineteenth century, Bunyan's spiritual autobiography, *Grace Abounding to the Chief of Sinners*, was published (and presumably read) more often in America than *Pilgrim's Progress*. See David Smith, "Publication of John Bunyan's Works in America," *Bulletin of the New York Public Library* (December 1962): 630–52; on Americanization of Bunyan, see Smith's *Bunyan in America* (Bloomington: Indiana University Press, 1966).
[12] The specific passage from Herber's "Farewell Sermon" and information about its popularity in the United States can be found in Allan Wallach's valuable essay " 'The Voyage of Life' as Popular Art," *The Art Bulletin* 59 (June 1977): 234–41.

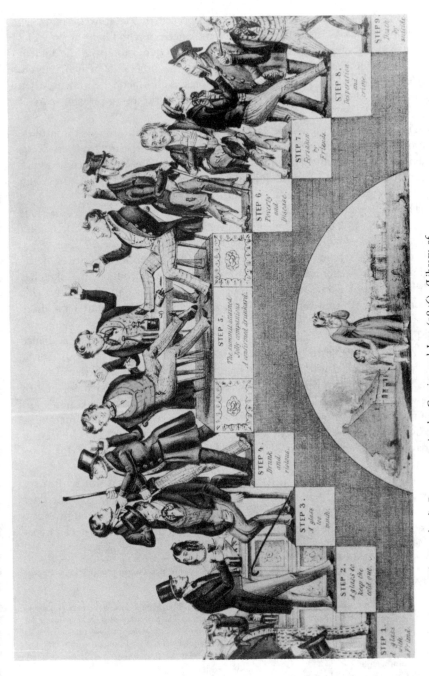

Figure 22. *The Drunkard's Progress*, a print by Currier and Ives (1846). (Library of Congress, Washington, D.C.)

STEP 1. *A glass with a Friend.*

STEP 2. *A glass to keep the cold out.*

STEP 3. *A glass too much.*

STEP 4. *Drunk and riotous.*

STEP 5. *The summit attained. Jolly companions. A confirmed drunkard.*

STEP 6. *Poverty and Disease.*

STEP 7. *Forsaken by Friends.*

STEP 8. *Desperation and crime.*

STEP 9. *Death by suicide.*

Johnson's "The Voyage of Life," which appeared in *The Rambler* in 1751. Johnson's essay was frequently reprinted in American schoolbook anthologies popular in the 1820s and 1830s. It begins with a quotation from the ancient Roman writer Seneca: "Life is a voyage, in the process of which, we are perpetually changing our scenes; we first leave childhood behind us, then youth, then the years of ripened manhood, then the more pleasing part of old age."[13]

This nautical metaphor pervaded American literature during the middle third of the nineteenth century, when the nation's maritime frontiers beckoned young men and the Hudson, Ohio, and Mississippi rivers teemed with steamboat traffic.[14] Cole himself began his *Voyage* series shortly after traveling on the Genesee River in rural, western New York.

The Cole paintings have taken an interesting historical voyage of their own. In 1839, Cole received a commission from the New York banker Samuel Ward, who died before the series was completed in the fall of 1840. Because Ward's heirs refused to permit extensive public exhibition of the paintings, Cole executed another set from memory and from original sketches while he was in Rome from November 1841 to May 1842. Ironically, this second set – painted for public viewing – virtually disappeared for more than a century.[15]

The original series – painted for a single patron – achieved a wide audience after the American Art Union bought it from Samuel Ward's heirs in 1848, the year of Cole's death. Later that year, a memorial exhibit of the paintings was attended by approximately 500,000 people, the equivalent of half of New York City's population. Within five months of the Art Union's announcement that it would distribute engravings of the series to members, its subscription list grew from less than 800 to more than 16,000, reflecting what the Reverend Gorham Abbott called the "magic influence of this series on the public mind."[16]

The original series, which hangs today in the Munson-Williams-Proctor Institute in Utica, New York, was purchased in 1849 for the Spengler Institute of New York City. In 1856, the Spengler Institute brought out a public edition of the series engraved by James Smillie at a cost of almost

---

[13] Cited by Michael Kammen, "Changing Perceptions of the Life Cycle in American Thought and Culture," *Massachusetts Historical Society Proceedings* 91 (1980): 41–42. Kammen probably overstates the influence of Johnson's essay on Cole.

[14] Kammen, "Changing Perceptions" (see n. 13), 44–45.

[15] The second set was exhibited in Boston, New York, and Philadelphia during the next two years. It was then sold to George K. Shoenberger of Cincinnati, Ohio. The paintings hung in his mansion for a century. After Shoenberger's death, his house was used as a sanitarium and eventually as part of Bethesda Hospital. In 1962, the series was "rediscovered" in the hospital's chapel and brought to the National Gallery of Art in 1971, where it hangs today. See "The Voyage of Life," anonymous National Gallery of Art mimeograph, 4–5.

[16] Gorham D. Abbott, Introduction to *The Voyage of Life: A Series of Allegorical Pictures* (Philadelphia: H. Cowperthwait, 1856), 3.

$20,000. The brochure that announced publication of this "American Pilgrim's Progress" contained Thomas Cole's own description of each age of life, along with glowing accounts of the engravings by William Cullen Bryant, Asher B. Durand, Frederick E. Church, various religious leaders, and several newspapers, magazines, and church publications.

Abbott boasted that the work was thoroughly American in its execution, scenery, and outlook. "It is an Allegory," he wrote, "the silent interpreter of which is in every heart. It is an Epic Poem – the hero, or heroine of which is the beholder. It is a Discourse of human life – its opening; its fascinations, temptations, trials, dangers; and to the Christian voyager, its peaceful, glorious end." According to Abbott, the series had an *"almost mysterious power"* to kindle the imagination of real voyagers in every stage of life. "Every human being feels that he himself is making this perilous and momentous voyage, and sees in one or another of the pictured passages before him, something suggestive of his own history, experience, or aspirations."[17]

In place of Bunyan's traditional metaphor of the path or road, Cole chose a river – a metaphor common in evangelical revivalism as well as in Romantic poetry. Cole's river of life moves inevitably to the sea through a fantastic natural landscape. The voyager faces no real choices – no City of Destruction to leave, no confusing crossroads to navigate, no false Worldly Wisemen to meet. Cole's *Voyage* is not about Christian conduct or complex moral choices in a confusing and dangerous social world. It is about keeping one's faith and surviving life's trials – in particular those of middle age.[18]

With the exception of the guardian angel, not a single image remains constant throughout the series. In *Childhood*, the sands of time begin falling through the hourglass perched on the bow of the voyager's boat; by *Old Age*, the hourglass has broken off. As in the early modern iconography, Cole focuses on the swift passage of individual "life time." Yet in his rendering, childhood, youth, and old age are all exempt from the trials of life. Not until mid-life do the swiftness of time and the realities of this world create feelings of loss and turmoil. Having survived with faith intact, the voyager passes serenely onto the ocean of death and immortality.

In *Childhood* (Fig. 23), the voyager emerges from a womblike cavern as sunrise bathes a lush, spring landscape. A guardian angel steers the laughing infant's boat through the narrow riverbanks.[19]

Although *Youth* (Fig. 24) was probably the most popular painting in the series, one wonders how contemporaries received Cole's intended message of youthful illusions. As the young man confidently takes the tiller and assumes

---

[17] Abbott, *Voyage of Life* (see n. 16), 1–4.
[18] See Joy Kasson, "The Voyage of Life: Thomas Cole and Romantic Disillusionment," *American Quarterly* 27 (March 1975): 42–56.
[19] Cole's accompanying descriptions of each age are included in Abbott, *Voyage of Life* (see n. 16), 5–6.

Figure 23. *The Voyage of Life: Childhood*, an oil painting by Thomas Cole (1842). (National Gallery of Art, Washington, D.C., Ailsa Mellon Bruce Fund.)

Figure 24. *The Voyage of Life: Youth*, an oil painting by Thomas Cole (1842). (National Gallery of Art, Washington, D.C., Ailsa Mellon Bruce Fund.)

control of his own destiny, the lofty trees, blooming plants, clear stream, towering mountains, and midday summer sky all suggest unbounded possibility. The youth does not yet see that the beautiful stream makes a sudden turn in the distance, descending rapidly over a rocky ravine.

In *Manhood* (Fig. 25), the raging river bears the voyager's boat over rapids on a dark autumn evening. The temptations of Suicide, Intemperance, and Murder lurk in the dark clouds above. His tiller broken, the bearded man prays, unaware that his guardian angel watches over him in the sky. The carved Hours, singing and smiling in the two previous scenes, weep. "Trouble is characteristic of the period of Manhood," wrote Cole. "In Childhood there is no cankering care; in Youth no despairing thought." Only when experience has taught men the realities of the world do they feel deep, abiding sorrow and realize their ultimate dependence on God.

In the last painting (Fig. 26), a white-bearded, bald old man arrives on a winter midnight at the place where the river of life empties into the ocean of eternity. He glides past a "few barren rocks" of old age, the last landmarks on the shore of this world. Guided over the deep waters by his guardian angel, he looks upward through the dark night toward an opening in the clouds, from which heavenly hosts descend on rays of divine light, welcoming him to the "Haven of Immortal Life."

For all its dazzling colors, magnificent natural landscapes, and apparent optimism, *The Voyage of Life* also evokes a dark sense of loss, anxiety, and helplessness. Its stark contrast between rich, detailed natural scenery and almost wooden, awkward human figures reflects more than Cole's mastery of landscape and lack of experience drawing figures. Cole's awkward human figures reflect a common feature of Victorian sentimentalism, which obscured the actual experience of pain, suffering, and evil in images of grand moral and religious ideals. This sentimental style, the immense scale, the intense colors and drama of the paintings concealed realities (like childhood sexuality or the trials of old age) that "civilized" morality found unpalatable.

In Cole's series, childhood, youth, and old age appear to be immune from life's vicissitudes. Childhood is protected and joyous rather than vulnerable and fallen.[20] Youth is brightly optimistic about the future. Old age, beyond the storms of life, is dead to this world and only waits to ascend into heaven. All the cares, trials, and dangers of life are collapsed into the turbulence of manhood. As the sands of time slip away, Cole's voyager learns that self-reliance is an illusion. He cannot steer his own craft. His only hope lies in faith and dependence on God. In the ages-of-life motif, middle age is clearly the prime of life. Its pyramid of stairs conveys the unbroken sequence and unity of life's course. Cole's middle-aged voyager, in contrast, is not at the

[20] On changing attitudes toward the death of young children, see Nancy Schrom Dye and Daniel Blake Smith, "Mother Love and Infant Death, 1750–1920," *Journal of American History* 73 (September 1986): 329–53.

Figure 25. *The Voyage of Life: Manhood*, an oil painting by Thomas Cole (1842). (National Gallery of Art, Washington, D.C., Ailsa Mellon Bruce Fund.)

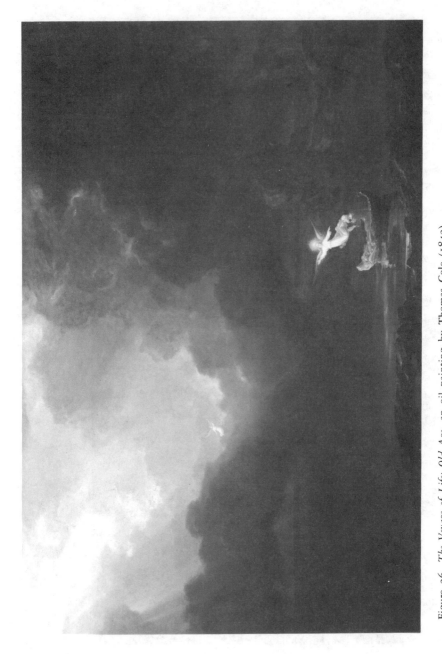

Figure 26. *The Voyage of Life: Old Age*, an oil painting by Thomas Cole (1842). (National Gallery of Art, Washington, D.C., Ailsa Mellon Bruce Fund.)

peak of his powers. He exhibits no skill or competence in negotiating the twists of fate.

By placing the four ages of life on separate canvases, Cole emphasizes differences and disjunction rather than continuity between stages.[21] He seems to offer a stark contrast between the sunshine of the first two canvases and the darkness of the last two. The bright hopes of life's morning seem to be dashed on the rocks of evening. But Cole's use of light and darkness is actually more subtle. The bright and innocent joy of childhood is qualified by the womblike cavern whose mysterious darkness occupies more space than the dawning rays of the sun. Similarly, the bright noon sky surrounding the bright "cloud built" palace that occupies the youth's attention is offset by a dark foreground from which he emerges and the misty, rocky ravine toward which he is (unknowingly) going.[22]

Although Cole includes darkness in all four paintings, he never depicts the full force of uncertainty, illusion, and anxiety. By placing the voyager's guardian angel in each painting, Cole tells his viewers that all is well despite unexpected rocks and turns in the river of life. The reward for faith is survival – a peaceful and passive old age, followed by beatific death and celestial afterlife.[23] The old man's survival does not bring with it the possibility of superior insight, knowledge, or wisdom – only the right to rest. Elaboration of this peaceful, powerless old age found its fullest expression in the preaching of Romantic evangelicals.

ROMANTIC RELIGION AND THE DUALISTIC VISION
OF OLD AGE

During the middle third of the nineteenth century, a Romantic style of religion replaced Scottish commonsense philosophy as the dominant force in evangelical Protestantism. The Romantic style contained three essential features: an emphasis on intuitive perception of truth through "feelings of the heart"; a theology that stressed the personality of Jesus over the moral order

---

[21] Individual depictions of the ages or decades of life, though not as common as the inclusion of all ages in one motif, have a long (and largely unexplored) history of their own. See, for example, Samuel Chew, *The Pilgrimage of Life* (New Haven, Conn.: Yale University Press, 1962), figs. 108–15; *Die Lebenstreppe* (see n. 1), 119–23; and Elizabeth Sears, *The Ages of Man* (Princeton: Princeton University Press, 1986), figs. 26–29, 35–38, 42, 45–51. The Staatliche Graphische Sammlung in Munich has several early modern series by Conrad Meyer, Balthasar Jenichen, and Tobias Stimmer.

[22] Here I am suggesting that Joy Kasson's emphasis on the contrast between the brightness of the first two ages and the darkness of the last two needs to be qualified.

[23] On the sentimentalization of death, see James H. Moorhead, " 'As Though Nothing At All Had Happened': Death And Afterlife In Protestant Thought, 1840–1925," *Soundings* 68 (winter 1984): 454–71; Philippe Ariès, *The Hour of Our Death* (New York: Knopf, 1981), 409–74; Ann Douglas, "Heaven Our Home: Consolation Literature in the Northern United States, 1830–1880," *American Quarterly* 26 (December 1974): 496–515.

of God; and a sentimental idealization of women, children, old age, death, and the family.[24]

In contrast to the paternal and authoritarian God of Nathaniel Taylor, Albert Barnes, Charles G. Finney, and Lyman Beecher, the God of the Romantics possessed maternal and affective qualities. The Romantics – men like Henry Ward Beecher, Phillips Brooks, Horace Bushnell, and Theodore Parker – also took more liberal positions on the Atonement, the nature of children, and biblical criticism.[25] At the same time, Romantics and revivalists shared the belief that individuals were free to work out their own fate and that God offered salvation freely to all who truly opened their hearts to his saving grace.

Romantic evangelicalism in the northeastern United States emerged during a period of clerical reorientation. By 1850, reacting to the disruptive zeal and chaotic style of revivalism and reform, many churchmen sought to strengthen the boundaries between the sacred church and the profane world, to reaffirm the church as a sanctuary where Christians might withdraw to renew the promise of salvation and their sense of the divine presence.[26] Even Finney, Lyman Beecher, and Barnes, the most ardent revivalists of the 1820s, participated in this conservative move to protect doctrine and devotion from external influences. During the 1830s and 1840s, music emerged as a central part of the evangelical service. Ministers increasingly stressed the emotive rather than the doctrinal and ecclesiastical aspects of faith. They structured their sermons not by formal argumentation but around a sequence of images or impressions designed to create Christian sentiments.

This devotional transformation also included changing notions of God and the Atonement. The God of seventeenth-century Puritanism had been utterly sovereign. He cared little for the feelings of men, demanded virtue and obedience beyond human capability, and had sent his only son to show his dislike of sin. The God of the second Great Awakening, though more merciful and perfectly just, remained a stern governor who demanded repentance and obedience. The God of Beecher and Bushnell, in contrast, was a father sensitive to human pain through the sufferings of Christ. Christ's love rather than God's command dominated the appeal of the Romantic minister.

Romantic ministers also encouraged more orderly and consistent religious emotions in their parishioners. During the revivalism of the 1820s, Lyman Beecher, Peter Cartwright, and Charles Finney had inspired powerful self-loathing, guilt, and hatred of sin. Revivalist conversion required an emo-

---

[24] William G. McLoughlin, ed., "Introduction," *American Evangelicals* (New York: Harper & Row, 1968).

[25] Theodore Parker, whose Unitarianism denied the necessity of supernatural regeneration, is discussed with the evangelicals because his preaching on old age belongs to the sentimental variety of Romantic Protestantism.

[26] Donald Scott, *From Office to Profession* (Philadelphia: University of Pennsylvania Press, 1978).

tionally painful and tumultuous struggle between a stern Father and a defiant child. In contrast, mid-nineteenth-century ministers and popular female writers viewed conversion as a tranquil voyage "from the nursery into the safe harbor of the church."[27]

By downplaying self-torment and aggressive or violent feelings, liberal and Romantic Protestant ministers helped define Christian piety as culturally female. They urged parishioners to become "ever more Christlike" – gentle, meek, forgiving, and humble. "Animal passions" stimulated in the masculine world of politics and business were split off from feminine "affections." This model may have proved appealing for congregations predominantly composed of women and older men.[28] It tended, however, to feminize old age as well as piety, thereby inhibiting young and middle-aged men from identifying with older men. The mid-Victorian retreat from intensity strengthened artificial boundaries between worldly passions and Christian affections, reinforcing a rigid division of sexual spheres. At the same time it solidified the emerging bifurcation of old age into a culturally female sainthood on one hand and masculine sin and decay on the other.

When Romantic ministers addressed older parishioners, they seldom used the traditional language of consolation. Theodore Parker and Henry Ward Beecher held the dominant view that sin was entirely voluntary and that a miserable old age was simply God's punishment for disobedience. Parker and Beecher painted an ideal old age tinged with passivity and nostalgia, rarely discussing either suffering or growth in late life.[29] Their emotive imagery often obscured and evaded the realities of sickness and physical decline. Phillips Brooks and Horace Bushnell, on the other hand, believed that sin was neither innate nor entirely voluntary but developed inevitably from the world's corrupting influence. They expressed more tolerance and sympathy for the disfiguring effects of time. They advised not passive acceptance but inner growth and openness to the unknown. Despite these differences, all the Romantic ministers paid less attention to old age itself than to laying the groundwork for it.

[27] Ann Douglas, *The Feminization of American Culture* (New York: Avon, 1977), 162–63.

[28] Although the research is scanty, some evidence suggests that women constituted two-thirds or more of most nineteenth-century congregations, with older men making up much of the remainder. On his travels through New England during the spring and summer of 1858, George Miller Beard made observations to this effect; see his "Private Journal," 87–95, Yale University Library, George Miller Beard Papers, Box 1, Series 2, folder 3. See Lumpkin, "The Role of Women in 18th Century Virginia Baptist Life," *Baptist History and Heritage* 8 (July 1973): 158–67; Howard Allen Bridgemen, "Have We a Religion for Men?" *Andover Review* 13 (1890): 388–96; Richard D. Shiels, "The Feminization of American Congregationalism, 1730–1835," *American Quarterly* 33 (spring 1981): 46–62.

[29] For Henry Ward Beecher's rare concessions to loss and suffering, see "The Blind Restored to Sight," in *Forty-Six Sermons* (London, 1885), 1:216; "Hindrances to Religious Life," in *Forty-Eight Sermons* (London: Dickinson, 1870), 2:175. My claim about the absence of consolation refers only to published sermons. Although it is impossible to be certain, I think it is quite likely that Parker and Beecher offered considerable comfort and consoling advice on ministerial visits to suffering aged parishioners.

YOUTH, MANHOOD, AND PREPARATION
FOR OLD AGE

In the early nineteenth century, Nathaniel Emmons had warned his parishioners to avoid hopes of long life and prepare for death. Romantics urged the reverse: to avoid thinking too much about death and prepare for long life and a ripe old age. "Now if you are young, that is presumptive evidence that God wants you to live," argued Henry Ward Beecher. "If you are middle-aged . . . that is evidence that God means you shall stand there." Beecher discouraged people from envisioning or imagining their deaths: "for a man, when everything connects him with the present, and the beat of his heart is 'Duty-work! Duty-work!' to torment himself with such questions . . . what supreme folly it is."[30]

When Beecher referred to torment, he was speaking from experience. Born in 1813, he grew up in a Connecticut town, where Calvinist church bells rang out the age of the newly deceased. Beecher lived much of his childhood in fear of damnation, unable to satisfy his father Lyman Beecher's demands for conversion.[31] In the early 1830s, the young Beecher attended Amherst College. As a theology student, Beecher rejected the frightening images of hell he had endured as a child. Though inspired by Amherst's revivalist President Heman Humphrey, Beecher also rejected the stern God of justice that Humphrey and his father preached so vividly. At Amherst he avidly studied the new science of phrenology, later popularized by his classmate Orson Squire Fowler. In phrenology, Beecher found intellectual authority for the view that a person's mind could be known and altered, thereby strengthening his belief in progress and human perfectibility.[32]

Beecher also rejected the old Puritan insistence on preparation for death. As a minister, he assured his congregants that God would send his saving strength to all who slipped or faltered along the way. Living properly enabled one to die properly. Phillips Brooks also warned against preparing for death "in a narrow and special sense. It is not good for a man to devote himself to preparation for dying," he asserted. "It is preparation for living that you need."[33]

---

[30] Beecher, "Strength According to Days," in *Forty-Eight Sermons* (see n. 29), 1:15–16.

[31] On Henry Ward Beecher and the impact of liberal Protestantism in America, see Kenneth Cauthen, *The Impact of American Religious Liberalism* (New York: Harper & Row, 1962); William R. Hutchison, *The Modernist Impulse in American Protestantism* (Cambridge, Mass.: Harvard University Press, 1976); William G. McLoughlin, *The Meaning of Henry Ward Beecher: An Essay on the Shifting Values of Mid-Victorian America* (New York: Knopf, 1970).

[32] Clifford E. Clark, Jr., *Henry Ward Beecher: Spokesman for a Middle Class America* (Champaign, Ill.: University of Illinois Press, 1978).

[33] Phillips Brooks, "The Power of an Uncertain Future," in *The Law of Growth and Other Sermons* (New York: Dutton, 1902), 54.

When they discussed spiritual development, Romantic ministers chose metaphors of organic growth more often than the journey. "To raise the great oak trees of human righteousness," argued Theodore Parker, "you want a deep, rich soil, and threescore, fourscore, fivescore summers and winters . . . an opportunity to grow great and ripen through."[34] Rather than an intense, crisis-ridden conversion, the Romantics preferred a gradual unfolding of the soul. They subtly naturalized the old Puritan view, asserting that the soul flowered naturally in a sequence unified and supervised by God.[35]

Organic metaphors emphasized the essential unity of the human life course, a unity that enabled ministers and reformers to teach young people that present conduct affected future life. "The man reaps in his old age as he sowed in his youth and manhood," asserted Parker. "If he has been faithful to his better nature, true to his conscience, and his heart and his soul, in his old age he often reaps a most abundant reward."[36]

Parker and the Romantics accepted the view that obedience to the natural laws of health and morality would bring long life, a healthy old age, and natural death. Like the revivalists, they also accepted the corollary: violation of natural law caused premature, wretched old age or early, painful death. Hence, two images of old age pervade these sermons: the gentle, ripe old age of the saint, and the nasty, disease-ridden, infirm old age of the sinner. Although ministers used masculine pronouns when speaking of old age, the old age of the saint was culturally feminized, while the old age of the sinner rarely betrayed a single feminine quality.

Like the revivalists, Romantics celebrated youth as the most favorable time for conversion. Yet they took a nurturing and lenient approach, stressing the opportunity to receive Christ's love rather than the need to obey God's command. Evoking the ancient analogy between a life and a day, Horace Bushnell urged youthful congregants to recognize their special religious abilities: "Call it the dew of thy youth, understanding well, that when thy sun is fairly up, it will, like dew, be gone."[37] Phillips Brooks similarly idealized the freshness and potential of the "true" young man: "He is the human creature in whom the best material of the world, which is manhood, exists in its best condition, which is youth."[38] The great advantages of youth

---

[34] Theodore Parker, "The Aged," in *The Works of Theodore Parker* (Boston: American Unitarian Association, 1910–1913), 10:190.

[35] Sydney E. Ahlstrom, *A Religious History of the American People* (New Haven, Conn.: Yale University Press, 1972), 611; Brooks, *Law of Growth* (see n. 33); Horace Bushnell, "Every Man's Life a Plan of God," in *Sermons for the New Life* (New York: Scribner, 1866).

[36] Parker, "The Aged" (see n. 34), 10:187.

[37] Horace Bushnell, "The Capacity of Religion Extirpated by Disuse," in *Sermons for the New Life* (New York: Scribner, 1866), 184.

[38] Phillips Brooks, "The Choice Young Man," in *The Light of the World and Other Sermons* (New York: Dutton, 1890), 90. In the same sermon, Brooks left open the possibility that youth might not be the

Figure 27. Photograph of Henry Ward Beecher. (Beecher Family Papers, Manuscripts and Archives, Yale University Library.)

lay in the "exhilaration of beginning," the "sense of starting," the freshness that seemed to wither so rapidly during the middle years of life.

The Romantics who celebrated youthful beginnings were among the first to address the stress of competitive urban life. As we know from various diaries and autobiographies, young men migrating to cities in search of fortune often experienced severe emotional turmoil and anxiety.[39] The middle-aged ministers who wrote and spoke so fervently about youth often yearned for its exemption from the renunciation and struggle of "manhood." Like Thomas Cole in his *Voyage of Life,* Romantics apparently idealized youth and old age to compensate for the emotional and spiritual toll of adult life.

"Men are hopeful when they are young . . . sad in middle age and glad to die when they are old," argued Beecher.[40] Speaking to young men at the Brooklyn YMCA, he warned that migration from the country involved the "greatest loss that the young can sustain . . . the loss of home . . . God's

best time of life: "If I am wrong in calling youth the best condition, at least it is a condition which has excellences and fascinations which are wholly its own."

[39] See Joseph Kett, *Rites of Passage* (New York: Basic Books, 1977), chap. 2; also Beard, "Private Journal" (see n. 28).

[40] Beecher, "Not Ashamed of the Gospel of Christ," in *Forty-Eight Sermons* (London: Dickinson, 1870), 1:190.

natural training ground." In the city, where the struggle for advancement discouraged fidelity, honesty, and thoroughness, alcohol, tobacco, and sexual indulgence abounded. "And this is a course," Beecher warned, "that grows worse with the years, and must in the end of life leave a man hopeless in old age."[41]

Parker compared "youth" and "manhood" in similar terms. The young man looked forward with great enthusiasm. "It is a hard world; he does not know it: he works little and hopes much. The middle-aged man looks around at the present. He has found that it is a hard world. He hopes less and works more."[42] Phillips Brooks lamented this "staining power of world" that turned bright and enthusiastic boys into guilty and desperate old men.[43]

Without religion, worldly experience was deforming. Horace Bushnell, who did not share Beecher's admiration of urban capitalist life, discussed its effects on spiritual growth: "[Worldly experience] murders the angel in us, and saves the drudge or the worm. The man that is left is but a partial being, a worker, a schemer, a creature of passion, thought, will, hunger, remorse, but no divine principle, no kinsman of Christ or of God."[44] The Romantics never developed a full-blown critique of a society increasingly devoted to the accumulation of individual wealth. They did, however, raise hopes for a beautiful old age that could emerge after a life of strenuous preparation.

Beecher believed that every individual possessed a right to old age – a patrimony of eighty years granted by God.[45] As Finney had argued, the power to shorten or lengthen life lay not with God but with the human being, who needed proper instruction for achieving a virtuous and happy old age. Occasionally, parental sins or accidents deprived a man of his old age. But the greatest number who died prematurely or found old age a "land of sorrow" did so out of their own ignorance or misconduct. "Old age has the foundation of its joy or sorrow laid in youth," Beecher emphasized to the young people in his congregation. "You are building at twenty. Are you building for seventy?"[46]

When Beecher preached a sermon entitled "Old Age," he devoted it almost entirely to advice about preparing for old age. Beecher divided his advice into four types: physical, secular, intellectual, and spiritual. Physical advice was the most important. Although nature, the "universal nurse," operated according to benevolent laws, most people wasted their physical patrimony

---

[41] Beecher, "Sermon to Young Men," in *Forty-Eight Sermons* (London: Dickinson, 1870), 1:49.

[42] Parker, "The Aged" (see n. 34), 10:185.

[43] Phillips Brooks, "An Evil Spirit from the Lord," in *Visions and Tasks and Other Sermons* (New York: Dutton, 1886), 299.

[44] Bushnell, "The Capacity of Religion" (see n. 37), 180.

[45] Beecher proclaimed old age as a natural right, arguing that "men are defrauded if they do not possess it." "Old Age," in *Forty-Six Sermons* (London, 1885), 1:236.

[46] Beecher, "Old Age" (see n. 45), 1:237.

by ignoring these laws and dissipating their vitality. Beecher imagined God as a banker and aging as the accumulation of physical capital: "Every immoderate draft which is made by the appetites and passions is so much sent forward to be cashed in old age. You may sin at one end, but God takes it off at the other."[47] With revivalists and health reformers, Beecher insisted that sinners would not live out half their days.

Although Phillips Brooks never used the metaphor of body as capital, he too shared a commitment to the "civilized" regimen. Brooks painted a frightening picture of the punishment awaiting those who violated nature's moral laws. The young man, he argued, who leads a "wild, unbridled life and thought himself happy in his dissipation" was actually "flinging away . . . health and vitality." It would not be long before the "worn-out young man settles down to a middle age of enforced and dreary decency, and expects an old age of imbecility and pain."[48]

Brooks believed that a man without God lost love, trust, and hope as he grew older. Cynical and careless, he eventually came "creeping into port, a wreck, with broken masts and rudder gone."[49] "Do you know," Brooks asked the young men of his Boston congregation, "that there are old men all through this city whose minds are powerless because of the wrong they did their bodies when they were . . . your age?"[50]

While Parker luridly described the old man of sin, he reserved his most punitive picture for the woman of vanity who has misused the three ages of her life. "Poor creature! In youth a worm; in womanhood a butterfly; in old age, your wings all tattered, your plumage rent, a 'fingered moth' – old, shriveled, sick, perching in nothing."[51]

Parker, an advocate of women's rights, is the only Romantic minister who explicitly envisioned the old age of women.[52] Romantics almost always portrayed the old sinner as a man. Confronted with such terrifying examples of miserable old age, young parishioners presumably listened attentively to the principles of preparation for old age. These boiled down to the hygienic rule of temperance in all things: regular habits of eating, drinking, and sleeping; abstention from liquor and coffee; total sexual abstinence outside marriage and sex within marriage only for purposes of procreation. "I hold

---

[47] Beecher, "Old Age" (see n. 45), 1:238.

[48] Phillips Brooks, "The Shortness of Life," in *The Purpose and Use of Comfort and Other Sermons* (New York: Dutton, 1878), 363.

[49] Phillips Brooks, "The Power of an Uncertain Future," in *New Starts in Life and Other Sermons* (New York: Dutton, 1896), 44.

[50] Phillips Brooks, "The Natural and the Spiritual," in *The Battle of Life and Other Sermons* (New York: Dutton, 1893), 249.

[51] Parker, "The Aged" (see n. 34), 10:195–96.

[52] Henry Ward Beecher, however, did attack those who used "that rude, unfeeling, and indelicate phrase, old maid." See "A New Year's Sermon," in *Forty-Eight Sermons* (London: Dickinson, 1870), 2:64 On ideas about beauty among older women, see Lois W. Banner, *American Beauty* (New York: Knopf, 1983), 219–21.

that no Christian parent can but be accountable to God for ignorance of the fundamental laws of health," asserted Beecher. "When I am king, none shall be married until they have passed through the catechism of natural health."[53]

After physical preparation for old age, Beecher encouraged "wisdom in secular affairs," a form of advice that none of the other Romantics offered. Invoking the Christian virtue of foresight, Beecher argued that provision for future contingencies constituted "obedience to God's law." Appealing to the male, bourgeois virtue of independence, he claimed, "It is part of wisdom to secure, in youth and manhood, a competency that shall keep old age from want. One of the conditions of manliness is that a man shall not be dependent upon anybody but himself."

Toward this end, Beecher urged frugality, savings, and even life insurance to provide for one's family after death. Although he acknowledged "something beautiful" in the thought of aged parents "leaning on" their children, Beecher counseled against fathers becoming dependent on their children. "There is something more beautiful," he argued, "in the thought of a man leaning upon his own staff. In youth you are cutting the staff that you are to lean upon in old age."[54]

Beecher praised the "mechanic, merchant, rover on the seas" who made and saved money. "You are doing right. Are you twenty-five, or thirty years of age, and have you said, 'I may live till I am sixty-five or seventy, and I must lay up resources for my later years'? . . . That is wise."[55]

Although Beecher claimed that "spiritual preparation" for old age was most important of all, he showed none of his ancestors' interest in reflection, self-examination, or meditation. Earthly wealth, he noted, was highly unstable, always changing hands. Heavenly treasures, on the other hand, were permanent, unchanging. The development of proper character, full of love and Christian fidelity, was the way to lay up such a treasure – a hedge against poverty on earth as well as bankruptcy in the "other life."[56]

For Beecher, "spiritual preparation" for old age consisted primarily of living with the "distinct consciousness that this is a 'joined life.' " He counseled his parishioners against envisioning their own deaths, implicitly rejecting the view that old age was a time of special preparation for death. Instead, he claimed that ideal old age was simply a time of minimal effort and confident expectation: "[A] man's whole life should be a preparation for dying," he asserted. "It is a beautiful thing for a man, when he comes into old age, to have no more preparation to make . . . waiting only . . . [to] pass from glory to glory."[57]

[53] Beecher, "Old Age" (see n. 45), 1:241.
[54] Beecher, "Old Age" (see n. 45), 1:243.
[55] Beecher, "Treasures in Heaven," in *Forty-Eight Sermons* (London: Dickinson, 1870), 2:11.
[56] Beecher, "Treasures in Heaven" (see n. 55), 8.
[57] Beecher, "Treasures in Heaven" (see n. 55), 8.

SENTIMENTALISM: SAINTLY OLD AGE AND
NATURAL DEATH

Nineteenth-century sentimentalism was part of the self-evasion of a culture at once committed to and disturbed by capitalist values of efficiency and productivity. In sermons, literature, advice books, and other forms of popular culture, sentimental writers placed great value on precisely those things – childhood, family life, motherhood, old age, death – whose meaning and value were threatened by marketplace competition and calculation.[58] Romantic ministers idealized the aged and painted them as symbols of an idyllic rural or revolutionary past. Such sentimental images masked devaluation of aging, fear of decline and dependency, and hostility toward elders. They embellished the positive pole in Victorian culture's divided vision of aging and old age.

For every old man whose misery constituted a damning judgment, Romantics depicted a positive counterpart. The kindly, old silver-haired grandfather was perhaps Parker's favorite representation of old age. Part of his sermon describing "Grandfather's Reveries" was reproduced in various aging manuals. The sermon depicts an "old, very old" man born in Boston at the end of the Revolutionary War. Grandfather's "back . . . is bent. In the street he sees crowds of men looking dreadfully young, and walking fearfully swift. He wonders where all the old folks are." Amidst the jostling crowd, Grandfather displays the fruits of a lifetime's manly piety with his dignity and good manners.[59]

At night, Parker's Grandfather sits by his "old-fashioned fire" after the family has gone to bed. He draws his "old-fashioned chair" close to the hearth. Nearby is a stand his mother once gave him. Candlesticks "also of old time" burn on the stand. Grandfather gazes into the low-burning fire, thinking of his children and grandchildren – the joy of his old age. "He takes out of his bosom a little locket: nobody ever sees it." Within are "two little twists of hair." The outer twist is transformed into a head of "ambrosial curls" as Grandfather remembers his young love and moonlight meetings with his long-dead wife. The inner twist, hair from his firstborn son, revives the memory of his wife's long and painful birthing. He yearns to be reunited with her in heaven: "How long O Lord? When lettest thou thy servant depart in peace, that mine eyes may see thy salvation?"[60]

Opposite the punitive picture of the old "woman of vanity," Parker painted his ideal old woman. She is a spinster, long ago desexualized by the loss of

---

[58] See Douglas, *Feminization of American Culture* (see n. 27), 11–12.

[59] Theodore Parker, "The Soul's Normal Delight in God," in *The Works of Theodore Parker* (Boston: American Unitarian Association, 1910–13), 6:182–83; and "The Aged" (see n. 34), 10:200–201.

[60] Parker, "Soul's Normal Delight" (see n. 59), 6:200–202.

a lover whom she hopes to meet again. Like Grandfather, Miss Kindly is "old, very old," and she has been "aunt to everybody as long as anyone can remember." For sixty years she ministered to the family. Now "her hands are thin, her voice feeble; her back is bent. She walks with a staff – the best limb of the three."[61]

When Henry Ward Beecher urged his congregation to avoid the ignorance or misconduct that made old age a "land of sorrow," he played on fears of dependency and social decline. "One dreads to see grey hairs in poverty, in beggary, dependent upon . . . charity. . . . One shrinks from old age when it is full of pains, when it is crippled, . . . helpless, hopeless, and hapless." Like Parker, Beecher placed his ideal of old age opposite the "sordid old man" whose life of sin made his life such a hideous spectacle. "There is nothing more beautiful than a serene, virtuous, and happy old age; and such an old age belongs to every individual's life, if he only knows how to build it."[62]

Beecher compared his ideal old age to a glorious sunset, shedding a golden light of virtue. Nathaniel Emmons had used the sunset metaphor as well; but for him, the beauty of piety as a "peculiar ornament" was that it "covered" moral and physical imperfections in old age. Beecher's virtuous old man, on the other hand, was distinguished by his independence and good health. Like Cole's painting of Old Age awaiting ascent to heaven, Beecher's ideal old age concealed harsh truths of poverty, sickness, and suffering in old age by appealing to feelings of guilt and nostalgia.[63]

Following popular health reformers, Romantic ministers elaborated the ideal of natural death as a quiet, painless, disease-free event – the perfection of old age. "The old lion, buffalo, eagle, elephant, dies as the apple falls from the tree, with little pain," asserted Parker.[64] Phillips Brooks, for example, described the "timeliness" of death in old age: "When a life has lived out its days in happiness, grown old with constantly accumulating joys, and then at last, before decay has touched it or the ground grows soft under its feet, the door opens and it enters into the new youth of eternity . . . is not death beautiful?"[65]

Whereas the descriptions of Parker and Brooks depicted natural death as the fulfillment of an organic life, Beecher depicted natural death in strictly accountable terms. A "true" old man, he claimed, should "die like a clock,

[61] Parker, "The Aged" (see n. 34), 10:197–200.

[62] Beecher, "Old Age" (see n. 45), 1:237.

[63] During the late nineteenth century, Dwight L. Moody, the most popular evangelist of his day, carried this imagery to its most lachrymose. For a discussion of Moody's sermons on aging and old age, see my "Past Meridian: Aging and the Northern Middle Class, 1830–1930" (Ph.D. diss., University of Rochester, N.Y. 1980), 148–66.

[64] Parker, "The Aged" (see n. 34), 10:187.

[65] Brooks, "Timeliness," in *Visions and Tasks and Other Sermons* (New York: Dutton, 1886), 253–54.

that goes on through the whole twenty-four hours, and until the very last beat" without disruption.[66] Beecher's clock metaphor, soon to be immortalized in Henry Clay Work's song "Grandfather's Clock" (1876), suggests how far the rationalization of time and the life course had proceeded since the sixteenth century.[67]

No longer a King of Terrors who struck down his victims at any age, death was fast becoming a kindly nurse who put old people to bed when their life's work was done.[68] Combining the power of God's grace (regeneration) and his natural laws of health, Romantic evangelicals helped shape the middle-class image of "normal" aging as masculine health, longevity, and natural death. All of these ministers shared the perfectionist belief in potential human holiness and emphasized that growth in grace might result in "entire sanctification" – replacement of animal passion and decay with the eternal power of the soul. Such perfectionism raised the possibility of escape from the punishment of infirmity. Whereas Calvinists considered disease and suffering to be ineradicable, Romantics, reformers, and revivalists did not consider these experiences a necessary or normal part of life.

At the same time, Romantics reinforced the Victorian dualism of old age. Their ideal of self-control and perfect health required a negative mirror image: the sinful old man suffering in a corrupt body. Puritan and New Divinity preachers had countenanced no such separation. For them, innate depravity meant that no man or woman could escape the punishment of an aging, decaying body. Accepting physical decline and disease, they had argued that piety and faith strengthened the aged to face their final trials, fulfill final obligations, and prepare for eternal life. The Romantics articulated no social obligation or usefulness for the aged. Their published sermons contain a great deal of advice about preparing for old age but almost no advice for the aged themselves. They assumed that preparing for old age was equivalent to preparing for death – the spiritual and social significance of both now hidden in a private, painless, secure transition to the next world.

[66] Beecher, "Old Age" (see n. 45), 1:242.

[67] See Rudolf Rezohazy, "The Concept of Social Time: Its Role in Development," *International Social Science Journal* 24 (1972), 23–26; E. P. Thompson, "Time, Work-Discipline, and Industrial Capitalism," *Past and Present* 38 (December 1967): 56–97; and Eviator Zerubarel, "Schedules and Social Control," in *Time and Aging*, ed. Ephraim H. Mizruchi, Barry Glassner, and Thomas Pastorello (Bayside, N.Y.: General Hall, 1982), 129–152.

[68] See the anonymous article "The Dying of Death," *Review of Reviews* 20 (September 1899): 364–65.

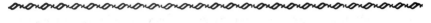

7

In a different voice: self-help and the ideal of "civilized" old age, 1850–1910

Old age is a large phrase. Most people know something of its reality at fifty. . . . When the descent of life is gradual, it is not usually painful, and the pilgrim lies down to rest . . . almost as one might go to sleep.

Harriet E. Paine

Those who in their prime neither nourished their spiritual nature nor cultivated their understandings, must expect to sink into dotage as their unlovely old age approaches.

Amelia Barr

When nineteenth-century evangelicals reinterpreted their religious heritage to accord with liberal capitalist values, they revised traditional Reformed ideas about aging, death, and the cycle of life. They rejected the introspective, acquiescent fatalism of Calvinism and championed each individual's right and ability to control his or her own life. Many portrayed life not as God's mysterious gift but as humankind's inalienable possession – property to be rationally invested and indefinitely perpetuated. Piety was transformed into the sum of civilized behavior; longevity into the dividend of properly invested physical capital; and death into a natural and peaceful transition from old age to eternal youth.

The evangelical alliance with bourgeois individualism, humanitarianism, and progress tended to celebrate the goals of the first half of life: education, expansion, efficiency, child-rearing, and social utility. The second half of life increasingly appeared as nothing more than the diminution of one's capacity to achieve these goals.

Evangelicals not only weakened the cultural significance of the last half of life, they also approached its physical and existential realities with faltering candor. Until the 1840s, when Arminian perfectionism came to dominate evangelical Protestantism, Northern ministers assumed that each age of life had its own tribulations and joys, rooted in the immutable and divinely ordained cycle of life. They agreed, as Nathaniel Emmons put it, that "no one can either read or hear the word of God properly and profitably without numbering their days aright, and realizing whether they are in the morning, meridian, or decline of life."[1]

Under the late Calvinist rendering of life's ages, each individual bore the responsibility to recognize his or her own old age, and to look to the Word of God for the duties and comforts appropriate to this last stage of life. Emmons, Lathrop, Porter, Van Rensselaer, and others emphasized the biblically sanctioned responsibilities of old age.[2] The aged were to spend the "residue of their days in praise, retirement and devotion." While stressing the physical infirmities and social losses of age, these ministers promised redemption and social integration in return for renunciation. In other words, they preserved goals, norms, and sanctions for easing people out of powerful positions and socializing them to a culturally viable old age that included the possibilities of frailty, sickness, and dependency.

By the middle third of the nineteenth century, this system was unraveling. An expanding society, committed to ever greater quantities of health and wealth, found it increasingly difficult to acknowledge "the cold friction of expiring sense," the complex and unmanageable dimensions of aging. One's physical, material, and spiritual condition in old age had become solely a matter of individual responsibility. Ironically, the Victorian vision of disease and decay in later life was harsher and more punitive than the old view, rooted in original sin. Rather than assume that everyone who lived long enough would become ill and bent with years as punishment for Adam's sin, Victorians assumed that everyone could be healthy and self-reliant in later life – unless they had personally sinned against God's laws of nature and morality. Hence poverty, disease, and frailty appeared to be shameful; they were visible signs of personal moral failure.

As we have seen, sentimental images strained to conceal fears of growing old and guilt at having deposed the authority of elders, as well as the sadness, anger, and suffering denied by the dualism of old age. Despite its evasions, however, Victorian culture recast the motifs of life's journey and its ages to create a new ideal of old age that remained powerful through the 1920s. This chapter traces the ideal – called here "civilized" old age – that emerged in the new advice literature that followed John Stanford's *The Aged Christian's Companion* (1829).

Socializing older people requires culturally viable ideals of old age, norms

---

[1] Nathaniel Emmons, "Piety A Peculiar Ornament to the Aged," in *The Works of Nathaniel Emmons* (Boston: Congregational Board of Publication, 1842), 2:492.

[2] For earlier examples, see Ebenezer Gay, *The Old Man's Calendar*, delivered in Hingham, Mass., August 25, 1781, reprinted in May 1846 by Jedidiah Farmer, Hingham, Mass.; Cotton Mather, *A Brief Essay on the Glory of Aged Piety* (Boston: n.p., 1726); Increase Mather, *Dignity and Duty of Aged Servants of the Lord* (Boston: n.p., 1716); and Samuel Willard, *A Complete Body of Divinity in Two Hundred and Fifty Expository Lectures on the Assembly's Shorter Catechism*, Sermon 180 (Boston: B. Green and S. Kneeland for B. Eliot and D. Henchman, 1726).

of proper behavior, and incentives for adopting them.[3] On all three counts, mid-century aging manuals confronted difficulty. Because they often began by addressing the decline of respect for age, these manuals shed considerable light on perceptions of generational relations in the urban middle class.

In early America, the obligation of youth to venerate age was balanced by the reciprocal obligation of age to "condescend" to youth. The old were to treat the young with decency, understanding, and respect.[4] Having transferred most of their worldly possessions and responsibilities to the next generation, the aged still had important religious tasks to fulfill and codes of behavior to follow. The decline of veneration and of cultural values esteeming the end of life therefore weakened the reciprocal obligations and norms of early modern generational relations.

As long as acceptance of death remained culturally sanctioned, the decline of patriarchy and veneration, along with the diminishing conceptual distance between old age and death, did not strip old age of all existential meaning and social responsibility. The slow "dying of death," however, ultimately removed this source of meaning in old age, since a culture that denies death as an integral part of life, and at the same time associates old age with death, must also deny that old age is an integral part of life.[5] This scenario did not fully unfold until the twentieth century, when the compromises of sentimentalism gave way to the hubris of scientific rationality. Between 1850 and 1910, the ideal of "civilized" aging forestalled the de-meaning of later life.

Writers of mid-century advice gave up considerable ground before they began. Lydia Sigourney (1791–1865), for example, sought to convince readers of *Past Meridian* (1856) that the "P.M.'s," whose "faces [turned] toward the setting sun" were "not utterly cyphers."[6] An advertisement in Connecticut's *Norwich Courier* approvingly noted that Sigourney attempted "to recall, if possible, those attributes of worth and true dignity, which in times past, compelled reverence and commanded influence for life in its decline."[7]

In her *Letters to Mothers* (1838), Sigourney had angrily noted the "diminution of respect" in "the treatment of the aged."[8] By 1856, she had abandoned the old ideal of veneration, instead urging her older readers to try to understand why "people are tired of us." In a democratic republic, the desire for equality was "neither peculiar nor reprehensible. . . . In an age when all

---

[3] Irving Rosow, *Socialization to Old Age* (Berkeley: University of California, 1974), chaps. 2–7.
[4] David Hackett Fischer, *Growing Old In America*, expanded ed. (New York: Oxford University Press, 1978), 29–32.
[5] On the "dying of death," see James J. Farrell, *Inventing the American Way of Death* (Philadelphia: Temple University Press, 1980), chap. 3.
[6] Lydia H. Sigourney, *Past Meridian* (New York: D. Appleton, 1856), iii, 10.
[7] Sigourney, *Past Meridian* (see n. 6), 348.
[8] Lydia H. Sigourney, *Letters to Mothers* (Hartford, Conn.: Hudson and Skinner, 1838), 185.

Figure 28. Portrait of Mrs. Lydia Huntly Sigourney (1791–1865), a watercolor-on-ivory miniature by Peter Kramer (1867). (Mead Art Museum, Amherst College. Gift of Judge and Mrs. Daniel Beecher [1955.163].)

slow movements are unpopular, speed in departure may possibly be counted among the graces . . . ."[9]

The popular magazine writer Nathaniel Willis took this logic one step farther. Because America was such a young and unsettled country, it was understandable that the aged constituted the "neglected portion of the great American family." But this was only a temporary and "unconscious" fault. Soon, he predicted, a maturing American culture would give "Old Age its preeminence. . . . The best armchair, by the fireside, the privileged room, with its warmest curtains and freshest flowers, the preference and first place in all groups and scenes in which Age can mingle – such is the proper frame and setting for this priceless picture in a home."[10]

The strongest response to America's preference for youth came from the Reverend J. B. Wentworth. Wentworth's essay "The Glories of Old Age,"

[9] Sigourney, *Past Meridian* (see n. 6), 24–25.
[10] Quoted by Sigourney, *Past Meridian* (see n. 6), 267–68.

published in S. G. Lathrop's *Fifty Years and Beyond: Or Gathered Gems for the Aged* (1881), criticized preachers and lyceum lecturers for presenting "the beau ideal of manhood" not as "the grave and reverend sire, with flowing beard and locks tinged with grey," but as "the stripling lover, with tender down upon his chin, and the mingled look of hope and passion gleaming from his eye." Wentworth rightly noted that lectures and sermons on the "model young man" left the impression that later life was simply "a dreary waste, unproductive and cheerless, characterized chiefly by rheumatism, imbecility, and decay."[11]

Aging manuals after 1850 betray an increasingly defensive tone. Whereas John Stanford had even-handedly portrayed old age as an "equal state of life," with its fogs and storms as well as its triumphs, later writers more often felt compelled (like contemporary gerontologists) to avoid the "negative" and emphasize the "positive" aspects of aging and old age. Cora Nourse, for example, argued that "there is nothing peculiar and essential to old age which we need to deprecate."[12] S. G. Lathrop claimed to see "no reason why the period of life at 'Fifty and Beyond' may not be rich in usefulness and abundant in its comforts and joys."[13] Similarly, when Margaret White published her anthology *After Noontide* (1888), she presented "a cheerful view of the afternoon of life, by bringing forth its pleasures, possibilities, and hopes."

Hoping to prevent older men from internalizing a sense of obsolescence, Margaret White, Lydia Sigourney, and Lydia Maria Child all quoted a passage from Mountford's *Euthanasy* (1848): "Useless, do you say you are? You are of *great* use. You really are. How are you useful? By being a man that is old. Your old age is a public good." Mountford tried to reassure old men that each positive interaction with a young person was valuable: "fellow-feeling with you ripens his soul for him."[14]

A defense of old age more popular than the mere affirmation of its existence was the recitation of its accomplishments. Emerson, Cora Nourse, John Hall, Child, Sigourney, and Wentworth all indulged this strategy.[15] They invariably listed older male (and occasionally female) artists, philosophers, writers, military men, scientists, and statesmen as evidence of the social

[11] J. B. Wentworth, "The Glories of Old Age," in S. G. Lathrop, *Fifty Years and Beyond; Or Gathered Gems for the Aged* (New York: F. H. Revell, 1881), 109.
[12] Cora S. Nourse, *Sunset Hours of Life* (New York: American Tract Society, 1875), 165–66.
[13] Wentworth, "Glories of Old Age" (see n. 11), 113.
[14] Margaret E. White, ed., *After Noontide* (Boston: Houghton Mifflin, 1888); Sigourney, *Past Meridian* (see n. 6), 138; Lydia Maria Child, *Looking Toward Sunset*, 4th ed. (Boston: Ticknor & Fields, 1866), 148.
[15] Ralph Waldo Emerson, "Old Age," *Atlantic Monthly* 9 (January 1862): 321; Nourse, *Sunset Hours* (see n. 12), 15; John Hall, "Some Noble Lives," in *Light at Eventide: A Book of Support and Comfort for the Aged*, ed. John S. Holme (New York: Harper Bros., 1871), 170ff.; Child, *Looking Toward Sunset* (see n. 14), 169; Sigourney, *Past Meridian* (see n. 6), 120; Wentworth, "Glories of Old Age" (see n. 11), 120ff.

value of old age. The most common names in this old-age hall of fame were Socrates, Plato, Bacon, Hobbes, Kant, Reid, Coke, Montesquieu, Copernicus, Cuvier, Humboldt, Franklin, Michelangelo, Saint Paul, Washington, Jefferson, and Adams.

If advice manuals conceded much to what Emerson called the "cynical creed of the market," they did not lack strategic reasons.[16] By loudly deploring the "diminution of respect" for age and the "unsightly irreverence" of the "crowding generation," they invoked nostalgia for the authority and security of earlier generations, transferring it onto a sentimental image of old age.[17] The power of this appeal in no way depended on realistic portraits of the democratic present or the patriarchal past. Rather, it successfully manipulated feelings of guilt and the need for reparation[18] in a society that increasingly freed men and women from physical parental presence while leaving them powerfully shaped by internalized parental influence.

The figure of the patriarch possessed a strong appeal in sentimental Victorian literature. In Sigourney's *The Young Lady's Offering* (1847), for example, the patriarch is like a totem set up to be worshipped in place of the deposed father. "He is the ancestor comfortably stowed away in the rocking chair, the male softened by the kindly touch of time."[19] In *Past Meridian*, one of Sigourney's "distinguished specimen[s]" reminds us that sentimentalism spread its mist over mothers and grandmothers too: "My earliest perceptions of the beautiful and holy were entwined with silver hairs, and I bless God that the fourteen first years of life were nurtured under their serene shadow."[20]

Advice manuals between 1850 and 1890 generally utilized sentimentalism to sanction their vision of ideal old age. Theodore Parker's idealizations of "Grandfather's Reverie" and "Aunt Kindly" found their way into several volumes. Lydia Maria Child, whose *Looking Toward Sunset* exhausted eighteen editions between 1864 and 1887, capitalized masterfully on sentimental portraits of old age. From the *Christian Examiner*, she lovingly quoted the story of "Old Uncle Tommy," who resembled Wordsworth's "The Old Cumberland Beggar." Old Uncle Tommy was beyond the storm and fierce strife of life's morning. His "clear blue eye" shone with the "undying light of immortality." Even though Tommy was old, poor, and ignorant, his "soul

---

[16] Emerson, "Old Age" (see n. 15), 320.

[17] On sentimentalism, I have been influenced by George B. Forgie, *Patricide in the House Divided* (New York: Norton, 1979); Ann Douglas, *The Feminization of American Culture* (New York: Avon, 1977); and Karen Haltunen, *Confidence Men and Painted Women: A Study of Middle-Class Culture in America, 1830–1870* (New Haven, Conn.: Yale University Press, 1982).

[18] See Melanie Klein and Joan Riviere, eds., *Love, Hate and Reparation* (New York: Norton, 1964).

[19] These are the words of Douglas, *Feminization* (see n. 17), 237. The figure of the patriarch also recurs in Lydia H. Sigourney's *Sketches* (Philadelphia: Kay and Biddle, 1834), and her *Water-Drops* (New York: R. Carter, 1848).

[20] Sigourney, *Past Meridian* (see n. 6), 52–53.

had attained a noble stature; there was a majesty about him which no mere earthly rank can impart."[21] Child also cited the "true story" of "old Aunty," "a worthy old woman, who sat in Washington Park, behind a table covered with apples and nuts," in order to feed and clothe her adopted orphans living in a New York boarding house.[22]

Like the Romantic evangelicals, aging advisers often portrayed the "passive virtues" of powerless old age. "Gray Hairs! Are they not associated in the mind with all that is tender and revered?" asked Cora Nourse. Bernard Barton's poem, "Beauty of Old Age," similarly eulogized "round benevolent old age."[23] Sigourney's poem "Mourning for Age" grieved for an aged father's "meek and helpless years" and for "wisdom's crown, so meekly worn."[24] Even J. B. Wentworth, who argued for the power and "Glories of Old Age," pictured the very old, whose "bent forms seem rather to be bowed down under that pressure of the sheaves of their wisdom and goodness than under the weight of their years and physical decrepitude."[25]

Whereas Stanford had argued that God reserved the most severe storms for the winter of life, sentimental writers preferred a different season. "Old age is the autumn of life, the time of ripeness," asserted Cora Nourse. "More than any other season, it should bear the stamp of perfectness."[26] Autumn, like evening, was a quiet, restful period – far from the crowded busyness of the summer day. "Rest weary soul!" wrote one anonymous poet. "Like a tired child upon its mother's breast, Rest, sweetly rest!"[27]

"CIVILIZED" OLD AGE

Alongside the Victorian domestication of death, and the cults of domesticity, true womanhood, and childhood innocence, sentimentalized old age took its rightful place. Yet we must not be misled by this popular image, which appealed to feelings of nostalgia, guilt, and the wish for security. Sentimentalism covered a multitude of sins: even as it softened the decline of veneration and justified the acceleration of generational displacement in the marketplace, sentimentalism provided a cloudlike sanction that helped to preserve important ideals, goals, and conventions of aging. Behind the mist

---

[21] Child, *Looking Toward Sunset* (see n. 14), 365–66; see also Child's version of J. P. Richter's "The Old Pastor and His Son" in *Looking Toward Sunset*, 441–53.

[22] Child, *Looking Toward Sunset* (see n. 14), 240–41.

[23] Bernard Barton, "Beauty of Old Age," in Holme, *Light at Eventide* (see n. 15), 305.

[24] Lydia H. Sigourney, "Mourning for Age," *Godey's Lady's Book* (January 1844): 25.

[25] Wentworth, "Glories of Old Age" (see n. 11), 135.

[26] Nourse, *Sunset Hours* (see n. 12), 7.

[27] Nourse, *Sunset Hours* (see n. 12), 244–45; see also Anonymous, "Too Old to be Useful," in *Nearing Home*, ed. William E. Schenk (Philadelphia: Presbyterian Board of Publications, 1868), 345; and A. K. H. Boyd, "At Evening Time It Shall be Light," in Holme, *Light at Eventide* (see n. 15), 24–25.

stood a compelling ideal of "civilized" old age – an ideal that often diverged from its sentimental legitimation.

We have seen how perfectionist and Romantic religious sermons created a bifurcated image of later life, drawing a thick black line between virtuous health and sinful decay. Addressing a wide range of age groups, especially young people, ministers held out the carrot of healthful, independent old age, and waved the stick of senile decay and dependence as incentives to proper conduct. Advice manuals, on the other hand, were addressed specifically to and often written by older people, usually women. Encouraged by proximity and self-interest to adopt a more integrated approach, these manuals found it more difficult to maintain that "good" people enjoyed a good old age, while "bad" people suffered a premature or miserable old age. As the crown of a lifetime's virtuous effort, "civilized" old age did not always live up to its billing.

Therefore, self-help manuals often made room for different aspects of "civilized" old age, which might yield a more integrated and varied experience. These fell into two basic categories: (1) the maintenance of health, character, usefulness, and activity as long as possible; and (2) the deepening of one's religious faith and spiritual life to offset physical and social losses. A minority of writers included the life review in this second category, instructing their readers to engage in retrospective and prospective reflections in order to reconcile themselves to the past and to reach hopefully into the future. Advice manuals did not correlate these different dimensions with specific chronological ages. Although writers assumed that men should begin "looking toward sunset" during their late forties and expect the darkness of evening at seventy, they left their readers to judge for themselves when a particular category of advice had become appropriate.

The first dimension of "civilized" old age was by far the most prominent. Writers generally preferred that older people follow the example of Grandfather's Clock, which kept on ticking perfectly until "the old man died" at ninety. The enormous popularity of Henry Clay Work's song, which sold 800,000 copies when first published in 1876, testifies to this ideal. Grandfather loved his clock since it displayed more punctuality and cheerfulness than anyone he could possibly hire. The clock followed Grandfather through the different stages of his life – never wasting time, always cheerful. "And its hands never hung by its side; But it stopp'd short, never to go again, when the old man died."[28]

Whereas John Stanford had urged gratitude for God's saving mercy and resignation to the inevitable pain and infirmity of old age, his successors viewed healthy, productive independence as the product of virtue. This

---

[28] See Bertram G. Work, ed., *Songs of Henry Clay Work* (1876; reprint, New York: Da Capo, 1974), preface, 178–80.

important corollary of a life devoted to accumulation proved more problematic for men than for women as the nineteenth century wore on. And the industrial working class, of course, possessed neither the economic autonomy nor the average longevity to fulfill this middle-class ideal. Nevertheless, advisers most often argued that longevity and cheerful self-reliance, not decay and dependence, crowned the life of those who followed the Christian way. Instruction for healthful aging invariably turned on the benevolence of natural law, whose most popular exemplar was the sixteenth-century Italian nobleman Luigi Cornaro.

As a young man Cornaro had strayed into disorderly living and sensual pleasures – "Habits common to young men of his class."[29] In 1504, at the age of forty, Cornaro suffered a serious breakdown in health; doctors predicted that he would not live two more years. Against great odds, Cornaro transformed himself into a model of simplicity, temperance, and regular living – a perfect model of "civilized" old age. This nobleman-turned-bourgeois lived to write four "Discourses on the Temperate Life" (at ages eighty-three, eighty-six, ninety-one, and ninety-five) before dying peacefully at ninety-eight.[30]

Cornaro's example warmed the hearts of health reformers and other Victorian moralists. Cora Nourse recommended the laws of health to those "who would not in their declining years become a burden either to themselves or others," and "who would preserve a happy independence and a gracious cheerfulness of spirit."[31] Lydia Child argued that Cornaro illustrated the "physical laws of our being," and urged "every man" to "study his own constitution, and regulate food, drink, and other habits in conformity thereto." All advisers agreed on the importance of moderate exercise in open air, regular hours of eating and sleeping, avoidance of all excess, and abstention from alcohol, tobacco, coffee, and other stimulants.[32]

Not surprisingly, writers linked health in old age to the maintenance of proper character. Child advised her readers to "restrain anger, and fretfulness, and keep all malignant or sensual passions in constant check. Banish melancholy, and do everything to promote cheerfulness. All these things have great influence over bodily health."[33] Aging manuals generally portrayed "civilized" old age as the culmination of a lifetime of self-denial.[34] "Among

[29] Child, *Looking Toward Sunset* (see n. 14), 256.

[30] The National Union Catalogue lists thirty-eight American editions of *La Vita Sobria* published between 1797 and 1938.

[31] Nourse, *Sunset Hours* (see n. 12), 83–84; see also Anonymous, "Excitement and Short Life," in Lathrop, *Fifty Years* (see n. 11), 47.

[32] See, for example, Sigourney, "Air," in *Past Meridian* (see n. 6), 64ff.; Child, "Hints About Health," in *Looking Toward Sunset* (see n. 14), 429ff.; and the following essays in Lathrop's *Fifty Years* (see n. 11): Reverend Robert W. Patterson, "The Preservation of Mental Vigor in Advanced Life"; W. S. Davis, "The Hygiene of Old Age"; and Joseph R. Richardson, "Old Age and How to Meet It."

[33] Child, *Looking Toward Sunset* (see n. 14), 260.

[34] Wentworth, "Glories of Old Age" (see n. 13), 131–32.

the highest accomplishments of age, are its dispositions," argued Sigourney. "It should daily cultivate the spirit to admire what is beautiful, to love what is good. . . . As the sensual pleasures lose their hold, the character should become more sublimated."[35]

The "civilized" ideal of aging character did not include the biblical injunction that older people maintain a distant demeanor worthy of patriarchal authority.[36] Apparently the liberal vision of generational relations had eroded the grave, somber ideal of aged behavior. Rather than unfeeling sobriety, advisers urged benevolence, good works, and cheerfulness above all else. Robert Patterson typified this advice: "A sombre temper," he wrote, was like a cloud darkening one's mental life. Patterson recommended a sunny or cheerful spirit – "essential not only to the buoyant elasticity of the mind in youth and middle life, but especially to its protracted vigor in later years."[37]

This advice to submit cheerfully was not without its opponents. In 1851, Mrs. C. M. Kirkland noted that "Growing Old Gracefully" was becoming a topic of dispute. To some, traditional rules for acting one's age seemed unnecessary and offensive. Kirkland angrily criticized those "very dull people" who almost seemed to favor sumptuary laws proscribing certain colors, forms, or ornaments of dress after a certain age, and who would probably "prohibit laughing, . . . liveliness, and joining in youthful pleasures . . . after the same period."[38] She revolted against pressures to step aside in favor of youth and to put ourselves in the way of becoming repulsive and censorious.

Despite their repudiation of caste, Americans, according to Kirkland, had constructed "the least dignified and the most offensive" of all caste systems – one based on age. "It would seem as if the national youthfulness had expressed itself in the maxims of social life, making it, by a supreme law of fashion, un-American to be anything but young." Undaunted, and unwilling either to pose vainly as an "aged butterfly" or to be "cast on the stream of time like [a] dead garland after a festival," Kirkland hoped to transcend stereotyped dualistic images. "Sadness and sweetness," she wrote, were not irreconcilable. They could be integrated within thoughtful and

---

[35] Sigourney, *Past Meridian* (see n. 6), 124; see also Reverend W. X. Ninde, "Characteristics Which Adorn Old Age," in Lathrop, *Fifty Years* (see n. 11), 239ff.; Reverend Glen Wood, "Christian Men and Their Work at Fifty and Beyond," in Lathrop, *Fifty Years* (see n. 11), 83ff.; Anonymous, "Sympathy and Selfishness," in Schenk, *Nearing Home* (see n. 27), 87ff.

[36] After reading well over two hundred articles, essays, poems, and sketches in manuals written between 1850 and 1900, I found only one author repeating Saint Paul's injunction that aged men be "grave" as well as "sober, . . . temperate, sound in faith, in charity, in patience" (Titus 2:2). This was Cora Nourse, who imbued the duty of "gracious and gentle condescension" with strong overtones of sentimentalism.

[37] Patterson, "The Preservation of Mental Vigor in Advanced Life" (see n. 32), 77; see also Rev. Reuben Smith, "Old Age Anticipated," in Schenk, *Nearing Home* (see n. 27), 64ff.; and William S. Plumer, "To An Old Disciple," in Schenk, *Nearing Home* (see n. 27), 288ff.

[38] C. M. Kirkland, "Growing Old Gracefully," *The Evening Book* (New York: Scribner, 1851), 251.

loving relationships that enabled people to continue growing and adapting to life's challenges.[39]

Virtually all writers linked the preservation of health and character to "useful activity." With the decline of the household mode of production and the gradual removal of older men from the work force, the philosophy of "staying in harness" proved increasingly difficult to practice. By 1905, one author felt the need to subtitle his advice book "The Value of Longevity Illustrated by Practical Examples." Colonel Nicholas Smith, himself near seventy and in poor health, described more than 130 *Masters of Old Age*. "To remain active members of society and continue to do our share of life's work is a matter of vital concern to those of us who are classed as elderly people," he wrote. "Of course, it is not always easy to dismiss the thought that we are growing old." For Smith, the key issue was to "keep our bodies so pure and active, and so preserve the integrity of our mental powers" that men between fifty and ninety could participate "in the full tide of the world's activities."[40]

Female authors also advocated the active life as long as possible. Lydia Child insisted that the "happiest specimens of old age are those men and women who have been busy to the last."[41] Adopting a "use it or lose it" perspective on mental and physical decay, Child called for constant exercise of one's capabilities. Along with others, Sigourney protested the expectation that the aged put themselves "decently away into some dark corner."[42] Since household work and women's capacity to perform it generally persisted longer than men's ability to secure paid employment, Child argued that "women undoubtedly have the advantage of men." A rigid sexual division of labor that assigned women to "home" and men to "work" allowed continued usefulness for older women.[43] In the mid-twentieth century, however, such domestic "usefulness" became a distinct disadvantage since Social Security benefits were based on market wages.[44]

In *Over the Teacups*, eighty-year-old Oliver Wendell Holmes insightfully noted the advantages of older women: "Women find it easier than men to grow old in a becoming way," he wrote. Women were grateful for the attention they received and entered easily into the spirit of younger lives.

[39] Kirkland, *Evening Book* (see n. 38), 249–50, 257, 260.

[40] Nicholas Smith, *Masters of Old Age* (Milwaukee: The Young Churchman Co., 1905), 1–2; for later thoughts of a "master" of old age, see Frank Moody Mills, *The Notings of a Nonagenarian* (Boston, 1926).

[41] Child, *Looking Toward Sunset* (see n. 14), 109.

[42] Sigourney, *Past Meridian* (see n. 6), 114.

[43] Sigourney, *Past Meridian* (see n. 6), 19. In 1910 Harriet E. Paine referred to her octogenarian female friends who sat all day sewing in their armchairs. "Perhaps this is the last generation that will ever see such work done," wrote Paine. "Even the young women who learn to sew now are not forced to it so constantly that it becomes a second nature, and their hand will lose its cunning much sooner in consequence." See *Old People* (Boston: Houghton Mifflin, 1910), 37.

[44] See Jill Quadagno and Madonna H. Meyer, "Gender and Public Policy," *Generations* (summer 1990): 64–66.

"With old men it is different. They do not belong so much indoors as women do. They have no pretty little manual occupations. The old lady knits her stitches so long as her eye and fingers will let her. The old man smokes his pipe, but does not know what to do with his fingers, unless he plays upon some instrument, or has a mechanical turn which finds business for them."[45]

If useful norms increasingly eluded older men and patriarchal norms were no longer appropriate, manuals advised men to hold on to whatever resources they had. The Reverend William S. Plumer counseled men to "retain exclusive control" of enough property to avoid poverty. "A dependent old age may be unavoidable, and when it is, should be borne submissively. But it is a great trial. If men will treat you well without property, they will also if you have your own means. The reverse is not *always* true."[46] Archibald Alexander similarly advised, "Make not yourselves dependent on the most affectionate and obedient children. They will be more affectionate and more respectful when you are not dependent."[47]

Lydia Child claimed that the best way to avoid sad feelings was to immerse oneself in some worthwhile activity. "If you are so unfortunate as to have nothing to do at home," exhorted Child, "then the moment you begin to feel a tendency to depression, start for the homes of others." Child urged men to saw and split wood for "some poor widow" and women to knit stockings, mend caps or bring flowers to an invalid.[48] An active feminist, abolitionist, writer, and reformer, Child spoke from experience.

In 1864, the year *Looking Toward Sunset* was published, the sixty-two-year-old woman left a partial list of her activities. That year, she "wrote 235 letters; read 28 books, made 25 needle books for freedwomen." She also "cooked 360 dinners and 362 breakfasts; swept the house 350 times," and omitted "innumerable jobs too small to be mentioned."[49] While working on the book, Child suffered from painful rheumatism and depression. Presumably, her spirits were lifted when the book sold 4,000 copies in the first few days and she received flattering letters from Whittier, Bryant, and Wendell Phillips.

Ten years later, when her husband died, Child ran up against the limits of her own advice – she had never shown an inclination to cultivate the rich inner life that some advisers advocated.[50] Without her husband to argue

[45] Oliver Wendell Holmes, *Over the Teacups* (Boston: Houghton Mifflin, 1891), 292–93.

[46] William Plumer, "To An Old Disciple," in Schenk, *Nearing Home* (see n. 27), 288.

[47] Archibald Alexander, "Reflections on Old Age," in Schenk, *Nearing Home* (see n. 27), 251–52.

[48] Child, *Looking Toward Sunset* (see n. 14), 169.

[49] Quoted in Kirk Jeffrys, "The Marital Career of Lydia Maria Child," *Feminist Studies* 2 (1975): 128, fn. 6.

[50] "Nothing is more healthy for the soul than to go out of ourselves and stay out of ourselves," wrote Child in *Looking Toward Sunset* (see n. 14), 176. "We thus avoid brooding over our own bodily pains, our mental deficiencies, or past moral shortcomings; . . . He who leads a true, active, and useful life has no time for such corrosive thoughts. All self-consciousness indicates disease."

Figure 29. Photograph of Lydia Child (ca. 1880). (American Antiquarian Society, Worcester, Mass.)

with and care for, or children to enjoy and symbolize personal continuity, Child's life became increasingly barren. "The future seems closed to me," she wrote Whittier, "but I am willing, just now, simply to wait. I greatly desire to be of some use in the world, during what remains to me of this existence, and I trust it will prove so."[51]

She stayed for a while with friends on Staten Island, but overly protective hosts virtually smothered her. Thereafter, she took up winter quarters in a Boston boardinghouse and spent her summers with a servant in her old home in Wayland, Massachusetts, until she died in 1889. Near the end of her life, she wrote a friend: "Here is my native Massachusetts, I feel like a hungry child lost in a dark wood. People are very kind to me, but I cannot banish the desolate feeling that I belong to nobody and nobody belongs to me."[52]

---

[51] Quoted in Helene G. Baer, *The Heart Is Like Heaven* (Philadelphia: University of Pennsylvania Press, 1964), 296.
[52] Quoted in Baer, *The Heart* (see n. 51), 303.

Writers like Child and Smith, who counseled unremitting activity and usefulness in later life – without advising people to develop compensations for the losses of aging – ultimately relied on the psychologically integrating effect of their moralizing. Even Nietzsche, the most relentless nineteenth-century critic of "civilized" morality, acknowledged the value of moral demands. "The essential thing in 'heaven and earth,' " he wrote in *Beyond Good and Evil*, "is apparently . . . that there should be long obedience in the same direction; there thereby results, and has always resulted in the long run, something which has made life worth living."[53]

SPIRITUAL ADVICE

The second category of advice – cultivating a rich inner life – complemented and addressed the limitations of the first. We have seen how, aided by popular prodigies of senescence, liberal capitalist values encouraged men to "master" old age rather than yield to it, to eliminate rather than explore the final stage of life. During the second half of the nineteenth century, the intellectual, emotional, spiritual, and religious sources of inner growth proved increasingly difficult to formulate. Nevertheless, a minority of writers – all operating within some variety of Christian belief – retained something of the Puritan view that old age was insupportable without religion.

"Those," wrote Amelia Barr in 1915, "who in their prime neither nourished their spiritual nature nor cultivated their understandings, must expect to sink into dotage as their unlovely old age approaches."[54] In "Sailing to Byzantium" (1928), Yeats made the same point:

> An aged man is but a paltry thing,
> A tattered coat upon a stick, unless
> Soul clap its hands and sing, and louder sing
> For every tatter in its mortal dress.[55]

The Reverend Reuben Smith's advice drew on the ancient metaphor of life's journey and on traditional Christian images of physical decline and spiritual growth. "You are now descending into the valley of declining years. That valley, we are persuaded, need not be dark if you but carry into it the lamp of true wisdom. There is what may properly be called, perhaps, the art of growing old."[56] The art of growing old required one not to deny that

---

[53] Quoted in Philip Rieff, *The Triumph of the Therapeutic* (New York: Harper & Row, 1966), 14.
[54] Amelia Barr, *Three-Score and Ten: A Book for the Aged* (New York: D. Appleton, 1915), 101–102.
[55] William Butler Yeats, "Sailing To Byzantium," in his *The Collected Poems* (New York: Macmillan, 1959), 191.
[56] Reuben Smith, "Old Age Anticipated," in Schenk, *Nearing Home* (see n. 27), 64.

"old age is an evil itself," but to submit to it and embrace the compensations promised in the Gospel.[57]

For Reuben and other evangelical advisers in this period, the art of growing old entailed piety, faith, and to some extent, a deepening spiritual life. Despite their optimism and investment in health, evangelicals did not place unlimited confidence in control of the physical body. The Victorian rendering of 2 Corinthians 4:16, "Though our outward man perish, yet the inward man is renewed day by day," merged sanctification with sublimation. "Unless we endeavour to *spiritualize* ourselves," wrote an anonymous author, "age *bodylizes* us more and more, and the older we grow the more we are imbruted and debased."[58] Similarly, John Gosman claimed that piety was "exempt from the decays of age";[59] and James Alexander claimed that "Christian confidence and hope confer a strength which is perfectly compatible with all . . . bodily weakness, decay, and pain."[60]

Others operated within the framework of liberal religion. Like Harriet E. Paine, they generally spoke from experience. "Old age is a large phrase," wrote Paine in her poignant and insightful *Old People* (1910). "Most people know something of its reality at fifty. . . . When the descent of life is gradual, it is not usually painful, and the pilgrim lies down to rest at the foot almost as one might go to sleep."[61]

Not so blessed, Miss Paine suffered prematurely from deafness, dim vision, and general infirmity before she died at sixty-four in 1909. "Nature had settled it that she should move perpetually in the mask of an age greater than her own," wrote one of her students at the Robinson Female Seminary. Harriet Paine amply appreciated the second category of instructions for achieving a "civilized" old age. As she had reason to know, the failures of body demanded deepening one's powers of mind: Gradual decline of the senses plunged older people into "worlds not realized" – worlds containing unexplored treasures for those who knew how to draw them out.[62]

Paine, however, was not immune from pressures to "master" old age. A retired woman who had worked all her life as a teacher, she wrote anxiously about the fate of those who outlived their ability to earn a living. Though she argued that "we must do our very best to guard against" dependence in old age, Paine acknowledged the growing problem of old-age poverty and

[57] Smith, "Old Age Anticipated," in Schenk, *Nearing Home* (see n. 27), 66; see also Archibald Alexander, "How to Die Safely," in Schenk, *Nearing Home* (see n. 27), 355–63.
[58] "Words in Season," in Schenk, *Nearing Home* (see n. 27), 319–20.
[59] John Gosman, "Piety Exempt From the Decays of Age," in Schenk, *Nearing Home* (see n. 27), 162.
[60] James Alexander, "Youth Renewed in Age," in Schenk, *Nearing Home* (see n. 27), 15–16; Archibald Alexander, "Councils to the Aged," in Schenk, *Nearing Home* (see n. 27), 115ff.; and Jacqueline Pascal, "Sanctification a Work of Time," in Holme, *Light at Eventide* (see n. 15), 146ff.
[61] Harriet E. Paine, *Old People* (Boston: Houghton Mifflin, 1910), 171.
[62] Paine, *Old People* (see n. 62), chap. 11, "The Inner Life of the Old."

favored pension legislation for the indigent old. Physical infirmity and dependence, she argued, called for a new stage of discipline. "Most of us struggle hopelessly for a while, exhausting ourselves in vain, and forget that real courage demands that we conquer ourselves, and not that we conquer old age, who is simply our conductor to a larger life than that we know." Under the most trying circumstances, Paine spoke of the need for friendship, "the renewal of emotion," and spiritual growth. In 1908, she wrote a friend that she had "been reviewing all the fine poetry I ever learned, to be prepared against days of greater dimness."[63]

More fortunate than Harriet Paine was the effervescent Amelia Barr, who wrote at eighty-four: "I wish to feel alive to the last moment, to preserve my vigor of mind and ready sympathy in all that happens. . . . " Such a "supple, joyous spirit," according to Barr, was "possible to those who have lived among things unseen, as well as things seen, who have kept every one of the strings of Life's harp in practice, and whose wellsprings of love and imagination lie too deep for the frost of Age to touch."[64]

Barr's observations at the Fifth Avenue Hotel in New York during the first decade of the twentieth century convinced her that the "wellsprings of love and imagination" in old men often dried up. "There is a painful forlornness about old men," she wrote. "They are with us but not of us, they are lonely with the young, they can form no new friendships, and they are willing to be gone." Wealthy, retired men seemed to "grow weary and bewildered in a new life that soon loses all interest for them. . . . [T]hey lose the grip of both lives and drift like a stray leaf on some idle backwater of life."[65]

Aging manuals often contained poetic variations on the theme of life as a spiritual pilgrimage. Holmes, Longfellow, Whittier, and Bryant were the most prominent of those who drew on personal encounters with their aging selves. Holmes, who in his late forties created a charming dialogue in which the "Professor" resists the encroachments of "Old Age," also wrote his best poetry in this period. In the last two stanzas of "The Chambered Nautilus" (1858), he wrote:

> Build thee more stately mansions, O my soul,
> As the swift seasons roll!
> Leave thy low-vaulted past!
> Let each new temple, nobler than the last,
> Shut thee from heaven with a dome more vast,
> Till thou at length art free,
> Leaving thine outgrown shell by life's unresting sea![66]

[63] Paine, *Old People* (see n. 62), 128–31, 6, xxvii.
[64] Barr, *Three-Score and Ten* (see n. 54), 2.
[65] Barr, *Three-Score and Ten* (see n. 54), 111–12.
[66] "The Professor's Paper," on old age, and "The Chambered Nautilus" both appeared in Oliver

Longfellow's poetry, especially "Morituri Salutamus," written for the fiftieth anniversary of his graduation from Bowdoin College, appeared in several advice books:

> Whatever poet, orator, or sage
> May say of it, old age is still old age.
> It is the waning, not the crescent moon;
> The dusk of evening, not the blaze of noon;
> . . . .
> What then? Shall we sit idly down and say
> The night hath come; it is no longer day?
> . . . .
> Something remains for us to do or dare;
> Even the oldest tree some fruit may bear;
> . . . .
> For age is opportunity no less
> Than youth itself, though in another dress,
> And as the evening twilight fades away
> The sky is filled with stars, invisible by day.

While some poets, like Holmes and Longfellow, urged new explorations, others – Bryant and Whittier, for example – envisioned a peaceful completion. Whittier, whose poem "My Psalm" found a prominent place in *Looking Toward Sunset*, suggested that old age was the end of the journey:

> I break my pilgrim staff, – I lay
> Aside the toiling oar;
> the angel sought so far away I welcome at my door.[67]

The most important element in advice to cultivate one's spiritual life was belief in the immortality of the soul.[68] Emerson expressed it this way: "I have heard that whenever the name of man is spoken, the doctrine of immortality is announced; it cleaves to his constitution. The mode of it baffles our wit, and no whisper comes to us from the other side."[69] In a more traditional evangelical formulation, William Adams explained how the "Gospel of our Redeemer" taught people how to live and die with cheerfulness. "It continually presents, what nothing else ever did or can, the sure method by which one may always, even to the very last day of life, be confident *that the best part of existence is yet to come.*"[70]

Some advisers preached an Arminian form of the Puritan search for signs of election. Interestingly, none of the six female writers studied here urged

---

Wendell Holmes, *The Autocrat of the Breakfast Table*, first published in 1858. In the edition I have used (London: Macmillan, 1903), see chap. 7, 152–80 and 98–99.

[67] Child, *Looking Toward Sunset* (see n. 14), 275.

[68] See George Frisbie Hoar, *Old Age and Immortality* (Worcester, Mass.: C. Hamilton, 1893).

[69] Emerson, "Old Age" (see n. 15), 336.

[70] William Adams, "Retrospect and Prospect," in Holme, *Light at Eventide* (see n. 15), 217.

Figure 30. Frontispiece from *The Voyage of Life: A Journey from the Cradle to the Grave*, compiled by S. L. Louis. (Chicago: J. A. Ruth, 1879.)

their readers to undertake a "review of life." Though they all viewed "the completion of our pilgrimage" as a passage to another world, Sigourney, Child, Nourse, White, Paine, and Barr advised a kind of passive waiting rather than an active introspection. "The waiting graces are beautiful," wrote Sigourney. "They imply readiness. . . . Let us have oil in our lamps, and cherish every gentle and holy affection."[71]

Several writers presented a sentimentalized life review.[72] Unlike Stanford,

---

[71] Sigourney, *Past Meridian* (see n. 6), 343; see also Barr, *Three-Score and Ten* (see n. 54), 240.

[72] See, for example, the following essays in Schenk, *Nearing Home* (see n. 27): Anonymous, "The Review of Life," 13–33; John Cosman, "Piety Exempt from the Decays of Age," 164; and Archibald

who had seen the review of life developing from years of spiritual renewal amidst life's most severe trials, these men began with the notion that "old age is the resting place in the journey of life."[73] Preparation for old age had become synonymous with preparation for death; there was no more serious spiritual work to be done.

The basic mechanism, however, remained essentially the same: Reviewing one's life involved both retrospection and anticipation in search of an inner reorganization. As William Adams put it, "Mature age is a hill from which one may look in opposite directions – backward and forward."[74] Looking backward over the "many windings of [one's] pathway through the world," through sin, sorrow, and confusion, an aged Christian's recollections brought humility, acceptance, renunciation. Looking ahead, the "weary pilgrim love[d] to let his imagination dwell upon the many mansions of his Father's house, where a place is being prepared for him."[75]

Perhaps the most interesting commentary on the psychic reintegrations of the life review appeared in Holmes's *Over the Teacups*. "We must not make too much of . . . exceptional cases of prolonged activity," he wrote. "[T]he great privilege of old age [is] getting rid of responsibilities." Freed from the harness, an old man could enjoy more intimate relations with "his Maker." The "faded frescos on the walls of memory" emerged more clearly and brightly than in earlier years. Unlike his expansive, forward-looking vision in "The Chambered Nautilus" (1857–58), the chambers of eighty-year-old Holmes's consciousness centered on memory: "In the midst of the *misery*, as many would call it, of extreme old age, there is often a divine consolation in recalling the happy moments and days and years of times long past."

Moreover, Holmes argued that the mind in deep old age did not expand progressively like "The Chambered Nautilus," leaving its past behind. Rather, mentation consisted of recollecting, repeating, and reweaving the material of a lifetime. Holmes compared consciousness to the layers of sand and pebbles on a beach. Pebbled thoughts were constantly washing up against one another, smoothing and shaping each other by long attrition. "When we think we are thinking, we are for the most part only listening to the sound of attrition between these inert elements of our intelligence."[76]

Despite the fragility of traditions emphasizing the achievement of a spiritual wisdom and the shrinking of the life review to encompass a generally tranquilized, sleepy old age and a guaranteed passage to eternal life, advice literature kept alive a mode of experience seriously endangered by an in-

Alexander, "Councils to the Aged," 115ff. See also these essays in Holme, *Light at Eventide* (see n. 15): C. J. Vaughn, "The Close of Life," 209ff; William Adams, "Retrospect and Prospect," 214ff; and James Bean, "Review of Life," 257ff.

[73] Anonymous, "The Review of Life," in Schenk, *Nearing Home* (see n. 27), 14, 16.
[74] William Adams, "Retrospect and Prospect," in Holme, *Light at Eventide* (see n. 27), 10.
[75] Anonymous, "The Review of Life," in Schenk, *Nearing Home* (see n. 27), 24.
[76] Holmes, *Teacups* (see n. 45), 35, 45, 10–11.

creasingly activist, instrumental, and scientific culture. The old Protestant vision of life as a voyage, with its emphasis on introspection, on receiving experience as well as actively molding it, on reconciling past and future in the present, on yielding one's life up to its Maker, provided an inwardly viable ideal of continuity and meaning. During the late nineteenth century, however, the accelerating pace of scientific discovery and of capitalist production further weakened this vision – and with it the incentives to grow old at all.

PART 3

Science and the ideal of normal aging

8

The aging of "civilized" morality: the fixed period versus prolongevity, 1870–1925

The pluck of the Anglo-Saxon is shown as much on the sick-bed as in Wall Street or on the battlefield. . . . The great men of history are . . . superior. . . . They live, for the same reason that they become famous. They obtain fame because they will not be obscure; they live because they will not die.

George Miller Beard

The human personality, incarnate, living on from century to century, conserving science, able to renew itself and resist all the vulgar agencies of decay and death, is the ideal human being, not a chain of parents and children.

Charles Asbury Stephens

If it be true that our precocious and unhappy old age is due to the poisoning of the tissues, . . . it is clear that agents which arrest intestinal putrefaction must at the same time postpone and ameliorate old age.

Elie Metchnikoff

Until the 1830s, American conceptions of aging were primarily shaped by the late Calvinist ideal, which paradoxically cherished health and strength yet also accepted decay and dependence on God. Aging was understood primarily as an ambiguous, uncertain, and difficult territory to be traversed on the journey of life. Elements of this ideal persisted in popular Protestant culture throughout the entire nineteenth century. During this same period, however, a new ideal rose to prominence, reflecting the Victorian impulse "to contain the life experiences of the individual from birth to death by isolating them as science."[1]

In constructing a "civilized" ideal of aging, antebellum ministers, reformers, physicians, and popular writers rejected the appreciation for human limits, the tension and contingency inherent in the orthodox view of life's journey. Their attempt to rationalize aging created a culturally powerful dichotomy that brooked neither ambiguity nor ambivalence. As we have seen, Victorian moralists split the last stage of life into two apparently

---

[1] Burton Bledstein, *The Culture of Professionalism* (New York: Norton, 1977), 55.

separate, controllable parts: the "good" old age of virtue, health, self-reliance, natural death, and salvation; and the "bad" old age of sin, disease, dependency, premature death, and damnation.

This bifurcation of aging and old age set up a historical dynamic in which popular perceptions would swing from one pole to the other. During the middle third of the nineteenth century, the positive pole held sway, its limitations less visible than its liberating qualities. The "good" old age of healthy self-reliance held a special attraction for actual or aspiring members of the entrepreneurial middle class, easing acute awareness of loss and failure, soothing anxiety about social and bodily decline. As long as old age remained a marginal social issue and sentimentalism provided emotional reparation, competition between these poles was largely suppressed. In the 1870s, however, the pendulum began to return. This chapter follows its movement toward the negative pole, reformulated by writers who referred to old age as the end point or *fixed period* of useful life.

When fixed-period theorists, pursuing a new ethic of efficiency, cooperation, and professional authority, envisioned old age as an unacceptable obstacle to progress, the antebellum denial of decline, dependency, and contingency returned with a vengeance. The "civilized" ideal, however, was far from dead; counterattacking with the movement for prolongevity, Victorian moralists struggled to repudiate the fixed-period doctrine and to reestablish the "good" old age of virtue, health, and self-reliance. Though seemingly contradictory, the fixed-period doctrine and the enthusiasm for prolongevity were both rooted in a single, bifurcated vision of aging. Both reinforced a way of thinking that would soon receive the scientific imprimatur of the "normal" (or physiological) and the "pathological."

THE FIXED PERIOD: BEARD, TROLLOPE, AND OSLER

During the last quarter of the nineteenth century, corporate,[2] state, and professional management of health began to replace individual hygiene and self-help as the principal means of accumulating "physical capital." Despite continued urban conditions of squalor and premature mortality, physicians and public health officials insisted that the old rewards of "civilized" morality were now within reach. Sanitary science, claimed Stephen Smith in his presidential address to the first annual American Public Health Association meetings in 1873, "revealed the stupendous fact that man is born to health

[2] Life insurance companies, for whom the relationship between dividends and longevity was more than a metaphor, devoted considerable attention to prolonging life and to perfecting the life table. See, for example, J. V. C. Smith and John H. Griscom, *The Two Prize Essays on the Physical Indications of Longevity, Written For The American Popular Life Insurance Company* (New York: American Popular Life Insurance Co., 1869).

and longevity (ca. 100 years), that disease is abnormal, . . . that death, except from old age, is accidental, and that both are preventable by human agencies."[3]

During the next fifty years, public sanitation did indeed contribute to rapidly falling infant mortality rates and significant increases in life expectancy at birth.[4] At the same time, however, the middle-class vision of self-reliant health and longevity foundered on the rocks of old age. By the end of the century, a cluster of interrelated developments – rapid demographic and sociogenic aging of urban immigrants,[5] perceptions of an accumulating scrap heap of older industrial workers,[6] the recognition of old age as a clinically distinct period of life,[7] and the early stages of an epidemiologic transition from infectious to degenerative diseases[8] – all tended to shatter the dreams of a "good" old age.

By promising to abolish pain and suffering in old age, "civilized" morality had essentially repressed decay and dependence, guaranteeing their return in heightened form. The following section will trace this return as it appeared after 1870 in the fixed-period doctrine. Whereas decline in old age had been ideologically and psychologically repugnant to the independent middle class of the antebellum period, the reconstructed professional and corporate middle class of the late nineteenth century found ample reason to acknowledge, and even exaggerate, the decays of nature.

The year after Stephen Smith urged public health professionals to rekindle the old struggle for national health and longevity, thirty-four-year-old George Miller Beard, a New York physician, began publicizing less sanguine views. In three lectures ("The Longevity of Brain Workers," "Legal Responsibility in Old Age," and "On the Decline of the Moral Faculties in Old Age"), later incorporated into his well-known *American Nervousness* (1881), Beard repudiated virtually all the popular health reform ideas about

---

[3] Stephen Smith, "On the Limitations and Modifying Conditions of Human Longevity, the Basis of Sanitary Work," *American Public Health Association Papers* 1 (New York: APHA, 1875), 2. Smith himself died at the age of ninety-nine; his final request to the APHA, adopted in 1922, was: "To send messengers of hope in a new scientific standard of long life." Quoted by Irving Fisher, "Lengthening of Human Life in Retrospect and Prospect," *American Journal of Public Health* 17 (January 1927): 1.

[4] See Louis I. Dublin, A. J. Lotka, and M. Spiegelman, eds., *Length of Life: A Study of the Life Tables* (New York: Ronald Press, 1949), chaps. 2, 3.

[5] Older immigrants constituted 30 percent of those over sixty-five in 1900 and turned up in increasing numbers in almshouses between 1880 and 1920. See U. S. Bureau of the Census, *Paupers in Almshouses* (Washington, D.C.: Government Printing Office, 1923).

[6] See Lee Welling Squier, *Old Age Dependency in the United States* (New York: Macmillan, 1912); and Isaac M. Rubinow, "The Old Man's Problem in Industry," in *Social Insurance* (New York: Holt, 1916), 301–17.

[7] Lilluth Kunkel, "American Medical Ideas About Old Age, 1793–1920," unpublished paper, Department of History, University of Wisconsin, 1979; and Carole Haber, *Beyond Sixty-Five: The Dilemma of Old Age in America's Past* (New York: Cambridge University Press, 1983), chaps. 3, 4.

[8] Abdel R. Omran, "The Epidemiologic Transition," *Milbank Memorial Quarterly* 49 (October 1971): 509–38.

Figure 31. Portrait of George Miller Beard. (George Miller Beard Papers, Manuscripts and Archives, Yale University Library.)

longevity and old age. No longing for patriarchal authority, no dreams of perfect health and universal self-reliance intrude into the professional world view of this New England son. Scientific investigation now revealed old age as an inevitable casualty in the great "race of life"; medical expertise would provide the appropriate standards of care. A new class consciousness pervades Beard's work, reflecting his membership in a growing professional middle class and its increasing social distance from a largely immigrant working class. As we will see, Beard's work foreshadows the progressive alliance between American medicine and industrial capitalist efficiency.

While a medical student at Yale, Beard collected material from the biographies of "nearly all the greatest names in history."[9] He computed the mean age at which these men and women accomplished their most original and creative work, followed their output over time, and derived the "law of the relation of age to work." Graphed with age on one axis and output on the other, the curve of Beard's law rose to a peak at age forty and declined sharply and continuously thereafter.[10] The shape of Beard's graph parallels the basic iconographic pattern of the ages of life – except that the peak of life has been reduced from fifty to forty, and the decline is both steeper and longer. The early modern imagery of animals, seasons, salvation, damnation,

[9] George Miller Beard, *Legal Responsibility in Old Age* (New York: Russells, 1874), 5.
[10] George Miller Beard, *American Nervousness* (New York: Putnam, 1881), 223.

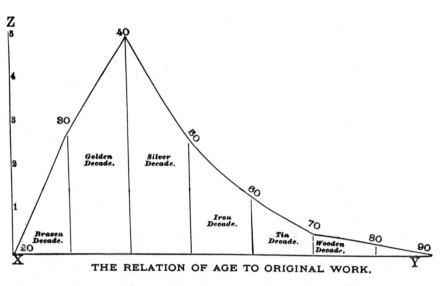

Figure 32. Illustration from *American Nervousness: Its Causes and Consequences*, by George M. Beard (New York: Putnam, 1881).

and eternity has disappeared, leaving the rise and fall of productive capacities as the sole criterion of meaning and value.

Beard announced that "seventy percent of the work of the world is done before forty-five, and eighty percent before fifty." Echoing the decline and degeneration of Hesiod's ages of the world, he labeled the six decades between twenty and eighty according to their level of productivity: "brazen," "golden," "silver," "iron," "tin," and (last and least) the "wooden" decade. Beard applied his concern for maximum efficiency to the production of children as well: "It should be noted also," he wrote, that in women, "the procreative function ceases between forty and fifty, just the time when physical and mental powers begin to decline, as though nature had foreseen this law and provided that the world should not be peopled by those whose powers had fallen from their maximum."[11]

It apparently pleased the young and ambitious Beard to find that great philosophers, religious leaders, statesmen, scientists, divines, generals, lawyers, physicians, artists, and writers had produced their most original work by the age of forty. His data implied that although old men still controlled "nearly all the wealth and prestige of the world," they did not really merit such power. Carrying the attack on arbitrary power to a new level, Beard lambasted "undue reverence" for age; it was a "barbarian folly," he argued, to believe that men were capable of governing others only when "their own

[11] Beard, *Legal Responsibility* (see n. 9), 7, 9.

165

brains have begun to degenerate, and the fires of youth have spent half their force." The "enormous stupidity and backwardness and red-tapeism of all departments of government everywhere" could be explained by the power of the aged.[12]

Beard complemented his statistics on age and work with a physiological view of aging that was far from rosy. Increased longevity might be a sign of progress, but its result – old age – seemed to be one of civilization's discontents. The curve of productivity simply mirrored the growth, maturity, and decay of the human organism as a whole; the "nervous, muscular, and osseous systems rise, remain, and fall together."[13]

Beard claimed that intellectual and moral decline was the rule in old age. Organic and functional changes in the brain caused the symptoms of querulousness, irritability, and avarice. Conservatism and cowardice rather than moral courage typified old age; happiness was a function of middle age. "The wind that blows on a hoary head never comes from a happy shore," he wrote, quoting Chateaubriand. Sounding like a secularized Cotton Mather, Beard noted that occasionally a man might avoid the general tendency of decay. A few fortunate individuals preserved their health, strength, reason, and moral courage; they "sailed into the harbor of old age freighted with well preserved treasures of virtue gathered during a voyage crowded with adventure, and difficulty, and peril."[14]

Unlike Graham or Alcott, Beard did not believe in natural death from old age. For him, death in old age was not a gentle cessation of unimpaired function, but a ten- to fifteen-year period of decline beginning with cerebral disease. Beard recommended plenty of sleep to conserve nerve force. Finally, however, dissolution and dependence were unavoidable. Since the moral and intellectual defects of old age were beyond individual control, Beard urged "especial kindness and charity for those in life's decline. . . . There should be at least as much charity for a tired brain as for a broken leg."[15]

As Beard anticipated, the view that physical, intellectual, and moral decline all commonly crowned a lifetime's effort did not sit well with contemporary opinion.[16] Popular health reform and "civilized" morality, rooted in the authority of the self-reliant individual, had resisted the notion of decay and dependence in old age. On the other hand, professional medicine and progressive social reform would soon find both scientific and ideological

[12] Beard, *Legal Responsibility* (see n. 9), 22; George Miller Beard, "On the Decline of the Moral Faculties in Old Age," a lecture to the Long Island Historical Society (n.p., n.d.), 3.

[13] Beard, *American Nervousness* (see n. 10), 249.

[14] Beard, *American Nervousness* (see n. 10), 252.

[15] Beard, "Moral Faculties in Old Age" (see n. 12), 4.

[16] In a private letter, Nathaniel I. Bowditch protested the "degrading tenor" of Beard's argument. *The Life and Correspondence of Henry I. Bowditch* (Boston: Houghton Mifflin, 1902), 2:302. For discussion in professional circles, see the editorial by S. W. Butler and D. G. Brinton, *Medical and Surgical Reporter* 29 (July 12, 1873): 30–32; and Beard's reply, *Medical and Surgical Reporter* 30 (April 4, 1874): 320.

reasons to minimize individual potency and emphasize decay and dependence in old age.[17] Beard's views would be commonplace (though not uncontested) by the turn of the century.

Popular health reformers, as we have seen, expressed a universal optimism about matters of health, sickness, and longevity. Any individual, regardless of social position, could achieve health and long life by following the laws of health. Using vital registration reports, Beard argued that the benefits of civilization redounded more to "brain-workers" than to "muscle-workers." Lawyers, clergymen, physicians, merchants, scientists, and literary men consistently outlived farmers, artisans, laborers, and industrial workers. Brain-workers lived and worked under better sanitary conditions; they pursued inherently healthful work in more comfortable settings. Those who worked with their hands, however, continually faced poverty and starvation without any control over their future – such was the short "life of the muscle-working classes of modern civilized society."[18]

Beard's acknowledgment of the class distribution of health and longevity was hardly a call for social justice; instead, it was an attack on the "mischievous theory" that brain work was incompatible with health and longevity. By repudiating this belief, Beard hoped to overcome one of the popular hurdles obstructing the development of the "new" middle class.[19] Too many college students, Beard argued, had abandoned plans for a professional career and returned to the farm or workshop. Nothing was more discouraging to young men of talent and noble ideals than the superstition that the life of an urban brain-worker led inevitably to exhaustion and premature death.

By later standards, Beard's work was methodologically sloppy and conceptually imprecise. In his enthusiasm to prove the longevity of brain-workers, Beard never discussed the registration reports he utilized; since these reports would have revealed the superior longevity of "muscle-working" farmers, perhaps he used them selectively. Regarding the "law of the relation of age to work," Beard never specified his sample (the number ranged, in various publications, from 750 to 1,000); nor did he share the calculations that presumably led to his conclusions.[20] Furthermore, Beard's dim medical view of the aging body and mind did not rest on the presentation of clinical evidence. Nevertheless, American physicians, assimilating the research of Charcot, would soon accept and elaborate Beard's position. With the pub-

---

[17] On professionalism's tendency to create dependency, see Bledstein, *Culture of Professionalism* (see n. 1); Ivan Illich, *Medical Nemesis* (New York: Pantheon, 1976); and Christopher Lasch, *Haven in a Heartless World* (New York: Basic Books, 1978).

[18] Beard, *American Nervousness* (see n. 10), 23, 435.

[19] On the emerging professional middle class after 1870, see Robert Wiebe, *The Search For Order* (New York: Hill & Wang, 1967). For discussion of the feminist contribution to this movement, see William Leach, *True Love and Perfect Union*, pt. 3 (New York: Basic Books, 1978).

[20] The data for Beard's conclusions can be found among his private papers at the Yale University Sterling Memorial Library.

lication of his "law," Beard deserves the dubious distinction of being the first to scientifically legitimate the reduction of human beings to their productive capacities.

There is an interesting congruence between George Miller Beard's life and his work. While he demystified the authority of "gray-haired seniors," Beard also placed intense competitive pressure on young men: "If the golden decade be near, as the law I have announced discloses," he wrote, "they must gird up their loins in great haste, else they find themselves beaten in the race of life."[21] After entering the new specialization of electrotherapy and neurology in 1866, Beard lectured and wrote at a furious pace while maintaining a busy practice. His major work, *Nervous Exhaustion* (1880), appeared when he was forty-one – just about on schedule. Since Beard celebrated the "race of life" rather than seeking to alter it or mitigate its effects, it is small wonder that he considered old age economically worthless, full of disease, and burdensome. In his lecture on "The Decline of Moral Faculties in Old Age," Beard suggested that it might be "a blessed thing to die young, or at least before extreme old age."[22] He died at forty-four – deprived of the opportunity to change his mind either in old age or about it.

The importance of Beard's thought about aging and old age lies in its unsentimental turn to the negative pole in the Victorian dichotomy of aging. The frightening, uncontrollable aspects of a "bad" old age – previously assumed to be avoidable given enough individual willpower – were being pushed into the cultural spotlight by new social and economic forces during the late nineteenth century. Anthony Trollope's satire *The Fixed Period* (1882) took up the shocking implications of these forces.

Trollope's futuristic novel is set in the late twentieth century on the imaginary island of Britannula – a republic that has recently gained independence from England and is considered the most humane and progressive nation in the world. In their far-sightedness, the young Britannulans agree on an entirely new solution to the problem of old people who outlive their usefulness and become a burden to themselves and society. According to the Fixed Period law, all citizens who reach age sixty-seven (the Fixed Period) are to be "deposited" in a special, honorary college known as Necropolis. For the benefit of both old and young, members of the college are to spend one year living in comfort, peaceful reflection, and social recognition, before being peacefully chloroformed and cremated. In this manner, older people will avoid the "imbecility and weakness of human life when protracted beyond its fitting limits" and depart under "circumstances of honor and glory."[23]

When the first man on the island reaches the age of the Fixed Period, he

---

[21] Beard, *Legal Responsibility* (see n. 9), 23.

[22] Beard, "Moral Faculties in Old Age" (see n. 12), 4.

[23] Anthony Trollope, *The Fixed Period* (Leipzig: B. Tauchnitz, 1882), 132, 142.

claims to be one year younger than his actual age. Although old Mr. Crasweller had enthusiastically supported the Fixed Period in his youth, he now irrationally persists in seeing himself as the victim of a cruel law. President Neverbend's assurances that he will be a pioneer and hero leave him strangely unmoved. Despite increasing popular opposition, Neverbend insists on the moral righteousness and social benevolence of the law. He proceeds to deposit Crasweller on the appointed day.

Just as the carriage conveying Neverbend and Crasweller nears the college, a British warship armed with a "250-ton steam-swiveller" races into the harbor. A few old loyalists had spinelessly informed the British, who quickly dispatched the navy to halt the ceremonies. "England, with unsurpassed tyranny," mourns Neverbend, "had sent out one of her brutal modern inventions, and threatened us all with blood and gore and murder if we did not give up our beneficent modern theory."[24] Crasweller is set free, amidst a jubilant crowd that had gathered to prevent his entry into Necropolis. Britannula is reduced to the status of a colony again, and Neverbend sails back to England, to be "deposited" in a London jail.[25]

Like Beard's law, Trollope's novel registers the tendency of an urban industrial society, where chronological age becomes a tool for regulating the life course and for managing generational replacement in primary labor markets. If a certain number of years mark the limit of human productivity, rationality, and efficiency, then no one who has passed this fixed period should be allowed to hold office or control land or other forms of wealth. Beard and Trollope stripped the veil of sentimentalism from the verdict of rationalist, secular, capitalist culture: Old age was irrelevant and burdensome.

Beard's work foreshadowed the legitimation of age discrimination and mandatory retirement, soon to be prominent features of large industrial and financial corporations as well as government bureaucracies.[26] Trollope's literary imagination reached further – he realized that the most efficient application of the fixed-period principle was not mandatory retirement but mandatory euthanasia. Ironically, the futuristic *Fixed Period* is set in the year 1980 – only a few years before Governor Richard D. Lamm of Colorado in fact suggested that sick, old people had an obligation to "die and get out of the way."[27]

---

[24] Trollope, *Fixed Period* (see n. 23), 180.

[25] Trollope, aged sixty-five when he wrote the novel, once described himself as a "writing machine." Shortly after beginning *The Fixed Period*, he wrote to his son: "Nothing really frightens me but the idea of enforced idleness" – the prescription for "honor" in his novel. True to his own satire, Trollope died before his sixty-eighth birthday. On the relationship between Trollope's last works and his own old age, see Robert Tracy, *Trollope's Later Novels* (Berkeley: University of California Press, 1978).

[26] See William Graebner, *A History of Retirement* (New Haven, Conn.: Yale University Press, 1980).

[27] *New York Times*, "Governor Lamm asserts elderly, if very ill, have a duty to die," March 29, 1984, A16.

Trollope's honorary college of Necropolis ingeniously accomplishes two contradictory purposes: to dispose painlessly and efficiently of all people who had outlived their usefulness; and to imbue the end of life with glory and distinction. By seeking to honor the occupants of Necropolis, Trollope suggests the collapse of moral and religious significance previously attributed to old age. As we have seen, early modern Protestantism conceived life as a spiritual pilgrimage whose significance transcended and outlasted one's capacity for work. Indeed, existence took on added meaning during a pilgrim's final season of probation and preparation for death.

An aging "civilized" morality placed increasing emphasis on prolongation rather than probation. By reducing human value to measurable productivity, by seeing longevity as a God-given right, and by evading the mystery and power of death, middle-class culture lost the power to envision aging both as decline *and* as the fulfillment of life. When it denied the precariousness of human life, literally embodied in the physical limitations of individuals, "civilized" morality severely weakened the Protestant tradition of pilgrimage, rooted in human imperfection and the search for ultimate meaning.

Trollope's college of Necropolis satirically sought a new rite of passage, a new tradition of wisdom and meaning in old age, based on the imminence and acceptance of death. Old age would be limited to one year of comfort and prestige – the rewards of a lifetime's productivity. This ludicrous scheme suggests that a culture overwhelmingly committed to material progress and the conquest of death had abandoned the spiritual resources needed to redeem human finitude and the end of life.

When William Osler delivered his final address to the Johns Hopkins University Medical School in February 1905, he could not have anticipated the furor that followed. Yet public response to the valedictory, entitled "The Fixed Period," would cause Osler considerable personal discomfort and plague his reputation long after his death in 1919. Osler, who at the age of fifty-six was leaving his position on the medical faculty, took the occasion to discuss the dangers of stagnation in a modern university. While regretting the sadness that accompanied a peripatetic professoriate, he extolled the intellectual virtues of constant change and new personnel. Academic progress, he argued, depended heavily on the youthful qualities of creative power, flexibility, and vitality. "It is a very serious matter in our young universities to have all of the professors growing old at the same time," he claimed. "In some places, only an epidemic, a time limit, or an age limit can save the situation."[28]

Osler admitted having two "fixed ideas . . . harmless obsessions" that nevertheless bore directly on the problem. Echoing Beard, Osler first asserted

[28] William Osler, "The Fixed Period," in *The "Fixed Period" Controversy*, ed. Gerald J. Gruman (New York: Arno Press, 1979), 381.

the comparative uselessness of men above forty years of age. The real work of the world, he argued, was done between the ages of twenty-five and forty – "these fifteen golden years of plenty, the anabolic or constructive period, in which there is always a balance in the mental bank and the credit is still good."

Osler's second fixed idea was the absolute "uselessness of men above sixty years of age." It would be an incalculable benefit to society, Osler said, if men stopped working at sixty. Jokingly, Osler referred to Trollope's "admirable scheme" of college and chloroform. Its advantages were obvious to anyone aware "of the calamities which may befall men during the seventh and eight decades." On the other hand, Osler teased, "Whether Anthony Trollope's suggestion . . . should be carried out or not I have become a little dubious, as my own time is getting so short."[29]

Actually, Osler's remarks contained little real cause for alarm. In practice, he advocated a system of pensions and retirement that followed logically from a competitive market and the increasingly widespread belief in the declining capacities of older men. According to Osler, there would be three stages to an ideal academic career: "study until twenty-five, investigation until forty, profession until sixty, at which age I would have him retired on a double allowance."[30] By the end of 1905, Andrew Carnegie, impressed by Osler's remarks, had founded the Carnegie Foundation for the Advancement of Teaching. Shaped by M.I.T. president Henry Pritchett, the Carnegie Foundation considered its pension system an indispensable tool for the advancement of teaching and research.[31]

Despite their seemingly innocent humor and practicality, Osler's remarks provoked a storm of outrage and controversy. The *New York Evening Globe*, perhaps in search of sensation, appeared to take the chloroform remark seriously. "The older men in America," it editorialized, "have reason to feel proud of the way the press has rallied to their support and deprecated the suggestion that they be chloroformed." Press reports of Osler's address were linked to as many as twenty suicides. New York City police took glove workman Herman Myron to Bellevue Hospital after Myron had informed his wife that Osler was following him "with intent to chloroform." The *Baltimore Sun* carried a story about old Sherman W. Link, found dead next to a bottle labeled chloroform. Link had recently been discussing Osler's remarks with his friends. Within a week of the valedictory, Osler had written a letter to the *New York Times* denying that he advocated chloroforming men over sixty.[32]

---

[29] Osler, "Fixed Period" (see n. 28), 381–83.
[30] Osler, "Fixed Period" (see n. 28), 383.
[31] Graebner, *History of Retirement* (see n. 26), 108–19.
[32] I have relied heavily on Graebner's account of the reaction to Osler's valedictory. The material quoted above appears in Graebner's manuscript, pp. 5–6, though not in the published version.

As William Graebner has shown, most of the agitation over Osler's address revolved around its chilling assessment of middle age and around the question of retirement. Harking back to an earlier era of individual enterprise and democratic medicine, the *New York Evening Mail* sought refuge in the old physiological capital metaphor. Men could remain vital and productive after forty, the *Mail* argued, "if they did not in youth apply to their nerves the 'hot and rebellious liquours' of over-effort, of over-strenuousness, of too much 'hustle.' . . . We each have our capital of energy. Dr. Osler seems to advise the prodigal expenditure of it in early life, and there he is unwise."[33]

Toronto physician John Ferguson sought to recover a "good" old age by reasserting the Victorian consensus about aging. According to Ferguson, decay in creative power was caused not by advancing age but by "wrong habits of life." Osler, he argued, knew full well that most people lived in a "pathological, not physiological, condition." Excess of eating, drinking, sleeping, alcohol, and other stimulants were the primary causes of the decay in later life.[34]

In his outrage at Osler's view of sexagenarians, James R. Angell, president of the University of Michigan, displayed little capacity for irony: "I would like to extend the time of a man's life instead of shortening it. The experiment of killing off old men has been tried in Africa for centuries, and I would suggest to the distinguished physician that civilization has not advanced very rapidly there."[35] The *Baltimore American*, *Denver Republican*, *Washington Post*, *Washington Times*, and various other newspapers carried stories with the increasingly familiar litany of accomplishments by older men.

Few observers supported Osler's notion of retirement, which quite logically appeared to Victorian morality as a kind of social euthanasia. Osler's address, however, correctly registered the drift of corporate capitalism; an economy and culture committed to rationality and productivity in increasingly large, bureaucratic forms of organization found it only rational to accelerate the rate of generational replacement. A fully developed ideological and institutional basis for retirement, however, awaited the intervention of social science and the state.[36]

Public uproar over Osler's valedictory reveals widespread anxiety and fear in the popular culture of aging at the turn of the century. Osler's half-joking remarks about *The Fixed Period* gave long-simmering conflicts outlet and means for public discussion. Two things are striking by their absence: women

---

[33] Graebner, *History of Retirement* (see n. 26), 6.

[34] Cited by Charles G. Roland, "The Infamous William Osler," *Journal of the American Medical Association* 193 (August 9, 1965): 100.

[35] *New York Times*, February 25, 1905, p. 5.

[36] The American Association for Labor Legislation, founded in 1906 by reform social scientists, initiated the drive for social insurance, which by 1935 had provided the legislative and ideological framework for retirement. See Roy Lubove, *The Struggle For Social Security* (Cambridge, Mass.: Harvard University Press, 1968).

and religion. Osler charged only men with worthlessness after sixty. In an aside, he indicated that old women's usefulness warranted sparing them the honor of euthanasia. The exclusion of middle-class women from the labor force seems to have eased their lives in old age. Closely tied to the household and family, female identity and utility apparently suffered little from the competitive pressures that haunted older men. Even dependency was easier to bear. Indigent aged women tended to fall into the gentler arms of private charity and family, while the cold dreariness of the almshouse more often awaited their male counterparts.[37] Public discussion of productivity and retirement revolved entirely around men, as if aging women deserved to be understood in entirely different terms.

Perhaps the most revealing aspect of the fixed-period controversy was its secular terrain. Virtually everyone took Osler on his own ground, arguing either that declining capacities disqualified old men for work, or (more commonly) that old men had important contributions to make. Following Beard, Osler entered the early stages of a debate that, although it stimulated important and continuing efforts to define the relationships between age and work, can have no final or authoritative answer.[38] The important point here is that by 1900, scientific assessments of efficiency and productivity had come to dominate public evaluation of old age. No one came forward to defend old men on the grounds that they had more important business to attend to – for example, meeting final obligations to God, family, and community. Almost no one, that is.

Amidst the decline of religious standards and beliefs, Felix Adler, leader of the New York Ethical Culture Society, opened the door to an existentialist understanding of old age. Roughly a year after Osler's address, Adler replied in a Carnegie Hall lecture entitled "The Spiritual Attitude Towards Old Age." Adler began by noting the unique influence of the physician in modern society, where confidence in a future life was waning and health began to appear as a kind of secular salvation.

According to Adler, the immense popular curiosity about Osler's remarks derived from two sources. First, declining belief in immortality led many people to cling more desperately to this life, creating anxiety and apprehension about its end. "Science has great authority; and if a scientist says that there are only twenty years of the three score and ten that are really flooded with sunshine, people listen attentively to him." Second, modern industry thrived on the competitive crowding out of the old and middle-aged to make way for the young. The privileges and lessons of old age had

---

[37] See U.S. Bureau of the Census, *Paupers in Almshouses* (see n. 5), 12–13.

[38] See W. A. Newman Dorland, "The Age of Mental Virility," *Century Magazine* 76 (1908). In the wake of the Osler valedictory, Beard's daughter, Grace Allen Beard, tried unsuccessfully to find a publisher to restate her father's views. See Grace Allen Beard, "A Discussion Re-Opened," unpublished manuscript, George Miller Beard Papers, Sterling Memorial Library, Yale University Library.

become obscured. "And worst of all the aged themselves often accept this opinion of themselves, as mere cumberers of the earth, creatures whom it were better to shelve."[39]

Adler criticized the "physicism" inherent in Osler's (and Beard's) ideas. This doctrine, which asserted that physical decline necessarily paralleled mental and moral decline, strengthened what Adler called the "current conception" of life. "The picture implied in the current conception of life is that of a hill with its upward and downward slopes. From youth to middle age we ascend, then reach the top, and after that descend." Here again we see the influence of early modern life-cycle iconography, now stripped of its traditional symbolism. As an alternative, Adler offered a "series of terraces, each higher than the last. From age to age, through ascent following on ascent, rising from power to power, from glory to glory, at last we do not stumble into a hole, but pass as it were into the open heaven."[40]

Adler's vision of spiritual ages relied not on divine grace but on the innate nature of human spirituality. Alone among those who replied to Osler, Adler made no attempt to judge the productivity or efficiency of the aged. Instead he defended old age on the ground that it embodied a central dimension of human existence. Old age was a time of "being," whereas youth and middle age were periods of "doing." Adler argued that honor and appreciation of old age depended on the realization that "the spiritual life is engendered in us through doing, but is manifested in being."[41]

Adler's search for a vision of aging that acknowledged productive decline and physical decay while seeking spiritual refinement and beauty is instructive. In conceiving youth and middle age as times of "doing" and old age as the time of "being," he apparently accepted the notion that the aged were economically worthless. Spiritual development grew not from exploration of unknown limits, but from renunciation and withdrawal. Without belief in God and the promise of immortality, Adler's "spiritual attitude towards old age" carried little popular appeal. And, as we have seen, the ideological hegemony of the American middle class rested on material progress and physical control rather than withdrawal and renunciation.

PROLONGEVITY AND REJUVENATION: THE LAST HOPE OF "CIVILIZED" MORALITY

Once the fixed-period doctrine had thoroughly shaken expectations of healthy, self-reliant longevity, the negative pole in America's dualistic im-

---

[39] Felix Adler, *The Spiritual Attitude Toward Old Age* (New York: Ethical Culture Society, 1906), 6, 16.

[40] Adler, *Spiritual Attitude* (see n. 39), 11, 12.

[41] Adler, *Spiritual Attitude* (see n. 39), 13.

agery of aging became ascendant. "Civilized" morality was in decline.[42] Infused with the anger and resentment of a decaying, male-centered, Protestant ethic, old age came to epitomize the previously unacknowledged, though always inexorable barriers to the American dream of limitless accumulation of health and wealth. The image of isolated, dependent, and deteriorating old age haunts popular writing at the turn of the century.[43]

It is not surprising then, that the heightened enthusiasm for prolongevity between 1890 and 1925 was coupled with an unambivalent hostility toward weakness or illness in old age. Unlike earlier supporters of life extension, prolongevity advocates in this period declared infirm old age (and in some cases, death) an unacceptable condition, and they proceeded with the struggle to defer or abolish it. Flourishing at precisely the moment that the aging culture of Anglo-Saxon, Protestant individualism was under continuous attack from women, labor, immigrants, and progressive liberals, the prolongevity movement held out a final hope that economic and social relations could yet be grounded in the biology of the autonomous male individual.

CHARLES ASBURY STEPHENS AND
NATURAL SALVATION

The life and work of Charles Asbury Stephens, a highly popular writer and enthusiast of life extension, exemplify in extreme form the appeal of prolongevity for many provincial mid-Victorians. Stephens was born near Norway, Maine, in 1844, the only son of a devout Methodist family whose ancestors had pioneered in the area. Stephens lost his father in the Civil War. He spent his adolescence and early adulthood working on his grandfather's farm, from which he freed himself after a long financial struggle, and completed his college degree at Bowdoin in 1869.[44]

In 1870, Stephens attracted Daniel Ford, the ambitious publisher of *Youth's Companion*, with his short children's stories reminiscing about farm and village life in the isolated setting of rural Maine. Stephens soon made his fortune writing for the *Companion*, which by 1885 had become the most popular periodical in America.[45] At the age of forty, he entered the Boston

---

[42] On the crisis of "civilized" morality, see Nathan G. Hale, *Freud and the Americans* (Baltimore: Johns Hopkins University Press, 1978), chap. 2.

[43] See W. Andrew Achenbaum, "The Obsolescence of Old Age," in *Old Age in the New Land* (Baltimore: Johns Hopkins University Press, 1978).

[44] Gerald Gruman, "C. A. Stephens – Popular Author and Prophet of Gerontology," *New England Journal of Medicine* 254 (April 5, 1956): 658–60; C. A. Stephens, *When Life was Young at the Old Farm in Maine* (Boston: The Youth's Companion, 1912).

[45] Gruman, "Prophet of Gerontology" (see n. 44), 659; Frank Luther Mott, *A History of American Magazines, 1865–1885* (Cambridge, Mass.: Harvard University Press, 1957).

University School of Medicine in order to write health articles for the magazine.

While in medical school, Stephens became absorbed in the biology of aging and death; he devoted much of the rest of his life to investigating their causes, motivated by a fervent belief in the possibility of human immortality. Stephens studied the histology of young and old dogs from tissue cultures taken at the New York City dog pound, attended biology courses at Woods Hole, and set up a research laboratory at his home in Norway, Maine.[46] In 1890, he sent out circulars to microscopists offering cash prizes for the best set of twelve slides demonstrating the different structures of capillary cells in young and old tissues. Over the next thirty years, he published and circulated the results of his laboratory research at his own expense.[47]

Like many mid-Victorians who migrated from family farms and small villages to increasingly large and secular cities, Stephens came to maturity when, as he put it, "the old faiths [were] fading out, like ghosts at dawn, when venerable 'soul doctrines' [were] falling into desuetude and discredit." He accepted the scientific consensus that death was "no longer the ladder to heaven, but the brink of unconsciousness," but with deep reluctance.[48] In 1905, Stephens wrote of an "everdeepening sadness" that followed the decline of Christian doctrines of immortality: "So much of solace has centered in it, so much consolation for the pangs of death; such sweet anticipation of future reunions with dear ones dead."[49]

Stephens felt that he lived "at humanity's darkest hour – the hour before dawn. We live too late to be buoyed and comforted by the illusions of religion, too soon to reach the goal and snatch our lives from the grasp of death."[50] Stephens nevertheless dedicated himself to medical research, to hasten the moment when natural would substitute for supernatural salvation: "Immortal life will be achieved by the aid of applied science; it is what the whole scheme of evolution moves forward to."[51]

For Stephens old age was as horrifying as death. Whereas sanitary reformers had argued, as did Charlton Lewis in 1877, that "the best symbol of progress is the venerable man, who, in a decaying body, preserves the energies of a wise, benevolent and vigorous mind,"[52] Stephens could not abide physical

---

[46] Gerald Gruman, "C. A. Stephens – a Pioneer of American Gerontology," *Geriatrics* 14 (May 1959): 332–36.

[47] The development of Stephens's thought can be traced through the following books, all published by The Laboratory at Norway Lake, Maine: *Living Matter* (1888); *Pluricellular Man* (1893); *Long Life* (1896); *Natural Salvation* (1903); *Salvation by Science* (1913); and *Immortal Life* (1920).

[48] Stephens, *Natural Salvation* (see n. 47), 113.

[49] Stephens, *Natural Salvation* (see n. 47), 124.

[50] Stephens, *Natural Salvation* (see n. 47), 127.

[51] Stephens, *Natural Salvation* (see n. 47), 127.

[52] Charlton Lewis, "The Influence of Civilization on the Duration of Life," *The Sanitarian* 4 (May 1877): 202.

decline. He found old age a condition of "grossness, coarseness, and ugliness," and described the aging body as "a sad, strange mixture of foulness and putrefaction in which the sweeter, purer, etheric flame of life struggles and smoulders." Stephens rejected the view that man would ideally die of a healthy old age, claiming instead that aging constituted a pathological process whose removal would lead to deathless life.[53]

Whereas hygienic reformers sought longevity in the economy of the body, Stephens sought immortality in the microeconomy of the living cell.[54] He opposed the evolutionary biologist August Weismann's theory that one-celled organisms were essentially ageless and deathless. Weismann had argued that old age and death entered the evolutionary world when multicellular organisms began to reproduce sexually, implying that human beings died shortly after producing and raising offspring because further prolongation of life served no species purpose.

According to Stephens, the sources of aging and death lay not in metazoan sexual reproduction, but in the imperfections of tissue cells. Observing the micropathology of aging in cuticle, bone, muscle, liver, heart, and capillary tissues, Stephens found that some older cells remained as large and healthy as younger ones. He concluded that, under proper conditions of nutrition and stimulation, the cell was a potentially deathless unit. This view received apparent confirmation in 1912, when Alexis Carrel, working at the Rockefeller Institute, successfully sustained the life of tissues taken from dead animals.[55]

In 1905, Stephens predicted that, within a few decades, humankind would perfect cellular nutrition and utilize vital energy for cellular restoration and maintenance. Such perfect nutrition and circulation of energy, Stephens believed, would lead to the spiritualization of life: "[T]his regimen, this higher sentiment of nutrition will come naturally . . . of itself with the hope of immortal life. Belly-greed, like sex-lust, will fade out as the sense of deathlessness grows."[56]

Antebellum health reformers had assumed that self-willed obedience to nature's benevolent laws would resolve the problems of aging, death, and generational succession. Faced with the harsh Darwinian view of nature, Stephens could not afford this assumption. Instead he sought to emancipate humanity from nature, harnessing science to the search for immortality. In effect, Stephens pushed the logic of "civilized" morality to its extreme point, revealing potential connections between repression of sexuality and the denial of death.

---

[53] Stephens, *Natural Salvation* (see n. 47), 235, 236, 3, 85, 89.
[54] Stephens, *Long Life* (see n. 47), 6.
[55] Alexis Carrel, "On the Permanent Life of Tissues Outside of the Organism," *Journal of Experimental Medicine* (May 1, 1912): 516–28.
[56] Stephens, *Natural Salvation* (see n. 47), 203, 210.

Once mankind had transcended the purely animal cycle of growth and decline, sexuality would disappear, since a chain of parents and children would no longer be essential to the perpetuation of life. Even more than his health reform forebears, Stephens staked everything on physical control, now enhanced by science and technology. Whereas they envisioned a bodily hygiene culminating in natural death, he imagined a cellular hygiene whose end product would be a race of individuals not only deathless, but also passionless, sexless, and childless.

There is little evidence to suggest that, as a protogerontologist, Stephens ever enjoyed much direct influence. He expanded the laboratory facilities at Norway, Maine, to house and equip fifty investigators in 1905, but plans to finance his large-scale research program collapsed. Most people attracted by the dream of longer life settled for less ambitious schemes. Stephens's thought did probe the still unresolved mysteries of biological aging; it also reflected something of the mood and direction of the turn-of-the-century prolongevity movement.

When Stephens spoke of humanity as "chronically tired" and of Aryans at the evolutionary edge of "a descending limb to the dark nadir of the fossil,"[57] he registered the broader sense of weakening energies, of human beings and gods grown old,[58] that characterized the crisis of "civilized" morality. In the undisciplined passions of urban masses and the unrestrained rapidity of industrialists, many Anglo-Americans saw the specter of social dissolution. The rising numbers of mid-Victorians who suffered from nervous exhaustion and who feared "forty and grey hair, and death and consumption and cancer," suggested the possibility of racial senescence.[59] Declining birth rates, alarming increases in chronic disease, and shrinking numbers and proportions of centenarians led J. H. Kellogg, the old sage of Battle Creek, to warn Congress in 1912: "We have been making ourselves believe that the tree is flourishing because of the great number of young sprouts at the bottom, while the main trunk is dying at the top. . . . The real measure of the physical vigor of a race is not the age at which the average man dies, but the proportion of individuals who attain great age."[60]

As these passages imply, individual and cultural fears of degeneration reinforced each other. It is no accident that Brooks Adams discovered the "law of civilization and decay" in an atmosphere of deep hostility to the

[57] Stephens, *Natural Salvation* (see n. 47), 195; Stephens, *Immortal Life* (see n. 47), 240.

[58] William S. Gilbert and Arthur Sullivan's first collaboration bore the title *Thespis, or The Gods Grown Old*. See F. W. Nietzsche's *The Gay Science* (New York: Random House, 1974) or Oswald Spengler's *The Decline of the West* (New York: Knopf, 1962).

[59] C. W. Saleeby, *Worry – The Disease of the Age* (New York: F. A. Stokes Co., 1907); "Race Senescence," *Popular Science Monthly* 63 (1903): 88–89.

[60] J. H. Kellogg, "Tendencies Toward Race Degeneration," Senate Document 648, 62d Congress, 2d. session, 1912; see Irving Fisher, *Report on National Vitality: Its Wastes and Conservation* (Washington, D. C.: National Conservation Commission, Government Printing Office, 1909).

organic processes of decline and death.[61] Amidst the declining authority of established institutions and ideas, the strident affirmations of prolongevity resound with a cultural cognitive dissonance. For those committed to the self-reliant liberalism of civilized morality, yet shaken by its deteriorating capacity either to explain the world or to command widespread respect, prolongevity offered a solution free of political or ideological challenge. Its attack on premature senility and physical degeneration enabled people to transfer diffuse anxieties onto comfortable terrain. The quest for a longer, healthier life seemed to resolve troubling existential and ideological questions in the familiar terms of bodily economy.[62]

FORMS OF PROLONGEVITY: PROFESSIONAL
SCIENCE, QUACKERY, AND HYGIENE

Efforts to rejuvenate and prolong life between 1890 and 1925 fall roughly into three (not always separate) categories: medical and surgical methods based on professional knowledge; fringe rejuvenation techniques marketed by various quacks and medical hustlers; and updated versions of hygienic reform. Most advocates of prolongevity considered aging a chronic disease, susceptible to treatment and eradication. All agreed that modern medical therapeutics and proper hygienic regimen could defer significantly, if not indefinitely, the onset of senile changes.

The first major figure to lend the authority of professional science to prolongevity was the peripatetic French-American, C. E. Brown-Séquard. Brown-Séquard, who lectured and practiced medicine on both sides of the Atlantic and in 1878 succeeded Claude Bernard in the chair of experimental medicine at the Collège de France, had long contemplated the possibilities in the common view that vital energy originated in the sex glands. In June 1889, the seventy-two-year-old neurologist announced to the French Society of Biology that he had successfully rejuvenated himself, using an extract of animal sexual glands. Popular Parisian newspapers immediately took up the news, initiating a campaign to finance the construction of an Institute of Rejuvenation.[63] Americans quickly followed suit.

In August, the *Cincinnati Lancet-Clinic* announced that "almost in the twinkling of an eye" the medical profession was faced with popular enthusiasm over Brown-Séquard's *Elixir of Life*, "the most striking phenomenon of the age." Day after day, newspapers carried interviews and testimonials

[61] Brooks Adams, *The Law of Civilization and Decay* (New York: Macmillan, 1896).

[62] This aspect of prolongevity may be considered the male counterpart to mind cure, which appealed especially to middle-class women faced with similar troubles. Donald B. Meyer, *The Positive Thinkers* (Garden City, N.Y.: Doubleday, 1965) has strongly influenced my thought along these lines.

[63] Eric Trimmer, *Rejuvenation: The History of an Idea* (London: Hale, 1967), 125.

to the wondrous power of the treatment. Readers were hungry for information about "what they hoped was a potent aphrodisiac and actual live forever business." Many flocked to physicians' offices and called for medical advice about "the new fountain of life that has brought hope to their fainting ears."[64]

Throughout the summer of 1889, newspapers, magazines, and medical journals printed a flurry of articles on the Brown-Séquard method. One drug company began producing a product called Spermine, a crystalline extract made from semen, calf's heart, calf's liver, and bull's testicles. Physicians all over the country reported that worn-out, debilitated patients became generally exhilarated and toned-up with testicular injections.[65]

Professional medical opinion ranged from scorn to cautious optimism. The conservative *Boston Medical and Surgical Journal* wrote: "There is no secret of rejuvenation, no elixir of youth. . . . We hope we may soon hear the last of Brown-Séquard's disgusting advice to old men. . . ."[66] Writing in the *North American Review*, former Surgeon General William Hammond called for further research: "There is nothing inherently impossible in a so-called 'elixir of life' – that is, in a substance that, when taken into the system, may so arrest the deteriorating influences of old age as to prolong life and render existence more tolerable."[67]

The Brown-Séquard sensation ended as quickly as it began. Rejuvenating effects of the injections may have stemmed from a placebo effect and proved temporary.[68] Yet serious scientists and physicians continued to pursue rejuvenation techniques along lines suggested by Brown-Séquard. In 1922, California surgeon L. L. Stanley injected crushed testicular substance into a series of 1,000 patients, described as "badly run-down." Stanley reported significant improvement in the appetite, weight, and emotional condition of his patients, and the method gained in popularity. By 1928, Dr. Albert Schneider, reviewing the whole field of rejuvenation, estimated that roughly 50,000 Stanley-type operations had been done in the United States, "with quite uniformly good results and without ill effects."[69]

Other efforts at renewing the "spermatic economy" followed the vasoligation technique developed by the Austrian physiologist Eugene Steinach in the early 1920s. The Steinach operation involved cutting and tying off

---

[64] Newell Dunbar, ed., *The Elixir of Life* (Boston: J. G. Cupples, 1889), 91–92.

[65] Dunbar, *Elixir* (see n. 64), 70.

[66] Unsigned editorial, "Is There an Elixir of Life?" *Boston Medical and Surgical Journal* 191 (August 15, 1889): 167–68.

[67] William A. Hammond, "The Elixir of Life," *North American Review* 294 (September 1889): 258.

[68] The effects of testosterone injections are still being studied by contemporary endocrinologists. Both "placebo" and physiological effects appear to be at work. I am grateful to Dr. Walter B. Meyer, Department of Psychiatry, University of Texas Medical Branch, for helpful conversations about this issue.

[69] Albert Schneider, "Rejuvenation," *Medical Review of Reviews* (April 1928): 53.

the vas deferens, thus eliminating the ejaculation of sperm from the testicles. By redirecting the sexual hormone back into the body, Steinach hoped to achieve general rejuvenation. Although not as common, an analogous operation for women involved the ligation of the fallopian tubes. Both operations purported to procure youthfulness at the cost of sterility. After ten years of experience with the "Steinach Therapy Against Old Age," Dr. Harry Benjamin of New York estimated a success rate of 75 percent with 1,000 cases, with results lasting from one to six years. He claimed that improved endocrine functioning after the operation had eliminated the subjective symptoms of exhaustion, insomnia, inability to concentrate, irritability, and lack of appetite. Objective improvements included lower blood pressure, renewed hair growth, improved skin texture, and improved eyesight and hearing.[70]

While prolongevity was used primarily to reinforce the self-reliant individualism of aging mid-Victorians, it also lent itself to other uses. Glandular rejuvenation techniques, for example, stimulated the minds of social engineers as well as the bodies of exhausted individuals. In 1928, Albert Schneider, who believed that active mental and physical life could be prolonged by at least 50 percent, noted a rumor that the German Reichstag was considering a law making gland transplants (pioneered by Serge Voronoff) compulsory "with a view to increasing human efficiency and . . . prolonging life." During the 1920s, over 5,000 inmates (both sexes) in various U.S. state penitentiaries "voluntarily" accepted glandular treatments in hopes of speeding their rehabilitation and restoration to society.[71]

Between 1890 and 1925, the war on old age drew some of its supplies from the time-honored tradition of quackery, which found a booming market in bogus rejuvenation methods.[72] Enterprising quacks sold a fantastic array of tonics, elixirs, advice, and assorted paraphernalia, luring their prey with the promise of renewed youth. Theophilius Noel, for example, came to Chicago in 1891 and began selling Vitae-Ore, an exotic mineral he claimed to have discovered in Mexico. Advertising in religious weeklies, Noel recommended his cure-all especially for those suffering from rheumatism, diabetes, Bright's disease, gout, and "stomach trouble." Chemical analysis revealed that Vitae-Ore consisted of Monsel's salt and epsom salt – the combination of which had netted over $200,000 by 1907.[73] Advertisements

---

[70] Trimmer, *Rejuvenation* (see n. 67), 472; Harry Benjamin, "Steinach Therapy Against Old Age," *American Medicine* (December 1932): 470.

[71] Schneider, "Rejuvenation" (see n. 69), 70, 72.

[72] On the interesting career of a quack surgeon from the late teens through the 1930s, see Jack D. Walker, "The Goat Gland Surgeon," *Journal of the Kansas Medical Society* 57 (December 1956): 749–55; and John L. Baeke, "A Critical Examination of the Works of Dr. John R. Brinkley," unpublished paper, Department of the History and Philosophy of Medicine, University of Kansas School of Medicine, March 15, 1983. I am grateful to Dr. Robert Hudson for bringing this material to my attention.

[73] American Medical Association, *Nostrums and Quackery* (Chicago: AMA Press, 1912), 1:459–51.

for El Zair, another exotic elixir of youth (consisting of epsom salt and vinegar), told of its power to sprout new hair on bald heads and to remove the "deeper seated waste matter" that caused old age.[74]

Specialists in sexual quackery appealed to the popular identification of sexual potency and manhood. The P. Presto Company, a mail-order operation out of Albany, Oregon, attracted attention with the following advertisement: "MEN OF ALL AGES – STOP GROWING OLD. You can recover and retain your youthful vigor and vitality without dangerous drugs and appliances. Our New Method tells how." Those who paid the two dollars for the "copyrighted new method" received graphic instructions on stretching the scrotum and testicles to strengthen and increase the blood and nerve supply to these organs.[75] In March 1919, a grand jury in Portland charged the proprietor of the P. Presto Company, Edward F. Lee, with using the mails to defraud the public; Lee was sentenced to eighteen months in a federal penitentiary.

Another charlatan of sexual health, Fred A. Leach, began his career selling vacuum developers for the enlargement of the male organ. After the U.S. Post Office Department issued a fraud order against him in 1908, Leach switched to a product known as "orchis extract – the greatest treatment known for weak men." A pamphlet advertising "orchis extract," allegedly a substance obtained from the testicles of rams, claimed that "careful and conscientious" use of the extract would relieve "pre-senility or premature old age." The pamphlet indicated that the extract had a revitalizing effect on the sex gland: "It is specifically indicated in cases of atrophy of the private organ so common in cases of sexual abuses."[76]

The widespread notion that masturbation and sexual intemperance led to premature old age provided quack establishments known as medical institutes with an ample supply of patients suffering from "Lost Manhood." Between 1900 and 1920, many large American cities housed such establishments, staffed by dubiously accredited physicians and their assistants. However predisposed we are to notice the humorous side of rejuvenation, these institutes force us to witness its pathos. One effective instrument of their grotesque exploitation of sexual guilt and anxiety was the spurious medical museum, displaying the horrors of "lost manhood" and venereal disease with vivid waxwork models, which seem to have generated some business. A former institute manager gave an exemplary case report to a Chicago newspaper man: One day a deaf, half-blind, bald, and toothless old man showed up at a medical institute. Convinced that a course of rejuvenation treatments could restore his manhood, he signed a contract and paid a large initial fee,

---

[74] American Medical Association, *Nostrums and Quackery* (Chicago: AMA Press, 1921), 3:124–25.

[75] Unsigned report of *JAMA*'s Bureau of Investigation, "The Propaganda for Reform," *Journal of the American Medical Association* (October 25, 1919): 1302.

[76] American Medical Association, *Nostrums and Quackery* (Chicago: AMA Press, 1921), 2:332–36.

insuring his return for more treatments. "We had to carry him down the stairs on the way out, but he went home with the belief for all his eighty-four years that he would be a boy again in a week."[77]

Along with professional and quack methods, the tradition of hygienic prolongevity also blossomed between 1890 and 1925.[78] During the ante-bellum period, hygienic reformers had focused broadly on the prolongation of life. For them, old age was a distant reward rather than a present concern. By the end of the nineteenth century, old age occupied a more central position, having emerged as the most intractable obstacle to the accumulation of individual health and wealth. Prolongevity hygiene in this period, there-fore, sought more desperately to prove that personal habits would guarantee a healthy old age. Its focus on aged prodigies reveals how closely the image of old age had become bound up with the fate of "civilized" morality.

The appeal of prolongevity hygiene rested heavily on popular identification with its heroes. As Carl Ramus put it in 1926,

Examples are more convincing than the most plausible theories and deductions. We may theorize as much as we like about the causes of aging and its prevention, but one genuine example of long retained youth has far more weight than a shelf full of books or innumerable opinions; it speaks not only for itself but for countless others potentially in the making.[79]

The articles and books of prolongevity hygiene teemed with aged prodigies who allegedly lived to fantastic ages or who rescued their decaying bodies from the cold terrors of death.[80] Despite poor documentation and lack of statistical measures, these success stories enjoyed considerable popularity. They appealed to a nostalgia for rural life and to the memories of one's grandparents, and appeared to confirm the central tenets of moral physiology and hygiene.

Studies of large numbers of very old people, initiated to shed more scientific light on the nature of longevity, proved equally comforting. In 1889, Clem-ent Hammond, associate editor of the *Boston Globe*, surveyed the character-istics of 3,500 New England men and women aged eighty or more. He learned that 95 percent were married, the great majority only once. The typical octogenarian had a light complexion, blue or gray eyes, and brown hair; had always been an early riser and retirer; and had eaten three regular meals a day, gotten plenty of outdoor exercise, and rarely ever drank anything more intoxicating than cider. Fully 86 percent of the men were farmers, artisans, professionals, merchants, or manufacturers; 66 percent of the women

---

[77] Trimmer, *Rejuvenation* (see n. 67), 76.

[78] Gerald Gruman, "The Rise and Fall of Prolongevity Hygiene, 1558–1873," *Bulletin of the History of Medicine* 35 (1961): 221–29.

[79] Carl Ramus, *Outwitting Middle Age* (New York: Century, 1926), 139.

[80] Ramus, *Outwitting Middle Age* (see n. 79). See also Horace Fletcher, *Fletcherism: What It Is; or How I Became Young at Sixty* (London: Seymour and Co., ca. 1915).

were farmers' wives, 87 percent of the remainder considered themselves housewives.[81]

Hammond did not draw the logical inference – that, to live beyond eighty, one should be born before 1810 to a rural, Anglo-Saxon, New England family, and belong to the independent middle class. Instead, like his British counterpart George Humphry, Hammond leaned toward the self-justifying view that personal habits alone explained differential longevity. Humphry, who published his results in the American *Popular Science Monthly* in 1885, had reached the same conclusion studying British octogenarians and centenarians.[82]

Hygienic writers on the "art of living two hundred years" generally explained old age in one of two ways: Either a man was as old as his arteries; or he was as old as his glands. The prescription for both vascular and glandular deterioration lay in a carefully followed hygienic regimen. William Kinnear, who wrote several magazine articles on the subject during the 1890s, followed the British physician C. W. De Lacy Evans. Evans had argued that the cause of aging lay in vascular deposits of earthy salts, which gradually blocked the delicate processes of nutrition and elimination. Kinnear helped popularize Evans's diet of fruits, fish, poultry, young mutton, and distilled water, designed to minimize the accumulation of calcareous salts.[83]

The principal advocate of the glandular explanation of aging, Austrian physician Arnold Lorand, based his work on "long study of the ... patriarchs of great age," a complete command of the medical literature of his day, and personal clinical experience.[84] Lorand, whose book *Old Age Deferred* exhausted four printings within fifteen months of its American appearance in 1911, believed that old age was a chronic disease, resulting from the degeneration of the ductless (endocrine) glands. He considered old age at sixty to be premature, the result of personal negligence. The properly regulated individual, he claimed, should live to ninety or a hundred in full possession of his or her powers.

Lorand prescribed "Twelve Commandments" for a "green old age." These included plenty of open air, sunshine, exercise, and deep breathing; a carefully regulated diet; daily baths and bowel movements, assisted by purgatives if necessary; porous cotton underwear, loose clothing, a light hat, and low shoes; early rising and retiring; six to eight hours of sleep in a dark, quiet room with an open window; one complete day's rest each week; avoidance

[81] Clement Hammond, "The Prolongation of Human Life," *Popular Science Monthly* 34 (1889): 92–101.

[82] George Humphry, "The Habits and Family History of Centenarians," *Popular Science Monthly* 32 (1887): 625–26.

[83] William Kinnear, "The Art of Living Two Hundred Years," *North American Review* 397 (1893): 755–58; William Kinnear, "Prolonging Life," *North American Review* 398 (1894): 635–40.

[84] Arnold Lorand, *Old Age Deferred: The Causes of Old Age and Its Postponement by Hygienic and Therapeutic Measures* (Philadelphia: F. A. Davis Co., 1912), 456.

of unpleasant emotions, discussions, or activities; careful sexual relations within marriage; and temperate use of alcohol, tobacco, coffee, and tea. If functioning of the ductless glands was weakened by age or disease, Lorand recommended a glandular transplant or injections, "but only under the strict supervision of medical men."[85]

Obedience to these commandments would guarantee perfect health. "A man with healthy ductless glands," wrote Lorand, "is the man who can face any emergency and, to a certain extent, direct fate at his own pleasure. Such a man can get practically everything he wants, and Napoleon was probably a man of such stuff. For such men there are no obstacles in the world."[86] Not even old age.

Prodigies of prolongevity, especially when they peddled the secrets of their power, sometimes enjoyed a fleeting celebrity status. Captain G. E. D. Diamond, allegedly born in Plymouth, Massachusetts, in 1796, found many eager readers for his book *The Secret of a Much Longer Life* (1906). Diamond added an unusual twist to his hygienic regimen: He claimed that rubbing olive oil into painful joints and bones prevented the stiffening processes of old age. At the well-oiled age of 110, Diamond asserted, "There is not a pain disturbing my body; not a joint ailing from rheumatic twinges; not a languid feeling of the nervous system; not a sign of heavy hearing."[87]

In 1912, another hygienic hero published his "story of an old body and face made young," complete with before-and-after photographs. At the age of fifty in 1889, prominent San Francisco businessman Sanford Bennett had looked like an old man. "I was . . . wrinkled, partially bald, cheeks sunken, face drawn and haggard, muscles atrophied, . . . and [had suffered] thirty years of chronic dyspepsia." In 1906, the *San Francisco Chronicle* noted his extraordinary physical rejuvenation by a method of hygiene and special exercises.[88] Anyone could accomplish this feat, according to Bennett. "The solution of the problem lies only in nature's principal methods of inducing health — sunlight, pure air, pure water, nourishing food, cleanliness and exercise."[89] (See Figs. 33 and 34.)

ELIE METCHNIKOFF AND THE PATHOLOGY
OF OLD AGE

All the basic aspirations of a beleaguered "civilized" morality may be found in the work of Elie Metchnikoff, the Nobel Prize-winning founder of modern

[85] Lorand, *Old Age Deferred* (see n. 84), chap. 56, 434–48.

[86] Lorand, *Old Age Deferred* (see n. 84), 410.

[87] G. E. D. Diamond, *The Secret of a Much Longer Life and More Pleasure in Living It* (San Francisco: n.p., 1906): 13.

[88] Sanford Bennett, *Old Age: Its Cause and Cure* (New York: Dodd, Mead, 1912): 32–33.

[89] Bennett, *Old Age* (see n. 88), 19.

Figure 33. Sanford Bennett at 50 (left) and at 72 (right). (From *Old Age: Its Cause and Prevention*, by Sanford Bennett [New York: Physical Culture Publishing Co., 1912].)

Figure 34. Using the stretching board. (From *Old Age: Its Cause and Prevention*, by Sanford Bennett [New York: Physical Culture Publishing Co., 1912].)

immunology. Metchnikoff's most enduring contribution to the world was his discovery of phagocytosis, the process by which phagocytes (white cells) attack and devour infectious bacteria. Born in southern Russia in 1845, Metchnikoff survived serious illness, depression, and two suicide attempts to assume a prestigious position at the Pasteur Institute in 1888. During the last twenty years of his life (1896–1916), Metchnikoff turned his attention to the pathology of old age and the prolongation of human life.

In his last two books, *The Nature of Man* (1904) and *The Prolongation of Life* (1907), Metchnikoff pursued the ideal of "orthobiosis" – a completely fulfilled life cycle, regulated by reason and knowledge. Metchnikoff's ideal, whose origins we have seen in the early modern search for an orderly and secure course of life, was built around the Enlightenment tradition of rational obedience to benevolent natural law. Metchnikoff acknowledged that certain "disharmonies" of the evolutionary process had emerged to prevent the normal course of healthy longevity and natural death. His book *The Nature of Man*, subtitled *Studies in Optimistic Philosophy,* called on modern science to transform these "disharmonies" into "harmonies." For those without religious consolation, who despaired over the irrationality and conflict of human life, Metchnikoff's work offered new hope. "If it be true that man cannot live without faith," wrote the English editor of *The Nature of Man*, "this volume, when the age of faith seemed gone by, has provided a new faith, that in the all-powerfulness of science."[90]

Like earlier health reformers, Metchnikoff confronted the question, Should we try to prolong human life?[91] The problem of old age, previously a distant if haunting issue, now assumed immediate practical importance. In France, Metchnikoff noted, many statesmen complained that the cost of supporting two million people over seventy years old was already too high. Why increase the burden of disease and dependency?

To these skeptics, Metchnikoff replied that he did not advocate prolonging live without modifying old age. He believed that life could be extended significantly *along with* the preservation of health and the power to work. "When we have reduced or abolished such causes of precocious senility as intemperance and disease, it will no longer be necessary to give pensions at the age of sixty or seventy years. The cost of supporting the old, instead of increasing, will diminish progressively."[92]

On the duration of human life, Metchnikoff offered no authoritative conclusions. He did, however, believe that centenarians were "really not rare." Either unaware of or unconvinced by W. J. Thoms's refutation of the claims of many celebrated centenarians, Metchnikoff accepted many cases of fantastic longevity that had been discredited thirty years earlier.[93] He expressed confidence, for example, that Kentigern, founder of the Cathedral of Glasgow, died at age 185 in 600, and that Pierre Zortray, a Hungarian "agriculturalist," died at the same age in 1724. Likewise, the celebrated case of Thomas Parr, examined by William Harvey and buried in Westminster Abbey in 1635 at the alleged age of 152, provoked little skepticism.[94] Metchnikoff's

---

[90] Elie Metchnikoff, *The Nature of Man* (London: Putnam, 1904), vii.

[91] Elie Metchnikoff, *The Prolongation of Life* (New York and London: Putnam, 1908), pt. 4.

[92] Metchnikoff, *Prolongation of Life* (see n. 91), 133–34.

[93] W.J. Thoms, *Human Longevity, Its Facts and Fictions* (London: J. Murray, 1873).

[94] Metchnikoff, *Prolongation of Life* (see n. 91), 86–88.

Figure 35. Dr. Metchnikoff in his laboratory. (From *Life of Elie Metchnikoff, 1845–1915*, by Olga Metchnikoff [Boston: Houghton Mifflin, 1921].)

uncritical acceptance of these alleged prodigies enabled him to argue that the scientific progress of the future would eliminate weakness and dependency and extend the average life expectancy to 140.

Since he believed that bacteriology could eliminate infectious disease, Metchnikoff argued that the old ideal of natural death might soon become a reality. And to the old description of natural death as free from disease and accident, Metchnikoff added a new element. He hypothesized that at the end of a completely fulfilled life, an instinct for death would replace the desire to live. This element, of course, was not entirely new. In the long struggle to soften and rationalize death, Metchnikoff's assertion of an instinct for natural death represents a scientized attempt to replace fear of death with calm anticipation.[95]

Metchnikoff's view of old age, his dietary prescriptions, and the popular response involved all three forms of *fin de siècle* prolongevity. When this

---

[95] Like his predecessors who pursued the ideal of natural death, Metchnikoff found little evidence to support his view. Throughout his life, Metchnikoff suffered from bouts of depression, fear of death, and suicidal tendencies. He looked in vain for the instinct of death when he died in 1916.

prize-winning scientist claimed that the disease of old age might be eliminated by harnessing bacteriology to the service of hygiene, he unwittingly
offered quackery a new market. According to Metchnikoff, the key to the
problem of senility lay in the digestive organs. Along with other mammals,
humans possessed a uniquely developed large intestine, which allowed them
to pursue a prey or evade an enemy for long periods of time without stopping
to evacuate the bowels. The accumulating waste matter, however, attracted
an abundance of bacterial flora, which produced "fermentations and putrefaction harmful to the organism."[96] The toxic substances from such putrefaction were absorbed into the rest of the body, stimulating the immune
system to attack its own weakened tissues. The voracious phagocytes not
only attacked invading bacteria, they also devoured nerve, hair, liver, and
kidney cells, creating the degenerative symptoms of old age.

Metchnikoff reasoned that reducing or fighting intestinal microbes
through dietary measures might inhibit putrefaction and reduce the degenerative effects of the overzealous phagocytes. Since soured milk, kefir, sauer-
kraut, salted cucumbers, and yogurt all contain large quantities of lactic
bacilli (bacteria that produce lactic acid), Metchnikoff believed that the
dietary habits of many cultures had impeded intestinal putrefaction for centuries. He recommended ingesting lactic bacilli to neutralize the toxins
produced by harmful bacteria. At fifty-three, Metchnikoff believed that his
own kidneys suffered from autointoxication; he adopted a strict diet of sour
milk and well-cooked food.[97]

In 1902, convinced of the rejuvenating qualities of sour milk, Metchnikoff
backed its production by a Parisian company, sparking an international sour
milk craze.[98] Though partly responsible for the unscrupulous use of his
theories, Metchnikoff's claims for science in *The Prolongation of Life* had been
more cautious. There, he acknowledged that science did not yet have an
adequate explanation of aging, "one of the chief problems of humanity." In
the meantime, he advised people to follow the regimen of civilized morality:
"[T]hose who wish to preserve their intelligence as long as possible and to
make their life cycle as complete and normal as possible under present
conditions, must depend on general sobriety and on habits conforming to
the rules of rational hygiene."[99]

Metchnikoff's views first achieved wide circulation in the United States
in 1905, when several writers used them to counter the pessimism of Osler's

---

[96] Metchnikoff, *Prolongation of Life* (see n. 91), 67.
[97] See Edwin E. Slosson, "Elie Metchnikoff," *Independent* 71 (December 7, 1911): 1235–50, for a
description of this diet; also, Metchnikoff, *Prolongation of Life* (see n. 91), 160–83.
[98] Metchnikoff, "A Few Remarks on Soured Milk" (New York: Lacto Bacilline Company, 1907);
C. A. Herter, "On the Therapeutic Action of Fermented Milk," *Popular Science Monthly* 74 (1904): 31–
42; and Trimmer, *Rejuvenation* (see n. 67), 88–89.
[99] Metchnikoff, *Prolongation of Life* (see n. 91), 183.

valedictory.[100] Writing in *McClure's*, Arthur E. McFarlane captured Metchnikoff's social message perfectly. The immunologist, McFarlane noted, believed that longer life would have its highest value in restoring "the old man to his rightful position in the world." Science now promised to bring forth healthy old age, "not age that is feeble and ailing, and miserably doubtful of itself."[101]

Metchnikoff appealed to a generation that found few public sources of consolation to soften the pain of its passing. By harnessing professional science to the old quest for health, self-reliance, and male authority, he promised to fulfill the ultimate dreams of mid-Victorian men whose individual destinies mirrored the destiny of classical bourgeois culture: "Again there may come back to us that ancient and peaceful weariness of the patriarchs of the Old Testament who, very full of their years, laid themselves down with their fathers."[102]

---

[100] Arthur E. McFarlane, "Prolonging the Prime of Life," *McClure's* 25 (September 1905): 541–51; T. D. A. Cockerell, "The Optimism of Science," *The Dial* 44 (May 1, 1908): 270–71; Sir Ray Lankester, "Professor Elie Metchnikoff," *Scientific American* 107 (July 13, 1912).

[101] McFarlane, "Prolonging the Prime" (see n. 100), 551.

[102] McFarlane, "Prolonging the Prime" (see n. 100), 551.

〜〜〜〜〜〜〜〜〜〜〜〜〜〜〜〜〜〜〜〜〜〜〜〜〜〜〜〜〜〜〜〜

9

Toward the scientific management of aging: the formative literature of gerontology and geriatrics, 1890–1930

We know absolutely nothing about the essence . . . of life; but we shall nevertheless regulate vital phenomena as soon as we know enough of their necessary conditions.

Claude Bernard

Senility is a state of physiological valetudinarianism. It requires special study, not as a pathological condition of maturity, but as an entity entirely apart from maturity.

I. L. Nascher

Scientific civilization has destroyed the world of the soul. But the realm of matter is widely opened to man. He must, then, keep intact the vigor of his body and of his intelligence. Only the strength of youth gives him the power to satisfy his physiological appetites and to conquer the outer world.

Alexis Carrel

FROM THE JOURNEY OF LIFE TO THE "NORMAL" LIFE COURSE

During the late nineteenth century, Victorian versions of life's stages and its journey – images that had sustained the dominant cultural meaning of aging for almost four centuries – appeared increasingly tired and trite. Many artists and intellectuals denounced Victorian ideals and virtues for creating respectable cowards rather than morally empowered individuals.[1] In urban

[1] For a brief sketch of cultural modernism, and its attack on Victorian respectability, see Jacques Barzun, *A Stroll With William James* (New York: Harper & Row, 1983), 180–98. On various aspects of cultural modernism, see Stephen Kern, *The Culture of Time and Space, 1880–1918* (London: Weidenfeld & Nicolson, 1983); Jackson Lears, *No Place of Grace* (New York: Pantheon, 1981); and Carl E. Schorske, *Fin-de-Siècle Vienna* (New York: Random House, 1981).

architecture and the visual arts, the old vocabulary of sacred symbols was uprooted. Eclecticism reigned in the marketplace of taste.[2]

On both sides of the Atlantic, modernist culture repudiated the rigid moralism and the static, obsolete imagery of the ages-of-life motif. Although Gauguin and other *fin de siècle* artists found innovative ways to represent the course of life, no new imagery took hold in popular culture.[3] Except for caricatures and advertisements, the ages-of-life motif had lost its popularity in urban areas by World War I, though it persisted in rural areas and around the Mediterranean past mid-century.[4]

As the ages-of-life motif disappeared in America, so too did the image of the lonely pilgrim. By 1910, American editions of *Pilgrim's Progress* were hard to find.[5] "Faith held out, but the paths grew dim," wrote Henry Adams in 1918, reflecting doubts about traditional eschatology. "The weary pilgrim [was led] into such mountains of ignorance the he could no longer see any path whatever, and could not even understand a signpost."[6] If the journey motif no longer mapped a secure route to salvation, it was still used to represent the quest for financial security in old age (see Fig. 37).

The loss of traditional symbols left many late-Victorian intellectuals feeling spiritually homeless. Existential doubt and anxiety affected even outwardly optimistic liberal Protestants like the Reverend Theodore T. Munger, who believed that "modern doubt" undermined the sense of reality. It "envelops all things in its puzzle – " he wrote in 1887, "God, immortality, the value of life, the rewards of virtue, and the operation of conscience. It puts quicksand under every step."[7]

By the early twentieth century, aging had been largely cut loose from earlier religious, cosmological, and iconographic moorings, made available for modern scientific scrutiny. Laboratory scientists and research physicians attempted to cast off religious dogma and mystery surrounding natural processes. Rejecting transcendent norms and metaphysical explanations, they

---

[2] Siegfried Giedion has called this process "the devaluation of symbols." See his *Mechanization Takes Command* (New York: Norton, 1969), 329–33. For another view of the breakup of traditional sacred symbols, see Howard Mumford Jones, *The Age of Energy: Varieties of American Experience, 1865–1915* (New York: Viking, 1971), chap. 3.

[3] In addition to the Gauguin painting *Where Do We Come From? What Are We? Where Are We Going?* (1897) reproduced here, see also Edvard Munch, *The Three Stages of Woman* (1894), reproduced in J. P. Hodin, *Edvard Munch* (New York: Thames & Hudson, 1985), 57.

[4] Even today, the motif lends itself nicely to the uses of banks and insurance companies. See Peter Joerissen and Cornelia Will, "Introduction," in *Die Lebenstreppe, Bilder der menschlichen Lebensalter*, kommission bei R. Habelt (Koln: Rheinland-Verlag, 1983), 9–10.

[5] See David E. Smith, "Publications of John Bunyan's Works in America," *Bulletin of the New York Public Library* (1962): 643, table 2.

[6] Cited in David E. Smith, *John Bunyan in America* (Bloomington: Indiana University Press, 1966), 13. Smith has provided an important linkage between the disappearance of the American wilderness and the decline of the conventional Pilgrim figure in American literature.

[7] Cited in Lears, *No Place of Grace* (see n. 1), 42.

Figure 36. *Where Do We Come From? What Are We? Where Are We Going?*, an oil painting by Paul Gauguin (1897). (Tompkins Collection, Museum of Fine Arts, Boston.)

Old Age Pensions

—Railroad Trainman

It Would Be a Welcome Detour!

Figure 37. The journey-of-life motif is used to depict the quest for financial security in a drawing from the *Railroad Trainman* (ca. 1925). (Martin P. Catherwood Library, New York State School of Industrial and Labor Relations Library, Cornell University.)

turned to biology in the hopes that nature itself contained authoritative ideals and explanations of old age.

The founders of modern gerontology and geriatrics set about discovering the laws of normality and pathology as applied to senescence. In doing so, they assumed that the biology of aging was a value-free realm of inquiry that could be neatly separated from cultural perceptions and values – an assumption that still prevails in the scientific study of aging. But medicine and science inevitably study biological processes that have previously been socially constructed.[8] Like disease and death, aging presents itself to scientific inquiry already encrusted with language, culture, and history.

[8] For an excellent review of recent works in the history of medicine that sustain these ideas, see Randall McGowen, "Identifying Themes in the Social History of Medicine," *Journal of Modern History*, forthcoming.

The scientific search for normal and pathological aging was therefore deeply infused with Victorian ideals and social realities. By the late nineteenth century, as we saw in the last chapter, the ideal of self-reliant, disease-free old age was in retreat. New medical pessimism, an increasingly elderly almshouse population, and middle-class fears of the poorhouse all worked to accentuate the negative pole in the American dualism of aging. In this ideological and social context, the formative literature of gerontology and geriatrics took shape.[9]

By the early twentieth century, new terms like *gerontology* (coined in 1904 by Elie Metchnikoff) and *geriatrics* (coined in 1909 by I. L. Nascher) reflected a growing international body of scientific literature. Scientists like Metchnikoff, C. S. Minot, Charles Manning Child, and Alfred Warthin formulated the first modern biological theories of aging. Research physicians like Alexis Carrel, Serge Voronoff, and Eugene Steinach experimented in the longevity of cells and in surgical methods of rejuvenating old (male) bodies. And physicians like Alfred Loomis (borrowing from Charcot), I. L. Nascher, and Malford Thewlis wrote the founding texts of American geriatrics. These men accumulated the intellectual capital that gerontology and geriatrics drew on after World War II, when they became formal fields of practice, research, and education.[10]

The formative literature of gerontology and geriatrics helped complete the long-term cultural shift from conceiving aging primarily as a mystery or an existential problem to viewing it primarily as a scientific and technical problem. As traditional religious images of life's course lost their binding power, the course of life itself became increasingly standardized and institutionalized. Gerontology and geriatrics helped define the place of old age in the "normal" life course. While the institution of mass retirement awaited the twentieth century, the definition of "normal" achieved its scientific imprimatur in the nineteenth century.

Early in the nineteenth century, French physicians introduced new clinical-pathological definitions of disease based on hospital research. The old classificatory and holistic medicine gave way to the search for specific, localized diseases – and to a new preoccupation with "normal" functioning. No longer was medicine concerned only with the cure of diseases. It embraced a new model of health or normality, against which various forms of pathology could

---

[9] For another reading of cultural modernism's influence on aging, see Gerald J. Gruman, "Cultural Origins of Present-Day 'Age-ism': The Modernization of the Life Cycle," in *Aging and the Elderly: Humanistic Perspectives in Gerontology*, ed. Stuart F. Spicker, Kathleen M. Woodward, and David D. Van Tassel (Atlantic Highlands, N.J.: Humanities Press, 1978), 359–87.

[10] It was not until Edmund Cowdry published the first edition of *Problems of Aging* (Baltimore: Williams & Wilkins, 1939), sponsored by the Josiah Macy, Jr., Foundation, that gerontology began to resemble its contemporary form, based on methodologically rigorous, multidisciplinary investigation. I am indebted to W. Andrew Achenbaum for bringing this point to my attention in a personal communication.

be understood. The medical polarity of normal/pathological came to play a new role in social life, authorizing medical men to articulate physical and moral standards for the individual and society.[11]

As the exercise of power in society became increasingly focused on organizing, controlling, and administering the human body,[12] medicine supplied a scientific standard of optimal functioning and of deviance. When aged Parisian paupers came to live and die in gigantic hospitals like Salpêtrière and Bicêtre, their bodies and corpses supplied the research material for the first geriatric treatises. The French clinicians who wrote those texts viewed aging as a quasi-pathological process of cell and tissue denegeration.[13]

German medical handbooks and encyclopedias reveal a similar medicalization and devaluation of old age from the late eighteenth to the early twentieth centuries.[14] In this literature, the possibilities for growth and development are restricted to the first half of life. As the old terminology associated with the ages of life disappeared from medical lexicons after the 1860s, the normative priority given to maximum functioning intensified. When Germany passed the first public social security legislation in 1889, pensions were considered necessary because of the supposed equivalency of old age and disability.[15] Bismarck considered them desirable because he thought a guarantee of material security in old age would reduce the risk of a working-class rebellion.[16]

In England and America, the word *senile* itself was transformed in the nineteenth century from a general term signifying old age to a medical term for the inevitably debilitated condition of the aged. Physicians in the United States joined welfare workers and social scientists in constructing a vision of old age as a clinically distinct phase of life requiring special professional attention and care. This view helped legitimate the first age-based mandatory retirement programs[17] and soon influenced the treatment of the aged in almshouses, hospitals, mental institutions and old age homes.[18]

[11] M. Foucault, *The Birth of the Clinic*, trans. A. M. S. Smith (New York: Pantheon, 1973), 34.

[12] M. Foucault, *The History of Sexuality*, vol. 1, trans. R. Hurley (New York: Pantheon, 1978).

[13] Carole Haber, *Beyond Sixty-Five: The Dilemma of Old Age in America's Past* (New York: Cambridge University Press, 1983), chap. 3; Peter N. Stearns, *Old Age in European Society* (New York: Holmes & Meier, 1976), chap. 3.

[14] Hans-Joachim Kondratowitz, "Die Medikalisierung des höheren Lebensalters," unpublished paper presented at a conference on *Medizin und Sozialer Wandel*, 1985.

[15] Hans-Joachim Kondratowitz, "Social and Administrative Definitions of Old Age," unpublished paper presented at a conference on The Elderly in a Bureaucratic World at Case Western Reserve University, Cleveland, 1983.

[16] G. A. Ritter, *Sozialversicherung im Deutschland und England* (Munich: Beck, 1983), 28–29, 38; see also Martin Kohli, "Retirement and the Moral Economy: An Historical Interpretation of the German Case," *Projektgruppe Biographie und Ruhestand*, Arbeitsbericht Nr. 3, 1986.

[17] As Brian Gratton has shown, the real drop in the participation of older workers in the U.S. labor force took place after Social Security benefits began flowing in the 1940s. Brian Gratton, *Urban Elders* (Philadelphia: Temple University Press, 1986). Mandatory retirement plans have never been the major determinant for a large percentage of retirement decisions. See also William Graebner, *A History of Retirement* (New Haven, Conn.: Yale University Press, 1980).

[18] Haber, *Beyond Sixty-Five* (see n. 13), chaps. 3, 4.

THE SEARCH FOR NORMAL AND
PATHOLOGICAL AGING

Rather than speculate about existential uncertainties or social values, the new scientific discourse of aging pursued presumably answerable questions with rigorous methods. In his landmark *Clinical Lectures on the Diseases of Old Age* (1861), for example, Jean Charcot claimed that physiology "absolutely refuses to look upon life as a mysterious and supernatural influence which acts as its caprice dictates, freeing itself from all law." At the same time, however, Charcot also acknowledged the limits of scientific inquiry. "It does not seek to find out the essence or the *why* of things. . . . It remembers that beyond a certain point, nature, as Bacon says, becomes deaf to our questions and no longer gives an answer."[19]

"From the time of Cicero to the time of [Oliver Wendell] Holmes," wrote Charles S. Minot in 1908, "numerous authors have written on old age, yet among them all we shall scarcely find any one who had title to be considered a scientific writer on the subject."[20] Minot probably had great fondness for Holmes, his former teacher at Harvard Medical School, but he had little use for Holmes's playful literary and satirical remarks about aging.[21] Minot's introductory remarks to *The Problem of Age, Growth, and Death* (1908) reflected a growing belief that biomedical science could someday turn the mysteries of the life cycle into solvable problems. Minot, who taught comparative anatomy at Harvard Medical School and had studied cellular biology in Carl Ludwig's laboratory in Leipzig, based his views on the "laws of cytomorphosis, . . . the change in structure which occurs not only in a single cell, but progressively in successive generations of cells."[22] Minot himself was not a dogmatic proponent of modern science as the royal road to eternal truth. He did, however, rightly point out that practical advice about aging had advanced very little since Cornaro's sixteenth-century hygienic treatise.

Minot's call for scientific research and his belief that science would develop a "solution to the problem of old age"[23] echoed a growing chorus on both sides of the Atlantic. Since the early nineteenth century, when elite French physicians in Paris established a clinical basis for geriatric medicine, the scientific study of aging had increasingly freed itself from the influence of speculative philosophy, ancient medical theory, and theology. Scientists discarded older theories based on the exhaustion of some vital element (e.g.,

---

[19] J. M. Charcot, *Clinical Lectures on the Diseases of Old Age*, trans. Leigh H. Hunt (New York: William Wood and Co., 1881), 13.

[20] Charles S. Minot, *The Problem of Age, Growth, and Death* (New York: Putnam, 1908), 1–2.

[21] See, for example, Oliver Wendell Holmes, *The Autocrat of the Breakfast Table* (New York: Macmillan, 1903), 158–59.

[22] Minot, *Age, Growth, and Death* (see n. 20), 249.

[23] Minot, *Age, Growth, and Death* (see n. 20), 38.

heat, moisture, energy) and focused their attention on progressively narrower, empirically observable changes taking place in organs, tissues, and cells.[24] In the late nineteenth century, experimental methodology began influencing the biomedical study of aging.

Formulated by Claude Bernard in 1865, the new experimental medicine narrowed its gaze to discover empirically and numerically specifiable laws of physiology, pathology, therapeutics, and prevention. A "living organism is nothing but a wonderful machine," declared Bernard. He warned scientists against wasting their time thinking about the origin, destiny, meaning, or purpose of living things. "If our feeling constantly puts the question *why*, our reason shows us that only the question *how* is within our range." Bernard's manifesto of experimental medicine exemplifies the growing intellectual split between science and humanistic thought, as well as a deeply instrumental attitude toward living processes: "We know absolutely nothing about the essence . . . of life; but we shall nevertheless regulate vital phenomena as soon as we know enough of their necessary conditions."[25]

After the mid-nineteenth century, biomedical science had less and less to say on the question of *why* we grow old and focused instead on *how* we grow old – searching, in other words, for the mechanisms of senescence and the pathology of old age. For a time, Darwinian theory seemed to answer the larger question. According to the evolutionary biologist August Weisman, aging and debility were adaptations that allowed new mutational responses to changing environments. Aging ensured the death of postreproductive organisms so as to make room for new adaptations.[26]

Despite its cultural resonance and social usefulness, this Darwinian explanation of why we grow old did not satisfy scientists who intensified their detective work in search of the basic cause or mechanism of senescence. Yet one after another, the primary suspects – hardening of the arteries, digestive putrefaction, endocrine functions, the immune system, the central nervous system, the cross-linkage of extracellular proteins in connective tissue – have proved incapable of committing the crime on their own. Today, many biologists believe that senescence is not a single process and has no direct cause but results from the inherent limitations of organic functioning.[27] The

---

[24] On the growth of medical thought about old age, see Haber, *Beyond Sixty-Five* (see n. 13), chaps. 3, 4; and Stearns, *Old Age in European Society* (see n. 13), chap. 3.

[25] Claude Bernard, *An Introduction to the Study of Experimental Medicine*, trans. H. C. Greene (1865; reprint, New York: Dover, 1957), 62, 83.

[26] August Weismann, *Essays upon Heredity and Kindred Biological Problems*, 2d ed. (Oxford: Clarendon, 1891).

[27] James Birren, "The Process of Aging: Growing Up and Growing Old," in *Our Aging Society*, ed. Alan Pifer and Lydia Brontë (New York: Norton, 1986), 263–81; Peter J. Mayer, "Biological Theories of Aging," *The Elderly as Modern Pioneers*, ed. Philip Silverman (Bloomington: Indiana University Press, 1987), 17–53; Edward L. Schneider, "Theories of Aging: A Perspective," in *Modern Biological Theories of Aging*, ed. Huber R. Warner (New York: Raven, 1987), 1–3.

ancients thought as much, but they had understood this within a cosmic framework that also made moral and spiritual sense of growing old.[28]

In contrast to the ancients, modern biomedical science set out to discover the laws of physiology and pathology in senescence, without reference to any explicit metaphysical view. In his *Clinical Lectures on the Diseases of Old Age* (1861), Charcot cited an enthusiastic colleague who predicted that science would someday attain "complete knowledge" of the normal man and of "all the secrets of the pathological condition."[29] Although this ideal presented a timeless, classless, and genderless vision of normality and pathology, it was in fact replete with these elements.

The polarity of the normal and the pathological dovetailed neatly with the middle-class dualism of aging. Hence it was not surprising that pathology was primarily documented among older immigrants and unemployed workers in almshouses, while normality seemed to reside in the lives of native-born middle- and upper-class elders. Equipped with the French biomedical paradigm of "the normal and the pathological"[30] and with Victorian culture's dualism of aging, physicians and scientists formulated the basic orientation that American gerontology and geriatrics have had ever since. That orientation is best described as "the scientific management of aging." Just as the new corporate managers in industry were learning to break down production into its smallest component parts and analyze and reorganize them for maximum efficiency,[31] so the new scientists of senescence aimed to analyze the economy of the aging body and regulate its vital functioning.

The search for normality and pathology in old age brought with it a rough division of labor. Basic scientists generally sought to discover the laws of physiology, normality, or health in old age; physicians wrote about the diagnosis and treatment of disease.[32] Generally unburdened by direct responsibility and care for older patients, basic scientists were likely to emphasize that science could ultimately prevent, retard, or even cure the symptoms of old age. Physicians, who regularly faced the realities of caring for older men and women, focused their writings on establishing and treating the distinctive diseases or pathology of old age.

Though seemingly gender-neutral, the search for normal aging had a decidedly masculine flavor. Working in their new research laboratories, male scientists searched for the cause of aging and the means of preventing senility.

---

[28] Thomas R. Cole and Mary G. Winkler, "Aging in Western Medicine and Iconography: History and the Ages of Man," *Medical Heritage* 1 (September/October 1985): 336–38.
[29] Charcot, *Clinical Lectures* (see n. 19), 4.
[30] Georges Canguilhem, *The Normal and the Pathological*, trans. Carolyn R. Fawcett (Boston: Reidel, 1978).
[31] See David Noble, *America By Design* (New York: Knopf, 1977); Daniel Nelson, *Taylor and Scientific Management* (Madison: University of Wisconsin Press, 1980).
[32] My notion of this division of labor is a rough, heuristic device, not a claim that it held true empirically in every case.

These men were often aging themselves, and personal concern about declining influence, sexual potency, and productivity is sometimes evident in their writings. They sought a "normal" old age that contained an unstated ideal of health or maximum functioning – the "good" old age of Victorian morality.

At the same time, however, clinical findings seemed to point in the opposite direction. This contradiction led to much confusion and some strained formulations, such as G. Stanley Hall's comment in 1922 that "typical old age is rare." No amount of effort, he wrote at age seventy-eight, could disguise the fact that "old age is now only too commonly a hateful and even ghastly thing."[33]

Not until the late 1920s did medical and scientific writers begin to realize that both cultural norms and statistical generalizations were built into the ambiguous concept of *normal*.[34] The British physician Sir Humphry Rolleston began his essay "Concerning Old Age" (1928) by distinguishing between "normal and cheerful" and "morbid, crabbed, and unhappy" forms of old age. A few pages later, he chooses his language more carefully: "[T]here are two kinds of old age: (i) the healthy old age, which I almost called normal . . . and (ii) the commoner, in which the body has not simply grown old, but shows the relics and results of past disease."[35]

The few physicians who ventured into the new territory of geriatrics worked with elderly patients in public welfare institutions. Physicians and almshouse superintendents sometimes acknowledged the difficulty of distinguishing between normality and pathology, or between paupers and hospital patients in large institutions. Yet belief in the benevolence of nature's laws and the persistence of the middle-class search for an orderly, healthy course of life made it difficult to do justice to the growing evidence that normality and pathology were inherently related and that their distribution was shaped by social class.

Medicine's growing intellectual and institutional power in the understanding and care of old age is best epitomized by the work of Jean Charcot. From 1881 (when it was translated into English and published along with clinical lectures by Alfred Loomis) until 1914 (when Nascher's *Geriatrics* appeared), Charcot's *Clinical Lectures on the Diseases of Old Age* was the major geriatric text in the United States. Charcot's book was based entirely on

[33] G. Stanley Hall, *Senescence, The Last Half of Life* (New York: D. Appleton, 1922), 202, 195.

[34] By the 1980s, biological gerontologists were using the term *normal* to mean universal. Normal aging and disease came to be seen on a continuum rather than as polarities. See Robert R. Kohn, "Aging and Age-Related Diseases: Normal Processes," in *Relations Between Normal Aging and Disease*, ed. Horton Johnson (New York: Raven, 1985); Jack Rowe, "Interaction of Aging and Disease," in *Aging 2000: Our Health Care Destiny*, vol. 1, ed. Charles M. Gaitz and T. Samorajski (New York: Springer-Verlag, 1985).

[35] Humphry Rolleston, "Concerning Old Age," in *Aspects of Age, Life and Disease*, ed. Humphry Rolleston (London: Kegan Paul, Trench, Trubner, 1928), 1, 29.

research and clinical work with poor elderly women at the Salpêtrière, an enormous medical poorhouse founded in 1656.

As chief of medicine, Charcot dominated the institution between 1862 and his death in 1893. During this period, the Salpêtrière was transformed into a modern medical hospital. Charcot presided over an unprecedented expansion of its scientific research and teaching facilities as well as a general purging of religious authority. Hundreds of old *soeurs-infirmières* were summarily replaced by licensed nurses. The names of medical and scientific figures replaced the old religious names of many hospital buildings. Obligatory church attendance was ended and the number of ecclesiastical personnel was reduced. Religious belief was reduced to a minor technique of medical therapeutics.[36]

Charcot's *Clinical Lectures* rarely gave much thought to the class or gender of the population on which they were based. Only at the outset of his introductory lecture on the "general characteristics of senile pathology" did Charcot concede "a strongly marked local coloring" to his observations. He described the 2,500 women then living at Salpêtrière as "belonging to the least-favored portion of society." Medically, they fell into "two very distinct categories. The first is composed of women . . . over seventy years of age . . . but who, in all respects enjoy an habitual good health, although misery or desertion has put them under the protection of public aid." Charcot viewed these women as exemplars of physiological old age. Their bodies formed the "materials which . . . serve us in making a clinical history of the affections of the senile period of life." The second category was composed of "women of every age – smitten for the most part, with chronic, and, by repute, incurable diseases, which have reduced them to a condition of infirmity."[37]

Charcot showed no interest in the cause of senescence, nor did he offer much in therapeutics beyond exercise, diet, and common drugs such as mercury and opium. His main concern was to describe the diseases of old age. Citing Hippocrates' analogy between the seasons and the ages of life, he called upon modern science to observe and describe the special characteristics of senile pathology. The diseases of old age could then be understood in relation to the "anatomical or physiological modifications which occur in the organism solely on account of age" rather than in relation to the physiological standards of adulthood.

Geriatric medicine, in other words, demanded norms of physiology and pathology based on old age as a stage of life. Charcot did concede that normal aging was not always distinguishable from disease. "We shall have to notice," he wrote, "that the textural changes which old age induces in the organism

[36] Mark S. Micale, "The Salpêtrière in the Age of Charcot: An Institutional Perspective on Medical History in the Late Nineteenth Century," *Journal of Contemporary History* 20 (1985): 703–31.

[37] Charcot, *Clinical Lectures* (see n. 19), 17.

sometimes attain such a point that the physiological and the pathological states seem to mingle . . . and to be no longer sharply distinguishable."[38] The paradigmatic polarity of normality and pathology, however, led him to treat this mingling as an anomaly or a temporary problem, solvable by advances in research design and techniques of observation.

When Abraham Jacobi, famed father of American pediatrics, introduced I. L. Nascher's *Geriatrics* in 1914, he welcomed it as America's "first modern comprehensive book on the normal and morbid changes of old age." Jacobi lamented that like the British, American physicians and scientists lagged far behind their French and German counterparts in the study of old age. He applauded Nascher's "scientific interest" and "humane sympathy," noting that Nascher "does not mean to take the sufferings of old and early death for granted, and for welcome dispensations of providence."[39]

The Viennese-born Nascher grew up in America and received his medical degree from New York University in 1885. After publishing several journal articles and coining the term *geriatrics*, Nascher was invited to lecture at the College of Physicians and Surgeons in Boston, at the Bennet Medical College of Chicago, and at Fordham Medical College. In 1917 his new "Geriatrics" section of the *Medical Review of Reviews* appeared with two hourglasses flanking the title.[40]

By 1920 he had created a specialty society, written over thirty articles on the subject, published two editions of his book, and interested several students in carrying on his work.[41] Despite these accomplishments, Nascher's hopes for geriatrics were unrealized when he died in 1944. Even today, geriatric medicine is a small, fledgling specialty, spurred more by gloomy forecasts of chronic disease and the need for long-term care than by enthusiasm about caring for the aged.

In 1914 Nascher attributed the scientific and medical neglect of old age to what he considered a typical attitude: "We realize that for all practical purposes the lives of the aged are useless, that they are often a burden to themselves, their family and to the community at large."[42] Nevertheless, Nascher went on, "the physician views the aged from a different standpoint. As a humanitarian, it is his duty to prolong life as long as there is life and to relieve distress wherever he may find it." Nascher also articulated the crucial distinction between problems and mysteries that would soon disappear from the discourse of gerontology and geriatrics. Scientifically minded phy-

[38] Charcot, *Clinical Lectures* (see n. 19), 20.
[39] Abraham Jacobi, "Introduction," in *Geriatrics*, ed. I. L. Nascher (Philadelphia: P. Blakiston's Son & Co., 1909), xvii.
[40] *Medical Review of Reviews* 23 (1917): 29.
[41] Joseph T. Freeman, "Nascher: Excerpts from His Life, Letters, and Works," *The Gerontologist* 1 (March 1961): 17.
[42] Nascher, *Geriatrics* (see n. 39), v-vi.

sicians, he wrote, would certainly find the "aged and their diseases" of utmost interest, since they presented "problems that are intimately bound up in the grand mystery of life and death."[43]

Until 1916, Nascher worked both in private practice and in the outpatient department of Mount Sinai Hospital. He was then appointed to the New York Department of Public Welfare, and became its chief physician from 1925 until his mandatory retirement in 1929. Two years later, he took charge of the 1,200 inmates of the New York Farm Colony.[44]

Nascher's hopes for geriatrics and his lifelong commitment to care of the aged – especially the aged poor – flew in the face of traditional American social welfare practices. Almshouses, which by the late nineteenth century were evolving into public old-age homes, had always been hampered by their inability to reconcile the conflicting goals of compassionate reform and deterrence. Since the antebellum period, institutionalized segregation of the indigent in almshouses had been premised on the (largely inaccurate) view that a clear distinction could be made between the "worthy" poor (the sick, elderly, and disabled who deserved a house of refuge) and the "unworthy" or able-bodied poor, for whom outdoor relief encouraged idleness and undermined self-reliance.[45]

The distinction between the "worthy" and the "unworthy" poor and the Victorian dualism of aging were both cut from the same cultural template: Individuals were solely responsible for themselves. Poverty and illness reflected individual failure. Hence, those unwilling to save for old age or to follow the bourgeois regimen of temperance and virtue could not expect to be coddled with pensions or health care in their dotage. Fear of disease, dependency, and the almshouse would enforce the ethic of work and self-reliance.

By Nascher's time, it had become clear that the almshouse, while it inspired fear of degradation by stigmatizing its inmates, could not slow the growth of poverty in urban capitalist society. Early hopes for transformation of character and compassionate haven gave way to the goals of preserving order and reducing costs. Custody replaced reform as the mainstay of institutional life. Poorhouses became symbols of brutality and corruption.[46] At the same time, children, the mentally ill, the deaf, the mute, and the blind were gradually transferred to specialized institutions, leaving the elderly and infirm (for whom nothing could presumably be done) behind. The sick and

---

[43] Nascher, *Geriatrics* (see n. 39), v-vi.

[44] Freeman, "Nascher" (see n. 41), 19.

[45] Michael B. Katz, "Poorhouses and the Origins of the Public Old Age Home," *Milbank Memorial Fund Quarterly: Health and Society* 62 (winter 1984): 118.

[46] David Rothman, *The Discovery of the Asylum: Social Order and Disorder in the New Republic* (Boston: Little, Brown, 1971), 30.

poor elderly — but especially the immigrant working class — were doubly damned by these developments and by late nineteenth-century pessimism about old age.

Between 1880 and 1920, the national proportion of the almshouse residents who were elderly rose from 33 to 66 percent. Cases of illness and insanity often went untreated.[47] At the same time, the foreign-born comprised about 25 percent of the aged population in the United States. But in major urban centers like New York, Chicago, Philadelphia, and Boston, immigrants made up anywhere from 50 to 75 percent of the elderly population.[48] They made up the majority of inmates (more men than women) in almshouses like the one on Blackwell's Island in New York City, where in 1929 dormitories contained a hundred or more beds squeezed so tightly together that the men could barely get in or out of them. Such institutions provided no bureaus, closets, or tables for personal possessions; between five and six hundred people ate together, and as many as thirty bathed together at one time.

When Homer Folks, commissioner of New York City's charities, announced in 1903 that the city almshouse would henceforth be called the Home for the Aged and Infirm, he attempted to bring a new dignity to the dependent aged who badly needed food, shelter, and medical attention. The new name and policy of the New York City almshouse initiated a national trend in the care of the elderly. Although this trend never succeeded in removing the stigma of pauperism from the new public old-age homes, it did signify and reinforce the growing perception that the frail and sick elderly should be cared for in separate institutions under medical supervision. As Homer Folks put it, the time had come "when the inmates of our almshouses should be considered as more related to hospital patients than paupers."[49]

Administrators and trustees of public homes for the aged often acknowledged that no clear distinction could be drawn between hospital patients and paupers — between the "old and infirm" and the "old and sick" who moved back and forth between medical and almshouse wards. This vagueness reinforced the ideological assumption that the "unworthy" elderly were full of pathology. Those who were by definition "worthy" (i.e., white Anglo-Saxon Protestant females) rarely were forced to conclude their lives in a public institution.[50]

---

[47] Cited in David Rothman, *Conscience and Convenience: The Asylum and Its Alternatives in Progressive America* (Boston: Little, Brown, 1980), 30.

[48] Gratton, *Urban Elders* (see n. 17), chap. 2. Gratton's figures are for the period 1890 to 1950.

[49] Cited in Haber, *Beyond Sixty-Five* (see n. 13), 87.

[50] See Mary Wilkins Freeman, "A Mistaken Charity," in *The Revolt of Mother and Other Stories*, 1st ed. (Old Westbury, N.Y.: Feminist Press, 1974); and Gratton, *Urban Elders* (see n. 17), 128–53. On the tendency for stereotypes of "others" to be represented as diseased, see Sander L. Gilman, *Difference and Pathology* (Ithaca, N.Y.: Cornell University Press, 1985).

Although Nascher spent some time in private and sectarian asylums for the aged, his views on the physiology and pathology of old age derived primarily from long clinical experience as a public welfare physician. Nevertheless, when he emphasized that old age deserved its own standards of health and disease, Nascher obscured the social and ideological dimensions of biological and medical categories. "Senility is a state of physiological valetudinarianism," he wrote. "It requires special study, not as a pathological condition of maturity, but as an entity entirely apart from maturity. . . . "[51]

Like Charcot, Nascher realized that geriatric medicine required a new understanding of the ages of life, in which each age had its own characteristic physiology and pathology. He distinguished between old age, which referred to progressive organic changes after mid-life, and senility (or advanced old age), the period "from the time when the mental and physical impairment begins to incapacitate the individual, to the complete decrepitude that ends in physiological death."[52]

Although not always explicit or consistent in his terminology, Nascher seemed to conceive of four ages of life: childhood, maturity, old age, and senility. The transition from old age to senility generally took place in the individual's late seventies or early eighties, a critical period known as the "senile climacteric."[53] Nascher ridiculed those who would evaluate the manifestations of one age by the standards of another: "A pulse of 120 in an infant does not mean tachycardia nor does limited reasoning power stamp the infant as an idiot. These conditions are natural and normal at that period of life although they are unnatural, abnormal and pathological in maturity."[54]

In the normal state of senility, for example, skin was "dry, lusterless, darker than in maturity, often pigmented, loose and thin, showing varicosed veins and tortuous arteries underneath." Hair tended to be thin and gray or white. Baldness was sometimes accompanied by excessive hair growth in unusual places. Nails became brittle and cracked. Impaired circulation and defective oxygenation often left extremities without adequate nourishment. Teeth fell out, jaw and facial bones changed shape with muscular atrophy, eyes became lusterless and acquired a gray ring around the cornea. "The attitude of age is well described as a slouch," wrote Nascher.[55] Stature diminished from compression of intervertebral disks, weakening skeletal musculature, exaggeration of spinal curvature, and flattening of the pelvis.

Some of the conditions Nascher attributed to normal senility would be considered diseases later in the century. Others would be considered mod-

---

[51] Nascher, *Geriatrics* (see n. 39), 496.
[52] Nascher, *Geriatrics* (see n. 39), 18.
[53] Nascher, *Geriatrics* (see n. 39), 18–21. Today the stages of old age and senility would be further divided and termed the "young old," the "old old," and the "oldest old."
[54] Nascher, *Geriatrics* (see n. 39), 11.
[55] Nascher, *Geriatrics* (see n. 39), 12–14.

ifiable (though not as completely as health reformers had advocated) by diet and exercise or by improved social support and opportunity to exercise autonomy. Declining bone density, for example, has since been defined as osteoporosis – a "disease," especially marked in women, that is to some extent preventable but not curable. Likewise, certain of Nascher's ideas about normal "senile changes in mentality" have been redefined as mental disorders treatable by pharmacological agents or psychosocial intervention.

The senile individual, Nascher observed, usually exhibited depression and lack of interest in things outside the self. Countenance ranged from expressionless to morose and resigned, to a haunting look of anxiety and fear. Nascher had little patience with the "optimistic platitudes" of philosophers or theologians. Infirm old people tended to be stubborn and perverse, terribly afraid of death, suspicious, and selfish. "The most prominent mental characteristic in old age is an overwhelming interest in self," he wrote, "a selfishness which gradually subordinates every other interest in life to the welfare of the individual."[56]

Nascher believed that with few exceptions, the same physiological changes took place in both men and women. Women showed more hair growth on the upper lip, more prominent decay of neck muscles, more abdominal fat deposits, and less marked curvature of the back. In women, mental changes appeared later and proceeded "to the extent of complete dementia far more often" than in men. At the same time, Nascher observed that women were "more readily resigned to the inevitable through their faith." Cheerfulness often brought a sympathy denied to their gloomy and disagreeable male counterparts.[57]

In classifying the diseases of old age and their relationship to the "senile organism," Nascher created a fivefold division: (1) primary senile diseases, which presented a clear alteration of "ordinary" anatomical or physiological changes; (2) secondary senile diseases, which resulted from these changes; (3) modified diseases, which presented symptoms in old age not present in maturity; (4) preferential diseases, which occurred most frequently in late life; and (5) diseases that were either rare in old age or did not present differently from maturity.

Nascher noted that his classification would require revision as knowledge of "normal senile conditions" and of the pathogenesis of diseases like gout, diabetes, cancer, and pernicious anemia increased. More importantly, he acknowledged that his first category – "abnormalities in the normal process of involution" – was a theoretical ideal rather than an empirically valid classification. Since biomedical science had no adequate "standard of senile conditions and no means of establishing a norm," he was forced to include

---

[56] Nascher, *Geriatrics* (see n. 39), 14.
[57] Nascher, *Geriatrics* (see n. 39), 16–17.

within this group many "ordinary senile degenerations . . . as nearly all produce discomfort or give rise to secondary pathological conditions."[58]

Despite the inability of clinicians to observe sharp distinctions between
physiology and pathology in old age, some biomedical scientists continued
to write as if this polarity could be read directly off the face of nature.
Although the clinical findings of geriatric medicine were uniformly depressing and even raised the possibility that aging itself was a pathological process,
the Enlightenment dream of a disease-free life cycle ending in natural death
found advocates in the exciting new fields of bacteriology and experimental
surgery.

In Chapter 8, we discussed Metchnikoff's theory of aging as a chronic
disease – a theory that was taught in American medical schools at least until
the late 1930s.[59] Metchnikoff's ideas in bacteriology were paralleled by
pioneers in experimental surgery. Alexis Carrel was a brilliant French physician who first succeeded in suturing blood vessels in 1902 and came to
work at the Rockefeller Institute for Medical Research in 1906. He agreed
with Metchnikoff about the degenerate state of old age in *fin de siècle* society.
Unlike Metchnikoff, however, Carrel warned against the dangers of prolonging diseased, paralyzed, weak, or insane lives. "Why should more years
be added to the life of persons who are unhappy, selfish, stupid, and useless?"
he asked. "The number of centenarians must not be augmented until we
can prevent intellectual and moral decay, and also the lingering diseases of
old age."[60]

Carrel's surgical and cell-culture experiments won him a Nobel Prize in
1912 as well as popular admiration. The seemingly immortal strain of cells
that he cultivated from the heart of an embryo chick actually outlived him.
Carrel took a basically eugenic approach to combating the destructive forces
of modern living. He believed that modernity had overridden natural selec-
tion by allowing individuals with chronic and genetic diseases to survive
and reproduce. He had little hope for procuring healthy longevity among
those already living, but advocated voluntary eugenics to give future generations a chance at normal old age. In *Man, The Unknown*, translated into
English in 1938, he formulated an almost mystical variation of the Enlightenment dream, in which a scientific elite would enable humanity to achieve
long life, freedom from disease, and spiritual advancement.

In the 1920s, other experimental physicians followed in the footsteps of
Brown-Séquard. Both Eugene Steinach, working in comparative physiology
in Austria, and Serge Voronoff, director of experimental surgery at the
physiology lab of the *Collège de France*, believed they had demonstrated that

---

[58] Nascher, *Geriatrics* (see n. 39), 66.
[59] I owe this information to Dr. William Schottstaedt, who was introduced to Metchnikoff's work at
the University of California at San Francisco Medical School in the late 1930s.
[60] Alexis Carrel, *Man, The Unknown* (New York: Harper Bros., 1935), 180.

older male organisms could be rejuvenated using the sex glands or hormones. Animal experimentation led to human application. Steinach, as we have seen, pioneered the operation of cutting and tying off the vas deferens in hopes of exchanging fertility for youthfulness.

These experiments reveal a desire to eliminate not only the diseases of old age but the decline of physical vitality in aging. In *The Conquest of Life* (1928), Voronoff, who did the first experimental work in glandular transplantation, heaped scorn on the ancient view of the ages of life. He had no use for the notion that every age has its privileges or that the dying out of passion in old age was a good thing. He rejected images of wisdom or of the serene, contemplative life. These were unacceptable substitutes for the real joys of intense activity and passion. "The alleged joys of old age," he wrote, "have been imagined to console us in our downfall, which is considered as inevitable and irremediable. Well, as a matter of plain fact, this notion is entirely false."[61]

The apparently optimistic views of Metchnikoff, Carrel, Steinach, and Voronoff, however, did not go unchallenged. In 1928, University of Michigan pathologist Alfred Warthin offered a more sobering ideal of normality. His Carpenter Lecture, given at the New York Academy of Medicine, defended the view of aging as "a combination of organ involutions [degenerative changes] and tissue involutions, shown histologically by well-defined tissue lesions and manifested clinically by descending function curves."[62]

Warthin had little patience for rejuvenation therapies or for notions of old age as a disease. Nor did he have a high opinion of contemporary theories of senescence. They were all, he wrote, "built upon insecure foundations. . . . Not a single one of all the theories . . . has a leg to stand upon; for the greater part they are pure hypotheses constructed about some single fact. . . . "[63] Warthin believed that these theories all shared the fundamental error of considering involution (or degeneration) to be qualitatively different from evolution (or growth).[64] In contrast, Warthin insisted that the processes of growth and senescence were inseparable and proceeded in tandem "from the time of the union of sperm cell and ovum." Just as the sperm lost its tail in the act of fertilization, so other cells, tissues, and organs lost their viability after fulfilling their biological functions. The exact "chemicophys-

---

[61] Serge Voronoff, *The Conquest of Life*, trans. G. Gibier Rambaud (New York: Brentano's, 1928), 73. See his chap. 6, "The Struggle Against Old Age," 71–75.

[62] Alfred S. Warthin, *Old Age, The Major Involution* (New York: Hoeber, 1929), 75. This lecture was first published in the *Bulletin of the New York Academy of Medicine*, and in the *New York State Journal of Medicine*.

[63] Warthin, *Old Age* (see n. 62), 160.

[64] Warthin, *Old Age* (see n. 62), 155–63. Warthin referred only in passing to Brown-Séquard's theory of sclerotic changes in vessels, Metchnikoff's theory of intestinal putrefaction, Horsley's theory of degeneration of the thyroid gland, and Lorand's theory of general degeneration of the ductless glands (in particular the thyroid, adrenals, and gonads).

ical" mechanism of senescence, he thought, could "be known only when we know the nature of the *energy-charge* and *energy release* of the cell."[65]

Like all other writers on the subject, Warthin acknowledged the "very great difficulty of distinguishing between physiologic involution and pathological conditions."[66] Warthin's view led logically to the idea that at least some physiological changes were themselves pathological, and could be labeled as such once they had reached a clinical level of impairment.[67] But he did not pursue this line of reasoning. Instead, he proceeded to list normal physiological changes in the skeleton, circulatory system, teeth, eyes, hearing, intellectual and spiritual life, digestive function, heart, respiration, bone-marrow and lymph system, urinary function, hair, and reproductive system.

After describing the physiological tissue changes (which he also termed "the primary pathology of age") of involution, Warthin then discussed the "secondary pathologic changes of old age" made possible by the structural alterations of the primary involution process. These diseases (like myocardial infarction, hypothyroidism, senile dementia, respiratory infections) accounted for nearly all deaths in the last third of life.[68]

Warthin believed that medicine could help treat or prevent some of this "secondary pathology of age," thereby allowing more individuals to achieve their full life span through physiological death. But he warned of the dangers. "There may be individuals who wish to live to the very limit of their biologic allotment, to pass the last decade or two of their descent to the grave in uselessness, nonproductive existence, dependency, in personal discomfort, and a burden to others. I personally am not of that sort," he wrote, preferring the Psalmist's limit: "and if by reason of strength, labor and sorrow they be four-score – yet is their strength, labor and sorrow; for it is soon cut off, and we fly away."[69]

Warthin scorned the "euphoric prophecy" of life extension advocates, showing that gains in life expectancy at birth (from thirty-five years in 1880 to fifty-four for men and fifty-six for women in 1920) had actually been accompanied by declines in life expectancy at age seventy-two and above. Sensitive to the need for "a philosophy of age," Warthin had searched in vain for literature or poetry "written from the viewpoint of the normal physiological conception of age and death."[70] Nevertheless, he singled out

---

[65] Warthin, *Old Age* (see n. 62), 162, 163.

[66] Alfred S. Warthin, "The Pathology of the Aging Process," *New York State Journal of Medicine* (November 15, 1928): 1354.

[67] This is the view of the contemporary pathologist Horton A. Johnson. See his edited volume *Relations Between Normal Aging and Disease* (New York: Raven, 1985). See also Rowe, "Interaction of Aging and Disease" (see n. 34), 247–57.

[68] Warthin, *Old Age* (see n. 62), 133–39.

[69] Warthin, *Old Age* (see n. 62), 183.

[70] Warthin, *Old Age* (see n. 62), 120.

a beautiful and haunting passage from the last chapter of Ecclesiastes for its "adequate word-picture of the closing days of human life."[71]

Warthin did not explain why he chose specific metaphors to convey aging as a normal physiological process, but his rhetoric and perspective are drawn from the ancients. He portrayed three acts of the "tragicomedy of human life" – evolution, maturity, and involution – in terms that closely parallel Aristotle's three ages of growth, stasis, and decline. A quote from Cicero's *De Senectute* concludes the book.[72]

Warthin also revised the image of the journey of life to convey his belief that aging and death were necessary for human adaptation over vast evolutionary periods. Rather than seeing the individual as a traveler on the river of life, Warthin imagined the "present river of life flowing through us" – either toward extinction or greater evolutionary development. The ultimate fate of living processes was of little concern. "What difference does either alternative make to us?" he wrote. "If we can see law, order and purpose in that infinitesimally small section of the life stream in which we find ourselves, there need be no concern as to a future we cannot understand."[73]

Despite important intellectual and scientific differences with other theorists, Warthin's views took their overall normative thrust from the same middle-class search for "normal" old age. When these men gazed into the mirror of nature, they rarely understood that they were seeing themselves. Hence the search for "normal" old age concealed its own class and gender dimensions as well as its role in relegating the aged to the margins of corporate industrial society. Like other founding fathers of modern gerontology and geriatrics, Warthin sought a philosophy of old age derived from its biology, assumed to exist in a pristine state of nature.

At the same time, however, scientists and physicians who founded modern gerontology and geriatrics did acknowledge their uncertainty about fundamental aspects of aging.[74] Why do we grow old and die? What is the meaning or purpose of aging? Like Warthin, they sometimes acknowledged that these were *meta*physical questions, not reducible to scientific method.

While the formative literature generally left room for the presence of mystery, it had no tolerance at all for the corresponding need for myth and religion – for metaphysical meaning and consolation.[75] Scientists railed

[71] Warthin, *Old Age* (see n. 62), 121; see Ecclesiastes 12:1–8.
[72] Warthin, *Old Age* (see n. 62), 184. "Whatever is natural must be accounted good. When death comes to youth, Nature is up in arms and revolts. Yet to old men, what is more natural than dying?"
[73] Warthin, *Old Age* (see n. 62), 15–16.
[74] For an excellent critique of the common conflation of biological senescence and human aging, see Stuart F. Spicker, "Philosophical Reflections on the 'Biology of Aging,' " in *Vitalizing Long-Term Care: The Teaching Nursing Home and Other Perspectives*, ed. Stuart F. Spicker and Stanley R. Ingman (New York: Springer, 1984), 29–45.
[75] On the essential and ineradicable human need for myth, see Leszek Kolakowski, *The Presence of Myth*, trans. Adam Czerniawski (Chicago: University of Chicago Press, 1989).

against old dogmas and myths that blocked understanding of potentially solvable problems. Because of their deeply instrumental orientation to aging, the founders tended to lose sight of the fact that aging is biographical as well as biological, that old age is an experience to be lived meaningfully and not only a problem of health and disease.[76] They could not have anticipated the profound cultural confusion that would arise from forgetting humans are spiritual animals and that growing old is full of both problems and mysteries.

Early gerontology and geriatrics also called for the creation of a new ages-of-life doctrine, based on scientific norms and ideals appropriate to the last stage of life. At the same time however, the founders borrowed their basic categories and values from the old Victorian dualism of aging. By authorizing maximum physical functioning as the ideal of normal aging, by denying that maximum functioning was a cultural as well as a biological norm, and by demonstrating that senescence involved an inevitable falling away from this ideal, scientific medicine most often lent its weight to the image of old age as pathological.

For both social and cultural reasons, then, aging was quickly becoming seen as a problem rather than part of a transcendent reality – a mystery that called for moral practice and spiritual transformation. An unwanted obstacle to the dream of unlimited individual health and wealth, old age was becoming a condition to be explained and regulated by scientific management. Provisions for the sick, frail, or dying elderly looked increasingly like "friendly gestures to the prisoners of [a] war against aging."[77] Nascher described the common view of old people: "Their appearance is generally unesthetic, their actions objectionable, their very existence often an incubus to those who in a spirit of humanity or duty take upon themselves the care of the aged."[78]

[76] See Spicker, "Philosophical Reflections" (see n. 74), 29–45.
[77] Henri Nouwen and Walter Gaffney, *Aging: The Fulfillment of Life* (Garden City, N.Y.: Doubleday, 1974), 17; Carole Haber, "Geriatrics: A Specialty in Search of Specialists," in *Old Age in a Bureaucratic Society*, ed. David D. Van Tassel and Peter N. Stearns (Westport, Conn.: Greenwood Press, 1986), 66–84.
[78] Nascher, *Geriatrics* (see n. 39), v–vi.

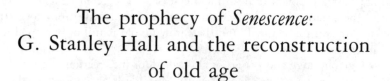

10

The prophecy of *Senescence*:
G. Stanley Hall and the reconstruction
of old age

Many of those who attain advanced years are battered, water-logged, leaky
derelicts without cargo or crew, chart, rudder, sail, or engine, remaining
afloat only because they have struck no fatal rocks or because the storms have
not yet swamped them.

G. Stanley Hall

Best for old people would be real jobs, real family relationships, real functioning in society. But if they cannot be given real lives, they must have
proxy ones.

George Lawton

In January 1921, an *Atlantic Monthly* article entitled "Old Age" opened
ominously: "After well-nigh, half a century of almost unbroken devotion to
an exacting vocation, I lately retired. . . . Now I am divorced from my world,
and there is nothing more to be said of me save the exact date of my death."
At seventy-seven, G. Stanley Hall, a professional psychologist and the founding president of Clark University, found nothing enjoyable about retirement.
"I really want, and ought, to do something useful and with unitary purpose.
But what, and how shall I find it?"[1]

Informed by a scientific world view, Hall sought to orient himself not by
taking his spiritual bearings but by checking his physical inventory. Visits
to several doctors convinced him that physicians knew very little about old
age. A bewildering array of advice provided little comfort or security. "Thus,
again, I realized that I was alone – indeed, in a new kind of solitude – and
must pursue the rest of my way in life by a more or less individual research
on how to keep well and in condition. In a word, I must henceforth and
for the most part be my own doctor."[2]

After months of "painful renunciation" verging on despair, Hall emerged
in a new mood of belligerency, eager to struggle against "ignorance, error,
and the sins of greed and lust." The "current idea of old age itself" headed

[1] G. Stanley Hall, "Old Age," *Atlantic Monthly* 127 (1921): 23, 24.
[2] Hall, "Old Age" (see n. 1), 24, 25, 31.

Figure 38. Photograph of G. Stanley Hall. (University Archives, Robert H. Goddard Library, Clark University, Worcester, Mass.)

the list of evils he had previously lacked the courage to attack. Hall sought the most authoritative and normative ideas of both life and death in the study of biology. The result was a secular jeremiad entitled *Senescence, The Last Half of Life* (1922) – a book whose tone of declension and vision of old age reveal large debts to Hall's Puritan ancestors and his rural mid-Victorian childhood.

For all its indebtedness to the past, *Senescence* is a prophetic book. At once a personal document, an aging manual, and a call to scientific study and professional service, *Senescence* is a rambling, often frustrating text.[3] Yet its

---

[3] For efforts to place *Senescence* in the history of psychology, see James Birren, "A Brief History of the Psychology of Aging," part 1, *The Gerontologist* 1 (1961): 69–77; J. C. McCullers, "G. Stanley Hall's Conception of Mental Development and Some Indications of Its Influence on Developmental Psychology," *American Psychologist* 24 (1969): 1109–14; J. M. A. Munnichs, "A Short History of Psychogerontology," *Human Development* 9 (1966): 230–45; Klaus F. Riegel, *Psychology of Development and History* (New York: Plenum, 1976); and J. E. W. Wallin, "A Tribute to G. Stanley Hall," *Journal of Genetic Psychology* 113 (1968): 149–53.

confusions and contradictions are revealing – not only of Hall's personal and intellectual life, but also of broader currents in American culture. The historical timing of Hall's life (1844–1924), his temperament, and his professional interests all prepared him both to experience the crisis of the "civilized" ideal of aging and to search prophetically for a resolution.

The alternating moods of despair and belligerency or exhilaration that Hall revealed in his *Atlantic Monthly* article (later included in *Senescence*) did not begin with his retirement from Clark University. Plagued by recurring feelings of worthlessness and isolation since childhood, Hall had suffered a prolonged psychic crisis in the 1890s. Within a few short years, Hall's parents died, his wife and daughter were accidentally asphyxiated, and his dream that Clark would emerge as a great modern university was dashed. In addition, when he reached the age of fifty in 1894, Hall had produced neither a major psychological work nor a coherent world view. Feeling haunted and oppressed by the "Great Fatigue" of death, Hall described the "early psychic symptoms of old age."[4]

By age sixty, Hall had apparently recovered from this malaise to produce his long-awaited *Adolescence* (1904), a monumental work that put forward his ideals of education, described adolescent development, and offered a theory of genetic psychology. Hall's work was saturated with the values and tensions of the nineteenth century. In particular, his idealized view of adolescence as the apex of human development – the period "before the decline of the highest powers of the soul in maturity and age"[5] – reflect values we have seen embedded in Victorian ideas about the ages of life.

Hall suffered from a sense of exhaustion and confinement that plagued many late nineteenth-century intellectuals who protested the spiritual impoverishment of modern civilization.[6] Searching for a source of regeneration and a unified world view, he turned to the theory of evolution for a biologically based ideal of human development whose optimum condition was health.[7] Echoing nineteenth-century evangelicals, *Adolescence* counterposed the purity and vigor of youth to the fragmented, deadening, and routinized qualities of urban industrial life. "There is really no clue by which we can thread our way through all the mazes of culture and the distractions of modern life save by knowing the true nature and needs of childhood and adolescence. . . . Other oracles may grow dim, but this one will never fail."[8]

Not surprisingly, this idealized oracle of adolescence did eventually fail. When his retirement in 1920 triggered a familiar cycle of depressive withdrawal followed by intense activity, Hall courageously turned to complete

[4] Dorothy G. Ross, *G. Stanley Hall* (Chicago: University of Chicago Press, 1972), 252–53.

[5] G. Stanley Hall, *Adolescence* (New York: D. Appleton, 1904), 2:361.

[6] Jackson Lears, *No Place of Grace* (New York: Pantheon, 1981).

[7] Ross, *Hall* (see n. 4).

[8] Quoted by Ross, *Hall* (see n. 4), 335.

his study (begun earlier during his mid-life crisis) of the last half of life. Confronting both a personal and social crisis of aging, Hall abandoned his earlier celebration of adolescence and struggled to find meaning in old age by deepening his understanding of evolutionary biology.

According to Hall's theory of "genetic" psychology, individual development recapitulated and paralleled the evolutionary development of the species.[9] In the years following World War I, Hall painted a gloomy picture of mankind facing conflict and decay on all sides. Deprived of the exhilarating sense of progress that had sustained it for generations, mankind was "drifting perilously close to the wrecking reefs." Here again, Hall's own aging paralleled the decline of classical bourgeois culture, intensifying the search for regeneration.

According to Hall, civilization itself had reached the age of senescence, paralleling a crisis of aging that confronted men who now lived longer and retired earlier than their forebears. "We are suffering chiefly from unripeness," he wrote. "The human stock is not maturing as it should."[10] Hall summoned science to the evolutionary task of stimulating the full flowering of human maturity. Truly ripe old age (or senectitude) had been a "slow, late, precarious, but precious acquisition of the race, perhaps not only its latest but also its highest product." Its modern representatives were pioneers whose task was to add "a new story to the structure of human life."[11]

A veritable prodigy of "well-conserved senectitude," Hall condemned the "antiquated scriptural allotment of three-score and ten years," claiming that the "man of the future" would plan twenty more years of activity. In explicitly patriarchal language, Hall called on older people (presumably men) to become "prophets" who could inspire, castigate, and "convict the world of sin, righteousness, and judgment. Thus, there is a new dispensation which gray-beards alone can usher in. Otherwise, mankind will remain splendid but incomplete."[12]

If Hall's fantasy of veneration resurrected by evolution suggests inner conflicts about his own supersession and death, these personal troubles also reflect broader public issues. *Senescence* poignantly registers the crisis of the "civilized" ideal of aging and prophetically forecasts a new kind of old age brought forth by scientific professionalism. Within little more than 500 pages, Hall unfolds a complicated program: He urges his readers to prepare wisely for old age while in their forties, "the dangerous age"; summarizes a large body of international research from biology, physiology, medicine, and social science; calls insistently for the development of gerontology, especially in the areas of physical and mental health; discusses his own research

[9] Ross, *Hall* (see n. 4).
[10] G. Stanley Hall, *Senescence, The Last Half of Life* (New York: D. Appleton, 1922), 407, 244.
[11] Hall, *Senescence* (see n. 10), 407.
[12] Hall, *Senescence* (see n. 10), 411, 409.

on the psychology of old age and death; and hammers away at his central message — that the aged have a vital yet unrecognized role to play in the modern world, a role requiring greater knowledge of the last stage of life. To appreciate the prophetic import of *Senescence*, we must see that its call for a "new story" atop the "structure of human life" forecasts the creation of old age as an institutionally separate stage of the modern life course.

Throughout the nineteenth century, the separation of work from the household and the expansion of wage labor had quickened the pace of generational replacement in the work force by substituting market competition for the rhythms and conflicts of the family cycle. As we have seen, Victorian morality, the cultural handmaiden of liberal capitalism, weakened older traditions emphasizing the religious, spiritual, and moral significance of the second half of life. After 1870, industrial capitalism further accelerated the pace of generational replacement by instituting hiring age limits and forced retirement.[13] Scientific professionalism, closely allied with corporate capitalism, deepened the assault on traditional esteem for the end of life.[14]

By the early twentieth century, the conjunction of shrinking roles in the family and the work force, increasing longevity, and waning existential significance generated an unstable space at the end of the life course. The resulting crisis, whose timing and impact varied considerably depending on class, sex, race, ethnicity, region, and religious perspective, seemed to require the reconstruction of a stage of life increasingly devoid of social purpose, cultural value, or material well-being.[15]

THE CALL FOR GERONTOLOGY

Hall understood that the crisis was symbolic as well as structural: "[T]he old-age problem is not merely economic, philanthropic, social, or even medical, but also . . . perhaps chiefly psychological." Like his gerontological successors, he sought essentially to rationalize and control old age rather than to change the economic structure and cultural milieu that made it so repugnant. "The future welfare of the race depends upon the development of an old age . . . [resulting from] a better knowledge and control of the conditions of this state of life."[16]

---

[13] William Graebner, *A History of Retirement* (New Haven, Conn.: Yale University Press, 1980). See also Brian Gratton, *Urban Elders* (Philadelphia: Temple University Press, 1986). Gratton has emphasized that labor force participation rates for older men only dropped substantially after the Social Security Act went into effect.

[14] See Christopher Lasch, *Haven in a Heartless World* (New York: Basic Books, 1977).

[15] W. Andrew Achenbaum, *Old Age in the New Land* (Baltimore: Johns Hopkins University Press, 1978), chap. 6 ; Michel Dahlin, "The Problem of Old Age, 1890–1920" (Ph.D. diss., Stanford University, 1980); David Hackett Fischer, *Growing Old in America*, expanded ed. (New York: Oxford University Press, 1978).

[16] Hall, *Senescence* (see n. 10), 244.

The crisis of aging cast doubt on Hall's belief that evolution, aided by science, would ensure human progress toward harmony and ultimate perfection. Many signs at the turn of the century suggested that old age indicated decay and degeneration rather than survival of the fittest. Perceptions of the uselessness of men after sixty and the alarming growth of poverty and of chronic disease rates in old age raised the prospect that the aged signaled the decay of Western civilization.

Though he never attempted a careful explanation of the "old-age problem," Hall pointed to the increasing pressure of "the advancing [generation] upon the receding generation" and the exhausting speed of an industrial economy. "The intensity of modern life with its industrial and managerial strain compels earlier withdrawal from its strenuosities. We live longer and also begin to retire earlier, so that senescence is lengthening at both ends." Surveying the response to Osler's valedictory address, Hall favored the work of W. A. Newland Dorland, who confined the validity of Osler's fixed-period ideas to manual laborers. Both Hall and Dorland considered old age one of evolution's choicest products – indicating survival of the fittest rather than impending extinction. If Osler was right, it was only because humankind had not outgrown the abnormally precocious habits of its "short-lived precursors." In the future, the modern human being would become more and more "an afternoon and evening worker."[17]

Unfortunately, the "excessive strains" of middle age blighted and dwarfed old age, stunting the higher late-developing powers so badly needed by modern society. The issue, again, became one of health. Hall agreed with Metchnikoff that man's "greatest disharmony" was now the "morbid nature and brevity of old age." In effect, he sought a revival of the positive pole in America's bifurcated imagery of aging: "The highest goal of all endeavor is to overcome the present degeneration of senescence, to cultivate physiological old age."[18]

Many contemporary observers, including the Roosevelt Conversation Committee, also feared a loss of vitality among older Americans. In *A Report on National Vitality* (1909), economist Irving Fischer summarized data that showed that while death rates below age forty fell substantially during the second half of the nineteenth century, death rates above age forty were increasing.[19] Gains in longevity during this period were limited to men and women below age sixty; degenerative diseases were on the rise.

"We are witnessing a race between two tendencies," wrote Hall, "the

[17] Hall, *Senescence* (see n. 10), 280, 6, 29.
[18] Hall, *Senescence* (see n. 10), 262.
[19] Irving Fisher, *A Report on National Vitality* (Washington, D.C.: Government Printing Office, 1909). Fisher reminded his readers that increased mortality at older ages could not be explained simply by the larger numbers who survived earlier deaths. Since old deaths increased faster than the number of old men, Fisher suspected that "the lives which have been saved by the hygiene of a generation ago are weak lives."

reduction of acute infections, such as typhoid, and increase of the chronic or degenerative disease, such as sclerosis, Bright's disease, etc..... We are freer from germs than our ancestors but our vital organs wear out sooner. And this degeneration of our bodies follows that of our habits."[20] A true Victorian moralist, Hall attributed much of the degeneration of senescence to sexual gratification that sapped vital energy and accelerated bodily decay. Most aging people clung to their fading youth, allowed themselves to indulge in "sexual recrudescences," and soon exhibited traits of senile narcissism. These erotic outbreaks, according to Hall, were dangerous to individual health, domestic happiness, and public morals.

On the other hand, the proper ideal of old age was "complete chastity, psychic and somatic." Hall argued that the old should epitomize purity. Only those "in whom asceticism and sublimation [had] . . . done their perfect work" could enjoy the consummate joys of old age, the "higher ideals of life and mind." Others would drift aimlessly, like "battered, water-logged, leaky derelicts . . . remaining afloat only because they have struck no fatal rocks."[21]

Interestingly, this concern with sexuality also infused the theories of evolution, microbiology, and physiology upon which Hall drew to explain the aging process.[22] With the German biologist August Weismann (1893), Hall believed that aging and death entered the world not through original sin but through evolution. Weismann denied that primordial unicellular organisms grew old or died – instead, they simply divided into two exactly equivalent parts, neither one older than the other. Since these rejuvenating divisions left no corpse behind, Weismann concluded that unicellular organisms were immortal.

The trouble began with the evolution of cell differentiation and specialization. As specialized cells developed higher powers, they lost their rejuvenating capacity and became subject to degeneration and death – all except the sex cells or germ plasm, which retained the pattern of endless growth and division, thus remaining deathless. According to Hall, senescence in humans began with the waning of reproductive power – the progressive loss of germ plasm or declining hormonal production of the sex glands. Final extinction of the *vita sexualis*, known as the climacteric, left old age stranded – the only stage of life unable to affect heredity. The aged, Hall wrote, live

[20] Hall, *Senescence* (see n. 10), 164.
[21] Hall, *Senescence* (see n. 10), 426, 377.
[22] C. M. Child, *Senescence and Rejuvenescence* (Chicago: University of Chicago, 1915); J. Loeb, "Natural Death and Duration of Life," *Science Monthly* 9 (1919): 578–85; Elie Metchnikoff, *The Nature of Man* (New York: Putnam, 1903); Elie Metchnikoff, *The Prolongation of Life* (New York: Putnam, 1908); Raymond Pearl, "The Biology of Death," *Scientific Monthly* 12 (1921); Eugene Steinach, "Biological Methods Against the Process of Old Age," *Medical Journal and Record* 125 (1927); Serge Voronoff, *Life: A Study of the Means of Restoring Vital Energy and Prolonging Life* (New York: Dutton, 1920); August Weismann, *Essays Upon Heredity and Kindred Biological Problems*, 2d ed. (Oxford: Clarendon, 1893).

"completely isolated from the main currents of the life of the race. They have already died racially or to the phylum and await only a second or individual death."[23]

Hall, then, explained aging as a consequence of multicellular functioning. With the evolution of higher organisms, not all somatic cells became highly specialized; white blood cells and connective-tissue cells, for example, remained quite primitive to accomplish their respective tasks of fighting infection and supporting the various organs. Hall's description of "the aging soma" contains a wonderfully revealing metaphor, associating senescence with the decline of bourgeois self-reliance.

Comparing the "primitive white blood cells and connective tissue cells" to "very robust, fecund proletarians," he charged them with incessantly "waging war upon the nobler, more professional and expert, but less independent cells which have sacrificed most of their cruder, pristine powers for service to the body corporate." Little by little, the higher cells succumbed to the "barbaric but vigorous cells" that made up the connective tissues. "We die because nature tends so strongly to develop the cruder type of cell. . . ." Biological aging, then, had become a kind of cellular class struggle in humans. Perhaps the higher, "more professional" cells could ingeniously develop some new mechanism for extending their domination. Discovery of the thyroid gland, whose secretions apparently checked "this aggression of the lower upon the higher cells," offered hope for an endocrinological solution.[24]

Discussing the *fin de siècle* enthusiasm for prolonging and rejuvenating life, Hall expressed cautious optimism that glandular and hormonal research might someday restore old age to the "main currents" of the human race. The work of Steinach and Voronoff suggested that injecting sexual hormones, ligating the vas deferens or Fallopian tubes, or implanting young gonads in old people could restore them to active functioning. Hall also experimented in various fads of prolongevity; he tried several dietary and hygienic measures – from Pohl's spermine tablets and vitamins to self-massage, olive oil, and exercises – apparently to no avail.

Hall was especially pleased with Steinach, who argued that "there is a false old age that has been imposed by civilization upon elderly people and given them a role they have more or less passively accepted." Foreshadowing the recent gerontological critique of stereotypes and age segregation, he expressed an angry solidarity with his older readers: "At no stage of life do we want more to be of service than when we are deprived of our most wonted opportunities to do so. We do not take with entire kindness to being set off as a class apart."[25]

[23] Hall, *Senescence* (see n. 10), 257.
[24] Hall, *Senescence* (see n. 10), 307, 308.
[25] Hall, *Senescence* (see n. 10), 302.

Despite his emphasis on biology, Hall did not expect biomedical research alone to transcend "false old age" or the "degeneration of senescence." As a genetic psychologist, Hall had long insisted that each stage of life had its "own feelings, thoughts, and wills, as well as its own physiology." The psychological task of senescence was to "construct a new self. . . . We must not only command a masterly retreat along the old front but a no less masterly advance to a new and stronger position, and find compensation for what old age leaves behind in what it brings that is new."[26]

What did old age bring that was new? Certainly not proximity to God, personal immortality, or eternal glory. These, according to Hall, were the necessary fictions of weak souls. Where were the compensations, if not in religion? He rejected the blandishments of rest, retirement, and reminiscence which he characterized as "senile regression." Hall argued that the normal tendency of old age was not letting go but taking hold of life – synthesizing experience, drawing the "moral of life," giving "integrity to the soul." Here, then, lay the compensatory source of a "new self," the psychological material for creating a new "outlook tower to guide the human race."[27]

But why was humanity suffering from "false" old age? What was stifling the "normal" developmental tendency to bring together life's lessons? In order to explain the psychological degeneration of senescence, Hall resorted to the old bifurcation of old age.[28] Just as bad habits explained the physiological degeneration of senescence, Hall invoked failure of will to explain why the "normal" psychic development from maturity to senectitude was generally arrested. Most men and women lacked the courage to confront their aging selves without delusion. After age forty, suffering from "meridional perturbations," they usually exhausted themselves trying to "seem younger . . . remain necessary, and circumvent the looming possibilities of displacement."[29] Self deception and overdrafts of vital energy created physiological and psychological bankruptcy.

Here, in the first academic discussion of the "mid-life crisis," Hall depicted the psychological trauma characteristic of a highly competitive, future-oriented society – a society that simultaneously lengthened life and drained it of substance. *Senescence*, after all, was subtitled *The Last Half of Life*, which Hall conceived essentially as a falling away from maximum power and ef-

---

[26] Hall, *Senescence* (see n. 10), 90, 403.

[27] Hall, *Senescence* (see n. 10), 427, 133.

[28] Hall's own research is methodologically split. "Years ago," he had visited homes for the aged, conversing with inmates and officials, and leaving little blue books for answers to questions. But these data, though "voluminous enough," supplied information that was "usually trivial, tediously and irrelevantly reminiscent," full of "pathos and pessimism." Hall concluded that "true old age" was not to be found in old-age homes and turned to a "few dozen" old, eminent, "cultivated" Anglo-Saxon Americans. Answers to questionnaires sent to this group supplied him with data that justified his vision of "true old age."

[29] Hall, *Senescence* (see n. 10), 367; G. Stanley Hall, "The Dangerous Age," *Pedagogical Seminary* 23 (1921): 275–94.

ficiency. On page 1, Hall compared life to a "binomial curve rising from a base line at birth and sinking into it at death."[30] Having adopted morale or maximum vitality as the chief goal of humanity, Hall could find little meaning or value in physical and mental decline.[31]

Given this perspective, Hall's vision of wisdom in old age remains hollow and unconvincing. Hall himself apparently derived little satisfaction from it. In the foreword to *Senescence*, he expresses "unique relief" at completing a study which he found increasingly depressing.[32] The wisdom that modern society reserves for old age, it seems, lies not in practical guidance or experienced judgment but in acceptance of historicity, contingency, and mortality.[33] As T. S. Eliot writes in *Four Quartets*,

> Do not let me hear
> Of the wisdom of old men, but rather of their folly,
> Their fear of fear and frenzy, their fear of possession,
> Of belonging to another, or to others, or to God.
> The only wisdom we can hope to acquire
> Is the wisdom of humility: humility is endless.[34]

And yet, modern culture, which prizes self-mastery, efficiency, and technical control almost exclusively, provides precious little nourishment for the seeds of such wisdom.

Hall must have sensed the thinness of his rhetoric, for he was not willing to let men and women face old age alone and unassisted. Without "initiators into the last stage of life," most people would never achieve his ideal of fully ripened senectitude. According to Hall, the world had "so far attempted almost nothing that could be called a curriculum for the later years of life – physical, intellectual, moral, social, or even hygienic or religious."[35] This claim, however, was untrue and highly misleading. Throughout Hall's lifetime, ministers and popular writers often served as "initiators" into older, religious "curricula" for the later years.

As we have seen, a flood of self-help literature poured into the marketplace during the nineteenth century.[36] Advice about aging occupied a very small but steadily growing place in this genre, which aimed at providing standards of conduct for a newly urban, middle-class readership. Generally written by older ministers or female authors, advice about aging shifted from a Calvinist to an increasingly liberal Protestant perspective during the nineteenth cen-

[30] Hall, *Senescence* (see n. 10), 1.
[31] G. Stanley Hall, *Morale: The Supreme Standard of Life and Conduct* (London: D. Appleton, 1920).
[32] Hall, *Senescence* (see n. 10), v.
[33] Erik Erikson, *Childhood and Society* (New York: Norton, 1963).
[34] T. S. Eliot, "East Coker," in *Four Quartets* (New York: Harcourt Brace & World, 1971), 26–27.
[35] Hall, *Senescence* (see n. 10), 427, 80.
[36] Ann Douglas, *The Feminization of American Culture* (New York: Knopf, 1977); Karen Haltunen, *Confidence Men and Painted Women* (New Haven, Conn.: Yale University Press, 1982).

tury. Allying itself with middle-class values of individualism and materialism, Protestant advice literature tended to celebrate the goals of the first half of life. By the early twentieth century, advice about aging had lost much of its appreciation for the mysteries of existence; writers and ministers struggled against the waning existential significance of aging and a weakening pattern of socialization to old age.

Hall's position reflects this erosion of Protestantism's vision of life as a spiritual journey. In effect, he was calling for a new "curriculum," based on science rather than religion. Gerontology was a regrettably young field of inquiry, but he believed firmly that future research in the biology, psychology, and medicine of senescence would lay the foundations for a socially useful reconstruction of the self in old age. Scientists and helping professionals would become the new "initiators" into the last stage of life.

THE RECONSTRUCTION OF OLD AGE AND THE RISE
OF THE AGING INDUSTRY

In the late twentieth century, we can appreciate the prescience of Hall's remarks. Authoritative understanding of old age is now attributed almost entirely to science – biological, medical, social. We are accustomed to the idea of aging as a problem that has many aspects and requires the intervention of trained professionals. Gerontologists regularly publish handbooks on various aspects of aging and methods of managing them.[37] Departments of gerontology offer advanced degrees for those who would make a career in the field.

Geriatrics is a growing part of undergraduate medical education, and several fellowships have been established for postresidency training. The National Institute of Aging and the Administration on Aging attest to federal commitment to research and social service. Aging as an area of professional study and social service has become a major influence on the way Americans conceptualize and experience the final years of life. The scientific study and management of aging has itself become an industry, linked to the regulation of the modern life course.

The creation of old age as the capstone of the institutionalized life course awaited the growth of the welfare state. Following the example of Germany[38]

---

[37] The third edition of the traditional Handbooks of Aging, under the editorial supervision of James E. Birren, was published in 1990 by Academic Press. See Edward L. Schneider and John W. Rowe, eds., *Handbook of the Biology of Aging*; James E. Birren and K. Warner Schaie, eds., *Handbook of the Psychology of Aging*; and Robert H. Binstock and Linda K. George, eds., *Handbook of Aging and the Social Sciences*. A *Handbook of Aging and the Humanities*, edited by Thomas R. Cole, David D. Van Tassel, and Robert Kastenbaum, will be published by Springer Publishing Company in 1991.

[38] Martin Kohli, "Retirement and the Moral Economy: An Historical Interpretation of the German Case," *Journal of Aging Studies* 1, no. 2 (1987): 125–44.

and other Western industrial democracies (e.g., Great Britain, 1908; Austria, 1909; France, 1910; the Netherlands, 1913), the United States instituted a national pension system in 1935 through the Social Security Act for retired workers.[39] Public pensions for retired workers helped prevent old-age pauperism,[40] cleared the labor market for younger workers,[41] and helped forestall more radical programs of social change.

In linking retirement benefits to a specific age, public pension systems provided the economic basis for a chronologically defined phase of life beyond gainful employment. By the mid-twentieth century, this "new" phase of life was becoming a mass phenomenon. Increasing life expectancy, the dramatic growth of the elderly population, the spread of retirement and the expansion of Social Security benefits transformed old age into the final stage of the institutionalized life cycle.[42]

A fuller understanding of the aging industry – and its role in creating old age as an institutionalized stage of life – awaits much more research, but it is safe to say that Hall would not have been pleased with the results. Psychologists who studied aging in the decade after Hall often documented and legitimated the separation of the old from the rationalized workplace of advanced capitalism.[43]

This separation resulted not from any ill intent on the part of the investigators, who generally took firm stands against age discrimination in industry. It followed, rather, from the goals and values inherent in the scientific investigation of mental functioning in later life. Much of this research, like the Stanford Later Maturity Study (funded by the Carnegie Corporation in the late 1920s and early 1930s), originated in the army's wartime methods of classifying and selecting manpower and in industrial management's drive to extract greater quantities of output from smaller quantities of labor time.[44]

The new "curriculum" that emerged in the mid-twentieth century was

---

[39] For a discussion of America's comparatively late and bifurcated social welfare system, see Jill Quadagno, *The Transformation of Old Age Security: Class and Politics in the American Welfare State* (Chicago: University of Chicago Press, 1989).

[40] Jill Quadagno, *Aging in Early Industrial Society* (New York: Academic Press, 1982).

[41] Graebner, *History of Retirement* (see n. 13).

[42] Gratton, *Urban Elders* (see n. 13); Kyriakos Markides and C. L. Cooper, eds., *Retirement in Industrialized Societies: Social, Psychological, and Health Factors* (London: Wiley, 1987).

[43] Josephine C. Foster and Grace A. Taylor, "Applicability of Mental Tests to Persons Over Fifty Years of Age," *Journal of Applied Psychology* 4 (1920): 39–58; H. E. Jones and H. S. Conrad, "The Growth and Decline of Intelligence," *Genetic Psychology Monographs* 13 (1933): 223–93; Walter R. Miles, "Measures of Certain Abilities Throughout the Life Span," *Proceedings of the National Academy of Sciences* 17 (1931): 627–33; Walter R. Miles, "The Correlation of Intelligence Scores and Chronological Age from Early to Late Maturity," *American Journal of Psychology* 44 (1932): 45–78; and Walter R. Miles, "Age and Human Ability," *Psychological Review* 40 (1933): 99–123. For an exception, see Lillien J. Martin and Claire DeGruchy, *Salvaging Old Age* (New York: Macmillan, 1930); and Martin and DeGruchy, *Sweeping the Cobwebs* (New York: Macmillan, 1933).

[44] Loran Baritz, *Servants of Power* (Middletown, Conn.: Wesleyan University Press, 1960); David Noble, *America by Design* (New York: Knopf, 1977).

premised not on vital participation in the public world but on virtual exclusion from it. Having helped ease the old out of the workplace, psychologists and other helping professionals channeled the needs of the old into the consumption of goods and services. Like George Lawton, spokesmen for the aging industry sometimes acknowledged that old people needed "real jobs, real family relationships, real functioning in society." Lecturing to a class of old-age professionals in 1943, Lawton starkly revealed the new "curriculum" for old age. "If they cannot be given real lives, they must have proxy ones," he claimed. "Nine million old people today . . . need schools, recreation centers, arts and crafts centers, sheltered work shops, adult playgrounds, marriage brokers, social clubs. They need bureaus for the exchange of services."[45]

By the 1940s, the outlines of a professional aging industry began to take shape in major urban areas across the country. Both the scientific study of aging and social services for the aged proliferated steadily, with the exception of the war years, which temporarily exempted older people from marginality. On the medical front, the U.S. Department of Public Health established a Unit of Gerontology; several state health departments initiated special programs for controlling chronic disease; Cleveland, Pittsburgh, St. Louis, New Haven, New York, Chicago, and Rochester, New York, undertook studies to determine the medical needs of their aged.[46]

After the passage of the Social Security Act, social workers, often employed in Old Age Assistance programs, began to define the casework needs of the aged.[47] A dozen major cities sponsored community surveys to define the social and emotional needs of the elderly and develop facilities for meeting them. By 1950, many had established recreational programs, generally supported by public welfare departments, settlement houses, park districts, and other community agencies.[48] Counseling centers and guidance clinics sprang up in Ann Arbor, Chicago, Minneapolis, and New York. These programs in turn generated a demand for trained personnel to carry out and expand them.

The service wing of the aging industry relied heavily for legitimation and planning on the research findings of its academic counterpart. Accordingly, social science in the 1940s shifted its focus away from old-age pensions and employment to problems of personal and social adjustment. The Social Science Research Council sponsored extensive research into these topics, under the direction of Ernest R. Burgess and Robert J. Havighurst of the University

---

[45] George Lawton, ed., *New Goals for Old Age* (New York: Columbia University Press, 1943), 32.

[46] Nathan Shock, *Trends in Gerontology* (Stanford, Calif.: Stanford University Press, 1951).

[47] Gertrude Smith, "What Are the Case-Work Needs of the Aged?" *Proceedings of the National Conference of Social Work*, Sixty-Fifth Annual Session (1939), 587–95.

[48] Oscar Schulze, "Recreation for the Aged," unpublished paper, Burgess Papers, Regenstein Library, University of Chicago (n.d.).

of Chicago.[49] After the Committee on Human Development was established at the University of Chicago in 1948, interest in life-span development gradually replaced the focus on adjustment in old age. The Chicago group led the way to the social psychology of aging, which developed quickly in the 1950s, largely through the committee's massive, decade-long research effort, the Kansas City Study of Adult Life, funded by the Rockefeller Foundation and the National Institute of Mental Health. Programs in social gerontology also emerged at Duke University and the University of Michigan.

Midway through the 1940s, gerontology and geriatrics societies were formed and began publishing their own journals. Various educational and training programs, both for old-age professionals and for lay persons hoping to "grow old successfully," sprang up in Ann Arbor, Berkeley, Chicago, and New York.[50] By 1950, the reconstruction of old age was well under way, although its financial foundation – soon to include private pension investment trusts, life insurance benefits in retirement, and increased federal support – had not yet solidified.[51]

The aging industry grew most rapidly after 1965, when Congress passed both Medicare and the Older Americans Act.[52] A host of new programs, organizations, and providers sprang up to serve the aged in one way or another. As Carroll Estes has shown, public policy basically defined old age as a problem in need of special services prescribed and provided by professionals. Perceived as dependent and isolated, old people were now subjected to age-segregated "solutions" that often undermined autonomous functioning.[53]

Although it would have dismayed him, G. Stanley Hall had anticipated many features of this "new story." He had seen the need to rebuild the unstable social space at the end of the life course generated by the widening gap between length of life and that portion of it spent working and raising a family. He had urged the scientific creation of a "curriculum" for the later years, attacked stereotypical notions of old age, and formulated his version of the tasks of "successful aging." And yet, Hall had not foreseen the dangers to individual autonomy, social justice, and existential integrity that lay in the scientific management of aging.

These dangers were already implicit in Hall's vision of a new old age brought forth by science. *Senescence* never clearly identifies the relationship

[49] R. S. Cavan et al., *Personal Adjustment in Old Age* (Chicago: Science Research, 1949); O. Pollak, *Social Adjustment in Old Age* (New York: Social Science Research Council, 1948).
[50] Shock, *Trends* (see n. 46).
[51] John Myles, *Old Age in the Welfare State: The Political Economy of Public Pensions* (Boston: Little, Brown, 1983); Peter Drucker, *The Unseen Revolution: How Pension Fund Socialism Came to America* (New York: Harper & Row, 1976); Gratton, *Urban Elders* (see n. 13).
[52] W. Andrew Achenbaum, *Shades of Gray* (Boston: Little, Brown, 1983).
[53] Carroll Estes, *The Aging Enterprise* (San Francisco: Jossey-Bass, 1980).

between those who would initiate old people into the last stage of life and the fully ripened aged who would occupy a vital role in the modern world. Being both a scientist and an old man, Hall apparently did not consider the problem. Yet, as the culture of professionalism insinuated itself into new areas of social life,[54] it claimed authority in the name of a scientific expertise that found little use for the wisdom of old age, however fully ripened. The very forces, in other words, that Hall summoned to unleash the full maturity of old age expropriated the authority of that maturity.

By attacking religious belief systems that were already compromised in their efforts to nourish and redeem aging and death, Hall unwittingly deepened the cultural void surrounding the end of life. But in spite of himself, Hall did not allow the scientific search for explanation and control to suppress his human search for meaning.

Although he scorned those "weak souls" who believed in God and personal immortality, Hall implicitly acknowledged the religious dimension in his own life. He concluded *Senescence* by printing, without comment, two poems: William Cullen Bryant's "Thanatopsis" and Alfred Tennyson's "Crossing the Bar." Tennyson's poem depicts the end of life:

> Twilight and evening bell,
>   And after that the dark!
> And may there be no sadness of farewell,
>   When I embark.
>
> For tho' from out our bourne of Time and Place
>   The flood may bear me far,
> I hope to see my Pilot face to face
>   When I have crost the bar.[55]

Why did Hall choose the language of poetry to complete a scientific study of senescence? Implicitly, it seems, he understood the limits of his vision of a new old age brought forth by science. Perhaps he was affirming unscientific truths he had learned as a child: We are all "weak souls" and life is, after all, a spiritual journey.

[54] Burton Bledstein, *The Culture of Professionalism* (New York: Norton, 1976).
[55] Hall, *Senescence* (see n. 10), 518.

Beyond dualism and control – reflections on aging in postmodern culture

There can be no stranger illusion – and it is an illusion we nearly all share – than this . . . that because the technique brought by science is more perfect than anything the world has yet known, it necessarily follows that we are . . . attaining to a profounder harmony of life, to a deeper and more satisfying culture.

Edward Sapir

Wholly unprepared, we embark upon the second half of life. . . . [W]orse still, we take this step with the false assumption that our truths and ideals will serve us as hitherto. But we cannot live the afternoon of life according to the programme of life's morning: for what in the morning of life was true will at evening have become a lie.

Carl Gustav Jung

There is no shortage of good days. It is good lives that are hard to come by. A life of good days lived in the senses is not enough. The life of sensation is the life of greed; it requires more and more. The life of the spirit requires less and less; time is ample and its passage sweet.

Annie Dillard

AGEISM AND ITS CRITICS

Beginning in the late 1960s, America witnessed a formidable effort to eliminate negative stereotypes of and prejudice toward older people. Academic gerontologists, humanists, health professionals, social workers, organized elders, and others attempted to debunk "myths" of old age and to substitute positive images of aging for negative ones. This movement, which attempted both to redress the social conditions of old age and to reform cultural sensibilities toward aging, relied heavily on the loose notion of ageism – conceived as the systematic stereotyping of and discrimination against older people, analogous to racism and sexism. The campaign against ageism accomplished a great deal in freeing older people from outmoded cultural constraints.

In some academic, professional, and government circles, however, the attack on ageism so quickly achieved the status of an enlightened prejudice that its limitations went unnoticed. Not the least of these limitations was that very little was really known about ageism – its origins, historical development, and social and cultural functions. Rather than settle for the conventional critique of ageism, uncritically invoked at the first hint of a negative feeling or idea about aging, it is important to refine our understanding of ageism – to probe its history and its limitations as a concept.

I suggest that the attack on ageism originated in the same chorus of cultural values that gave rise to ageism in the first place. Ageism and its critics represent the alternating, dominant voices of an American fugue on the theme of growing old – a fugue in which successive singers have performed variations of the same parts since the early nineteenth century. As a result, ageism and its critics have much more in common than is generally realized.[1] By placing the attack on ageism in this historical perspective, we can become more aware of its conceptual limitations, its existential evasions, and its moral and political dangers.

The term *ageism* was coined in 1968 by the psychiatrist Robert Butler, who subsequently emerged as the most influential and prolific opponent of prejudice and age discrimination against the elderly.[2] Butler directed the National Institute on Aging from its inception in 1974 until 1982, when he moved to Mount Sinai Hospital in New York to head a department of geriatrics and adult development. His Pulitzer Prize-winning *Why Survive?* (1975), probably the most widely read exposé of aging in the United States, did much to popularize the notion of ageism. According to Butler, ageism is a "deep and profound prejudice against the elderly," manifested in stereotypes and myths, outright disdain or dislike, or simply in subtle avoidance of contact. Discriminatory practices against people simply because they are old, Butler argued, allowed society to ignore the condition of those who are old and poor, even as it allowed individuals to distance themselves from fears of their own aging and death.

Critics of ageism aimed their fire primarily at the negativity, futility, fear, and hostility that presumably pervaded the culture of aging in the United States during the 1960s and 1970s. Social researchers documented the widespread acceptance of negative stereotypes while striving to abolish

---

[1] I am deliberately overgeneralizing about "critics of ageism" to make my point. For notable exceptions, see Richard A. Kalish, "The New Ageism and the Failure Models: A Polemic," *The Gerontologist* 19 (1979): 398–402; and Robert H. Binstock's 1982 Kent Lecture, "The Aged as Scapegoat," *The Gerontologist* 23 (April 1983): 136–43.
[2] Robert N. Butler, "Age-ism: Another Form of Bigotry," *The Gerontologist* 9 (1969): 243–46.

them.[3] According to Butler, the very idea of chronological aging was itself a myth, since advancing years bring more individuality and diversity than uniformity. Other discredited myths typified the old person as conservative, unproductive, disengaged, inflexible, senile, serene, poor, sick, or in a nursing home.[4]

The term *ageism* obviously derived its cultural resonance from contemporary movements for racial and sexual equality. Unfortunately, we still do not have the careful, critical scholarship that might justify or illuminate its analogies to racism and sexism.[5] They may be deeply flawed and misleading. At a minimum, however, we must be skeptical of the liberal assumption underlying these analogies – that age is irrelevant, that old people differ from young people only in their chronological age. As we have seen, traditional thought about the ages of life presupposed the opposite. In age, as in race and sex, the Scylla of prejudice is never far from the Charybdis of denial of human differences – differences that need to be acknowledged, respected, and cherished.

As a conceptual tool, ageism suffered from the same intellectual parochialism that plagued social gerontology generally in the 1970s. It was neither informed by broader social or psychological theory nor grounded in historical specificity. On the one hand, myths and stereotypes were often treated as if they were scientific hypotheses to be falsified. "Facts" and "reality" were invoked against "myths" and "fancy."[6] This naive empiricism, however, could not explain why people continued to believe such obviously false stereotypes; nor could it explain why until quite recently so much biomedical and social science research served to reinforce and legitimate negative stereotypes.

On the other hand, many who emphasized the social and cultural "construction" of old age[7] were unwilling to acknowledge their own participation in an alternative mythology – refurbishing the positive pole in the old American dualism of aging. During the 1970s, an emerging consensus among health professionals, social workers, and researchers insisted on a view that was the mirror opposite of ageism: Old people are (or should be) healthy, sexually active, engaged, productive, and self-reliant.[8]

---

[3] See Erdman B. Palmore, "Attitudes Toward the Aged," *Research on Aging* 4 (1982): 333–48, which surveyed the findings of over one hundred studies in this area.

[4] See Robert N. Butler, *Why Survive?* (New York: Harper & Row, 1975), chap. 1; Louis Harris and Associates, *The Myth and Reality of Aging in America* (Washington, D.C.: National Council on Aging, 1977).

[5] One exception is Jack Levin and William Levin, *Ageism and Discrimination Against the Elderly* (Belmont, Calif.: Wadsworth, 1980). These authors argue, with minimal success in my view, that prejudice and discrimination are based on the minority group status of the elderly.

[6] See, for example, Clark Tibbits, "Can We Invalidate Negative Stereotypes of Aging?" *The Gerontologist* 4 (1979): 10–20; or Harris and Associates, *Myth and Reality of Aging* (see n. 4).

[7] For example, Anne Foner, ed., *Age in Society* (Beverly Hills, Calif.: Sage, 1976); Matilda White Riley, "Aging, Social Change, and the Power of Ideas," *Daedalus* 107 (1978): 39–52.

[8] For examples, see James Fries and Lawrence Crapo, *Vitality and Aging* (San Francisco: Freeman,

Contrary to the assumptions of scientific management, the cultural significance of myths and stereotypes runs far beyond their epistemological status as empirically false beliefs. Stereotypes are a universal means of coping with anxieties created by our inability to control the world. Education and study will never eliminate stereotypes but can enhance self-reflection, reveal the ideological uses of stereotypes, and help minimize their deforming effects.[9] Stereotypes are embedded in larger archetypes, ideals, or myths that societies use to infuse experience with shared meaning and coherence. The key to understanding any particular mythology lies in figuring out how it attempts to satisfy the human quest for meaning in a specific context.

As this book has shown, middle-class American culture since the 1830s has responded to the anxieties of growing old with a psychologically primitive strategy of splitting images of a "good" old age of health, virtue, self-reliance, and salvation from a "bad" old age of sickness, sin, dependency, premature death, and damnation. Rooted in the drive for unlimited individual accumulation of health and wealth, this dualism has hindered our culture's ability to sustain morally compelling social practices and existentially vital ideals of aging.

From this perspective, the empiricist debunking of myths of aging was another sign of the widely perceived impoverishment of meaning in later life. Ironically, mainstream gerontology's reified conception of aging (as a process whose "meaning" amounts to the sum of its empirical parts) intensified this impoverishment. At the same time, the fashionable activist mythology of aging perpetuated the same failure of meaning.

Ageism and its critics, then, need to be understood in relationship to each other, in light of their common social and cultural history. As we have seen, this history begins with the transition to Victorian morality in the northern United States. Before 1800, when most men and women lived in families and communities regulated by religious and social principles of hierarchy, dependency, and reciprocal obligation, acknowledgment of the intractable sorrows and infirmities of age remained culturally acceptable. In Chapters 3 and 4, for example, we saw that New England Puritans constructed a dialectical view of old age – emphasizing *both* the inevitable losses and decline of aging *and* hope for life and redemption. According to the late Calvinist ideal (which persisted in some areas down to the middle of the nineteenth century), old age normally entailed physical, mental, and moral deterioration. Pain and chronic disease were considered part of man's punishment for the sin of Adam. Prolongation of life and usefulness into

1981); Alex Comfort, *A Good Age* (New York: Crown, 1976); and Frances Tenenbaum, *Over 55 Is Not Illegal* (Boston: Houghton Mifflin, 1979).
  [9] See Sander L. Gilman, *Difference and Pathology* (Ithaca N.Y.: Cornell University Press, 1985), chap. 1.

old age constituted a "distinguishing favor" – a rare exemption from the ills of unrenewed human nature granted by an inscrutable God.

Today this view would be attacked as ageist, negative, or hopeless; but for the orthodox believer it offered an alternative to despair. Physical decay expressed the flawed nature of humanity and underscored dependence on God – the real source of hope – and drove home the necessity of piety. In the tradition of Reformed Christianity, the pious old were "visible monuments of sovereign grace," revealing the Lord's righteousness, his faithful support and comfort of friends. God's grace did not alter the signs of physical decay. It transformed their meaning. With the tested and refined piety of old age came the strength and courage to face one's condition openly and to fulfill final obligations.

During the late eighteenth and early nineteenth centuries, the revolt against patriarchy and communalism struck hard at old age, a convenient symbol of hierarchical authority. If old age in America had only suffered the usual misfortune of being identified with an old order, the impact might have been short-lived. But old age not only symbolized the old order, it represented a blind spot in the new morality of self-control. As we saw in Part 2, the primary virtues of Victorian morality – independence, health, success – required constant control over one's body and physical energies. The decaying body in old age, a constant reminder of the limits of self-control, came to signify precisely what bourgeois culture hoped to avoid: dependence, disease, failure, and sin.

The rise of liberal individualism and of a moral code relying heavily on physical self-control marked the end of early American culture's ability to hold opposites in creative tension, to accept the ambiguity, contingency, intractability, and unmanageability of human life. Initiated by antebellum revivalists, Protestantism's overwhelming commitment to Victorian morality deeply compromised its existential integrity and consequently its approach to aging and death. Buoyed by faith and the vision of life as a spiritual journey, early American believers had sought strength and personal growth by *accepting* frailty and decline in old age. Hope and triumph were linked dialectically to tragedy and death. This existential integrity was virtually lost in a liberal culture that found it necessary to separate strength and frailty, growth and decay, hope and death. A society overwhelmingly committed to material progress and the conquest of death abandoned many of the spiritual resources needed to redeem human finitude.

Impelled by their perfectionism in physical and spiritual matters and by their belief in the power of the individual will, Victorian moralists dichotomized and rationalized experience in order to control it. Ideological and psychological pressures to master old age generated a dualism that retains much of its cultural power today. Rather than acknowledge ambiguity and contingency in aging, Victorians split old age into sin, decay, and dependence on the one hand, and virtue, self-reliance, and health on the other. According to the consensus constructed by revivalists, Romantic evangelicals, and popular health reformers between 1830 and 1870, anyone who lived a life of hard work, faith, and self-discipline could preserve health and independence into a ripe old age; only the shiftless, faithless, and promiscuous were doomed to premature death or a miserable old age.

Throughout much of the nineteenth century, the positive pole of this dualism, the myth of healthy self-reliance, remained culturally dominant. But that century also witnessed the demise of the old Protestant vision of life as a spiritual voyage and the rise of a scientific world view. By 1900, scientific assessment of efficiency and productivity had come to dominate public evaluation of old age. While decline in old age had been ideologically repugnant to the self-employed shopkeepers and artisans of the "old" middle class, the reconstructed professional and corporate middle class of the late nineteenth and early twentieth centuries found ample reason to acknowledge, if not exaggerate, the degenerative characteristics of aging.

In Part 3, we came to appreciate some of the ironic consequences of the "scientific management of aging." Often with the best of intentions, academic and helping professionals reinforced and legitimated age discrimination and the separation of older workers from the increasingly rationalized workplace of advanced capitalism. In order to win support for new programs of social insurance, reformers had to break the power of the old Victorian consensus by showing that many old people were truly needy and sick through no fault of their own. Between 1909 and 1935, social reformers, academics, and helping professionals often stereotyped old people as sick, poor, and unable to support themselves. The myth of healthy self-reliance was replaced by its opposite.

Until the late 1960s, most gerontological research and practice reinforced this negative pole in the dualism of old age. Unlike the nineteenth-century version, the scientific view did not hold old people responsible for their failings. Modern science amply documented the inevitable declines in physiological capacity, mental ability, and overall health that accompanied aging. While Victorian morality had insisted that all properly disciplined individuals could attain health and self-reliance in old age, professional science offered a secularized version of Calvinism's view of aging as unrelieved deterioration. In place of piety and divine grace, gerontology and geriatrics offered scientific knowledge and professional expertise as the path to salvation.

Between the 1920s and the 1960s, the reconstruction of old age (which became the capstone of the institutionalized life course) proceeded on the assumption that most old people cannot contribute significantly to the "real world" (i.e., the labor market). Social policy often defined the elderly as clients or patients in need of professional expertise and intervention. As Social Security benefits became more generous, older people retreated or were moved to the margins of society.

In the atmosphere of the Vietnam War and movements for social justice, a new consciousness began crystallizing among organized elders, who were gaining considerable political clout. The movement to reform popular views of old age began among these older people, and their allies in gerontology, advertising, the media, labor, and business. The campaign against ageism enjoyed considerable success, particularly in expanding the range of choices for the middle-class elderly.

Unfortunately, champions of the "new" old remained bound to the same false dichotomies and coercive standards of health that had historically plagued middle-class views. The same drive for accumulation of individual health and wealth, the same preoccupation with control of the body that gave rise to ageism in the nineteenth century, informed the attack on ageism. In repudiating the myths of dependence, decay, and disease, critics did not transcend the dualism of old age.

Apart from its class bias and its empirical deficiencies, the attack on ageism perpetuated the existential evasiveness of its Victorian forebears. The fashionable positive stereotype of old age showed no more tolerance or respect for the intractable vicissitudes of aging than the old negative stereotype. While health and self-control had been previously understood as virtues reserved for the young and middle-aged, they were increasingly demanded of the old as well. As in the nineteenth century, however, unrealistic optimism about growing old gave way to exaggerated pessimism. Yet the new images that surfaced in the 1980s suggest the old dualism had lost some of its power to shape perceptions of aging in American culture.

GENERATIONAL EQUITY AND THE SPECTER OF AN AGING SOCIETY

By the late 1970s, a specter was haunting the United States – the specter of an aging society.[10] Awareness that the national population was aging blended silently into fears of nuclear holocaust, environmental deterioration, military and economic decline, social conflict, and cultural decadence. The "first new nation,"[11] apparently a declining empire, no longer seemed exempt from Old World destinies. Youthful optimism and belief in limitless prog-

---

[10] I am drawing here from Harry R. Moody's excellent portrait of "the specter" of an aging society; see his *Abundance of Life: Human Development Policies for an Aging Society* (New York: Columbia University Press, 1988), chap. 2, "The Specter of Decline: Fear of an Aging Society," 12–32.

[11] See W. Andrew Achenbaum's astute essay, "The Aging of 'The First New Nation,' " in *Our Aging Society: Paradox and Promise*, ed. Alan Pifer and Lydia Bronté (New York: Norton, 1986), 15–32.

ress, qualities the nation ironically tried to recapture in 1980 by electing its oldest president, appeared increasingly incongruous in a society confronting limits on all sides. The mood of pessimism – the loss of faith in a secure and better future – was particularly strong among many who were then reaching middle age. "Such is youth," as Santayana put it, "til from that summer's trance we wake to find Despair before us, Vanity behind."[12]

Awakening from a privileged youth spent amidst the unprecedented prosperity that followed World War II, the baby boom generation (nearly one-third of the total U.S. population) found itself the first in American history that could not count on surpassing its parents' station in life. Prohibitive housing prices, high interest rates, sluggish economic growth, and glutted job markets turned confident expectations of upward mobility into a gloomy view of the future. This pessimism was not unfounded: Massive trade deficits, the continuing decline of the U.S. manufacturing sector, and the low wages paid to most workers in the growing service sector of the economy raised considerable doubt that younger workers would achieve anything like the rising standard of living their parents enjoyed in the 1950s and 1960s.[13]

Beginning in the late 1970s, these frustrations and a growing disenchantment with welfare-state liberalism gave a new and surprising political color to images of aging and intergenerational relations. Critics of Social Security and Medicare blamed the deteriorating condition of children and families on the "graying of the federal budget" (more than half of the federal domestic budget was being spent on the elderly) and raised the possibility of intergenerational warfare between young and old. After 1985, these views were widely publicized by an advocacy group known as Americans for Generational Equity, which argued that society was displacing current costs onto future generations and ignoring its obligations to children and the unborn. The group traded on the image of a powerful gerontocratic lobby, ruthless in its pursuit of hard-earned tax dollars to buy mink coats, golf carts, and condos.[14]

Until the early 1980s, the elderly had enjoyed a privileged status among welfare-state beneficiaries – built on the image of old people as poor, frail, and dependent.[15] But as the generational equity campaign portrayed them as politically powerful, selfish, and potentially dangerous, the dynamics of interest-group liberalism were turning against them. In February 1988, for example, the cover of *Time* magazine sported a vigorous elderly couple smiling all the way to the tennis court. The caption read: "And now for the fun

---

[12] Cited by Achenbaum, "Aging of 'The First New Nation' " (see n. 11), 24.

[13] See the neoconservative economist Peter Peterson's article "The Morning After," *Atlantic Monthly* (October 1987): 43–69.

[14] Sheila Kaplan, "The New Generation Gap: The Politics of Generational Justice," *Common Cause Magazine* (March/April 1987): 13–15.

[15] See Moody, *Abundance of Life* (see n. 10), 122–42.

234

years! Americans are living longer and enjoying it more – but who will foot the bill?"

In the 1980s, most of the retired elderly received generous public entitlements, while younger workers generally payed (directly or indirectly) one dollar in seven of their earnings to the Social Security system. According to polls, young people continued to support the system even though surprisingly few believed that it would provide adequately for them when they reached retirement. They had heard forecasts of the future bankruptcy of Social Security. They knew that there would be a smaller ratio of workers to retirees when they left the labor force. Saddled with a staggering national debt, surprised by the unexpected longevity of their elders, frightened by the rising medical costs of an aging population, many felt as if they were "born to pay."[16]

The late twentieth century, of course, is not the first era to turn its disappointments and anxieties into anger against old age. Nor is it the first to infuse fear of old age and denial of death with ideological and political meaning. We have seen that amidst the late nineteenth-century crisis of Victorian morality and the decline of classical liberalism, old age in America came to symbolize an intractable barrier to the dream of limitless accumulation of health and wealth. Middle-class fears of the poorhouse were heightened by the alarming growth of pauperism among older immigrants and the urban working class. Aging mid-Victorian American men raised the specter of "race suicide" as evidence of low birth rates, divorce, and chronic illness among Anglo-Saxon Protestants seemed to contrast with the fecundity and hardiness of foreign-born urban masses.

In the late twentieth century, old age has again emerged as a lightning rod for the storms of liberal capitalism and of middle-class identity. This time, it is the middle-aged baby boomers who are most susceptible to neoconservative Cassandras who forecast intergenerational Armaggedon and the bankruptcy of the federal government. Fears about declining fertility[17] and the burden of an aging population merge with the fiscal and ideological crises of the welfare state. Personal anxieties about growing old are conflated with pessimism about the future. Critics and commentators represent the aging of our social institutions with metaphors of decline, exhaustion, and collapse. Our aging society does indeed bring with it unprecedented problems, but the specter of old age obscures its possibilities.[18]

For one thing, the current pessimism overlooks the enormous triumph

---

[16] See Phillip Longman, *Born To Pay: The New Politics of Aging in America* (Boston: Houghton Mifflin, 1987).

[17] See, for example, Ben Wattenberg, *The Birth Dearth* (New York: Pharos Books, 1987).

[18] For a wide range of perspectives on the problems and possibilities of "our aging society," see Pifer and Brontë, *Our Aging Society* (see n. 11).

Epilogue

represented by the democratization of longevity, as well as the considerable success of welfare-state policies for older people. For another, it relies on the negative pole in the dualism of old age and ignores the self-fulfilling nature of those aging policies that define the elderly as socially redundant. Perhaps most important of all, it obscures the vast potential for social productivity and human fulfillment inherent in what Harry R. Moody calls our new "abundance of life."

For the first time in history, most people can expect to live into the "long late afternoon of life." Whereas American life expectancy at birth in 1900 was about forty-nine years, today's children will live an average of about seventy-five years (seventy-one for men, seventy-eight for women). This increase represents two-thirds of all the gains in life expectancy achieved since the emergence of the human species! Since 1968, mortality among the elderly has fallen substantially, suggesting that we are not yet reaching the limits of the human life span. While individuals are living longer, they are also having fewer children, creating an older population. In 1920, 4.6 percent of the U.S. population was aged sixty-five or older. In 1984, this figure had reached 11.8 percent. By 2030, when the baby boom cohort is passing through old age, at least one in five Americans will be elderly.[19]

Not only are more people living longer, but in the American welfare state they are also healthier and more financially secure than ever. It is true that the middle-class elderly have received the bulk of federal spending and that poverty and disease among the very old, women, and minorities are more recalcitrant than ever.[20] But since the 1960s, liberal Social Security benefits have reduced poverty among the elderly from an average of 35 percent to less than 14 percent. Thanks to Medicare and Medicaid, more older people are able to see physicians and to receive long-term care.

American aging policy still does not meet the health or income needs of an important minority of elders;[21] but it has been far more successful than programs designed for children and young families, and has avoided the deep funding cuts that other social programs received during the Reagan era. In the 1990s, however, aging policy faces a series of problems that neither liberal (more professional intervention, more entitlements, more taxes) nor conservative (marketplace solutions: more self-reliance, more savings) perspectives adequately address.[22] Generational equity is only the most

[19] See Jacob S. Siegel and Cynthia M. Taeuber, "Demographic Dimensions of An Aging Population," in Pifer and Brontë, *Our Aging Society* (see n. 11), 79–110.
[20] For a historical treatment of the class basis of welfare policy for the elderly, see Jill Quadagno, *The Transformation of Old Age Security: Class and Politics in the American Welfare State* (Chicago: University of Chicago Press, 1988).
[21] See Robert Crystal, *America's Old Age Crisis: Public Policy and the Two Worlds of Aging* (New York: Basic Books, 1982).
[22] See Moody, *Abundance of Life* (see n. 10), chaps. 6, 7, for a penetrating discussion of the limits of both liberal and conservative social policies for the elderly.

visible and widely publicized of these problems, which are rooted in the decline of American military and economic power, the legitimation crisis of the liberal welfare state, and the aging of our population. In addition, the question of justice between the old and the young is linked to the "spiritual situation" of our age[23] – in particular our culture's inability to provide convincing answers to deeper existential questions like the quality of life in old age, the unity and integrity of the life cycle, and the meaning of aging. While the middle-class elderly have become healthier, more financially secure, and more politically potent, they nevertheless suffer from the cultural disenfranchisement imposed on old people in general. "Growing old," says a character in Anthony Powell's *Temporary Kings*, "is like being penalized for a crime you haven't committed." Having satisfied the social requirements of middle age and avoided or survived many previously fatal diseases, older people are often able to live ten or twenty years beyond gainful employment. But then what? Is there something special one is supposed to do? Is old age really the culmination of life? Or is it simply the anticlimax to be endured until medical science can abolish it?

We must acknowledge that our great progress in the material and physical conditions of life has been achieved at a high spiritual and ethical price. Social security has not enhanced ontological security or dignity in old age. The elderly continue to occupy an inferior status in the moral community – marginalized by an economy and culture committed to the scientific management of growth without limit.

Only recently have economic and political conditions turned this apparently academic question into an urgent public issue. In rebuilding a moral economy of an extended life course,[24] we must not only attend to questions of justice within and between different stages of life, we must also forge a new sense of the meanings and purposes of the last half of life.

This will require a new and integrated appreciation of aging that transcends our historical tendency to split old age into positive and negative poles. As we have seen, since the early nineteenth century, American culture has characteristically oscillated between attraction to a "good" old age (the healthy culmination of proper middle-class living) and repulsion from a "bad" old age (punishment for immoral, unhealthy behavior). We can no longer afford this dualism, which feeds both the false pessimism and the superficial optimism in contemporary discussions of our aging society.

Ironically, contemporary biomedical science itself contains the seeds of a

[23] See Jurgen Habermas, ed., *Observations on the Spiritual Situation of the Age*, trans. Andrew Buchwalter (Cambridge, Mass.: MIT Press, 1984).

[24] See Martin Kohli, "Retirement and the Moral Economy: An Historical Interpretation of the German Case," *Journal of Aging Studies* 2 (1987): 125–44; Meredith Minkler and Thomas R. Cole, "Political Economy and Moral Economy: Not Such Strange Bedfellows," in *Critical Perspectives on Aging: The Political and Moral Economy of Growing Old*, ed. Meredith Minkler and Carroll L. Estes (Amityville, N.Y., 1991), 37–49.

new integration. The more scientists learn about the biology of aging, the clearer it becomes that the Enlightenment dream of a disease-free life cycle cannot be realized. As Jack Rowe has shown, the relationship between "normal" aging and disease can be conceptualized along a continuum. At one end aging can be clearly separated from disease, while at the other end the two shade into one another. In the middle, physiology and pathology interact in complex and surprising ways.

At the former end, senescence brings virtually no physiological changes. The volume of red blood cells, for example, does not change significantly with age; therefore, a low hematocrit in an old person cannot be attributed to "old age" but results from some (often treatable) disease. In the middle of the continuum, physiologic changes make certain diseases more or less likely or more or less severe. Other changes alter the clinical presentation of disease. Still others mimic specific diseases. High levels of blood sugar in old people, for example, are sometimes mistaken for diabetes.[25]

At the opposite end of the continuum, we find physiological changes that, beyond a certain point, become labeled diseases. Such changes are normal in the sense that they occur in everyone, yet they are harmful and eventually cause clinical debility. For example, normal changes in the eye, if they proceed far enough, lead to cataract formation and blindness. Arteriosclerosis, the normal thickening of the walls of the major arteries, can eventuate in cerebrovascular disease or stroke. Accumulated chemical damage caused by random errors in DNA replication can lead to cancer or atherosclerosis. "Even if cardiovascular aging and cancer could be controlled," writes Horton Johnson, "life expectancy would be changed only marginally because sooner or later . . . changes in the immune system and in the mechanical properties of the lungs would . . . lead to 'the old man's friend,' pneumonia."[26]

This knowledge by itself, however, will not change long-term cultural habits. In fact, the dominant biomedical ideal of "successful aging," articulated by Jack Rowe and supported by the MacArthur Foundation, simply acknowledges the diversity hidden within the category of "normal" aging and then uncritically reasserts the old wish for maximum physiological functioning as the criterion of success.[27] By this criterion, however, we are all destined to live in fear of failure. As with the old Calvinist search for signs of election, we can never know whether we will be healthy enough to be "saved." By transforming health from a means of living well into an end in itself, "successful" aging reveals its bankruptcy as an ideal that cannot ac-

---

[25] Jack Rowe, "Interaction of Aging and Disease," in *Aging 2000: Our Health Care Destiny*, vol. 1, ed. Charles M. Gaitz and T. Samorajski (New York: Springer, 1985).
[26] Horton A. Johnson, ed., *Relations Between Normal Aging and Disease* (New York: Raven, 1985), vii.
[27] See, for example, John W. Rowe and Robert L. Kahn, "Human Aging: Usual and Successful," *Science* 237 (July 1987): 143–49.

commodate the realities of decline and death.[28] To create genuinely satisfying ideals of aging, we will have to transcend our exclusive emphasis on individual health and find renewed sources of social and cosmic connection.

We must criticize the dualism of old age in all its forms. It reflects the traditional middle-class hope that bad things don't happen to good people. No matter how good our hygienic regimen *or* our medical care, our place on the biological continuum between "normal" aging and disease is only partly controllable.[29] We are all vulnerable to chronic disease and death. This vulnerability, once accepted, can become the existential ground for compassion, solidarity, and spiritual growth.

We must also break with our habit of using old age as a metaphor for the success or failure of various political and ideological agendas. This does not mean that our search for more adequate ideals of aging should be "value-free" — as if continued scientific research and technology could eliminate all conflict, mystery, and suffering in late life. Rather, we need social criticism and public dialogue aimed at creating socially just, economically sound, and spiritually satisfying meanings of aging.

We need, for example, to criticize liberal capitalist culture's relentless hostility to physical decline and its tendency to regard health as a form of secular salvation. We need to revive existentially nourishing views of aging that address its paradoxical nature. Aging, like illness and death, reveals the most fundamental conflict of the human condition: the tension between infinite ambitions, dreams, and desires on the one hand, and vulnerable, limited, decaying physical existence on the other — the tragic and ineradicable conflict between spirit and body. This paradox cannot be eradicated by the wonders of modern medicine or by positive attitudes toward growing old. Hence the wisdom of traditions that consider old age both a blessing and a curse. As Ronald Blythe puts it: "Old age is full of death and full of life. It is a tolerable achievement and it is a disaster. It transcends desire and it taunts it. It is long enough and far from long enough."[30]

TOWARD A POSTMODERN LIFE COURSE: RESYMBOLIZING THE AGES OF LIFE AND THE JOURNEY OF LIFE

Despite the continued cultural dominance of the scientific management of aging, there are signs that the modern quest for a rational, healthy, and

---

[28] For a provocative critique of the meaning of success for the American middle class, see Loren Baritz, *The Good Life* (New York: Knopf, 1988).

[29] See Fries and Crapo, *Vitality and Aging* (see n. 8), for a popular view of health and aging that fails to acknowledge vulnerability and contingency, therefore reinforcing the old dualism.

[30] Ronald Blythe, *The View in Winter* (New York: Harcourt Brace Jovanovich, 1979), 29.

orderly life course has reached a limit – or at least a turning point. A growing number of people have criticized the rigidity of traditional age norms and the segmentation of lifetime into the "three boxes" of education, work, and leisure.[31] We may be witnessing the emergence of a postmodern course of life, in which individual needs and abilities are no longer entirely subordinated to chronological boundaries and bureaucratic mechanisms.[32]

As we have seen, the modern course of life was born amidst the anxiety and upheaval of the Renaissance and Reformation eras, when the imagery of the ages and journey of life assumed an almost numinous quality amidst European urban middle classes struggling for social and religious identity. The burgeoning iconography of the life course played an important role in helping people imagine individual lives as a sequence of age-linked roles and activities, always linked to the prospects for eternity.

This temporal perspective encouraged the development of individual virtues like self-control, thrift, and long-range planning. It also defused awareness of social inequalities based on class, wealth, gender, or political power. French Revolutionary moralists, for example, envisioned a society where individuals would be divided only according to the natural order of the ages; every individual could expect to run the course from dependent child to active adult to honored elder.[33] American republicanism proclaimed the autonomy and equality of each mature generation.

Set free from older bonds of status, family, and locality, middle-class individuals increasingly came to view their lives as careers – as sequences of expected positions in school, at work, and in retirement. Since the nineteenth century, this pattern of expectations has become both statistically and ideologically normative, constituting what Martin Kohli aptly calls a "moral economy of the life course."[34] By the third quarter of the twentieth century, Western democracies had institutionalized this "moral economy" by providing age-homogeneous schools for youthful preparation, jobs organized according to skills, experience, and seniority for middle-aged productivity, and publicly funded retirement benefits for the aged who were considered too slow, too frail, or too old-fashioned to be productive.

The modern course of life developed as an essential instrument for the maintenance of social order. Supported by the state and administered by experts, the institutionalized life course is under attack from those who call

---

[31] See, for examples, Richard Bolles, *The Three Boxes of Life* (Berkeley: Ten Speed Press, 1979); Fred Best, *Flexible Life Scheduling: Breaking the Education-Work-Retirement Lockstep* (New York: Praeger, 1980); and Ralf Dahrendorf, *Life Chances: Approaches to Social and Political Theory* (Chicago: University of Chicago Press, 1979).

[32] See Mike Featherstone and Mike Hepworth, "Ageing and Old Age: Reflections on the Postmodern Life Course," in Bill Blytheway et al., eds., *Becoming and Being Old: Sociological Approaches to Later Life* (London: Sage, 1989), 143–57.

[33] David Troyansky, *Old Age in the Old Regime* (Ithaca, N.Y.: Cornell University Press, 1989).

[34] Kohli, "Retirement and the Moral Economy" (see n. 24), 125–44.

for an "age-irrelevant" society as well as from the generational equity movement. It is also increasingly experienced as a new form of domination and a source of alienation. The ideal of a society legitimately ordered by the divisions of a human lifetime is now under siege in large part because its view of old age is neither socially nor spiritually adequate and because the social meanings of life's stages are in great flux.[35]

Recent critiques of aging in the modern life course have also reflected a dawning awareness that aging is much more than a problem to be solved. In some quarters, it is becoming clear that accumulating health and wealth through the rationalized control of time and the body is an impoverished vision of what it means to live a life. In 1964, Erik Erikson noted that "as our world-image is a one-way street to never ending progress . . . our lives are to be one-way streets to success — and sudden oblivion."[36]

This truncated vision of the stages of life and its preoccupation with maximum performance help us understand F. Scott Fitzgerald's haunting comment that "there are no second acts in American lives."[37] It provides a response to Alfred Kazin's wonder about "why we have been so oppressed by the sense of time . . . why our triumphs have been so brittle."[38] Since roughly the 1920s, in the absence of culturally powerful, existentially vital images of the ages *and* the journey of life, the middle-class American vision of aging has amounted to a kind of perpetual middle age, at once valued above and disconnected from childhood and old age.[39] Such a vision is blind to the real problems of the aged, problems that can make the old akin to the young, as suggested in a children's poem by Shel Silverstein:

> Said the little boy, "Sometimes I drop my spoon."
> Said the little old man, "I do that too."
> The little boy whispered "I wet my pants."
> "I do that too," laughed the little old man.
> Said the little boy, "I often cry."
> The old man nodded, "So do I."
> "But worst of all," said the boy, "it seems

[35] See Bernice L. Neugarten and Dail A. Neugarten, "Changing Meanings of Age in the Aging Society," in Pifer and Bronte, *Our Aging Society* (see n. 11), 33–51; Matilda White Riley and John W. Riley, Jr., "The Lives of Older People and Changing Social Roles," *Annals of the American Academy of Political and Social Science* 503 (May 1989): 14–28; Neil Postman, *The Disappearance of Childhood* (New York: Delacorte, 1982); and Marie Winn, *Children Without Childhood* (New York: Pantheon, 1983).

[36] Erik Erikson, "Human Strength and the Cycle of Generations," in *Insight and Responsibility* (New York: Norton, 1964).

[37] Quoted in Alfred Kazin, *On Native Grounds*, 1st ed. (New York: Reynal and Hitchcock, 1942), x.

[38] Kazin, *On Native Grounds* (see n. 37), x.

[39] See David Riesman, "Some Clinical and Cultural Aspects of Aging," *American Journal of Sociology* 59 (January 1954): 379–83.

Grown-ups don't pay attention to me."
And he felt the warmth of a wrinkled old hand.
"I know what you mean," said the little old
  man.[40]

Along with growing awareness of the need to revalue the stages of life has come a renewed appreciation for the journey of life.[41] As with Matthew Arnold and Alfred Tennyson in the late nineteenth century, the value of life's journey is increasingly sought in the actual process of discovery rather than in the traditional pattern of Christian teleology.[42] The various impulses to move *toward* something as one grows older – a unity of understanding, God, expiation of guilt, renewal of innocence, or restoration of self – have become more manifest. The literal complexity of contemporary patterns of travel suggests the metaphor of a maze rather than a journey. "The passage of being human," wrote Abraham Heschel in 1972, "leads through a maze: the dark and intricate maze we call the inner life . . . it is an exuberance that goes on, frequently defying pattern, rule, and form. The inner life is a state of constantly increasing, indefinitely spreading complexity."[43]

Margaret Morganroth Gullette suggests that since the mid-1970s, a new genre – the "mid-life progress novel" – has been invented by writers like Saul Bellow, Margaret Drabble, Anne Tyler, and John Updike. Although she does not comment on the historical resonance of the term *progress*, Gullette shows that these authors have created middle-aged protagonists who free themselves from preoccupation with the loss of youthfulness and discover the "gifts reserved for age."[44] Constance Rooke suggests that contemporary writers in the United States, Britain, Canada, and the old Commonwealth countries are creating a genre based on completion of life – the *Vollendungsroman*, a contemporary counterpart of the old *Bildungsroman*, a genre of novels of starting out in life.[45]

The discovery of a previously suppressed dimension of fairy tales, called "elder tales" by Allan Chinen, further suggests the growing search for ideals of transformation, self-transcendence, and wisdom that are not limited by

---

[40] Shel Silverstein, "The Little Boy and the Old Man," in *A Light in the Attic* (New York: Harper & Row, 1981), 95.

[41] See, for example, the essays in John Raphael Staude, ed., *Wisdom and Age* (Berkeley: Ross Books, 1981).

[42] See Georg Roppen and Richard Sommer, *Strangers and Pilgrims, An Essay on the Metaphor of Journey* (Bergen: Norwegian Universities Press, 1964), chap. 4.

[43] Abraham Heschel, *Who Is Man?* (Stanford, Calif.: Stanford University Press, 1972), 39. Heschel's powerful address to the 1961 White House Conference on Aging anticipates much of the concern with spirituality and aging in the 1990s. His address is reprinted as "To Grow In Wisdom," in *The Insecurity of Freedom* (New York: Schocken, 1966), 70–84.

[44] Margaret Morganroth Gullette, *Safe At Last In the Middle Years* (Berkeley: University of California Press, 1988).

[45] See Constance Rooke, "Old Age in Contemporary Fiction: A New Paradigm of Hope," in *Handbook of Aging and the Humanities*, ed. Thomas R. Cole, David D. Van Tassel, and Robert Kastenbaum (New York: Springer, forthcoming).

the values of healthy functioning and success.[46] New collections of short stories about aging,[47] new roles for older people on the silver screen,[48] the founding of a Center for Creative Retirement at the University of North Carolina at Asheville, the growth of pastoral and theological concern about aging,[49] a growing academic awareness of the importance of diversity in aging[50] – these are only some of the signs that as the modern era comes to a close,[51] significant elements in American culture are recovering the existential ground of aging and its possibilities for human development.

Vital postmodern ideals of aging will require a kind of cultural *bricolage*: taking valuable bits and pieces of our cultural inheritance and arranging them in new ways to meet current needs, circumstances, and particular communities. In this process, we would do well to recall the power of the ancient Greek tragedians. Their themes of fate and mutability, mortality and finitude, suffering and wisdom, pose a sharp contrast to the world view of modern science. The tragedians resisted the human propensity toward reductionism, toward problem solving that neglects the intractable complexities of the world. They insisted that knowledge is rooted in ignorance, that ignorance is rooted in mortality, and that all wisdom is incomplete.[52]

In particular, Sophocles' *Oedipus at Colonus* possesses special resonance for late twentieth-century culture. While it certainly cannot be adopted as "our" ideal, Sophocles' vision remains compelling: Aging is a moral and spiritual frontier because its unknowns, terrors, and mysteries cannot be successfully crossed without humility and self-knowledge, without love and compassion, without acceptance of physical decline and mortality, and a sense of the sacred. This requires a delicate reciprocity in which individuals must be

[46] Allan Chinen, *In The Ever After* (Wilmette, Ill.: Chiron, 1989).

[47] See, for example, Constance Rooke, ed., *Night Light: Stories of Aging* (Toronto: Oxford University Press, 1986); and Dorothy Sennett, ed., *Full Measure: Modern Short Stories on Aging* (St. Paul: Graywolf, 1988).

[48] Popular motion pictures with elderly characters in the late 1980s and early 1990s included *Cocoon, The Whales of August, A Trip to Bountiful, Driving Miss Daisy,* and *Dad.*

[49] Within the last decade the *Journal of Religion and Aging* (1984), the *Journal of Judaism and Aging* (1986), and the *Journal of Religious Gerontology* (1983) were founded. In 1988, a brief bibliography for gerontology instruction, *Theology and Aging,* was compiled by Henry Simmons, Vivienne Walaskay, and Barbara Payne, and was published by the Association for Gerontology in Higher Education. In the fall of 1990, an issue of *Generations,* edited by James Ellor and myself, was devoted to the theme of aging and spirituality. See also Henry C. Simmons, "Religious Education of Older Adults: A Present and Future Perspective," *Educational Gerontology* 14 (1988): 279–89; Eugene C. Bianchi, *Aging as a Spiritual Journey* (New York: Crossroad, 1982); and Shrinivak Tilak, *Religion and Aging in the Indian Tradition* (Albany: State University of New York Press, 1989).

[50] Scott A. Bass, Elizabeth A. Kutza, and Fernando M. Torres-Gil, eds., *Diversity in Aging* (Glenview, Ill.: Scott, Foresman, 1990).

[51] My views on modernity and postmodernism have been strongly influenced by Stephen Toulmin, *Cosmopolis: The Hidden Agenda of Modernity* (New York: Free Press, 1990). For a valuable introduction to the debate about postmodernism, see Steven Connor, *Postmodernist Culture* (Oxford, England: Blackwell, 1989).

[52] J. Peter Euben, ed., *Greek Tragedy and Political Theory* (Berkeley: University of California Press, 1986), 40.

willing to persevere on the tragic journey to self-knowledge and communities must be willing to tolerate the unknown, the fearfully alien old person.

The modern scientific culture of aging resembles Oedipus as a younger hero, the brilliant problem solver who neglected the existential ground of his greatness. Like the young Oedipus, we study the ages of life to control the facts of human existence in time and space. And like the young Oedipus, we have suppressed the mystery and fatedness of the course of life by construing it as a technical problem. As a result, old age in our culture too often appears like a season without a purpose; old people too often appear only as strangers, not also as pilgrims. Like the aging Oedipus, however, a growing element in our contemporary culture seeks not to avoid but to transform its fate into a journey to self-knowledge and reconciliation with finitude.

In her book *Women and Spirituality*, Carol Ochs has argued that the journey metaphor in Western spiritual writings contains a male bias that does not accord with women's experience. This is an important criticism. Yet I believe that Ochs has put the case too strongly.[53] She misses the journey of Christiana in *Pilgrim's Progress* and does not acknowledge the nonlinear and nonteleological forms the metaphor has taken since the late nineteenth century.

As we have seen, Christiana's journey — unlike Christian's — retained the traditional pattern of physical decline and spiritual growth. Her passage across the River of Death marked the triumph of an aged heroine, albeit one still inescapably limited by her impure flesh and earthly relationships. Ironically, feminist theologians in the late twentieth century have inverted the normative implications of Bunyan's tale. Traditional male-centered spirituality, they would argue, is inadequate in its exclusive emphasis on individuation, its preoccupation with distant goals, and its devaluation of the body. In contrast, they offer a vision that implicitly revalues Christiana's experience — a spirituality that prizes experience, that embraces the aging body as a sacred space, and that emphasizes nurturing and coming into relationship.[54] The contemporary irony of *Pilgrim's Progress* lies here: An aging woman's body and her earthly relationships, which appeared to Bunyan as impediments, today offer precisely the ground for a recovery of spirituality in later life.

The most striking contemporary resymbolization of the ages and journey of life is Jasper Johns's popular series of paintings, *The Seasons* (1986–87), perhaps the first time that a serious American artist in the twentieth century has brought together these ancient motifs. *The Seasons* also marks the first

---

[53] See Carol Ochs, *Women and Spirituality* (Totowa, N.J.: Rowman & Allanheld, 1983).

[54] Elizabeth Dodson Gray, ed., *Sacred Dimensions of Women's Experience* (Wellesley, Mass.: Roundtable, 1988); Carol P. Christ, *Diving Deep and Surfacing: Women Writers on the Spiritual Quest* (Boston: Beacon, 1980); Nelle Morton, *The Journey is Home* (Boston: Beacon, 1985); and Christine Downing, *Journey Through Menopause: A Personal Rite of Passage* (New York: Crossroad, 1987).

time that Johns, known for his emphasis on the fragmented and incomplete nature of existence, has represented a virtually whole human figure in his work.[55] These paintings inevitably suggest a comparison with Thomas Cole's *The Voyage of Life.*[56]

Johns's four ages are represented by the four seasons and by an arm that moves around a clocklike circle. The symbols of his journey are taken from a little-known Picasso, *Minotaur Moving His House* (1936), in which the Minotaur pulls a cart containing all of his possessions – his individual experience. Unlike Cole's Everyman, a mysterious shadow, drawn from a tracing of Johns himself, dominates each of the four canvases.

The Minotaur myth offers a clue to the shadowy, bewildered postmodern traveler, uncertain of his direction, destiny, and self. In order to get through the maze guarded by the Minotaur, Theseus received a thread from Ariadne with which to retrace his steps. The artifacts and influences represented on each canvas make up the artist's thread to his individual past. A ladder and rope tying these artifacts to the cart appear throughout the series, as do the stars (also borrowed from Picasso) that once guided ancient travelers. The series is an autobiography of the painter's life as an artist, placed in the context of the seasons of life.

Johns's *Spring* (Fig. 39) is represented not like the rosy, springtime morning of Cole's childhood, but as a rainy night. Rain unifies all but a child's shadow, which appears in the foreground. Traced from a friend's son, the shadow child appears frail and vulnerable but also (like the larger shadow) featureless and therefore mysterious.[57] The child is not laughing but sees the world through the tears of the spring rains. This child's world is filled with ambiguous images and visual puzzles like Wittgenstein's *Duck-Rabbit*, W.E. Hill's *My Wife and My Mother-in-law*, and silhouette/goblets seen through rain-drenched window panes. Johns retains the traditional image of a budding branch, symbolizing new beginnings and growth. The ladder is in a horizontal, traveling position. A taut rope holds the collected objects firmly, enabling the artifacts of childhood to move into the next season of life.

In *Summer* (Fig. 40), the rain has cleared and the buds of childhood have developed into the leaves of youth. The hand of time has moved from a child's upward reach to the young person's outstretched position. The shadow has left the center of the canvas to make room for the productive world of

---

[55] See Deborah Solomon, "The Unflagging Artistry of Jasper Johns," *New York Times Magazine*, June 19, 1988, 20–23, 63–65.

[56] I am grateful to Dale L. Meyer for her collaboration, reflected in the following jointly written interpretation of *The Seasons*. A more detailed version of our analysis can be found in Thomas R. Cole and Dale L. Meyer, "Aging, Metaphor, and Meaning: A View From Cultural History," in *Aging and Metaphor in Science and the Humanities*, ed. Gary Kenyon, Jans Schroots, and James Birren (New York: Springer, 1991), 57–82.

[57] B. Rose, "Jasper Johns: *The Seasons*," *Vogue* (January 1987): 193–99, 259–60.

Figure 39. *The Seasons: Spring*, encaustic on canvas by Jasper Johns (1986). (© Jasper Johns/VAGA, Visual Artists and Galleries Association, New York, 1990.)

the artist's experience on the right-hand panel. Johns's American flag, an earlier work that catapulted his career onto center stage in the New York art world, appears here and in *Fall* and *Winter* as well. The Mona Lisa refers both to Leonardo and Marcel Duchamp.

The jigsawlike background, on which cups of the American ceramicist George Ohr are mounted, is traced from a fragment of Matthias Grünewald's Issenheim Altarpiece, *The Temptation of Saint Anthony* (1513–15). The fragment shows a hideous demon who looks to be in utter agony, his body covered with plague sores.[58] Unlike the demons that appear only in *Manhood*

[58] Mark Rosenthal, *Jasper Johns: Work Since 1974* (Philadelphia: Philadelphia Museum of Art, 1988).

Figure 40. *The Seasons: Summer*, encaustic on canvas by Jasper Johns (1985). (© Jasper Johns/VAGA, Visual Artists and Galleries Association, New York, 1990.)

in Cole's series, portions of the Grünewald fragment appear in all four of Johns's canvases, suggesting that each season of life has its hidden demons. In *Summer*, life's artifacts remain securely held by the taut rope, the ladder still at an angle for traveling.

In *Fall* (Fig. 41), we see the strongest similarity between Johns's and Cole's depictions of life's seasons. Both artists see the mid-life period as full of crisis, turmoil, and despair. But Johns provides a distinct sense of physical decline – the ladder broken, the rope slack, cups and goblets tumbled to the bottom of the canvas, the branch broken and hanging limply. The shadow has split, separating to the sides of the painting. The center is ominous and

Figure 41. *The Seasons: Fall*, encaustic on canvas by Jasper Johns (1986). (© Jasper Johns/VAGA, Visual Artists and Galleries Association, New York, 1990.)

chaotic. Marcel Duchamp's stark profile has replaced the Mona Lisa. In place of the American flag looms a Swiss avalanche sign with skull and crossbones.

The geometric shapes, present in all four canvases, have risen to the top of the painting, obliterating the stars. The cold, hard facts of life and death, symbolized by the realm of geometry, come to play a dominate role in mid-life.[59] Whereas Cole's figure looked to God in his despair, Johns's looks to human constructs such as math and science for order and assurance. There seems to be a fundamental difference in the artists' intentions. Where Cole

[59] Rosenthal, *Jasper Johns* (see n. 58), 96.

Figure 42. *The Seasons: Winter*, encaustic on canvas by Jasper Johns (1986). (© Jasper Johns/VAGA, Visual Artists and Galleries Association, New York, 1990.).

had a normative intent, admonishing that in mid-life one ought to look to God, Johns is more descriptive, suggesting pictorially that during times of crisis we allow our constructs to assume such importance that they can even blot out the stars. He leaves us to evaluate for ourselves how we ought to proceed. The hand of time no longer reaches up or out, but points downward toward the toppled cups and vases lying in a heap.

In *Winter* (Fig. 42), the ladder has been repaired and the rope once again holds the objects tightly to it. Neither the shadow nor the collection of images is split. The double images are gone. There is a sense that necessary repairs have been followed by clarity and acceptance of reality. The arm of the clock has dropped down in a clockwise direction for the first time. Perhaps we spend the greater part of our lives fighting against the clock, trying to deny our limitations and the physical process of our aging. Finally, at the end of life we may accept reality and go with the clock. *Winter* was inspired by a poem by Wallace Stevens entitled "The Snowman."[60] The snowman in Johns's painting resembles a child's drawing on a chalkboard, suggesting the links between old age and childhood.

Here, at the journey's end, the mended ladder rests in an *upright* position. A tool that Johns has carried along the way, the ladder can finally achieve its purpose only when it has stopped moving. It points upward, enabling him to reach beyond what he has been able to attain on his own. It is directed toward the stars, the ancient symbol of spirituality. Vincent van Gogh mused over this metaphor around the time he painted *Starry Night*:

Why, I ask myself, shouldn't the shining dots of the sky be as accessible as the black dots on the map of France? Just as we take the train to Tarascon or Rouen, we take death to reach a star. One thing undoubtedly true in this reasoning is that we cannot get to a star while we are alive, anymore than we can take a train when we are dead.[61]

Cole's *Voyage* is about keeping one's faith and surviving the trials of modern life. Johns's *Seasons* is about questions of identity, change, and meaning in our perplexing and foundationless postmodern world. Where Cole makes statements about the stages of life's journey, Johns asks questions. The viewer becomes engaged in the quest for meaning when he or she begins to struggle with the puzzles and paradoxes presented on the canvases. There seem to be no right or wrong answers to Johns's questions. Whereas Cole's viewer is passive, Johns's is an active participant. His art is created only when someone looks at it. The struggle for interpretation is what makes the experience and gives it meaning. And this wrestling with experience is what makes up the course of life, from beginning to end.

Yet Johns's *Seasons* does not leave his viewers utterly at sea. His vision requires resurrection of the past and the reworking of traditional archetypes to help guide us into our uncertain future. Each of his images changes throughout the series. Each change brings some new meaning to the work. This working and reworking is Johns's autobiography, except for *Winter*, a depiction of his imagined future. Thus, Johns suggests that reweaving a collective past into the present and reweaving a personal past into each stage of life are essential means of preparing for one's journey into the unknown future.

---

[60] Wallace Stevens, "The Snowman," in *The Palm at the End of the Mind: Selected Poems*, ed. Holly Stevens (New York: Vintage, 1972), 54.

[61] Cited in Mary Winkler, "Walking to the Stars," Cole, Van Tassel, and Kastenbaum, *Handbook of Aging* (see n. 45).

Johns's depiction of the journey and seasons of life speaks to the complexity and ambiguity of aging in an emerging postmodern culture. *The Seasons* is a contribution to a pluralistic dialogue about life's meanings. He offers no simple prescription, no romantic vision of a proper way to grow old, no promise that we will be unscathed by life's vicissitudes. By weaving the ages and journey of life into reconstituted symbols of personal, social, and cosmic meaning, Johns suggests one way for postmodern aging selves to cultivate existential nourishment. Somehow, we must find other ways to integrate the ancient virtue of submission to natural limits with the modern value of individual development for all.

It remains to be seen whether we can build postmodern courses of life that are both socially just and fulfill our needs for love and meaning. Neither Johns nor Cole is especially helpful here, since both work with individualistic images stripped of social relations. Bunyan's Christiana may be a more useful reminder that each stage, each cycle, each journey of life is lived in relation to others. At the beginning, we are what we are given. By mid-life, when we have finally learned to stand on our own two feet, we learn that to fulfill our lives, we are called "to give to others, so that when we leave this world we can be what we have given."[62] Death, from this perspective, can be made into our final gift. "We belie it daily," wrote Florida Scott Maxwell at age eighty-five, "but is it not possible that by living our lives we create something fit to add to the store from which we came? Our whole duty may be to clarify and increase what we are, to make our consciousness a finer quality. The effort of one's entire life would be needed . . . to return laden to our source."[63]

[62] Henri Nouwen and Walter J. Gaffney, *Aging: The Fulfillment of Life* (New York: Doubleday, 1974), 13.
[63] Florida Scott Maxwell, *The Measure of My Days* (New York: Knopf, 1968), 40.

Index

Index

Index

minister of (Nathaniel Emmons), 57–66
and patriarchal ideal, 49
and perspective on aging, xxvi
and pilgrimage (journey-of-life motif), 34

Quidor, John, 76

Rabbi Akaviah ben Mahalalel, xxxiii
Reagan era, 236
Reformation, *see* Protestant Reformation
rejuvenation, 174–5
retirement by contract, 11
Return of Rip Van Winkle, The (Quidor), 76f
revivalist, revivalists, 79
and attitudes toward aging, 85
and conversion, 82
and images of old age, 83, 84
Rhetoric (Aristotle), xxxii, 6
Rights of Man, The (Paine), 56
"Rip Van Winkle" (Irving), 74–6, 83, 113
Rolleston, Sir Humphrey, 200
Romantic evangelicals, 128, 134, 145
and last half of life, 139
and "manhood," 132
and ministers' ideals of natural death, 137
and "normal" aging and natural death, 138
and preparing for old age, 138
and youth, 131
Romantic images of old age, 74
Romantic religion, Victorian, 110–27
Romantic religion and dualistic vision of old age, 127–9
Rosenmayr, Leopold, xix
Rostow, Irving, xix
Rush, Benjamin, 101
and ameliorating diseases of old age, 103–4

"Sailing to Byzantium" (Yeats), 152
Salpêtrière Hospital, Paris, 196
salvation, natural, 175–9
Santayana, George, 234
Schneider, Dr. Albert, 180
Seasons, The (Johns), 244–51
Seneca, 120
Senescence, The Last Half of Life (Hall), 213, 215, 220
and old age as institutionally separate stage of modern life course, 216
sentimental images of old age, 74, 83, 114
Shakespeare, William, 24
Shephard, Thomas, 36
Shew, Joel, 99
Sigourney, Lydia Huntly, 141, 143, 144, 148, 149
portrait, 142f
Smith, Colonel Nicholas, 149
Smith, Stephen, 162

and national health and longevity, 163
Social Security Act and System, 224, 234–6
Some Thoughts on Education (Locke), 54
Sophocles
Oedipus at Colonus, xxxiii, 243
Oedipus Rex, xxxiii
spiritual advice, 152–8
spiritual development, and Romantic ministers, 131
spiritual growth and physical aging, 47
spiritual journey, erosion of Protestantism's vision of life as, 222
Spring from *The Seasons* (Johns), 245, 246f
stages of life
in antebellum America, 81
and institutionalized old age, 223
modern view of, 241
need to revalue, 242
reconstruction of, 216
revising, 81
spiritual, of New England Puritans, 36
Victorian versions of, 191
and women (Christiana in *Pilgrim's Progress*), 47
see also ages of life
staircase as image of life course, 111
Stanford, John, 140, 143, 145, 146
The Aged Christian's Companion, 67
late Calvinist style of, 86
Steinach, Eugene, 180, 195, 207, 208, 219
Stephens, Charles Asbury, 175–8
as enthusiast of life extension, 175
Summer from *The Seasons* (Johns), 245, 247f

Taylor, Nathaniel, 61, 81, 82, 85, 128
"Ten Ages of This World, The" (Gengenbach), 18
Tennyson, Alfred, 242
"Crossing the Bar," 226
Tetrabiblos (Ptolemy), 6
"Thanatopsis" (Bryant), 226
Thewlis, Malford, 195
Thomas, W. J., 187
Trall, Russell, 99, 101
on natural death, 109
Trap des Ouderdoms, and iconography of life course of couples, 26, 28
Trollope, Anthony
The Fixed Period, 168
honorary college of Necropolis of, 170

Van Beusecom, François, 26
Van Gogh, Vincent, 250
Van Rensselaer, Cortlandt, 86, 87, 88, 140
vegetarianism and health, 100
veneration, 141
Victorian era

259